T0292836

Get the eBook FREE!

(PDF, ePub, Kindle, and liveBook all included)

We believe that once you buy a book from us, you should be able to read it in any format we have available. To get electronic versions of this book at no additional cost to you, purchase and then register this book at the Manning website.

Go to https://www.manning.com/freebook and follow the instructions to complete your pBook registration.

That's it!
Thanks from Manning!

Functional Design and Architecture

EXAMPLES IN HASKELL

ALEXANDER GRANIN

MANNING
SHELTER ISLAND

Manning Publications Co.
20 Baldwin Road
PO Box 761
Shelter Island, NY 11964

Development editor:	Dustin Archibald
Technical editor:	Arnaud Bailly
Review editor:	Kishor Rit
Production editor:	Andy Marinkovich
Copy editor:	Lana Todorovic-Arndt
Proofreader:	Melody Dolab
Technical proofreader:	Thad Meyer
Typesetter:	Tamara Švelić Sabljić
Cover designer:	Marija Tudor

ISBN 9781617299612
Printed in the United States of America

To my wife.

brief contents

iv

contents

preface

You're probably looking for new insights into what you already know about software design, or you might be wondering how to build real programs in functional languages such as Haskell, Scala, Elm, PureScript, F#, or OCaml. Perhaps you've always wanted to get a complete picture of software engineering in Haskell, or maybe the idea of having a methodology unifying all the main concepts of functional programming has attracted your attention. All of these reasons motivated me to write this book: I realized how big the knowledge gap was and that I desperately needed to fill in this gap for my day-to-day functional job.

This book uses Haskell as a model language. The choice was deliberate because it's the most iconic functional language with a rich type system. It could have been Scala or OCaml, but unfortunately, I am not proficient enough in those languages. The ideas are universal, and Haskell allows me to present them in a concise and easy-to-follow way.

This book has a long story behind it. I started this book with Manning Publications at the beginning of 2016, but the process stalled out. At that time, I had completed a lot of supporting projects and examples. I also discovered a bunch of new concepts that I refined through several years of successful production usage.

In 2020, I self-published the first writing of *Functional Design and Architecture* (https://leanpub.com/functional-design-and-architecture). I received many great reviews from my readers and reached out to Manning to see whether they would be interested in publishing it in the completed form. This book is the result.

This edition significantly differs from the first edition in the teaching material used, but the topics and approaches are identical. The core idea and the concept also remained the same, which is software design with statically typed functional languages. I rewrote the first half completely and made many improvements in the second half; it is now more polished and better organized, so you don't have to read the earlier version. I personally love both, nevertheless.

Long story short, this book is what I've been working on for more than eight years, and I truly believe the final product does a great job of shedding light on the subject. Many interesting ideas are presented here; however, one book can't cover everything there is to know about functional programming for designing software. A lot of interesting stuff was left behind, and we likely need 20 additional ground-breaking books to cover everything. I will continue writing more books, so let's keep in touch to develop this knowledge together!

acknowledgments

This book wouldn't be what it is today without the contribution of many, and I am grateful to everyone who participated in the process.

A heartfelt thanks goes to the pioneers of functional programming. Your innovative ideas and foundational work have been instrumental in shaping this field and, by extension, this book. Your efforts have made all the difference.

I also extend my gratitude to the trailblazers of software engineering. Your dedication to establishing and advancing this discipline has paved the way for professionals like me to grow and innovate. Your legacy is evident in every chapter of this work.

To my readers, both past and present, your support has been invaluable. Your feedback, questions, and enthusiasm have not only motivated me but also played a crucial role in refining this book. Your contribution is deeply appreciated.

Thank you to the team at Manning Publications who were so invaluable in making this edition of the book a reality. Your professionalism and belief in me are truly appreciated. Thanks also to my technical editor, Arnaud Bailly, who has been developing software and helping teams develop software in various technologies, contexts, and roles for nearly three decades. Arnaud's experience was a great help in making sure everything in the book works as it should.

Special thanks go to all the reviewers who helped refine and polish this manuscript: Adrian Bilauca, Andrei Formiga, Andres Sacco, Charles Earl, Daut Morina, David Cabrero, David Paccoud, Ernesto Garcia Garcia, Filip Mechant, German Gonzalez-Morris, Joel Holmes, Jose Luis Garcia Baltazar, Kai Gellien, Kelvin Chappell, Kent R. Spillner, Kevin Cheung, Luca Campobasso, Makarand Deshpande, Marco Perone, Mike Tedeschi, Mikkel Arentoft, Nikita Dyumin, Phillip Sorensen, Richard Tobias, Robert Walsh, Roberto Casadei, Rohinton Kazak, Satej Kumar Sahu, Tony Mullen, Walt Stoneburner, and William E. Wheeler. Your input and expertise have been vital in ensuring the clarity and quality of the final product.

In essence, this book is a collaborative effort, and I am grateful to everyone who was part of this journey.

about this book

Fundamental mainstream software engineering books are readily available, and we all know how important they have been for establishing the software engineering industry. While most of these books address object-oriented programming (OOP), this book expands the knowledge base to functional languages.

I wrote *Functional Design and Architecture* to help developers build big, high-quality applications from end to end in functional languages and with functional reasoning. The book talks about functional design patterns, old and new, discussing various application architectures suitable for languages such as Haskell, Scala, and OCaml. It also introduces a number of best practices to follow, incorporating them into a bigger picture of software engineering with functional ideas. You'll also find various design principles from both the mainstream and functional world, which all form the core of the methodology I craft in this book—functional declarative design (FDD).

This book pioneers several concepts, such as free monads as true functional interfaces and the hierarchical free monads approach. It also builds on object-oriented design principles such as SOLID for functional settings. I also provide you with new ways of domain modeling, be they collection requirements with mind and concept maps or using interpretable embedded domain-specific languages as a main tool to maintain complexity. The book contains this and even more, but the main idea is based on pragmatism. You'll rarely find a book that talks about functional programming in such a practical and informal style, free from unnecessary math fleur and approachable to a wide audience. This book proves that functional programming can be a useful tool for serving businesses.

Who should read this book?

This book is intended for software developers and architects looking to enhance their skills by learning a comprehensive and complete methodology of software design with deep and interesting ideas coming from the functional world. Although Haskell is a model language, and some prior knowledge is assumed, the book is comprehensive, so its ideas can be applied to other statically typed functional languages such as OCaml, F#, PureScript, Elm, Scala, and even C++! The first half of the material is simplified to address a wider audience of developers, so it is quite helpful even if Haskell is not your favorite language.

If you're interested in learning Haskell, I recommend checking out these excellent Manning resources:

- Philipp Hagenlocher, *Learn Haskell by Example,* www.manning.com/books/learn -haskell-by-example
- Will Kurt, *Get Programming with Haskell,* www.manning.com/books/get -programming-with-haskell

If you want to expand your knowledge even further, the following is a great resource:

- Vitaly Bragilevsky, *Haskell in Depth,* www.manning.com/books/haskell-in-depth

How this book is organized: A roadmap

This book is organized into five parts. In the first four parts, we'll talk a lot about domain-specific languages, domain-driven design, interpretable languages, design principles, design patterns, and the new methodology of functional declarative design (FDD). Part five continues this discussion, but the perspective is slightly different, as we will focus on designing real-world software.

Part 1 offers an introduction to functional declarative design:

- *Chapter 1*—This chapter establishes the foundation for further discussion. It explains the main notions of software design, such as complexity, design principles, and design patterns. In addition, it introduces the terminology we'll be using throughout the book.
- *Chapter 2*—In this chapter, I define my methodology, that is, functional declarative design. The chapter is organized as reference material listing topics pertaining to the methodology.

Part 2 creates a minimum viable product:

- *Chapter 3*—We start building a spaceship control software application with simple functional approaches and then form the initial set of business requirements for our software.
- *Chapter 4*—Focusing on end-to-end design, we continue to develop the application by designing a skeleton that includes all the needed parts and a proper architecture.

Part 3 delves into domain-driven design:

- *Chapter 5*—This chapter opens a discussion of domain modeling with embedded domain-specific languages. This approach is superior when it comes to addressing business domains properly and keeping complexity low.
- *Chapter 6*—In this chapter, I introduce free monads using knowledge from the previous chapter. With free monads, domain modeling becomes truly powerful.

Part 4 addresses stateful and reactive applications:

- *Chapter 7*—Here, we learn more about organizing stateful applications and maintaining state with direct approaches, such as argument-passing state and mutable references. Then we move to state monads.
- *Chapter 8*—This chapter covers the actor model and basics of multithreaded concurrent architectures. We also finish developing our spaceship control software by making a simulator environment for it.

In part 5, we work on designing real-world software:

- *Chapter 9*—We move to the development of the concurrent application framework using the knowledge we've acquired and learn about additional architectural and design approaches.
- *Chapter 10*—Here, we craft several important subsystems of the framework, including, among others, logging and a state management subsystem.
- *Chapter 11*—This chapter discusses type-level programming and addresses the task of key–value databases for the framework.
- *Chapter 12*—We continue talking about databases and the related design patterns, such as higher-kinded data (HKD). This time, we implement a subsystem for relational database access.
- *Chapter 13*—In this chapter, we deal with one of the hardest problems in programming, error handling. We also talk about various ways of implementing dependency injection in functional languages.
- *Chapter 14*—We work on an HTTP service and application on top of the framework we've just developed. We discuss ways of organizing the business logic so that the code is properly layered, decoupled, and testable.
- *Chapter 15*—This final chapter contains a thorough discussion of various testing approaches, such as property-based testing, functional and unit testing, and others—all in the context of the approaches we've learned in the book.

You might find the code in part 5 a bit more advanced, although not overly difficult. However, it may motivate you to learn Haskell at a deeper level.

I recommend reading the book sequentially. The main narratives connect the chapters, and the chapters complement each other, helping you travel more easily through this magical world.

About the code

This book contains many examples of source code, both in numbered listings and in line with normal text. In both cases, source code is formatted in a `fixed-width font like this` to separate it from ordinary text. Occasional *italic* highlights commonly refer to an important term or topic that I want to call attention to. Often, we had to modify the format of the original source code to fit the book's pages. This involved adding new line breaks and adjusting the indentation. In a few instances, even these changes were not sufficient, leading us to use line-continuation symbols (➥) in the code listings. Furthermore, we sometimes omitted comments from the source code in the listings, particularly when the accompanying text already describes the code. Many listings are also accompanied by code annotations to emphasize key ideas and concepts. You'll also see many graphics in the text, which I enjoyed creating, as they clarify the subject matter and facilitate learning.

You can get executable code snippets from the liveBook (online) version of this book at https://livebook.manning.com/book/functional-design-and-architecture. The complete code for the examples in the book is available for download from the Manning website at www.manning.com/books/functional-design-and-architecture and from GitHub at https://github.com/graninas/Functional-Design-and-Architecture.

There are two big projects we'll be building in this book, in addition to many small ones. If you visit the Manning-Publications folder, you'll find the project buildable with stack, a popular Haskell build tool. In the BookSamples folder, you'll find many subprojects organized similarly to the sections of the book for easy navigation. For example, section 6.1.1 has the corresponding subproject, as well as the whole section 6.2, and so on.

What wasn't demonstrated in the code samples was showcased with the two complementary projects:

- *Andromeda*—Andromeda is a standalone application simulating a system for controlling spaceships. It corresponds to parts 2, 3, and 4 (that is, chapters 3 through 8). This field is known as supervisory control and data acquisition software (SCADA), and it's rather big and rich. We certainly can't build a real SCADA application, but we'll try to create a simulator to demonstrate the ideas of domain-driven design (DDD). We'll track all the stages of software design, from requirements gathering to a possibly incomplete but working simulator application. In other words, we'll follow a whole cycle of software creation processes. You don't have to be proficient in SCADA because you'll be given all the information necessary to solve this task. Writing such software requires touching on many topics, so it's a good example of the different sides of functional programming. (See Andromeda, SCADA-like system for controlling spaceships at https://github .com/graninas/Andromeda).

- *Hydra*—Hydra represents an application framework for building concurrent and multithreaded web services, backends, and console applications. We'll talk about design patterns, approaches, and practices that help to structure our code properly to simplify it and make it less risky. We'll see how to build layered applications and write testable, maintainable, and well-organized code. While building a framework and some demo applications, you'll deal with many challenges you might expect to meet in the real world: relational and key–value database access, logging, state handling, and many more. (See the Hydra application framework in Haskell at https://github.com/graninas/Hydra.)

These projects have slightly different architectures but share some common ideas, which will help us examine the same concepts from many different viewpoints and thus better understand when and how to apply them.

I'm happy to see you here, and I promise you'll get all this and even more. Everything has its own goal and its own place in this material. The discipline of software engineering in static functional languages now has a thorough, careful, and consistent exposition. I wish you a good reading experience!

liveBook discussion forum

Purchase of *Functional Design and Architecture* includes free access to liveBook, Manning's online reading platform. Using liveBook's exclusive discussion features, you can attach comments to the book globally or to specific sections or paragraphs. It's a snap to make notes for yourself, ask and answer technical questions, and receive help from the author and other users. To access the forum, go to https://livebook.manning .com/book/functional-design-and-architecture/discussion. You can also learn more about Manning's forums and the rules of conduct at https://livebook.manning.com/ discussion.

Manning's commitment to our readers is to provide a venue where a meaningful dialogue between individual readers and between readers and the author can take place. It is not a commitment to any specific amount of participation on the part of the author, whose contribution to the forum remains voluntary (and unpaid). We suggest you try asking the author some challenging questions lest their interest stray! The forum and the archives of previous discussions will be accessible from the publisher's website for as long as the book is in print.

about the author

ALEXANDER GRANIN is a senior software engineer and architect with over 15 years of experience. He is an international speaker, researcher, and book author. Functional programming has been his love and passion. His mission is to empower developers with practical insights and build a comprehensive software engineering discipline for functional programming.

about the cover illustration

The figure on the cover of *Functional Design and Architecture* is captioned *Walaque*, or "Man from Wallonia, Belgium," taken from a collection by Jacques Grasset de Saint-Sauveur, published in 1797. Each illustration is finely drawn and colored by hand.

In those days, it was easy to identify where people lived and what their trade or station in life was just by their dress. Manning celebrates the inventiveness and initiative of the computer business with book covers based on the rich diversity of regional culture centuries ago, brought back to life by pictures from collections such as this one.

Part 1

Introduction to functional declarative design

The first part of this book will introduce you to the intricate and fascinating world of software design, exploring its principles, challenges, and methodologies. Software design transcends mere coding. It is the art and science of translating domain models and requirements into efficient, maintainable code structures. This section sheds light on the pivotal role of software design in managing complexity, the importance of choosing appropriate tools and approaches, and the nuances of different programming paradigms. We examine object-oriented design (OOD) and functional declarative design (FDD), discovering how these frameworks guide decision-making and shape the architecture of software projects.

As we venture further, the focus shifts to the engineering approach in software development, emphasizing systematic, educated, and conscious decision-making over haphazard coding practices. This part of the book underscores the importance of understanding software architecture, the art of making informed decisions at various levels, and the value of domain-specific languages in functional programming. The aim is to equip you with a broad understanding of methodologies, practices, and patterns essential for effective software design and architecture that will help you navigate the complexities of both object-oriented and functional paradigms with ease and proficiency.

What is software design?

This chapter covers

- Establishing the idea and intuition behind software design
- Finding similarities and dissimilarities between object-oriented and functional design
- The concepts of functional design
- General design principles

Software engineers deal with many universal concepts, such as requirement analysis, design of domain-specific languages, modularization and project organization, layering, SQL and key–value database support, multithreading, concurrency, logging, building frameworks, domain modeling, and testing. Developers who choose statically typed functional languages such as Haskell, Scala, F#, OCaml, Elm, or Pure-Script generally have fewer resources for learning design principles that maximize the benefits of those languages in addressing common challenges.

This book explores software design and architecture within statically typed functional languages by introducing a systematic approach called *functional declarative design* (FDD). FDD is a full development cycle methodology along the lines of object-oriented design (OOD), which introduces functional application architectures, design patterns, design principles, and a new architectural design pattern called *hierarchical free monads* (HFM).

This book is intended for any developer who wants to sharpen their software design skills, those who want to make their functional code better, and those who want to create command-line applications, web services, critical software, games, business applications, and more. By reading this book, you'll acquire the knowledge senior software engineers and software architects should possess.

1.1   Why functional programming?

You may be asking, why functional programming? Good question. I could answer that functional programming techniques can make your code safer, shorter, and better in general. I could also say that some problems are much easier to approach within the functional paradigm. Moreover, I could argue that the paradigm is just as deserving as others.

But perhaps the main reason I argue for functional programming is that it brings a lot of fun to all aspects of development, including the hardest ones. You've probably heard that parallel and concurrent code is where functional approaches shine. This is true, but it's not the only benefit. In fact, the real power of functional programming is in its ability to make complicated things much simpler and more enjoyable because functional tools are highly consistent and powerful. Considering this, many problems you might face in imperative programming are made simpler or even eliminated. Certainly, functional programming has its own problems and drawbacks, but learning new ideas is always profitable because it gives you more opportunities to find better techniques or ways of reasoning.

In this chapter, you'll find a definition of software design, a description of software complexity, and an overview of known practices. The terms introduced here will show that you may already be using some common approaches, and if not, you'll get a bird's-eye view of how to approach design thinking in three main paradigms: imperative, object oriented, and functional. It is important to understand when functional programming (sometimes called FP) is better than OOP and when it's not. We'll look at the pros and cons of traditional design methodologies and then see how to build our own.

In this book, I assume you have some prior knowledge of functional programming. Most of the examples are written in Haskell, and knowing a little bit of Haskell will make the examples easier to follow. If you want a quick introduction to Haskell, there are many good books from which to choose, such as Philipp Hagenlocher's *Haskell Bookcamp* (www.manning.com/books/haskell-bookcamp) and Will Kurt's *Get Programming with Haskell* (https://mng.bz/yo4E).

Now let's begin by answering the question, "What is software design?"

1.2   Software design

When constructing programs, we want to obey certain requirements to make the program's behavior correct. But every time we deal with our complex world, we experience the difficulties of describing the world in terms of code. We can just continue developing, but at some point, we will suddenly realize that we can't go further because of overcomplicated code. We should pause and make a significant refactoring of the project. Otherwise, we risk getting stuck completely and failing to meet the requirements. There seems to be a general law of code complexity that symmetrically reflects the phenomenon of entropy: *any big, complex system tends to become bigger and more complex.* But if we try to change some parts of such a system, we'll encounter another problem that is very similar to mass in physics: *any big, complex system resists our attempts to change it.*

Software complexity is the main problem developers deal with. Fortunately, we've found many techniques that help decrease this problem's acuteness. And there is a general name for these techniques and activities—software design.

Software design is the process of implementing business requirements with a systematic engineering approach. It's aimed at accomplishing goals. The result of software design can be represented as software design documents, high-level code structures, diagrams, or other software artifacts.

To keep a big program maintainable, correct, and clear, we structure it in a certain way. First, the system's behavior should be deterministic because we can't manage chaos. Second, the code should be as simple as possible because we can't maintain Klingon manuscripts.

You might say that many successful systems have an unjustifiably complex structure. True, but would you be happy to support code like that? How long can you endure working on complex code that you could be designed better? You can try the Fizz-Buzz Enterprise Edition project, which has an enormous number of Java classes to solve the classic problem FizzBuzz (https://mng.bz/2K99).

A small portion of these classes, interfaces, and dependencies is presented in figure 1.1. Imagine how weird this object-oriented code is!

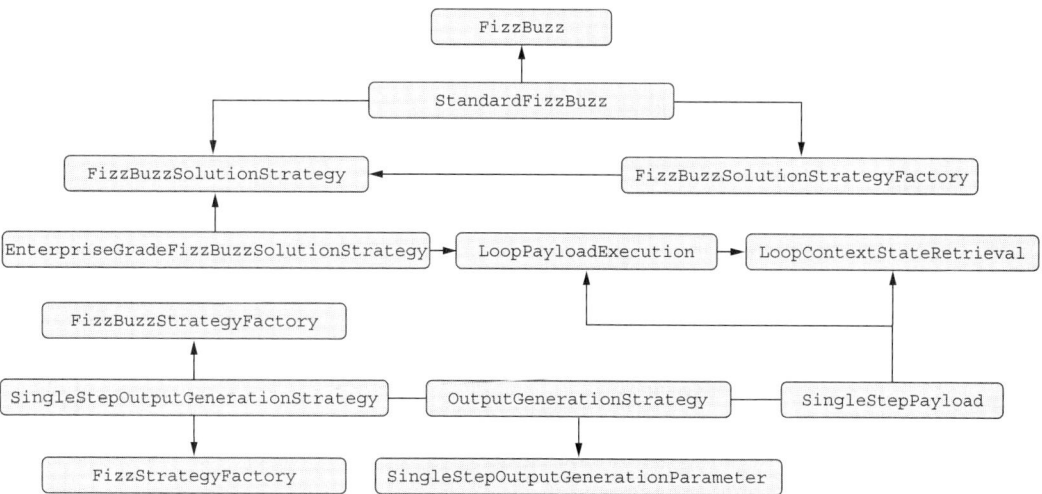

Figure 1.1 FizzBuzz Enterprise Edition class diagram (an excerpt)

So does going functional mean you're guaranteed to write simple and maintainable code? The answer is no. Like many tools, functional programming can be dangerous when used incorrectly. You can consider the following paper as evidence, where the same FizzBuzz problem is solved in a functional yet mind-blowing manner: "FizzBuzz in Haskell by Embedding a Domain-Specific Language" (https://mng.bz/1GKy).

That's why software design is important even in Haskell or Scala. But before you design something, you need to understand your goals, limitations, and requirements. Let's examine these now.

1.2.1 Requirements, goals, and simplicity

Imagine you are a budding software architect with a small but ambitious team. One day, a man knocks at your office door. He introduces himself as a director of Space Z Corporation. He says that they have started a big space project recently and need some spaceship management software. What a wonderful career opportunity for you! You decide to contribute to this project. After discussing some details, you sign an agreement, and now your team is an official contractor of Space Z Corporation. You agree to develop a prototype for date 1, to release version 1.0 by date 2, and to deliver major update 1.5 by date 3. The director gives you a thick stack of technical documents and contact details for his engineers and other responsible people so you can explore the construction of the spaceship. You say goodbye, and he leaves. You quickly form a roadmap to understand your future plans. The roadmap—a path of what to do and when—is presented in figure 1.2.

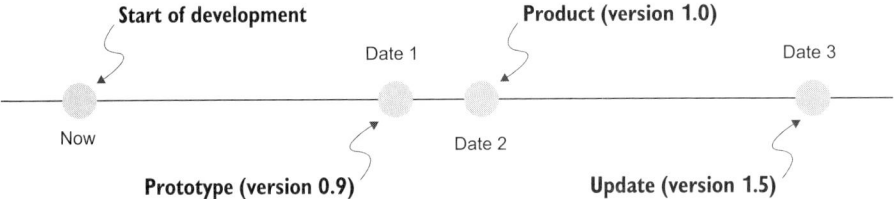

Figure 1.2   Roadmap of the development process

To cut a long story short, you read the documentation inside and out and gather a bunch of requirements for how the spaceship software should work. At this point, you are able to enter the software design phase.

As the space domain dictates, you must create a robust, fault-tolerant program that works correctly all the time, around the clock. The program should be easy to operate, secure, and compatible with a wide component spectrum. These software property expectations are known as *nonfunctional requirements*. Also, the program should do what it is supposed to do: allow an astronaut to control the ship's systems in manual mode, in addition to fully automatic mode. These expectations are known as *functional requirements*.

Functional requirements are the application's requirements for functionality. They describe a full set of things the application should do to allow its users to complete their tasks. Correspondingly, nonfunctional requirements are requirements for the application's general properties: performance, stability, extensibility, availability, amounts of data it should be able to process, latency, and so on.

You must create a program that will meet the requirements and will not necessitate rewriting from scratch—a very challenging task, with deadlines approaching. Fortunately, you understand the risks. One of them is overcomplicated code, and you would like to avoid this problem. Your goal is not only to create the software on time but to update it on time, too; therefore, you should still be comfortable with the code after a few months.

It is even worse if it's not you but some of your colleagues who jumped into the project recently. How would they improve the code when they feel completely lost? The more sophisticated the code is, the less chance it will get better with time. Overcomplicated code will cost much more, or equally, it will be less maintainable. Based on the experience obtained from practice, I can draw a graph of this regularity (see figure 1.3).

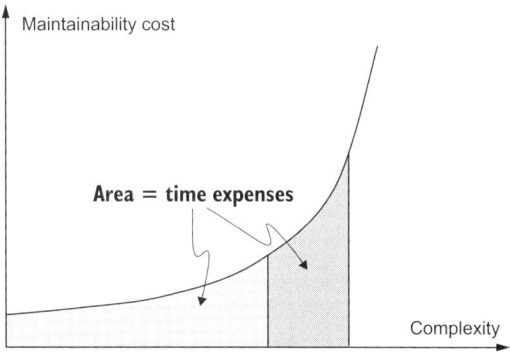

Figure 1.3   Maintainability cost vs. complexity

Of course, the picture is not scientifically accurate. It's just our feelings about and experience with how projects evolve. But look at the picture: simpler code slowly degrades because simplicity lowers the cost of its support, and we can spend additional resources on refactoring or testing.

Designing simple yet powerful code takes time, and it often involves compromises. You will have to maneuver between these three success factors (there are other approaches to this classic problem, but let's consider this one):

- *Goals accomplished*—Your main goal is to deliver the system when it's needed, and it must meet your customer's expectations: quality, budget, deadlines, support, and so on. There is also a goal of keeping risks low and being able to handle problems when they arise.

- *Compliant with requirements*—The system must have all the agreed-on functions and properties. It should work correctly.
- *Constant simplicity*—A simple system is maintainable and understandable; simple code allows you to find and fix bugs easily. Newcomers can quickly drop into the project and start modifying the code.

Although fully satisfying each factor is your primary meta-goal, it is often an unattainable ideal in our imperfect world. This might sound fatalistic, but it actually gives you additional possibilities to explore, such as factor execution gaps. For example, you might want to focus on some aspects of fault tolerance, even if this means exceeding a deadline by a little. Or you may decide to ignore some spaceship equipment that you know will be out of production soon. The compromises themselves can be represented by a radar chart (see figure 1.4).

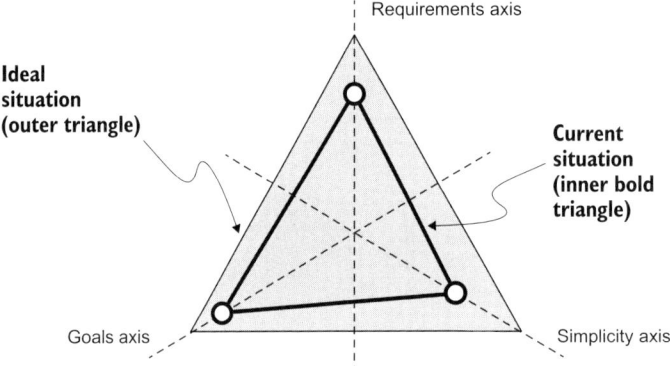

Figure 1.4   Compromising between simplicity, goals, and requirements

You can read the chart like this: the inner triangle is advancing toward the outer triangle when we're developing our product. But not all the directions are advancing at the same pace, so we see some goals achieved and requirements met given the lower costs of simplicity. Maybe it's what we want, and maybe it's not, but that's our current situation.

Software design is a risk management process. Risks affect our design decisions and may force us to use tools and practices we don't like. We say the risk is low when the cost of solving problems is low. We can list the typical risks that any software architect deals with:

- *Low budget*—If we can't hire a good software architect, we can't expect the software to be of production quality.
- *Changing requirements*—Suppose we've finished a system that can serve a thousand clients. For some reason, our system becomes popular, and an increasing number of clients are coming. If our requirement was to serve a thousand clients, we'll face problems when there are millions of clients.

- *Misunderstood requirements*—The feature we have been building over the last six months was described poorly. As a result, we've created a kind of fifth wheel and lost time. When the requirements were clarified, we were forced to start over again.

- *New requirements*—We created a wonderful hammer with nice features like a nail puller, a ruler, pliers, and electrical insulation. What a drama it will be someday to redesign our hammer to give it a striking surface.

- *Lack of time*—Lack of time can force us to write quick and dirty code with no thought for design or for the future. It leads to code we're likely to throw in the trash soon.

- *Overcomplicated code*—With code that's difficult to read and maintain, we lose time trying to understand how it works and how to avoid breaking everything with a small change.

- *Invalid tools and approaches*—We thought using our favorite dynamic language would boost the development significantly, but when we needed to increase performance, we realized it has insuperable disadvantages compared to static languages.

- *Invalid tools and approaches, again*—We thought using our favorite statically typed language would boost the development significantly, but when we needed to fix the acting code right on the production server, we realized it is not that simple compared to dynamic languages.

At the beginning of a project, it's important to choose the right tools and approaches for your program's design and architecture. Carefully evaluated and chosen technologies and techniques can make you confident of success later. Making the right decisions now leads to good code in the future. Why should you care? Why not just use mainstream technologies like C++ or Java? Why pay attention to the new fashion today for learning strange things like functional programming? The answer is simple: parallelism, correctness, determinism, and simplicity. Note that I didn't say *easiness* but *simplicity*. With the functional paradigm comes the simplicity of reasoning about parallelism and correctness. That's a significant mental shift.

> **NOTE** To better understand the difference between easiness and simplicity, I recommend watching the talk "Simple Made Easy" (or "Simplicity Matters") by Rich Hickey, the creator of the functional language Clojure and a great functional developer. In his presentation, Hickey speaks about how this difference affects whether we write good or bad code. He shows that we all need to seek simplicity, which can be hard but more beneficial than the easy paths we often follow.

You'll be dealing with these challenges every day, but what tools do you have to make these risks lower? In general, software design is that tool: you want to create an application, but you also want to decrease any potential problems in the future. Let's continue walking in the mythical architect's shoes and see what software design is.

1.3   *Essential and accidental complexity*

You are meditating on the documentation. After a while, you end up with a set of diagrams. These diagrams show actors, actions, and the context of those actions. Actors—figures in the pictures—trigger actions. For example, an astronaut starts and stops the engine in the context of the control subsystem. These kinds of diagrams (*use case diagrams*) come from the Unified Modeling Language (UML), and you've decided to use them to organize your requirements in a traditional way. One of the use case diagrams is presented in figure 1.5.

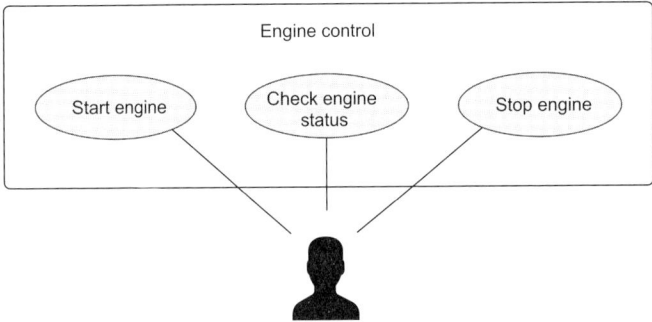

Figure 1.5   Use case diagram for the engine control subsystem

Use case diagrams are a part of UML, which is primarily used for object-oriented design. But looking at the diagram, can you say how they are related to OOP? In fact, use case diagrams are paradigm agnostic, so they can be used to express requirements regardless of the implementation stack. However, we will see how some UML diagrams lead to imperative thinking and can't be used directly in functional declarative design.

Thinking about the program's architecture, you notice that the diagrams are complex, dense, and detailed. The list of subsystems the astronaut will work with is huge, and there are two or three instances of many of those subsystems. Duplication of critical units should prevent the ship's loss in case of disaster or technical failure. Communication protocols between subsystems are developed in the same vein of fault tolerance, and every command carries a recovery code. The whole scheme looks very sophisticated, and there is no way to simplify it or ignore any of these problems. You must support all the required features because this complexity is an inherent property of the spaceship control software. This type of unavoidable complexity has a special name: *essential complexity.*

The technical documentation contains a long list of subsystem commands (see table 1.1). They are called the *spaceship application programming interface* (spaceship API), and are essentially native, raw calls of some kind written in a low-level language such as C.

Table 1.1 Spaceship API

Command	Native API function
Start boosters	`int send(BOOSTERS, START, 0)`
Stop boosters	`int send(BOOSTERS, STOP, 0)`
Start rotary engine	`core::request::result`
	`request_start(core::RotaryEngine)`
Stop rotary engine	`core::request::result`
	`request_stop(core::RotaryEngine)`

The table reveals a variety of coding styles for various devices, each of which is attributed to its own manufacturer. These functions must be called somewhere in your program, but mixing different styles might make your project too messy. Your task is to hide these native calls behind an abstraction, which will keep your program concise, clean, and testable. Also, new devices and new APIs can suddenly appear on the horizon.

After some meditating, you write down several possible architectural decisions to abstract the calls:

- No abstractions. Native calls only.
- Create a runtime mapping between native functions and higher-level functions.
- Create a type-level compile-time mapping between native functions and type-level entities. (Side note: How should this work?)
- Wrap every native command in a polymorphic object (command pattern).
- Wrap the native API with a higher-level API (OOP interfaces or functional interfaces), and unify the syntax.
- Create a unified embedded domain-specific language (eDSL).
- Create a unified external domain-specific language (DSL).

Aside from the actual meaning of these notions (which we're about to learn in this book), it's obvious that every solution has its own mechanism and even philosophy. Some of the mechanisms are expected to be more complex than others. For example, the type-level compile-time mapping will be too difficult to implement. This complexity has nothing to do with essential complexity; it's artificial and comes from our tools. This type of complexity is known as *accidental complexity* (sometimes called *incidental complexity*).

Accidental complexity is not an inherent property of the domain; it didn't exist before you created the code itself. When you write unreasonably tricky code, you increase the accidental complexity. When you choose more difficult solutions without a proper justification, you increase the accidental complexity. Figure 1.6 compares two imaginary solutions consisting of various technologies that contribute to both complexities. As it's apparent from the image, solution A weighs a lot more than solution B.

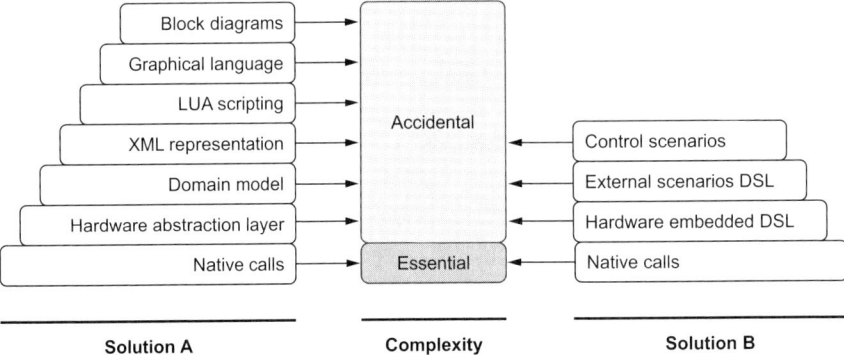

Figure 1.6   Accidental and essential complexity of two solutions

Handling complexity is an art of balance. Avoiding abstractions can reduce code maintainability and lead to excessive coupling. Conversely, indulging in overdesign when creating new abstractions introduces unnecessary accidental complexity and hinders code maintainability. The main task of software design is to keep the accidental complexity as low as possible, but not at the expense of other factors. In this sense, software design is a creative activity because you always search for the best solution. There is no general path to it, and you are the only person who defines what is best in particular cases. "Best" is not "perfect." Maybe the perfect solution doesn't even exist. That's why we want to know software design best practices and patterns: they make us more conscious and provide a framework for reasoning about our decisions.

Object-oriented design is this framework, just for object-oriented languages. An example of OOD is presented in figure 1.7. It's a class diagram from UML corresponding to the use case diagram in figure 1.5.

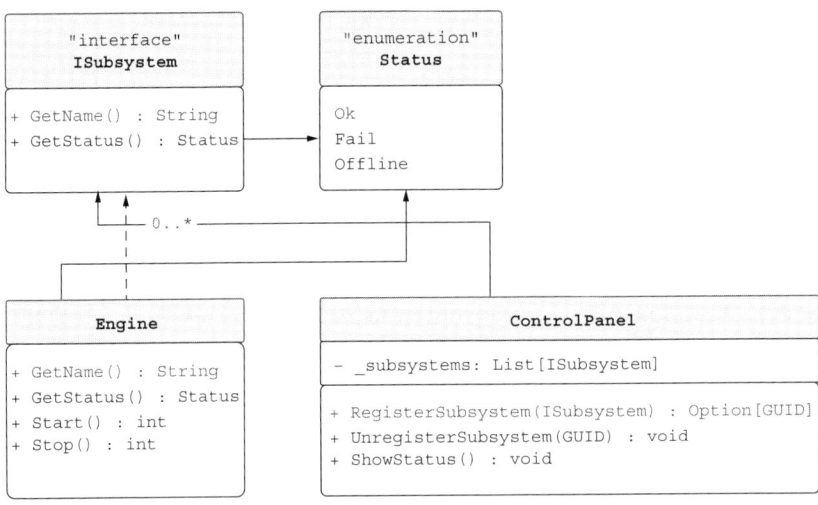

Figure 1.7   OOD class diagram for the engine control subsystem

This diagram describes the high-level organization of a small part of the domain model. There is an interface (ISubsystem), an implementation (Engine), a client class that uses the interface (ControlPanel), and some auxiliary enumeration Status. The system can operate by doing those tasks: starting and stopping engines, bookkeeping subsystems, and doing other stuff.

Class diagrams may be the best-known part of UML, which has been widely used in OOD recently. Class diagrams help object-oriented developers communicate with each other and express their ideas before coding. An interesting question here is how applicable UML is to functional programming. We traditionally don't have objects and state in functional programming—does that really mean we can't use UML diagrams? The short answer: we can, at least some of them. But maybe you'll find the custom diagrams I'm proposing in the book more appropriate for your FP code.

Not everything from the object-oriented world fits well with functional programming. Specific features of an object-oriented language, or some tricky techniques based on the fundamental OOP concepts, can't be applied directly. But more abstract notions and ideas can and should be considered in the functional design. Here, we will take only a brief tour of some major design principles known in mainstream design: low coupling and high cohesion. This is all about keeping complexity manageable in OOD and, in fact, in other methodologies.

1.3.1 Low coupling, high cohesion

As a team leader, you want the code your team produces to be of good quality and suitable for the space field. You've just finished reviewing some of your developers' code, and you are in a bad mood. The task was extremely simple: read data from a thermometer, transform it into an internal representation, and send it to the remote server. But you've seen some unsatisfactory code in one class. The following listing in Scala shows the relevant part of it.

Listing 1.1 Highly coupled object-oriented code

```
object Observer {
  def readAndSendTemperature() {
    def toCelsius(data: native.core.Temperature) : Float =    ← Conversion function
      data match {
        case native.core.Kelvin(v)  => 273.15f - v    ← Invalid conversion formula
        case native.core.Celsius(v) => v
      }

    val received = native.core.thermometer.getData()    ← Real device is engaged
    val inCelsius = toCelsius(received)
    val corrected = inCelsius - 12.5f    ← Defective device, magic constant
    server.connection
        .send("temperature", "T-201A", corrected)    ← Magic constants
  }
}
```

Look at the code. It has a bad design. Why? First, the conversion algorithm hasn't been tested at all. We know this because the code contains an error in converting from Kelvin to Celsius. The right formula should be `v - 273.15f`. Fixing this in only one place would be easy, but it's real trouble if there are many. Second, the code can't be tested at all because it talks to the external systems directly. You need a real thermometer connected and a real server online to evaluate all the commands. You can't do this in tests. Third, it violates the *single responsibility principle* (SRP) by doing too much and knowing too much. The magic constants make it fragile and too specialized. The code assumes that it will query a defective thermometer and even tries to fix the measurement. But what if it's a good thermometer? Should we rewrite the code again?

The problem with this class is that it's highly coupled with the outer systems, which makes it unpredictable and untestable. The code has a low cohesion; in other words, its responsibility is blurred, and its internals try to do extrinsic things. Solving these problems requires introducing new levels of abstraction. You need interfaces to hide native functions and separate the responsibilities from each other. You probably want an interface for the transformation algorithm itself. Interfaces break high coupling and allow for a better responsibility distribution. After refactoring, your code could look like this.

Listing 1.2   Loosely coupled object-oriented code

```scala
trait ISensor {                                          ◄─┐  Interface for
  def getData() : Float                                     │  reading a sensor
  def getName() : String
  def getDataType() : String
}

trait IConnection {                                      ◄─┐  Interface for sending
  def send(dataType: String, name: String, data: Float)     │  data to a server
}

final class Observer (val sensor: ISensor,              ◄─┐  Injecting
                      val connection: IConnection) {        │  dependencies
  def readAndSendData() {                               ◄─┐  Conversion of
    val data = sensor.getData()                            │  temperatures
    val sensorName = sensor.getName()                       │  goes to this
    val dataType = sensor.getDataType()                     │  implementation.
    connection.send(dataType, sensorName, data)
}}
```

Here, the `ISensor` interface represents a general sensor device, and you don't need to know much about that device. It may be defective, but your code isn't responsible for fixing defects; that should be done in the concrete implementations of `ISensor`. `IConnection` has a small method to send data to a destination: it can be a remote server, a database, or something else. It doesn't matter to your code what implementation is used behind the interface. A class diagram of this simple code is shown in figure 1.8.

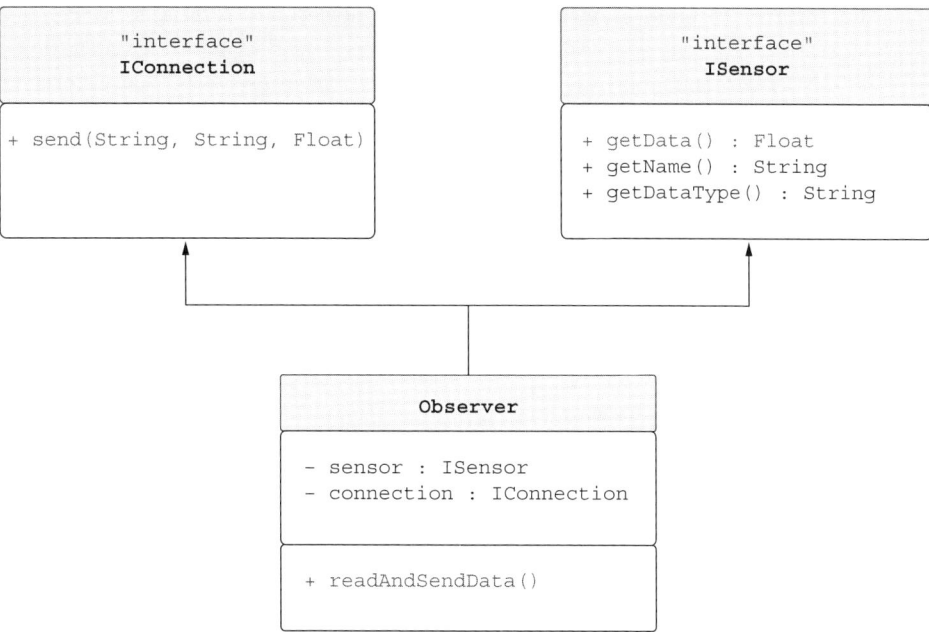

Figure 1.8 Class diagram of listing 1.2

Achieving low coupling and high cohesion is a general principle of software design. Do you think this principle is applicable to functional programming? Can functional code be highly coupled or loosely coupled? Both answers are yes. The following listing gives you some sense of this. It's functional code in Haskell. Still, it exhibits exactly the same problems as the code in listing 1.1.

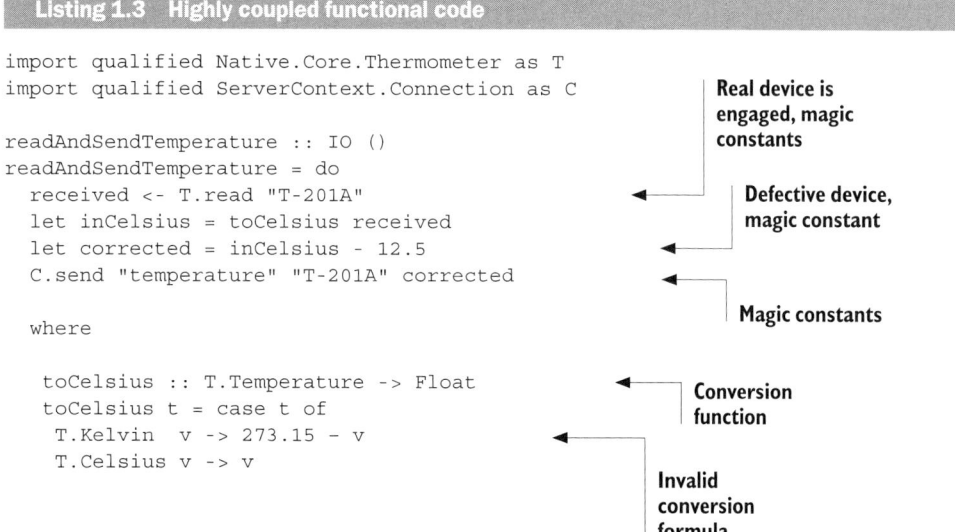

Listing 1.3 Highly coupled functional code

```
import qualified Native.Core.Thermometer as T
import qualified ServerContext.Connection as C

readAndSendTemperature :: IO ()
readAndSendTemperature = do
  received <- T.read "T-201A"
  let inCelsius = toCelsius received
  let corrected = inCelsius - 12.5
  C.send "temperature" "T-201A" corrected

  where

  toCelsius :: T.Temperature -> Float
  toCelsius t = case t of
   T.Kelvin  v -> 273.15 - v
   T.Celsius v -> v
```

Real device is engaged, magic constants

Defective device, magic constant

Magic constants

Conversion function

Invalid conversion formula

Functions read and send talk to the native device and remote server. They evaluate side effects for this purpose. The problem here is finding a better way to deal with side effects. There are good solutions in the object-oriented world that help to keep code loosely coupled. The functional paradigm tries to handle this problem in another way. For example, the code in listing 1.3 can be made less tightly coupled by introducing a domain-specific language (DSL) for native calls. We can build a scenario using this DSL so the client code will only deal with the DSL, and its dependency on native calls will be eliminated. How to design such a language and how to make it work will be a very central topic of the next few chapters, along with other brilliant patterns and idioms in functional programming. I've said that no one approach gives you a silver bullet, but the functional paradigm seems to be a really good try.

1.3.2   *Interfaces, inversion of control, and modularity*

Functional programming provides new methods of software design, but does it invent any design principles? Let's deal with this. Look at the solutions in listings 1.1 and 1.2. We separate interface from implementation. Separating parts from each other to make them easy to maintain rises to a well-known general principle: *divide and conquer*. Its realization may vary depending on the paradigm and concrete language features. As we know, this idea has come to us from ancient times, when politicians used it to rule disunited nations, and it works very well today—no matter what area of engineering you have chosen.

Interfaces in object-oriented languages such as Scala, C#, or Java are a form of this principle too. An object-oriented interface declares an abstract way of communicating with the underlying subsystem without knowing much about its internal structure. Client code depends on abstraction and sees no more than it should: a little set of methods and properties. The client code knows nothing about the concrete implementation it works with. It's also possible to substitute one implementation for another, and the client code will stay the same. A set of such interfaces forms an *application programming interface* (API).

For our purposes, we'll think of an API as a contract that describes the operations, inputs, outputs, and underlying types of a software component independent from its implementation. Consequently, you can change the way a component is implemented without compromising its interface. A good API makes it easier to develop a program by providing all the building blocks, which are then put together by the programmer without specific knowledge of the implementation of each block.

Introducing an interface and forcing client code to use it instead of a direct implementation is a known and important technique. It's so important that it has a name: *inversion of control* (IoC). With IoC, our code becomes more robust and reliable. It's also a way to make it testable and more readable.

It's like a theatre. Actors can replace each other behind the scenes (they are the implementations). The actors are all different. They all are people with their own lives and their own aspirations. But the spectator (client code) won't realize that because on the scene, they all will have the same dress and makeup (interface, abstraction) and will behave according to a predefined screenplay (behavior contract).

An example of this is shown in the following listing. This code complements the code in listing 1.2.

Listing 1.4 Interfaces and inversion of control

```
final class Receiver extends IConnection {
  def send(dataType: String, name: String, data: Float) =
    server.connection.send(dataType, name, data)
}

final class Thermometer extends ISensor {
  val correction = -12.5f
  def transform(data: native.core.Temperature) : Float =
    toCelsius(data) + correction

  def getName() : String = "T-201A"
  def getDataType() : String = "temperature"
  def getData() : Float = {
    val data = native.core.thermometer.getData()
    transform(data)
  }
}

object Worker {
  def observeThermometerData() {
    val t = new Thermometer()
    val r = new Receiver()
    val observer = new Observer(t, r)
    observer.readAndSendData()
  }
}
```

- Specific receiver
- Specific sensor
- The implementation is aware of the defect of this sensor.
- Constants are now hidden.
- The worker that knows what implementations we need
- Observer from listing 1.2 that only works with interfaces

The full class diagram of listings 1.2 and 1.4 is presented in figure 1.9.

Now we are going to do one more simple step. Usually, you have a bunch of object-oriented interfaces related to a few aspects of the domain. To keep your code well organized and maintainable, you may want to group your functionality into packages, services, libraries, or subsystems. We say a program has a *modular* structure if it's divided into independent parts somehow. We can conclude that such design principles as modularity, IoC, and interfaces help us to achieve our goal of low software complexity. So far, we've discussed OOD in short. But what about functional design?

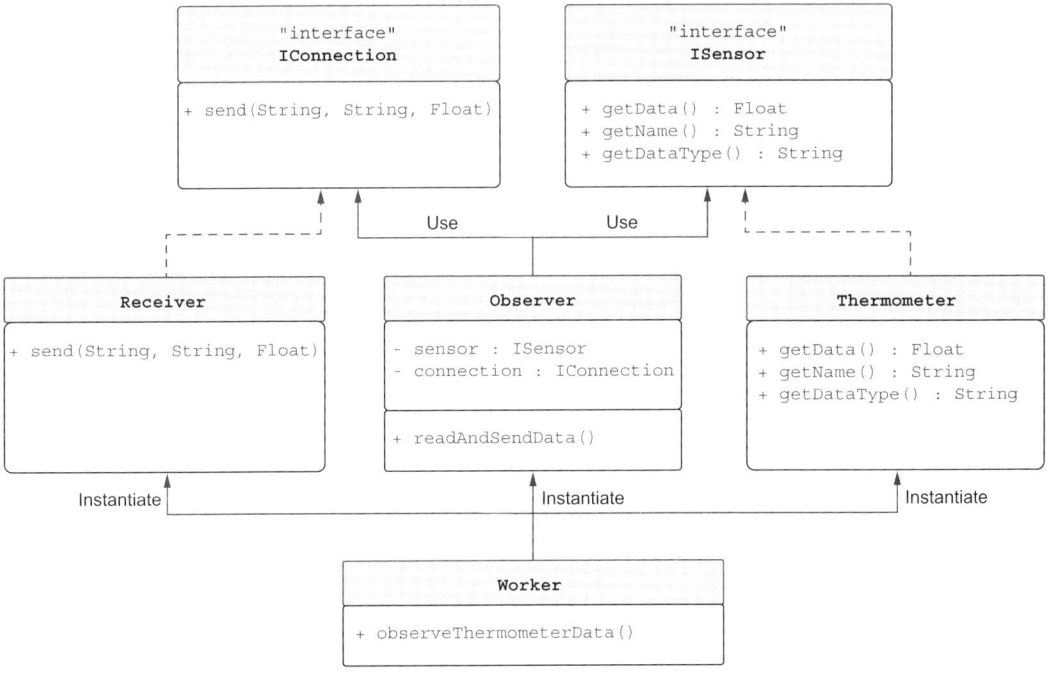

Figure 1.9   Full class diagram of listings 1.2 and 1.4

1.3.3   *Functional design*

Any time we read articles on OOD, we ask ourselves the following: Is the functional paradigm good for software design too? What are the principles of functional design, and how are they related to object-oriented principles? For example, can we have interfaces in functional code? Yes, we can. Does that mean that we have IoC out of the box? The answer is yes again, although our functional interfaces are somewhat different because functional is not object oriented, obviously. A functional interface for communication between two subsystems can be implemented as an algebraic data type and an interpreter. Or it can be encoded as a state machine. Or it can be monadic. Or it could be built with type classes. OOP is good, but it has to do a lot to keep complexity low. In functional programming, there are many interesting possibilities that may offer advantages over what the object-oriented paradigm provides. The functional paradigm also introduces a new principle of software design: finding the essence of some domain means finding its mathematical invariants, which then can be emphasized to get the correct behavior of the domain as a consequence.

When designing a program in the functional paradigm, we must investigate our domain model, its properties, and its nature. This allows us to generalize the properties to functional idioms (for example, functor, monad, or zipper; we'll meet the first two later in the book). The right generalization gives us additional tools specific to those concrete functional idioms already defined in base libraries. This dramatically increases the power of code.

For example, we have a list of names, `names :: [String]`. From functional programming, it is known that lists can be mapped with a function that converts every element into another type. The resulting list preserves the length of its predecessor, but the type of elements changes. This idea of mapping lists and other data types while preserving their internal structure is called a functor. The `names` list therefore is a functor that should obey this behavior as well, and being a functor means there are various abstract operations that work for all functors. For example, we calculate the lengths with the `fmap` function, a function to iterate over any valid `Functor`:

```
import Data.Functor (fmap)

-- fmap :: (a -> b) -> [a] -> [b]          ◄─── Generic fmap function
                                                defined for every Functor

names :: [String]                          ◄─── Initial list
names = ["Alice","Bob", "Trudy"]

lengths :: [Int]                           ◄─── Resulting list
lengths = fmap length names
                                           Using the fmap function
-- lengths: [5,3,5]                         to convert the list
```

Later on, we refactor the `names` list into a list of possible names with the `Maybe` type:

```
data Maybe a
  = Just a
  | Nothing

maybeNames :: [Maybe String]
maybeNames = [Just "Alice", Just "Bob", Nothing]
```

Then we realize that the `Maybe`, being quite different from a list, is also a functor and has its own `fmap` defined for it. Now, instead of manually recursing over the `maybeNames` list and every element of it, we traverse both with double `fmap`, thus relying on their `Functor` natures:

```
maybeLengths :: [Maybe Int]
maybeLengths = fmap (fmap length) maybeNames

-- maybeLengths: [Just 5,Just 3,Nothing]
```

And then we might discover even more interesting properties that enable an even bigger set of tools. Like anything new, functional programming comes with its own set of vocabulary, concepts, and design principles. As you move forward, you'll quickly become used to these new ways of thinking, and my methodology, called functional declarative design (FDD), will help you navigate across this world. With this methodology, I wanted to do what mainstream methodologies do: shape the discipline of software design, provide ready solutions, and establish a baseline with which to compare our decisions. Let's now see how software design works for imperative, object-oriented, and functional paradigms because you'll see that the ideas, being very high level, can be transferred from one paradigm to another.

1.4 *Design in mainstream paradigms*

In the early computer era (roughly 1950–1990), imperative programming was a dominant paradigm. Almost all big programs were written in C, Fortran, COBOL, Ada, or another well-used language. Imperative programming is still the most popular paradigm today for two reasons: first, many complex systems (like operating system kernels) are idiomatically imperative; second, the widely spread object-oriented paradigm is imperative under the hood. Let's see how these two have evolved with time.

1.4.1 *Imperative design*

Imperative programming is a type of programming that focuses on how a program flows, allowing for changes in data and the use of side effects. In simpler terms, this approach involves giving the computer step-by-step instructions on how to alter information. Within imperative programming, we can employ techniques such as loops (repeated actions), mutable plain old data structures (changeable basic data groups), pointers (variables that hold memory addresses), procedures (sets of instructions to perform specific tasks), and eager computations (immediately calculating results).

In essence, when we talk about imperative programming, we're referring to a style that is often procedural or structured. This means that the focus is on laying out the sequence of steps the program needs to take rather than emphasizing the final outcome.

Imperative design in programming refers to how a program is organized, employing techniques such as risky type conversions, changing variables destructively, or introducing side effects to achieve specific low-level characteristics in the code. For instance, these methods might aim to make the code utilize the CPU cache efficiently or reduce instances where data needs to be fetched from slower memory locations.

Has the long history of the imperative paradigm produced any design practices and patterns? Definitely. Have we seen these patterns described as much as the object-oriented patterns? It seems we haven't. Despite the fact that OOD is much younger than bare imperative design, it has been much better described. But if you ask system-level developers about the design of imperative code, they will probably name techniques such as modularity, polymorphism, and opaque pointers. These terms may sound strange, but there's nothing new here. In fact, we already discussed these concepts earlier:

- *Modularity* is what allows us to divide a large program into small parts. We use modules to group behavioral meaning in one place. In imperative design, it is a common thing to divide a program into separate parts.
- *Opaque data types* allow a subsystem to be divided into two parts: an unstable private implementation and a stable public interface. Hiding the implementation

behind the interface is a common idea of good design. Client code can safely use the interface, and it never breaks, even if the implementation changes someday.

- *Polymorphism* is the way to vary implementations under the unifying interface. Polymorphism in an imperative language often simulates an ad hoc polymorphism from OOP.

For example, in the imperative language C, an interface is represented by a public opaque type and the procedures it is used in. The following code is taken from the Linux kernel file as an example of two opaque types—MYPROCOBJECT and MYPROCTYPE:

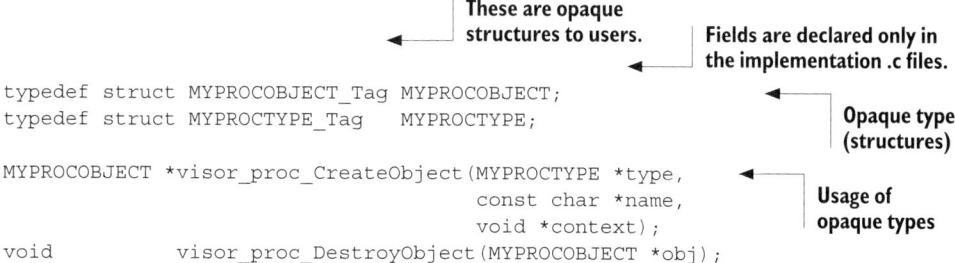

```
typedef struct MYPROCOBJECT_Tag MYPROCOBJECT;
typedef struct MYPROCTYPE_Tag   MYPROCTYPE;

MYPROCOBJECT *visor_proc_CreateObject(MYPROCTYPE *type,
                                      const char *name,
                                      void *context);
void          visor_proc_DestroyObject(MYPROCOBJECT *obj);
```

These are opaque structures to users.

Fields are declared only in the implementation .c files.

Opaque types (structures)

Usage of opaque types

Low-level imperative language C provides full control over the computer. High-level dynamic imperative language PHP provides full control over the data and types. But having full control over the system can be risky. Developers have less motivation to express their ideas in design because they always have a short path to their goal. It's possible to hack something in code—to reinterpret the type of a value, cast a pointer even though there is no information about the needed type, use some language-specific tricks, and so on. Sometimes it's fine, and sometimes it's not, but it's definitely not safe and robust. This freedom requires good developers to be disciplined and pushes them to write tests. Limiting the ways a developer could occasionally break something may produce new problems in software design. Despite this, the benefits you gain, such as low risk and good quality of code, can be much more important than any inconveniences that emerge. Let's see how OOD deals with lowering the risks.

1.4.2 Object-oriented design

What is OOD? In short, it is software design using object-oriented languages, concepts, patterns, and ideas. Also, OOD is a well-investigated field of knowledge on how to construct big applications with low risk. It focuses on the idea of "divide and conquer" in different forms. OOD patterns are intended to solve common problems in a general, language-agnostic manner. This means you can take a formal, language-agnostic definition of the pattern and translate it into your favorite object-oriented language. For example, the *adapter pattern* shown in the next listing allows you to adapt a mismatched interface to the interface you need in your code.

Listing 1.5   Adapter pattern

```
final class HighAccuracyThermometer {
  def name() : String = "HAT-53-2"
  def getKelvin() : Float = {
      native.core.highAccuracyThermometer.getData()
  }
}

final class HAThermometerAdapter (
    thermometer: HighAccuracyThermometer)
  extends ISensor {
    val t = thermometer

    def getData() : Float = {
        val data = t.getKelvin()
        native.core.utils.toCelsius(data)
    }
    def getName() : String = t.name()
    def getDataType() : String = "temperature"
}
```

Thermometer class
to adapt to a
different interface

Adapter

The instance of
the high accuracy
thermometer

New method that
adapts the interface
of the thermometer

What's happening here is that we have some high-precision thermometer, namely the
HighAccuracyThermometer class, but we can't implement it for the ISensor interface. The two don't agree on what unit to use for temperature: Celsius or Kelvin. So we
create HAThermometerAdapter, which will convert one unit into another, while dealing with the mismatched thermometer. Figure 1.10 shows the Adapter design pattern
as it is presented in the "Gang of Four" book.

NOTE   *Design Patterns*, a book by Erich Gamma, Richard Helm, Ralph Johnson,
and John Vlissides (Addison-Wesley, 1994), is informally called "Gang of Four"
or just "GoF." It introduces two dozen general patterns with descriptions and
explanations of how and when to use them. This book has a systematic approach
to solving common design problems in object-oriented languages.

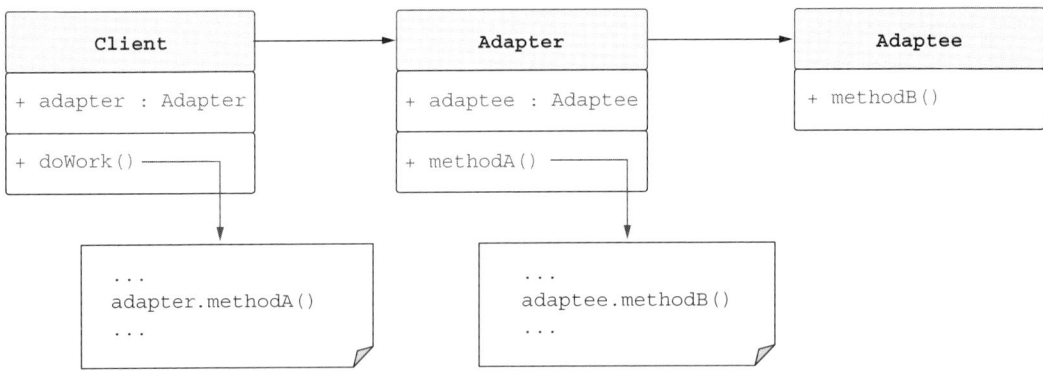

Figure 1.10   The Adapter design pattern, a class diagram from UML

Understanding object-oriented patterns is crucial for any skilled developer today. However, advancements from a functional approach in programming languages are proving to be more effective in solving problems compared to specific object-oriented patterns. Certain patterns, such as command or strategy, often involve intricate structures with numerous classes, making the code complex. Interestingly, you can achieve the same functionality as these patterns using higher-order functions, lambdas (small anonymous functions), and closures (functions along with their encompassing environment).

Functional solutions tend to be more concise and easier to maintain and understand because they consist of small, independently functioning functions that work well together. In fact, many object-oriented patterns can surpass the limitations of object-oriented languages, regardless of their intended use.

So we can define object-oriented patterns as well-known solutions to common design problems. But what if you encounter a problem no one pattern can solve? In real development, this dark situation dominates over the light one. The patterns themselves are not the key thing in software design, as you might be thinking. Note that all the patterns use interfaces and IoC. These are the key things: IoC, modularity, and interfaces. And, of course, design principles.

1.4.3   *Object-oriented design principles*

Let's consider an example. Our spaceship is equipped with smart lamps with program switchers. Every cabin has two daylight lamps on the ceiling and one utility lamp over the table. Both kinds of lamps have a unified API to switch them on and off. The manufacturer of the ship provided a sample code for how to use the lamps' API, and we created one general program switcher for convenient electricity management. Our code is very simple—it only has an interface, two implementations, and a client function:

```
trait ILampSwitcher {                          ◄─── Lamp interface
  def switch(onOff: bool)
}

class DaylightLamp extends ILampSwitcher        ◄─── Implementation 1
class TableLamp     extends ILampSwitcher        ◄─── Implementation 2

def turnAllOff(lamps: List[ILampSwitcher]) {    ◄─── Client code that is aware
  lamps.foreach(_.switch(false))                     of the interface but not
}                                                    of the implementations
```

What do we see in this code? Client code can switch off any lamps with the interface `ILampSwitcher`. The interface has a `switch()` method for this. Let's test it! We turn our general switcher off, passing all the existing lamps to it, and a strange thing happens: only one lamp goes dark, and the other lamps stay on. We try again, and the same thing happens. We are facing a problem somewhere in the code—in the native code, to be precise, because our code is extremely simple and clearly has no bugs. The only option we have to solve the problem is to understand what the native code does. Consider the following listing.

Listing 1.6 Concrete lamp code

```
class DaylightLamp (n: String, v: Int, onOff: Boolean)          Implementation 1
  extends ILampSwitcher {
    var isOn: Boolean = onOff
    var value: Int     = v
    val name: String   = n
    def switch(onOff: Boolean) = {
      isOn = onOff
    }
}

class TableLamp (n: String, onOff: Boolean)                     Implementation 2
extends ILampSwitcher {
  var isOn: Boolean = onOff
  val name: String   = n
  def switch(onOff: Boolean) = {
    isOn = onOff
    // Debug: will remove it later!
    throw new Exception("switched")                             Unexpected exception
  }
}
```

Stop! You see this? The manufacturer's programmer forgot to remove the debug statement from the method `TableLamp.switch()`. In our code, we assume that the native code will not throw any exceptions or do any other strange things. Why should we be ready for unspecified behavior when the interface `ILampSwitcher` tells us the lamps will be switched on or off and nothing more?

The guarantees that the `ILampSwitcher` interface provides are called a *behavior contract*. We use this contract when we design our code. In this particular situation, we see the violation of the contract by the class `TableLamp`. That's why our client code can be easily broken by any instance of `ILampSwitcher`. This doesn't only happen with the assistance of exceptions. Mutating a global state, reading an absent file, working with memory—all these things can potentially fail, but the contract doesn't define this behavior explicitly. Violation of an established contract of the subsystem we try to use always makes us think that something is badly implemented. The contracts must be followed by implementation; otherwise, it becomes really hard to predict our program's behavior. This is why so-called *contract programming* was introduced. It brings some special tools into software design. These tools allow us to express the contracts explicitly and to check whether the implementation code violates these contracts or is fine.

Let's show how the contract violation occurs in a class diagram (figure 1.11).

When you use a language that is unable to prevent undesirable things, the only option you have is to establish special rules that all developers must comply with. And once someone has violated a rule, they must fix the mistake. Object-oriented languages are impure and imperative by nature, so developers have invented a few rules, called *object-oriented principles*, that should always be followed to improve the maintainability and reusability of object-oriented code. You may know them as the *SOLID* principles.

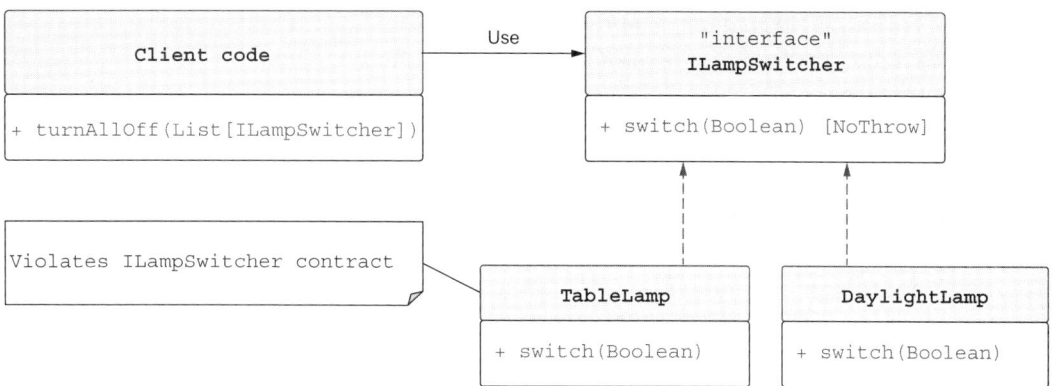

Figure 1.11 Class diagram for listing 1.6 illustrating contract violation by `TableLamp`

> **NOTE** Robert C. Martin first described the SOLID principles in the early 2000s. SOLID principles allow programmers to create code that is easy to understand and maintain because every part of it has one responsibility, is simplified with interfaces, and respects the contracts.

In SOLID, the L stands for the Liskov substitution principle (LSP). This rule prohibits situations like the one described here. LSP states that if you use `ILampSwitcher`, then the substitution of `ILampSwitcher` by the concrete object `TableLamp` or `DaylightLamp` must be transparent to your code. In other words, your code shouldn't be specifically updated for this substitution. There should always be a supposed correct behavior you may rely on, it should be manifested in the interfaces, and no implementations have a right to violate it. `TableLamp` obviously is a criminal here. It throws an unexpected exception and breaks the client code.

In addition to the LSP, SOLID contains four more OOP principles. The components of the acronym are presented in table 1.2.

Table 1.2 SOLID principles

Initial	Stands for	Concept
S	SRP	Single responsibility principle
O	OCP	Open/Closed principle
L	LSP	Liskov substitution principle
I	ISP	Interface segregation principle
D	DIP	Dependency inversion principle

It seems DIP, ISP, and SRP correspond to the ideas of IoC, interfaces, and modularity, respectively. We need these in our functional programs, as well as other SOLID principles. Unfortunately, they are mythologized as OOP-only, but actually, all of them are applicable to imperative and functional design. They are applicable to any possible engineering that has the notions of interface and implementation, including, for example, electric circuits. This is why we should be comfortable with these principles.

> **NOTE**   We talked about low coupling, high cohesion, and polymorphism earlier, and those are among the General Responsibility Assignment Software Patterns (GRASP). GRASP incorporates other OOD patterns too, but they aren't so interesting to us from a functional programming point of view. If you want to learn more about OOD, you can read a comprehensive guide by Craig Larman, *Applying UML and Patterns* (3rd Edition, Prentice-Hall, 2004).

1.5   *Software design in functional languages*

The first functional language was born in 1958 when John McCarthy invented Lisp. For 50 years, functional programming lived in academia, with functional languages primarily used in scientific research and small niches of business. With Haskell, functional programming was significantly rethought. Haskell (created in 1990) was intended to research the idea of laziness and problems of strong type systems in programming languages. However, the functional paradigm also brought in functional idioms, which are typical ways of writing code, rich with highly mathematical and abstract ideas. These concepts have become a signature feature of the entire functional programming style.

No one imagined that pure functional programming would arouse interest in mainstream programming. But programmers were beginning to realize that the imperative approach is quite deficient in controlling side effects and handling state, so it makes parallel and distributed programming painful.

The time of the functional paradigm had come. Immutability, purity, and wrapping side effects into a safe representation opened doors to parallel programming heaven. Functional programming began to conquer the programming world. You can see a growing number of books on functional programming, and all the mainstream languages have adopted functional programming techniques such as lambdas, closures, first-class functions, immutability, and purity. How do these ideas change our vision of software design? Let's see.

1.5.1   *Immutability, purity, and determinism*

In functional programming, we love immutability. We create bindings of variables, not assignments. When we bind a variable to an expression, it's immutable and just a declaration of the fact that the expression and the variable are equal and interchangeable. We can use either the short name of the variable or the expression itself with no difference.

Assignment operation is destructive by nature: we destroy an old value and replace it with a new one. It is a fact that a shared mutable state is the main cause of bugs in parallel or concurrent code. In functional programming, we restrict our freedom by prohibiting data mutations and shared state, so we don't have this class of parallel bugs at all. Of course, we can do destructive assignments if we want: Scala has the `var` keyword, and Haskell has the `IORef` type. However, employing these imperatively (in a step-by-step manner) is generally discouraged. This approach deviates from functional programming principles and can lead to unpredictability, known as nondeterminism. Sometimes it's necessary, but more often, the mutable state should be avoided.

In functional programming, we love pure functions. A pure function doesn't have side effects. It uses arguments to produce the result and doesn't mutate any state or data. A pure function represents deterministic computation: every time we call a pure function with the same arguments, we get the same result. The combination of two pure functions gives a pure function again. If we have a "pyramid" made of such functions, we have a guarantee that the pyramid behaves predictably on each level. We can illustrate this by code:

```
def max(a: Float, b: Float) : Float = {
  math.max(a, b)
}

def calc(a: Int, b: Int, c: Float) : Float = {
  val sum = a + b
  val average = sum / 2
  max(average, c)
}
```

Also, it is convenient to support a pyramidal functional code: it always has a clear evaluation flow, as shown in figure 1.12.

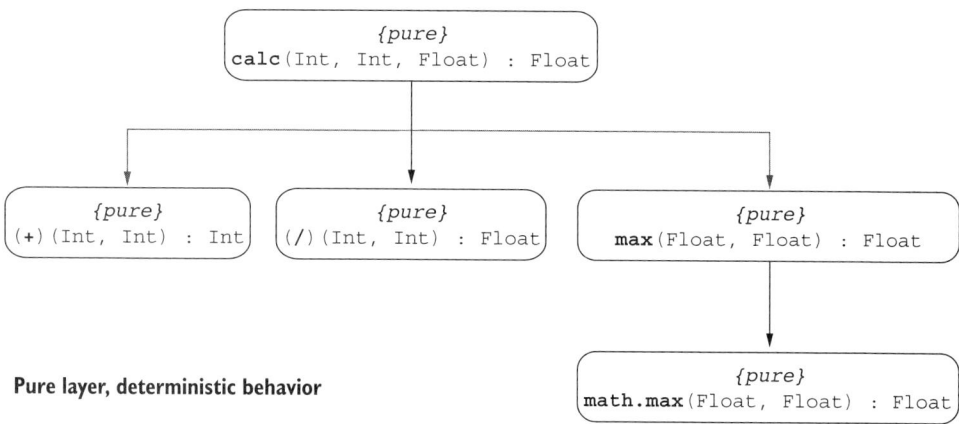

Figure 1.12 Pure pyramidal functional code

We give arguments a, b, and c to `calc`, and the function returns the max of `average` and c. If a year later we give the same arguments to the function `calc`, we will receive the same result.

There are languages that support purity as a language feature. Haskell, PureScript, and Idris have this separation embedded into the type system. You can ensure a function is pure by just looking at its type, for example, the max function:

```
-- Haskell, PureScript:
max :: Float -> Float -> Float                    ◄──── Definitely pure

-- Scala:
def max(a: Float, b: Float) : Float               ◄──── The purity status is unknown.
```

It's impossible for Haskell's max to do anything dangerous because the compiler becomes unhappy when it sees the Float return type that is not a type for side effects (the IO type in Haskell, the Effect type in PureScript). Any impure call in max breaks compilation:

```
launchMissile :: IO ()                            ◄──── Impure IO function

max :: Float -> Float -> Float                          Won't compile:
max a b = launchMissile        -- Dangerous!      ◄──── Float is not IO
```

Most languages lack this feature and do not restrict the developer to invoke side effects anywhere in the program. The Scala's compiler will be humbly silent about this:

```
def max(a: Float, b: Float) : Float = {
  launchMissile()            -- Dangerous!        ◄──── Impure call, side
  math.max(a, b)                                        effect, compiles well
}
```

The idea to declare side effects explicitly in the return type was a breakthrough in functional programming. The IO type has even more interesting properties that will help us in software design. Every function with return type IO may do impure calls; as a result, it can only be called from other impure functions, which in turn can be invoked from top impure functions until it all comes to the main function, which is impure too. This is how impurity infects all code, function by function, layer by layer. This also makes a code pyramidal; it's just a pyramid with two layers. The next listing demonstrates a complete program for printing the biggest number of the two, and you can easily track all the impure calls.

Listing 1.7 Pure functions and impure routines

```
max :: Float -> Float -> Float
max a b = if a > b then a else b                  ◄──── Pure computation
                                                        (the if expression)

printNumber :: Float -> IO ()
printNumber n = putStrLn ("Biggest number: " ++ show n)   ◄──── putStrLn is impure.

printMaxNumber :: Float -> Float -> IO ()         ◄──── Impure function
printMaxNumber n1 n2 = do
  let maxN = max n1 n2
  printNumber maxN

main :: IO ()                                     ◄──── The topmost
main = printMaxNumber 3.14 2.71                          impure function
```

A better illustration of a pyramidal code is presented in figure 1.13.

Pure layer, deterministic behavior

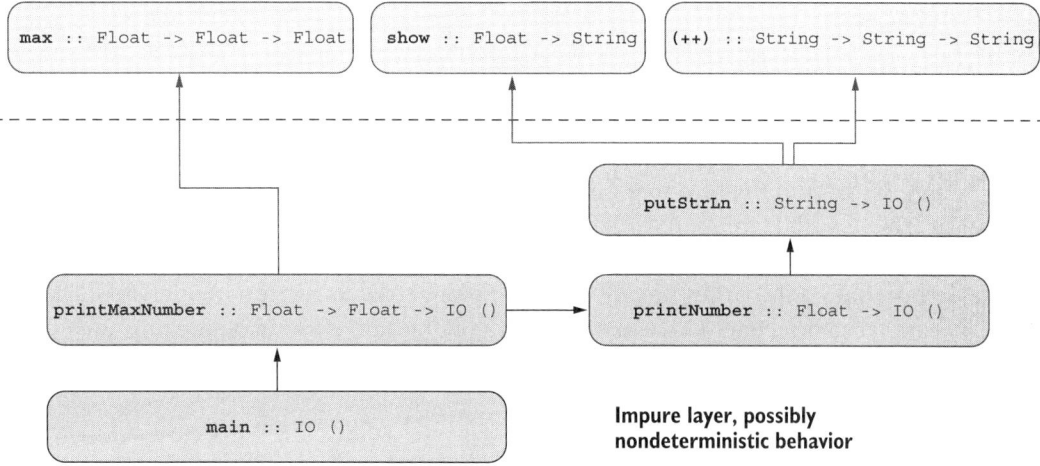

Figure 1.13   Impure pyramidal functional code

Lack of basic guarantees is the problem. If there is no purity mechanism in a language, we can't rely on the compiler. We must be careful and self-disciplined with our own and third-party code. There is always a temptation to relax personal standards of code quality and start dropping side effects here and there. This makes functional programming harder because impure functions do not compose well.

It's interesting that typed functional programming goes far beyond this technique of purity and develops a bunch of new approaches to checking guarantees at the compile time. Let's see what place static type systems play in functional software design.

1.5.2   Strong static type systems

Although OOP introduces new ways to express ideas in design (classes, object-oriented interfaces, encapsulation, and so on), it also tries to restrict the absolute freedom of the imperative approach. Have you used a global mutable state, which is considered harmful in most cases? Do you prefer a static cast checked in compile-time, or are you fine with a hard unmanaged cast, the validity of which can't be verified by the compiler? C++ developers know very well how difficult it is to find a code that is crashing the program due to some vague unmanaged cast. In imperative and object-oriented programming, it's common to debug a program step-by-step with a debugger. Sometimes, this is the only debugging technique that can give you an answer about what's happening in the program.

But lowering the need for a debugger (and thus limiting ourselves to other debug techniques) has a positive effect on program design. If everything is clear at first sight, then there is nothing to debug step by step. In fact, step-by-step debugging often becomes a way to write code and replaces the very idea of software design. A lazy developer would rather drop some code and debug the behavior instead of designing the behavior explicitly. The debugger makes you rely on hope; the design gives you sureness.

So how could we replace step-by-step debugging? The answer is static type systems and a good compiler. An expressive static type system can be a language of correctness that we use to design valid-by-construction programs. Certain type-level design techniques are intended to teach the compiler to gatekeep whole classes of errors. The more we go into the type level, the more errors and incoherencies the compiler sees, and the more bad things it can prevent at the design phase of the development. Consequently, step-by-step debugging becomes less needed.

But that's only part of the argument. Haskell helps us catch potential errors before we even run our code. This can save us a lot of time and effort in debugging and ensure that our programs are correct and reliable. Let's consider a small example:

```
data Shape = Circle Double
           | Rectangle Double Double
```

This defines a data type `Shape` with two constructors: `Circle` and `Rectangle`. The `Circle` constructor takes a `Double` argument representing the radius of the circle, while the `Rectangle` constructor takes two `Double` arguments representing the width and height of the rectangle.

Now let's say we want to write a function that calculates the area of a given `Shape`. We can do this with the following function:

```
area :: Shape -> Double
area (Circle r)      = pi * r^2
area (Rectangle w h) = w * h
```

This function takes a `Shape` as input and returns a `Double` representing the area of that shape. The implementation uses pattern matching to extract the relevant values from the `Shape` input and calculate the area accordingly.

Let's say we accidentally call the area function with an argument that is not a Shape, such as an integer:

```
area 5
```

If we try to compile this code, we will get a type error like this:

```
Couldn't match expected type 'Shape' with actual type 'Integer'
```

This means that we cannot call the area with this argument, and we need to fix the code accordingly, without triggering the debugger.

This leads us to a technique of designing software against the types. We define the types of top-level functions and reflect the behavior in them. If we want the code to be extremely safe, we can lift our behavior to the types, which forces the compiler to check the correctness of the logic. This approach, known as *type-level design*, uses such concepts as *type-level calculations*, *advanced types*, *linear types*, and *dependent types*. You may want to use this interesting (but not so easy) design technique if your domain requires the absolute correctness of the code. In this book, I'll discuss a bit of type-level design too.

1.5.3   Patterns and idioms

Software design has its own special vocabulary, so before we move on, let's look at two terms we'll use frequently: pattern and idiom. Although these two ideas are similar, we'll differentiate them in the following way.

A *design pattern* is an external solution to certain types of problems. A pattern is an auxiliary compound mechanism that helps to solve a problem in an abstract, generic way. Design patterns describe how the system should work. In particular, OOD patterns address objects and mutable interactions between them. An OOD pattern is constructed by using classes, interfaces, inheritance, and encapsulation.

An *idiom* is the internal solution to certain types of problems. It addresses the natural properties of the object and the immutable transformations of those properties. The idiom describes what the object is and what inseparable mathematical properties it has. Functional idioms introduce new meanings and operations for domain data types.

Some functional patterns and idioms have been incorporated into mainstream paradigms. Let me give you some quick examples; more detailed and more informative lists are waiting for you in the second chapter:

- *LINQ in C#, streams in Java, and ranges in C++*—These are examples of the functional approach to data processing.
- *Monads*—This concept deserves its own mention because it can reduce the complexity of some code (for instance, eliminating callback hell or making parsers quite handy).
- *Functional (monadic) Software Transactional Memory (STM)*—This approach to concurrency is based on a small set of concepts that are being used to handle a concurrent state and do not produce extra accidental complexity. In contrast, raw threads and manual synchronization with mutexes, semaphores, and so on usually turn the code into an unmanageable, mind-blowing puzzle.
- *Declarative embedded domain-specific languages (declarative eDSLs)*—These are not really an invention of the functional world, but they seem more applicable here. Writing in a functional language often feels like inventing the most convenient and expressive eDSL for a particular task. You can create declarative eDSLs in any object-oriented language as well, and this is a truly powerful tool for reducing complexity.

Functional developers have researched these and other techniques a lot. They've also found analogs to interfaces and IoC in the functional world. They did all that was necessary to launch the functional paradigm into the mainstream. But there is still one obstacle remaining. We lack the answer to one important question: How can we tie together all the concepts from the functional programming world to design our software? Is it possible to have an entire application built in a functional language and not sacrifice maintainability, testability, simplicity, and other important characteristics of the code?

1.5.4   *Monads*

Most books about functional programming spend a lot of time discussing monads, and we will meet many of them soon. In Haskell, monads are everywhere. You can do many things with monads: layering, separating side effects, mutating state, handling errors, and so on. Monads are amazing and very powerful!

For now, when we talk about a monad, imagine it as a framework that outlines a series of procedures in a computation, effectively managing tasks such as input–output operations, changing states, and other effects that might not always be pure or unchangeable. In the realm of functional programming, a monad serves as a fundamental concept. It enables you to distinctly separate data from the actual computing processes.

> **NOTE**   I assume some prior knowledge of monads and functional programming. If you'd like to refresh your knowledge, read appendix A (Plenty of monads), appendix B (Stacking monads with monad transformers), and appendix C (Word statistics example).

You may be wondering whether we should think of a monad as a design pattern or a functional idiom. As it turns out, the monad resists falling cleanly into one category.

For example, any functional list is a monad, whether you know this fact or not. "Monadic" is simply a mathematical property of a functional list. This is an argument in favor of "monad" being a functional idiom because, according to our definition, the idiom describes what the object is and its inseparable mathematical properties.

But from another perspective, a monad is a design pattern because the monadic mechanism is built somewhere outside the problem (in monadic libraries, to be precise). As an illustration of what expressivity gives us by knowing the internal properties of something, consider the code that returns the initial letter of a specific user from a certain database:

```
getUserInitials :: Int -> Maybe Char
getUserInitials key =
  case getUser key users of                    ← Case switch with
    Nothing   -> Nothing                          two options
    Just user -> case getUserName user of
      Nothing    -> Nothing                    ← Another case switch
      Just name -> Just (head name)               with two options
```

The program requests a user by the primary key from the external storage `users`, gets the name, and returns the first letter of it. Every operation may eventually fail, so both getting functions return the `Maybe` result that is either success (`Just something`) or `Nothing`:

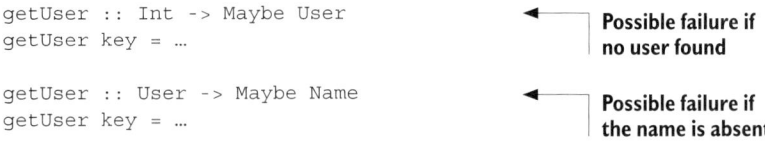

```
getUser :: Int -> Maybe User            ← Possible failure if
getUser key = …                           no user found

getUser :: User -> Maybe Name           ← Possible failure if
getUser key = …                           the name is absent
```

In `getUserInitials`, we experience some boilerplate in the form of the two `case … of` blocks. It is two levels of nesting, both doing the same thing: pattern matching over two `Maybe` values. Let's see if we can write this better using the monadic property of the `Maybe` type:

```
getUserInitials' :: Int -> Maybe Char
getUserInitials' key = do
  user <- getUser key users
  name <- getUserName user
  Just (head name)
```

The first case switch is hidden here.

The second case switch is hidden here.

Here, we refactored in terms of the results' mathematical meaning. We don't care what the functions `getUser`, `getUserName`, and `head` do or how they do it; it's not important at all. It's of the `Maybe` type, and the `Maybe` type can be supplemented with monadic behavior. This is why we were able to convert multiple stairs-like case switches into a concise do notation: the `Maybe` monad wraps these switches internally and allows the monadic code to stay simple while doing exactly the same.

The example with `Maybe` demonstrates that the process of functional design requires you to adopt a new way of thinking. When we design programs functionally, we are researching the properties of the domain model to relate them to functional idioms. When we succeed, we have all the machinery written for the concrete idiom in our toolbox. There are many of them: functors, applicative functors, monads, monoids, foldables, traversables, comonads, zippers. That's a lot of tools! I'll cover a few of them in the book, but the topic is much wider than that. I'll at least show you that functional programming is not just about lambdas, higher-order functions, and closures. It's also about composition, declarative design, and functional idioms that are applicable in many languages, not necessarily functional ones: Scala, Haskell, Lisp, Clojure, F#, OCaml, and even C++, C#, and Java. I hope you enjoy the journey!

Summary

- Software design is the process of translating domain models and requirements into high-level code structures to achieve specific goals.
- The main task of software design is to control accidental complexity.
- Software complexity is a major challenge for developers, but there are techniques that can help reduce it.
- The more complex the code is, the more costly it will be to maintain.
- It is important to choose the right tools and approaches for a project's design and architecture to ensure success.
- Object-oriented design is a reasoning framework for object-oriented languages that can help guide decisions.
- Functional declarative design is a reasoning framework for functional languages that also helps in decision-making.

- FDD is a subset of the declarative approach, and it puts imperative and object-oriented paradigms away to achieve declarative thinking.

- Imperative, object-oriented, and functional paradigms are related and should be understood to make conscious design decisions.

- UML is a widely used object-oriented design tool that can help developers communicate and express their ideas before coding.

- Software design principles are universal across different paradigms. Apply them to make the code less complex, less risky, and better.

- Low coupling and high cohesion are two major design principles that help keep complexity manageable in OOD and other methodologies.

- A functional program can be both highly coupled and loosely coupled, just like any other code.

- Functional programming emphasizes immutability, binding variables instead of assigning them, and avoiding shared mutable state and side effects.

- A functional paradigm comes with its own design principles. You can be a more qualified software engineer in Haskell, PureScript, Scala, F#, and Elm if you know them.

- Inversion of control, modularity, and interfaces are all about one general principle of software design—divide and conquer.

- The essential part of functional programming is the careful handling of side effects.

- The use of a static and strong type system in an object-oriented language can help developers eliminate errors during the design phase.

- Use the SOLID principles for reasoning about your design decisions, even in functional languages.

The basics of functional declarative design

This chapter covers

- Software architecture
- Functional design tools, ideas, and approaches
- Shaping the surface of functional declarative design
- Practicing simple eDSLs

High-level requirements and business environments are never the same for different business tasks. Budgets, technology stacks, available resources—all of them are very situational. We can't predict everything. If some idea works better here, it can fail under other circumstances. The object-oriented paradigm addresses graphic user interfaces nicely, while making it very difficult to build concurrent applications. Imperative code will be the fastest on average, but its safety will require much more effort than functional languages can take.

We can't predict everything, but we can at least reduce risks and costs by having patterns, architectures, common practices, and reasoning frameworks ready. Knowing a principle frees us from remembering the details. Knowing a methodology frees us from unnecessary, risky, and costly occasional research. Functional languages such as Scala and Haskell offer a different perspective on how to construct applications. Even within Scala, there are at least three schools of doing things: Scala-as-Java, Scala-as-Scala, and Scala-as-Haskell. Yet there is a conceptual apparatus that we can try to shape in this chapter. I call it *functional declarative design* (FDD), a methodology that is the closest counterpart of *object-oriented design* (OOD). It's an umbrella term for the practices I recommend: all of them constitute a consistent, complete, and reasonable approach, but this is not the only design philosophy possible. There are others as well (see, for example, *Railway Oriented Programming* by Scott Wlaschin at https://fsharpforfunandprofit.com/rop/), but in some sense, they can be fit into FDD easily, as they represent only a fraction of the whole engineering discipline for functional languages.

Figure 2.1 sheds some light on the meta-structure of FDD and OOD.

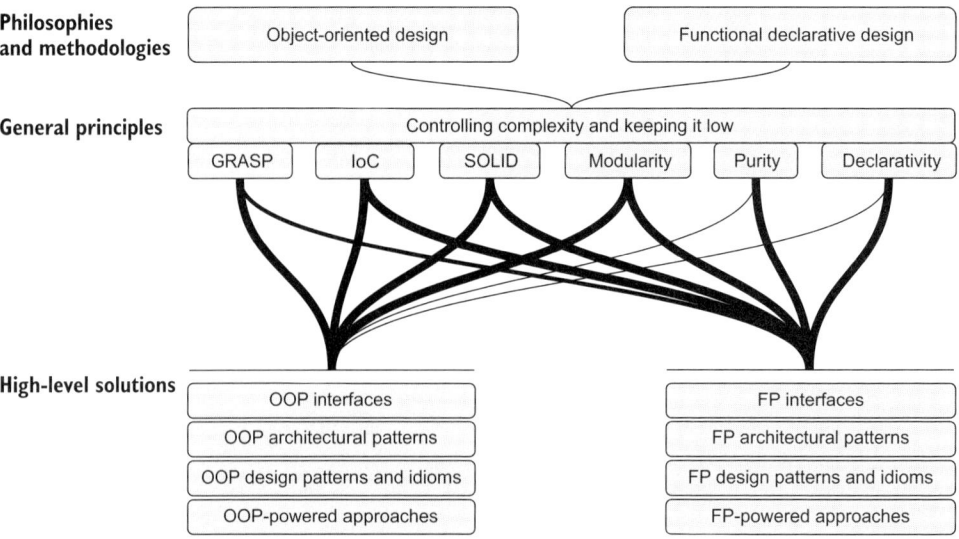

Figure 2.1   OOD and FDD

Both OOD and FDD gravitate toward complexity and provide similar tools for designing software: interfaces, design patterns, and approaches. The design principles such as modularity and purity may, in principle, be applied in both worlds, but the thickness of the lines shows what principles work best for OOP or FP.

It's the world of practical concepts and ideas that you can meet in Haskell, Scala, and other functional languages. Consider this chapter as a navigation map across this world, and read it as reference material, or skip it and return later if you'd like to proceed with the actual project we'll be building in the book.

2.1   *The engineering approach*

When newcomers join our team, we can easily include them in the project because we have different artifacts left after the design process: application architectures, design diagrams, requirement documents, program interfaces, and domain-specific languages. Newcomers see the big picture and can navigate across the project. That's how the engineering approach solves the problem of knowledge transfer.

But the main goal of this reasoning is certainly the product quality. Good, nicely engineered code allows us to rework the parts independently, without breaking the rest of the application. The risks are low, the complexity is low, and the components are reasonably decoupled from each other and can be observed by a human mind. The engineering approach is important because software becomes much more complicated every year.

2.1.1 *Software architecture classification*

We'll start with a clarification. Recently, we introduced the term *software architecture*. While it's too broad on its own, we'll use it sometimes as a synonym for *application architecture*, which is a narrower term. When we're talking about better-structured code, it's the architecture of an application (for example, a Google Docs mobile application). When we're trying to make various services friends, it becomes a solution architecture (a Google Docs mobile application, Google Docs web service, and all the infrastructure behind it). There are other levels above that—for example, *enterprise architecture*, which is about developing several products in relation to each other (the whole Google Drive functionality integrated with Google Docs, Google Sheets, Google Slides, and everything behind it, including its relation to Google Accounts). Figure 2.2 introduces these architectures organized hierarchically.

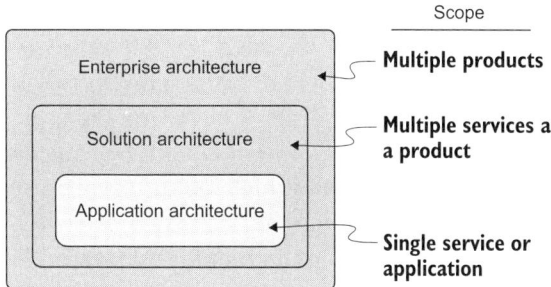

Figure 2.2   Different types of architecture in software engineering

To draw a line between them, let's see what questions can be asked when developing the solution architecture:

- What are the main business components of the whole solution? Web portal, mobile application, backend for services?
- Do we need a service-oriented approach (and therefore a service-oriented architecture)?
- Should it be monolith or microservices?

- Will it be a complex of distributed applications? If so, do we need our own communication protocol, or is it fine to take any existing one?
- Should a big enterprise-level database be included to secure the future growth of the product? Postgres? MS SQL Server? Oracle?
- Plus, NoSQL database for caching or fast replicas? Redis, Cassandra? MemcacheDB?
- Should we have a message broker in the middle? RabbitMQ, ZeroMQ? Apache Kafka?
- What is the data flow between these components?
- How can we store data reliably? Do we need event sourcing?
- How can we process data reliably? Maybe using a specific architecture pattern, particularly command and query responsibility segregation (CQRS)?
- How can we deal with the difficulties of distributed systems such as the CAP theorem?

You can see that there are many topics here, most of which I'm not even familiar with. At this level, we can still apply functional ideas to a solution architecture—a functional reactive pipeline made of services or an object-oriented actor model, but in general, the notion of a programming paradigm does not have any significant effect here. In contrast, choosing the paradigm, or rather, the core principles for code structuring is crucial for an application architecture to age properly. This is what we'll focus on.

So what are other considerations for an application architecture? Imagine we're talking with someone who knows programming in depth. Even if they've never seen a particular program, they can make assumptions about the largest concepts it comprises. Let's take Minesweeper as an example. This application has a graphic user interface (GUI), a field of bombs and numbers, some rules for bombs, and a scoring dashboard. We might assume that the application has a monolithic structure, with bare WinAPI calls for drawing and controlling the GUI, in which the logic is encoded as transform functions over a 2D array of predefined values (Bomb, Blank, and numbers from 1 to 8). Figure 2.3 shows this structure.

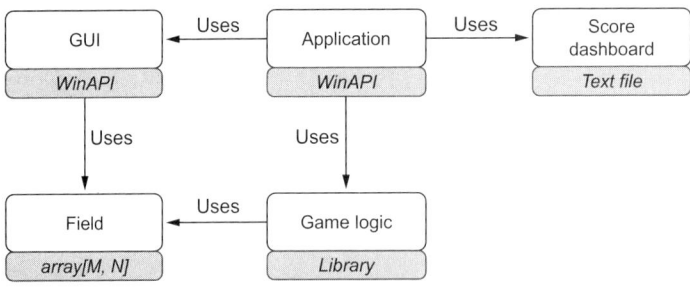

Figure 2.3   Architecture of the Minesweeper game

Another example is Minecraft. It's a little more challenging to say what the game code looks like. It's way more complex than Minesweeper. But we can make some assumptions by observing external symptoms of the internal mechanisms. The game has a GUI, server and client parts, networking code, 3D graphics logic, a domain model, an AI solver, a database with game objects, world-generation logic, game mechanics, and lots of fans. Each of the parts (except the fans, of course) is implemented in the code somehow. If we imagine that we are Minecraft developers, we can

- Implement 3D graphics using OpenGL
- Use relational database SQLite
- Have a Lua scripting layer for the AI
- Encode game logic in pure functions
- Mix it all together with some spaghetti code in Java

Clearly, we won't get into the implementation details; instead, let's look at the top level of the code structure only, which we can visualize in a diagram (figure 2.4).

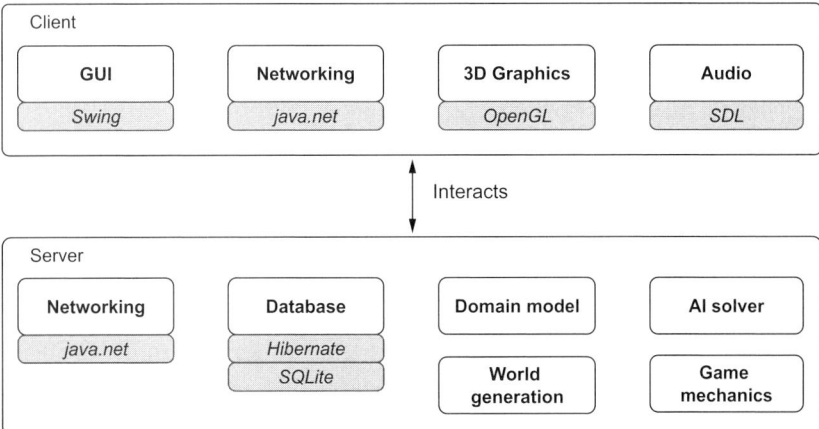

Figure 2.4   Possible architecture of Minecraft

This is an application's architecture. So architecture is the high-level structure of an application of a software system—a description of its structure, behavior, and properties, as well as the motivation behind the decisions that have led to this architecture.

Decisions we make on the architecture level affect all aspects of our program. The cost of mistakes is high because it's often impossible to change an architectural choice. Consider the diagram in figure 2.5.

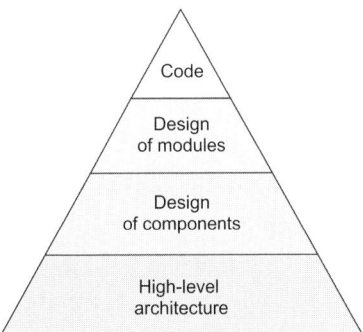

Figure 2.5   Levels of software design

The lower the level where decisions are made, the higher the cost of possible mistakes. Invalid decisions made about architecture are a widespread cause of project deaths.

Unfortunately, there are no holy tablets with step-by-step guides on how to create a good architecture, but there are some common patterns and practices that help us obey the software requirements. By following these practices, it's possible to make a raw sketch of architecture, but every project has its own unique characteristics, and so will every architecture. For more information on architectures, see *Software Architecture Guide* by Martin Fowler (https://martinfowler.com/architecture/).

When it's unclear whether the architectural solution is good enough, try to remember the following three things: there are goals to be accomplished, requirements to be satisfied, and complexity to be eliminated. Good architecture should address these characteristics well.

2.1.2   *Design tools and abstractions*

It seems that functions (either first class or higher order) are the only abstraction all functional languages have in common. It all starts with combining functions and applying them to functions, or functions to simple values. Both Clojure and lambda calculus prove that only this abstraction has expressiveness powerful enough for designing entire applications. But most of the languages offer extra features beyond just functions and lambdas, and there is a reason for that—abstractions can strengthen or weaken the design if they fit well or are completely misplaced.

Take templates in C++ as an example. This feature has an awkward syntax and is therefore hard to use. Constructing a fragile house of cards with templates in C++ is a high art of avoiding deadly traps! By doing this, the developer wants to achieve an abstraction that solves the problem, but the taller the house, the more likely it will crash. Abstractions over abstractions are over-engineering, and they tend to leak.

> **DEFINITION**   A leaky abstraction is an abstraction that reveals implementation details instead of hiding them. It solves part of the problem, while resisting changes that are supposed to solve the whole problem. A leaky abstraction affects refactoring badly, and it not only seeps into the client code but also spreads over

the project like a tide. A leaky abstraction brings more complexity to the code than it removes.

Abstractions can be more or less compound. Initially, functional languages were more function focused, but any modern language also has a lot of features beyond functions. These features, be they only syntactic sugar or something more involved, give you great freedom to produce various abstractions.

Common functional programming elements include lambdas, regular functions, and higher-order functions that take other functions as inputs or produce new functions as results. But at the design level, you would rather abstract from bolts and nuts to more general instruments—to advanced functional idioms. Haskell, for example, suggests a set of concepts inspired by category theory, and it's believed that these abstractions don't leak because of their mathematical nature. In practice, they can leak, though, because nothing is perfect in grounded software engineering.

So what are these idioms and patterns? You'll find informal definitions of them right after the schematic view in figure 2.6.

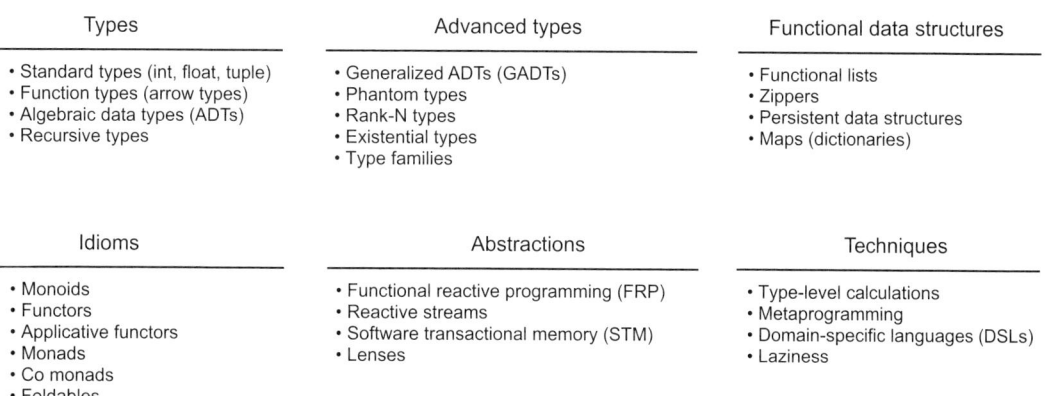

Types	Advanced types	Functional data structures
• Standard types (int, float, tuple) • Function types (arrow types) • Algebraic data types (ADTs) • Recursive types	• Generalized ADTs (GADTs) • Phantom types • Rank-N types • Existential types • Type families	• Functional lists • Zippers • Persistent data structures • Maps (dictionaries)

Idioms	Abstractions	Techniques
• Monoids • Functors • Applicative functors • Monads • Co monads • Foldables • Traversables	• Functional reactive programming (FRP) • Reactive streams • Software transactional memory (STM) • Lenses	• Type-level calculations • Metaprogramming • Domain-specific languages (DSLs) • Laziness

Figure 2.6   Classification of functional ideas

You'll encounter many of these important terms and functional pearls, and the following definitions should help you form a kind of intuition required to design functionally:

- *Standard types*—These include int, float, tuple, function types (also known as types of functions or arrow types), and so on. In functional programming, almost every design starts by constructing a type that reflects the domain. When you have a type of something, you know how it can be used and what properties it has:

```
type PersonName = (String, String)
johnDoeName, janeDoeName :: PersonName
johnDoeName = ("John", "Doe")
janeDoeName = ("Jane", "Doe")
```

- *Algebraic data types (ADTs)*—An ADT is a composite type consisting of sum types (also known as *variant types*), and every sum type can be composed with a product type (also known as a *tuple* or *record*). ADTs are widely used in functional programming for designing domain models or any kind of data structure:

```
type Age = Int
data Person = Person { name :: PersonName, age :: Age }
johnDoe, janeDoe :: Person
johnDoe = Person johnDoeName 32
janeDoe = Person janeDoeName 31
```

Algebraic data type having two fields

- *Recursion and recursive data types*—While it is the only way to iterate over things in pure functional programming, recursion also permeates many functional idioms. Interestingly, without recursion in the level of types, it would be hard to represent, for example, a list data type in a static type system:

```
data List a = Cons a (List a) | Nil

persons :: List Person
persons = Cons johnDoe (Cons janeDoe Nil)
```

Recursive ADT

Custom list with two items

- *Data structures and containers*—Designing a good domain model sometimes means choosing from a number of data structures to better reflect the essence of the domain. *Maps (dictionaries), sets, lists, graphs, vectors (arrays),* and other structures inhabit every program, including a program written in a functional language:

```
type SocialSecurityNumber = String

personsDict :: Map SocialSecurityNumber Person
personsDict = Map.fromList
  [ ("111-11-1111", johnDoe)
  , ("222-22-2222", janeDoe) ]
```

Converting an associative list of (key, value) into a map

- *Lenses*—Modifying an immutable data structure isn't possible. Instead, we recreate the structure to have a modified one. If the updated value is buried too deep within a hierarchical data structure, then we first unroll the structure layer by layer, make the change, and then roll everything back. But this process can quickly turn code into a boilerplate mess, making it difficult to read and understand. Lenses provide a useful abstraction for modifying data structures of any depth, all while keeping the code concise and readable. With lenses, you can avoid manually unwrapping and rewrapping complex data structures, which makes it easier to work with them in a clean and organized way. If you're looking to simplify your code and streamline your workflow, lenses are an excellent tool to consider:

```
type Suffix  = String
type PersonTitle = (Suffix, PersonName)

personName :: PersonTitle -> PersonName
```

```
personName title = view _2 title
```

> **_2 is a lens for accessing the second element of the tuple with the 'view' combinator.**

```
getFirstName1 :: PersonTitle -> String
getFirstName1 title = view _1 (personName title)
```

> **_1 is a lens for accessing the first element of the tuple.**

```
getFirstName2 :: PersonTitle -> String
getFirstName2 title = view (_2 . _1) title

-- getFirstName ("Mr.", johnDoeName) == "John"
```

> **Same, with two lenses combined with the dot combinator**

- *Meta-programming*—In many programming languages, including functional ones, meta-programming involves manipulating abstract code that declares what some unwritten code should be. When the compiler encounters this manipulation, it generates additional code at compile time based on these instructions. While meta-programming can be a powerful tool for design, the output produced by the compiler is implicitly embedded into your code, making it difficult to discern what code was actually generated. Despite this challenge, with careful use, meta-programming can greatly enhance the expressiveness and flexibility of your codebase:

```
data Person = Person { _name :: PersonName
                     , _age :: Age }
```

> **The underscore prefix is a Haskell convention for making lenses.**

```
person = Person ("Jane", "Doe") 31

makeLenses ''Person
```

> **Template Haskell (metaprogramming) function call to create lenses for Person**

```
getFirstName :: Person -> String
getFirstName person = view (name . _1) person
```

> **The name lens is generated with Template Haskell.**

```
-- getFirstName janeDoe == "Jane"
```

- *Domain-specific languages (DSLs)*—A DSL represents the logic of a particular domain by defining its structure, behavior, naming, semantics, or possibly syntax. The benefits of a DSL are reliability, reducing the complexity of the domain, clearness of code to nonprogrammers, ease of getting things right, and difficulty of getting things wrong:

```
data Actions
  = SendMoney { to :: Person, amount :: Money }
  | InviteToParty { attendees :: List Person }
  | ScheduleMeeting { with :: Person, when :: DateTime }
```

- *Functional idioms: monoids, functors, applicative functors, comonads, arrows, and others*—These idioms are intrinsic mathematical properties of some data types.

Once we've revealed a property of our data type (for example, our ADT is a functor), we gain the next level of abstraction for it. Now our type belongs to the corresponding class of types, and all the library functions defined for that class will work for our type too. We can also create our own library functions for general classes of types:

```
data List a = Cons a (List a) | Nil                        ◄──  Custom functional list
                                                                type (recursive)
instance Functor List where                                ◄──  Functor instance
  fmap f Nil       = Nil                                    ◄──  for the list type
  fmap f (Cons a l) = Cons (f a) (fmap f l)     ◄──
                                                                fmap function for
persons :: List Person                                          an empty list
persons = Cons johnDoe (Cons janeDoe Nil)                       fmap function for the tail

personsAges :: List Age
personsAges = fmap age persons                    ◄──          List of Person converted
                                                                to List of Age
-- personsAges == Cons 32 (Cons 31 Nil)
```

- *Monads*—Monads are mechanisms for combinatorial value transformation when it's not only value transformation but something else over that. If you want to work with a value, and it can eventually become null (in terms of Java), then we'd better consider it "a possibly absent value" rather than "a possibly null instead of the value." This gives us the idea of the Maybe type (Option in Scala). But it's no longer convenient to process many Maybe values naively with boilerplate. This is where the Maybe monad mechanism helps a lot. There are many monads: IO, State, Reader, Writer, Maybe, List, Either, STM, Free. All have their own internal mechanisms and effects, but dealing with one monad is very similar to dealing with another, thanks to the abstract monadic interfaces and syntactic sugar (the do-notation in Haskell and for-comprehension in Scala). Perhaps no functional designer can avoid inventing monads irrespective of their intentions. As this is a place of struggle for many, it would be good to have one more explanation of monads. Check out appendix A to improve your knowledge of monads and their usage:

```
getPerson :: SocialSecurityNumber -> Maybe Person
getPerson ssn = Map.lookup ssn personsDict               Maybe values are
                                                         bound monadically
areNamesakes :: Maybe Bool                               with do-notation.
areNamesakes = do
  p1 <- getPerson "111-11-1111"                    ◄──
  p2 <- getPerson "222-22-2222"
  let namesakes = (view (name . _2) p1) == (view (name . _2) p2)
  pure namesakes

-- areNamesakes == Just True
```

- *Monad stacks, monad transformers*—Monads can be seen as extra effects for regular functional code. Two effects can't coexist for the same code—for example, doing impure sequential input–output operations (IO monad) and unwrapping Maybe values (Maybe monad) isn't possible inside a single do-block. Either this or that—the do-block is strictly specialized. But with the help of monad transformers, merging two monads into a compound monad becomes possible. Monad transformers nest one monad into another with no limit on the nesting depth. This action, therefore, forms a monad stack, which is a monad itself. Monads and monad stacks have a significant share in the Haskell codebases. We'll definitely learn a bunch of design patterns based on monadic stacks. To find more about monad transformers, consider appendixes B and C:

```
getPersonFromFile :: SocialSecurityNumber -
                   > StateT (Maybe Person) IO ()
getPersonFromFile ssn = do
  contents <- liftIO (readFile "persons.txt")      ◄──  IO action is used in the
                                                        StateT stack with the
                                                        help of lifting.
  case (readMaybe contents) of
    Nothing -> pure ()
    Just personsDict -> do
      let mbPerson = Map.lookup ssn personsDict
      put mbPerson                                  ◄──  StateT monad is used to
                                                        put the value into the
                                                        StateT's context.
```

It was quite easy to provide real-world examples for each concept from this list. Yet, in Haskell, there are concepts that are even more challenging to learn:

- *Laziness*—In the hands of a master, laziness can be a powerful design technique. With laziness, for example, it's possible to transform one graph to another effectively without touching some nodes if they are not used in the program. How does this work? You might write code that looks like it transforms a big structure but actually doesn't. After that, you can compose such heavy transformations, but in fact, when they finally go to evaluation, only a small part of the chained transformations will be evaluated—no more and no less than you need.

- *Nonstandard complex types: existential types, phantom types, and Rank-N types*—We won't define these here, but you should know that sometimes it's possible to enforce your code by enclosing additional information in your types so the compiler will be checking code validity all the time while you are compiling the code.

- *Generalized algebraic data types (GADTs)*—The GADT is an extension of the ADT in which nonstandard complex types are allowed. GADTs allow us to lift some logic and behavior to the type level and also solve some problems in a more generic way. We'll see a couple of use cases for them in the book.

- *Type-level calculations and logic*—Type-level calculations are types too. Why? This is the further development of the idea of getting correctness from types. Correct behavior can be achieved either by testing code and debugging it or by lifting the logic to the type level and proving its correctness via the compiler. Haskell and Scala have many features for type-level calculations: type classes, phantom types, rank-N types, type families, GADTs, recursive types, meta-programming, and so on. Learning such unusual concepts for design can be a mind-blowing experience!

Type-level design is yet to be structured as an engineering discipline. For now, I can recommend this interesting book on Idris, a Haskell-like functional language but with a type system that reaches very advanced grounds: Edwin Brady's *Type-Driven Development with Idris* (Manning, 2017; https://mng.bz/PZ0g).

Finally, functional programming comes with high-level abstractions and approaches that can be used for architecting the applications:

- *Software transactional memory (STM)*—STM represents a model of concurrent state with safe transactions for its modification. Unlike concurrent data structures, STM represents a combinatorial approach, so combining models gives us another STM model. One of the biggest advantages of STM is that it can be implemented as a monad, so you can construct your model monadically and even embed STM into other monads.

- *Functional reactive programming (FRP)*—FRP is a style of reactive programming merged with functional ideas. In FRP, the notion of time-varying values is introduced. If some other value depends on the first one, it will be automatically updated. These values have a special name: *signals* (or *behaviors*). Every event is mapped to a form of a signal, as it can occur, change, repeat, and disappear—it's a time-dependent value. Any logic can then be bound to the signal as a reaction. By having a reactive model composed of signals (often called a *reactive network*) and actions, it's possible to support GUIs and complex business logic in functional programs.

- *Functional reactive streams*—This abstraction addresses similar purposes as FRP. A reactive stream is a continuous stream of events arranged by time. Streams (and thus the events that have occurred) can be mapped, merged, divided, and zipped, forming new types of streams. Every change or absence in a stream can be bound to an action. The streaming model implements the data flow concept. For more information, see *Parallel and Concurrent Programming in Haskell* by Simon Marlow (O'Reilly Media, Inc., 2013; https://mng.bz/JZeP), *Functional and Reactive Domain Modeling* by Debasish Ghosh (Manning, 2016; https://mng .bz/wxqW), and Stephen Blackheath and Anthony Jones' *Functional Reactive Programming* (Manning, 2016; https://mng.bz/qOqE).

- *Functional architectural design patterns*—When designing an application architecture, it's important to think in terms of molecules rather than atoms and electrons. In the mainstream world, there are many architectural design patterns such as MVC (Model–View–Controller) and MVVM (Model–View–ViewModel). In addition, functional programming has its own unique set of design patterns, which are essential to building high-quality applications. In particular, developers working with Scala and Haskell often rely on the Final Tagless approach (known as mtl in Haskell), as well as other patterns such as the ReaderT monad, Service Handle pattern, Free Monad pattern, and various effect systems. This book introduces each of these patterns, providing a detailed comparison so that you can choose the best approach for your application. By learning from these functional design patterns, you can build software that is more modular, scalable, and maintainable.

I've described the most important patterns, but I'll leave detailed explanations for later, at least for those patterns that we'll be touching directly.

2.1.3 *Top-down iterative development process*

In chapter 1, we discussed the phases of the development process, which follow one another until we reach a ready application. We started with requirements analysis. This is the process in which we try to understand the domain in which we want to program. We collect problems, facts, and notions by reading documentation and talking with engineers. We want to know what we should create. The software design phase comes after that. We translate requirements into a form suitable for developers to begin writing code. In this phase, we design the software architecture, composing it from big independent parts and high-level design patterns. When the big picture is done, we implement details in the code. That's why we call this approach *top-down*: we start from top-level concepts of the domain and descend to the details of low-level code. The whole process is described in figure 2.7.

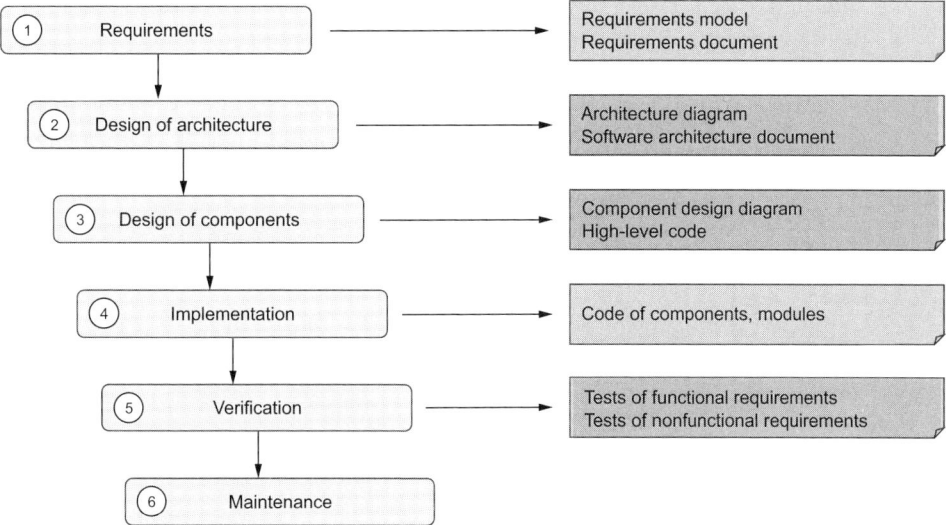

Figure 2.7   The waterfall model of software development

Although we can't return to the previous phase, this flow is an idealization of the development process. It has a well-known name: *the waterfall model*. In real life, we'll never be so smart as to foresee all the hidden pitfalls and prevent them before the next phase starts. For example, we may face problems in phases 2, 3, and 4 if we miss something in the initial requirements phase. For this exact reason, the waterfall model is barely followed in production. In contrast to the waterfall model, agile models have been invented. They are iterative and very adaptive. Without going too deep into this theme, we'll adopt some iterative and incremental models for our learning projects; however, consider the waterfall model as a reference to what activities exist in the software development process.

> **NOTE**   In its way, the waterfall model has undergone many iterations aimed to make it less resistant to eventual switches between phases. You need to know the waterfall model or its modifications to understand what you're doing now and to avoid wasting time while trying hard to fit your activities into some blocks on a piece of paper.

Better models allow you to return to the previous phases iteratively so you can fix any problems that may have occurred. In functional programming, the iterative top-down approach seems the best choice for the initial design. You start from a high level—for example, a function

```
type Problem  = <task description>
type Solution = <desired result>

solveProblem :: Problem -> Solution
```

and then descend into the implementation. Before attacking the problem in code, you need to collect requirements and design the architecture and separate subsystems.

Designing with diagrams in FDD aims to reveal points of interest, show hidden pitfalls, and elaborate a rough vision of how to overcome problems. Returning to diagrams at any stage of development is normal because something will always need to be specified or changed. Figure 2.8 shows the whole design process.

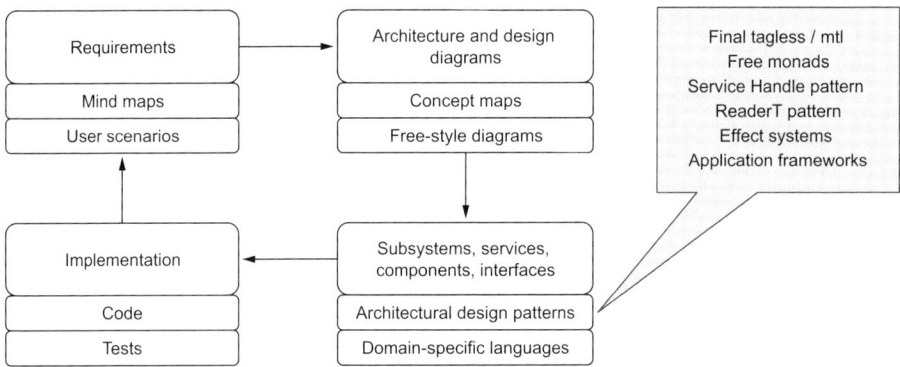

Figure 2.8   Iterative architecture design process in FDD

In reality, the number of different methodologies is huge. Every team lead establishes their own practices in their team. Every software architect goes down a unique path before they can be effective enough and stick to the techniques of design they like the most. No need to learn this as a theorem; the only point I want to make is that a conscious developer should be systematic.

2.1.4 Collecting requirements

In general, we need a comprehensive, consistent, and clear description of the task we want to solve. This will serve as a feature reference for developers and, much more importantly, an agreement with the customer as to what properties the system should have. Let's call this description a *requirements model*. A requirements model is a set of detailed, clear, and well-structured descriptions of what properties an upcoming product should have. The process of requirements modeling aims to collect the requirements and represent them in a form accessible to all project participants.

While creating the requirements model, you may feel like Sherlock Holmes. You're trying to extract actual knowledge from your customer, from experts, from the documentation provided, from examples, and from any other sources of information available. You have to be discerning because the facts you're getting are often very unclear; some of them will be contrary to each other and even to common sense. This is normal because we're humans, and we make mistakes. Don't hesitate to ask questions when you need clarification. What's worse? Spending more time on requirements analysis or wasting that time creating something vague and useless?

There are many possibilities for creating a requirements model. When you're done, you will have a software requirements document or, less formally, a set of well-formed requirements available to both developers and the customer. We'll take a brief look at them here:

- *Questions and answers*—This is the best method of investigating what the customer wants to have done. Questions can vary about the purpose of the software, domain terms and their meaning, expectations regarding functionality, and so on. The main disadvantage of questions and answers is the lack of a convenient information structure.

    Q: Should the Minecraft application support multiplayer?

    A: It's the central idea.

    Q: Should it be a classic client-server architecture or a distributed nodes network?

    A: Classic client-server architecture would be enough.

- *Use case diagrams*—A use case diagram (see figure 2.9) shows what actions the actor can do with a subsystem within some logical boundary. An actor can be a user or another subsystem. As mentioned in chapter 1, use case diagrams are part of UML, a standard that suggests a strong structure for the diagrams. Use case diagrams can be used as the agreement between you and your customer about what functionality the program should have. For our intention to design software using a functional language, use case diagrams don't help much because they don't allow us to reveal the domain's functional properties.

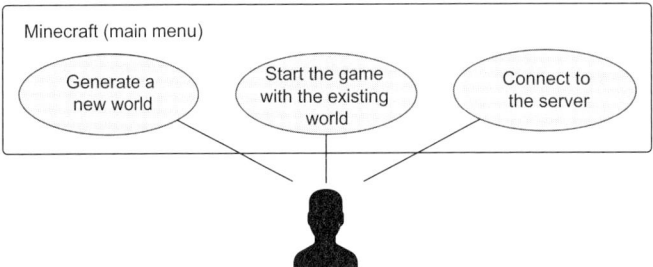

Figure 2.9   Use case diagram for the main menu of Minecraft

- *User scenarios*—These scenarios describe a user solving a particular problem step by step with the help of the application we're constructing. Scenarios may have alternative paths—input conditions and output conditions the system should meet before and after the scenario, respectively. User scenarios can follow use case diagrams or be an independent part of the requirements model. They are written informally, so you and the customer can verify that you understand each other. User scenarios have a good and focused structure and are concrete and comprehensive:
  - *User scenario*—Generating a new random world.
  - *Preconditions*—The game is launched.
  - *The user opens a generation window*—They either enter a specific seed for the random generator or configure the desired properties of the world: the surface/ocean ratio, the number of biomes, the density of forests, and other parameters. When this is done, the user initiates the generation itself.
  - *Postconditions*—a new world is generated.
- *Associative mind maps*—A mind map is a tree-like diagram with notions connected associatively. Mind maps are also called *intellect maps*. There are no standards or recommendations for how to dump your mind in a diagram because this is a highly personal process. The associative nature of mind maps extracts associations regarding a concrete notion. Mind maps are useful in software analysis, and they help us understand requirements from an FDD perspective. See the next section for a detailed explanation.

You may use any of these four tools of analysis. Questions and answers, user stories, and use case diagrams are well known, so we'll skip explanations here to have a deeper look at mind maps. As said earlier, associative diagrams seem to be the most suitable tool for brainstorming, but they aren't the only ones. You'll see how information can be organized in the mind map model, where each diagram reflects a part of the domain with a granularity that can be adapted to your needs.

2.1.5 Requirements in mind maps

In the FDD methodology, brainstorming is the preferred method for gaining a deep understanding of things. You'll learn some design diagrams that force you to think associatively and, I believe, lead you to functional solutions for architecture problems. But first, you need to prepare for this journey because you should understand your domain before you can construct the architecture. Welcome to the world of requirements analysis with mind maps.

Brainstorming is very unordered, which is why the results often have a free form. Mind maps are not so chaotic and yet are not as rigid as user stories or use case diagrams. We want to keep our diagrams focused on the goal: a description of a small part of the domain that's short but not so short as to miss important points that can affect the design.

A simple mind map I got after brainstorming Minecraft is presented in figure 2.10.

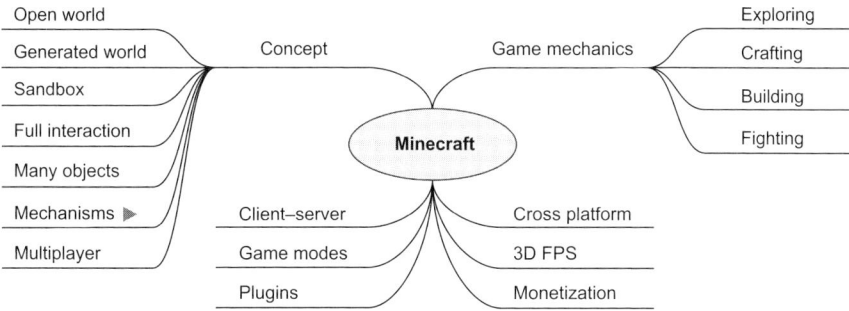

Figure 2.10   Level 1 mind map

It has the big topics of the game, with a promise to expand them later. After some elaboration, I got more detailed mind maps for several topics, as shown in figures 2.11 and 2.12.

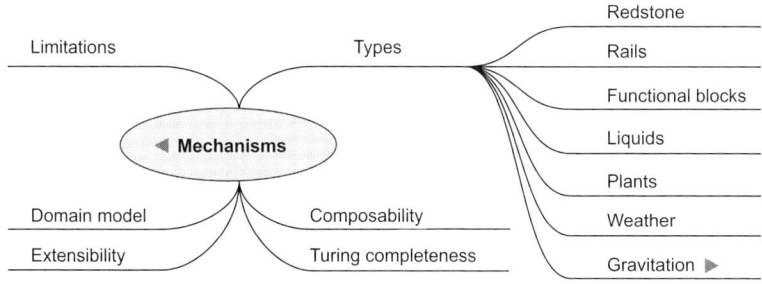

Figure 2.11   Level 2 mind map

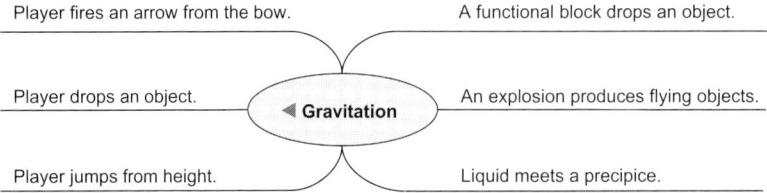

Figure 2.12 Level 3 mind map

As you can see, mind maps are trees of notions, although this is not strictly required. Relations between leaves and branches are allowed, so mind maps may carry much more information than just notions. I might have the domain organized imperfectly on these mind maps, and I might have missed something, but at least I know important terms and can navigate across the domain easily.

I like mind maps very much; they've helped me arrange my knowledge many times.

2.2 *Application architecture*

I'm going to flesh out the application architecture as it's seen from a functional programming's perspective. Is it in any way different from application architectures backed with object-oriented programming? We'll see.

Imagine developers who know nothing about your architecture. Can they easily understand its underlying ideas? Will they have trouble using the DSLs? Can they break something? How can you be sure the types you have elaborated on are good enough? And what is "good enough" architecture? Let's think. The architecture of the functional application is good if it is at least

- *Modular*—The architecture is separated into many parts (for example, subsystems, libraries, frameworks, or services), and every part has a small set of strongly motivated responsibilities.
- *Simple*—All parts have clear and simple interfaces. You don't need much time to understand how a specific part behaves.
- *Consistent*—There is nothing contradictory in the architectural decisions.
- *Expressive*—The architecture can support all of the known requirements and many of those that will be discovered later.
- *Robust*—Breaking one separate part shouldn't lead to crashes.
- *Extensible*—The architecture should allow you to add new behaviors easily if the domain requires it.

In functional programming, it's good to have an architecture in two forms:

- *Topology of layers, modules, and subsystems*—This can be either described by diagrams or implemented in the project structure. The hints as to how to define functionality for modules lie in our requirements model, and we will extract them from mind maps directly.

- *DSL interfaces for domain model, subsystems, and services*—A set of DSLs on top of a subsystem can be thought of as the functional interface of that system. We can use model-driven development to build DSLs for our domain model.

2.2.1 Architecture layers

In OOD, a *layer* is a set of classes grouped together by architectural purpose. We can also say a layer is a slice of the architecture that unites components with one high-level idea or acting on the same level of abstraction. In any matter, a layer is a logical division, not something physical.

What layers do we know of? There are several in OOD, and FDD suggests a few new ones. Let's revise the OOD layers:

- *Application layer*—This layer is concerned with application functioning and configuration, for example, command-line arguments, logging, saving, loading, environment initialization, and application settings. The application layer may also be responsible for threading and memory management.
- *Service layer*—In some literature, *service layer* is a synonym for *application layer*. In FDD, it's a layer where all the service interfaces are available.
- *Persistence (data access) layer*—This layer provides abstractions for storing data in permanent storage; it includes object-relational mappers (ORMs), data transfer objects (DTOs), data storage abstractions, and so on. In FDD, this layer may be pure or impure depending on the level of abstraction you want in your application. Purity means this layer's services should have functional interfaces and there should be declarative descriptions of data storage. The actual work with real data storage will be done in the interoperability layer or in the business logic layer.
- *Presentation (view) layer*—This layer provides mechanisms for building GUIs and other presentations of the application (for example, a console or web UI). It also handles input from the user (mouse or keyboard), from graphic and audio subsystems, and possibly from the network.
- *Domain model layer*—This layer represents a domain model in data types and DSLs and provides logic to work with. In FDD, it's a completely pure layer. Cases where it's impure should be considered harmful.
- *Interoperability layer*—This layer was born from the idea of providing one common bus that all the layers should use for communications without revealing the details. It often manages events, and in bigger systems, this can become an independent standalone message broker system. In FDD, this layer can be represented either by reactive code (FRP or reactive streams) or pipelined impure code (streams, pipelines, or compositions of impure, low-level functions, for example).
- *Business logic layer*—This layer should be considered as a superstructure over the interoperability layer and other layers. It consists of behavioral code that

connects different parts of the application together. In FDD, the business logic layer is about scenarios and scripts. Business logic is aware of interfaces and DSLs that the subsystems provide, and it may be pure. Business logic scenarios can be translated to impure code that should work over the interoperability layer.

Figure 2.13 brings everything into one schematic view.

Application layer	Domain model layer	Persistence layer
• Save/load • Configuration • Initialization • Plugins • Resources • Threading • Error handling • Lifecycle management	• Domain model • Domain logic	• Mapping to data model • CRUD • Store/load • Transactions • Error handling
Business logic layer	**Interoperability layer**	**Presentation layer**
• User scenarios • Parsers • Translators • Serialization • Logging • Error handling • Threading • Lifecycle management • Connection sessions • Networking	• Validation • Error handling • Impure logic evaluation • Threading • Event handling • Reactive logic • Interaction with other layers	• GUI • Input/output • Audio • Graphics

Figure 2.13   Layers: descriptions and responsibilities

Simultaneously, the idea of purity in FDD gives us two other layers that we mentioned before:

- *Pure layer*—This layer contains pure and deterministic code that declares behavior but never evaluates it in an impure environment.
- *Impure layer*—In this layer, any impure actions are allowed. It has access to the outer world and also has some means to evaluate logic declared in the pure layer. The impure layer should be as small as possible.

The pure layer can be quite a utility—just data transformations, nothing else. I won't be wrong if I say that every program has a number of calls of the library functions (for example, operations with strings or with numbers). However, I would avoid calling the ocean of these functions a layer. It doesn't have any design purpose. A more reasonable candidate for being a layer should be somehow involved in design activities.

By treating the whole program this way, we'll inevitably encounter the essence of functional programming: encoding actions by pure values and then interpreting these values with an impure interpreting machine. We do this all the way down in Haskell, and we're therefore building various kinds of eDSLs. The very spirit of Lambda Calculus blesses us for this encoding reasoning, so let's go for it.

2.2.2 *Embedded domain-specific languages*

Embedded domain-specific languages are my passion. I've constructed dozens and dozens of them, more or less domain oriented and more or less sophisticated, with all kinds of machinery inside. And every time I've done so, they've turned an unspeakably difficult domain into an understandable and accessible one. In this section, I'll introduce you to a typical pattern that we'll be exploiting a lot in this book.

The language will be intended for dealing with a smart home. Everyone can install intelligent thermometers and barometers outside the window to monitor the weather. A simple script in this language should read the measurements and send them somewhere—for example, to a chatbot.

All the methods will be encoded as an algebraic data type, and the whole script will be pure. Listing 2.1 demonstrates the language and the script. Notice that the language has five methods only, but the script may combine them in a sequence to achieve the needed effect. This particular design has a lot of flaws, including some inconsistency in the language and a possibility of screwing things up, but still.

Listing 2.1 Domain-specific language for a smart house

```
type ThermometerName = String
type BarometerName = String

data Language
  = ReadThermometer ThermometerName          Available methods
  | ReadBarometer BarometerName              to perform
  | ReportTemperature
  | ReportAtmospherePressure
  | ClearData

type Script = [Language]                     List of language methods represents
                                             a domain-specific script
script :: Script
script =
  [ ReadThermometer "Garage"                 A specific script that
  , ReadThermometer "Near the road"          does something useful
  , ReadThermometer "House"
  , ReadBarometer "Garage"
  , ReadBarometer "House"
  , ReportTemperature
  , ReportAtmospherePressure
  , ClearData
  ]
```

Once we pass the script to an interpreter, the latter will connect the pure actions to the impure external calls. Assuming we have a couple of libraries to interact with the devices, we can write it. Unfortunately, the interpreter will be long, as it must account for every action in the DSL. Also, it should be stateful and impure, which complicates the code even more. The entry point into the interpreter will be the following function:

```
interpreter :: Script -> IO ()
interpreter acts = interpret [] acts

interpret :: [Measurement] -> Language -> IO ()
```

It takes a script and traverses all its steps one by one, while connecting them to effective actions. It also maintains some state with the first argument of the interpret function. In our case, this state will be a list of measurements obtained during the script's evaluation. The interpreter has an internal data structure for it, which is an implementation detail we don't want to know in our script:

```
data Measurement
  = TemperatureCelsius ThermometerName Float
  | PressureAtmUnits BarometerName Float

isTemperature (TemperatureCelsius _ _) = True
isTemperature _ = False
isPressure (PressureAtmUnits _ _) = True
isPressure _ = False
```

Listing 2.2 gives you an excerpt of the interpreter's code. You can try reading it and ask whether it is clear or understandable. In contrast to the script, the interpreter is recursive, and it's monadic in the IO monad. Some shenanigans happen around the external libraries. This all may look too messy, but that's the implementation. Fortunately, we only need to write the interpreter once and hide all this complexity from the scripts.

Listing 2.2   Interpreter for the language

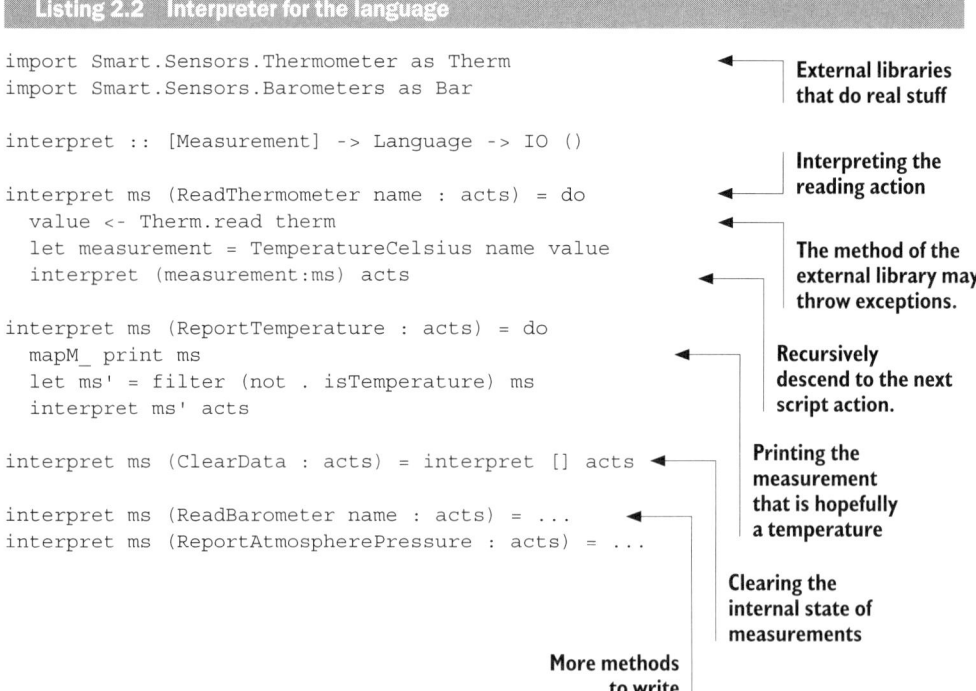

```
import Smart.Sensors.Thermometer as Therm        ◄──── External libraries
import Smart.Sensors.Barometers as Bar                  that do real stuff

interpret :: [Measurement] -> Language -> IO ()
                                                        Interpreting the
interpret ms (ReadThermometer name : acts) = do  ◄──── reading action
  value <- Therm.read therm                      ◄────
  let measurement = TemperatureCelsius name value       The method of the
  interpret (measurement:ms) acts                ◄────  external library may
                                                        throw exceptions.
interpret ms (ReportTemperature : acts) = do
  mapM_ print ms                                 ◄────  Recursively
  let ms' = filter (not . isTemperature) ms            descend to the next
  interpret ms' acts                                   script action.

interpret ms (ClearData : acts) = interpret [] acts ◄──  Printing the
                                                        measurement
interpret ms (ReadBarometer name : acts) = ...   ◄────  that is hopefully
interpret ms (ReportAtmospherePressure : acts) = ...    a temperature

                                                        Clearing the
                                                        internal state of
                                                        measurements

                          More methods
                             to write
```

Suppose we have the `Script` from the previous listings, and we want to add a logging call to each of the actions. We want to save effort and nerves and take only the minimal effort to support this case. What can we do?

There are at least three solutions:

- Update the existing interpreter. Add a logging function to each branch of it. The initial script won't be polluted by logging calls, but still, every step will be logged.
- Put the existing interpreter into a more high-level interpreter. Make logging calls in the external one, while the internal interpreter should only process the methods. The initial script will also stay the same.
- Add one more eDSL for logging, and wrap every single constructor of the `Language` ADT into it. Then, add a wrapping interpreter that will be descending to the currently existing one. We will be able to specify what methods to log from our script.

The first option with putting a `log` method into each interpreter branch is simple:

```
interpret ms (ReportTemperature : acts) = do
  mapM_ print ms
  let ms' = filter (not . isTemperature) ms

  log ReportTemperature                          ◀─┐ Log action
                                                    │ somehow
  interpret ms' acts
```

The second option requires some work. We already have two interpreting functions—a public one (`interpreter`) and an internal one (`interpret`)—and they are already organized hierarchically. What would moving the logging calls up one level look like? There is an obstacle in the previous code that prevents this from refactoring, so we should fix it first. Namely, we should move the responsibility of recursion from `interpret` to `interpreter`. Extracting them will make the design better. The following listing shows a new outer interpreter.

Listing 2.3   Outer interpreter

```
interpreter :: Script -> IO ()
interpreter acts = interpreter' [] acts
                                                   ◀─┐ Helper function
interpreter' :: [Measurement] -> Script -> IO ()  ◀─┐
interpreter' ms (act : acts) = do                     │ Interpreting a
  ms' <- interpret ms act                          ◀─┘ single action

  log act                                          ◀─┐ Logging the
                                                    │ action somehow
  interpreter' ms' acts                            ◀─┐
                                                       │ Recursively
                                                       │ descend to
                                                       │ other actions.
```

For recomposing the `interpret` function, we should make it return the list of updated measurements from every case instead of performing the recursion. It still interacts with the external library when needed, though:

```
interpret :: [Measurement] -> Language -> IO [Measurement]
interpret ms (ReadThermometer name) = do
  value <- Therm.read therm
  let measurement = TemperatureCelsius name value
  pure (measurement:ms)

interpret ms ClearData = pure []
```

The `[Measurement]` parameter here works as an immutable interpreter state. We'll elaborate on various approaches to state handling in chapter 7.

The final solution would be redesigning the language itself by adding specific methods for logging. I won't implement it to the working state but just share some design ideas in the form of scenarios.

Listing 2.4   Scenario with logging possibilities

```
script :: LoggingLanguage
script =
  [ Log (ReadThermometer "Garage")
  , Log (ReadThermometer "Near the road")
  , Log (ReadThermometer "House")
  , NoLog (ReadBarometer "Garage")
  , NoLog (ReadBarometer "House")
  , NoLog ReportTemperature
  , NoLog ReportAtmospherePressure
  , NoLog ClearData
  ]
```

In this script, we made the logging language to wrap the device control methods. That's certainly strange and may suggest the logging language is king. An attempt to fix this might lead to a script like the following.

Listing 2.5   Another scenario with logging possibilities

```
script :: [(Method, Log)]
script =
  [ (ReadThermometer "Garage", Log)
  , (ReadThermometer "Near the road", Log)
  , (ReadThermometer "House", Log)
  , (ReadBarometer "Garage", NoLog)
  , (ReadBarometer "House", NoLog)
  , (ReportTemperature, NoLog)
  , (ReportAtmospherePressure, NoLog)
  , (ClearData, NoLog)
  ]
```

In fact, the variety of eDSL designs is huge, and exploring this space can be a joyful activity. We'll develop this idea in future chapters; in particular, I'll teach you how to adopt the free monad to make your own powerful languages, so keep learning!

2.2.3 *Modularization of applications*

We want our code to be loosely coupled. Remember the general principles of design: divide logic, and be happy with smaller parts. In FDD, we're achieving this by introducing functional interfaces, as much as in OOD with its OOP interfaces and abstract classes. In my FDD methodology, I'm paying the most attention to free monads as functional interfaces, the only complete and full-fledged counterpart of OOP interfaces. Under some circumstances, free monadic languages can even simulate OOP classes with inheritance, encapsulation, and dynamic polymorphism (dynamic dispatch).

In general, free monads are a mechanism for making declarative, abstract, monadic, and interpretable languages. They are also value level, in contrast to other functional interfaces (such as ReaderT, Final Tagless / mtl, and effect tracking systems in Haskell):

- *Declarative*—A free language will describe several steps or actions declaratively. A scenario built from these actions will also be declarative. The scenario declares the steps or actions to be performed, but nothing will be evaluated until it is interpreted.

- *Abstract*—A free language, while serving as an interface, should only reflect the most important aspects of a domain or subsystem, without relying on or including implementation details.

- *Monadic*—A scenario will be monadic, meaning that it will be sequential and also compatible with all the monadic tools, such as do-notation, generic monadic functions, and monad stacks.

- *Interpretable*—A scenario in a free language can be passed to an interpreter that knows how to sequentially traverse all the steps and perform useful actions for each of them. Interpreters are implementations of a free language, and they are responsible for handling specific implementation details.

- *Value level*—A free monadic interface will be a first-class citizen, and so will interpreters. A method of a free interface can take another free interface and can return another free interface as a result.

In fact, we were very close to a free monadic eDSL with the `Language` for reading thermometers or barometers. `Language` is interpretable, abstract, and declarative. It's not yet monadic, though, and this is why we had to put the actions into a list, not into a do block. But with free monads, it's possible to convert it so that a scenario (script) could look as shown in the following listing.

Listing 2.6 A possible free monadic scenario

```
script :: Language ()
script = do                                    ◄─────── Language is a
  readThermometer "Garage"                               monad.
  readThermometer "Near the road"
  readThermometer "House"              Do-notation
  readBarometer "Garage"               works nicely for
                                       Language.
```

```
readBarometer "House"
reportTemperature
reportAtmospherePressure
clearData
```

This scenario looks much better than the previous ones, right? And nothing can stop us from having two interpreters for the Language eDSL—one with logging and another one without logging:

```
interpreter :: Language -> IO ()

loggingInterpreter :: Logger -> Language -> IO ()
```

I'm omitting the language itself and leaving this topic for later.

What free monadic interfaces bring into the application architecture is the separation of concerns. Similarly to OOP interfaces, free monadic interfaces introduce *subsystem boundaries*, which are illustrated in figure 2.14.

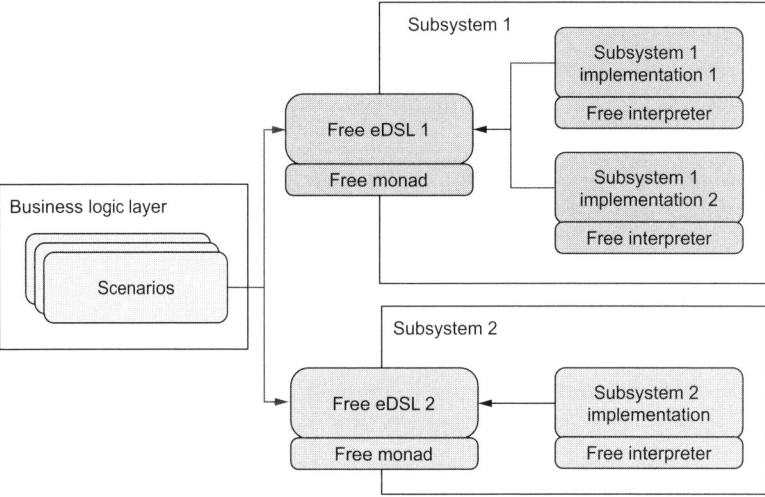

Figure 2.14   Subsystem boundaries

The two subsystems don't know about each other, and they can even relate to the different layers: subsystem 1 connects the application to the relational databases, whereas subsystem 2 is about the graphical user interface. The application layer here talks to the interpreters, which in turn execute free monadic languages. There is no limitation on how the interpreters act. They can be subordinate to the application as libraries, or they can have their own threads and be in-program actors. The boundaries between the subsystems now lie between the free monadic eDSLs. The only place where the languages come together is the business logic layer. We define free monadic scripts abstracted from real subsystems as much as we do with OOP interfaces.

In this architecture approach, it becomes clear that free monadic eDSLs should interact somehow when this makes sense. If we want to place the methods of the two free languages into the same script, this script should know about both of the languages. This is where the idea of free monad effect systems occurs, but it occurs in the community, not in FDD. I'm proposing another way that is simpler and quite enough to do impressive things. Free monadic languages can be nested. Methods of a language can refer to other languages, and this helps to build hierarchies of free monads. I call this approach *hierarchical free monads (HFM)*. Figure 2.15 is their schematic representation.

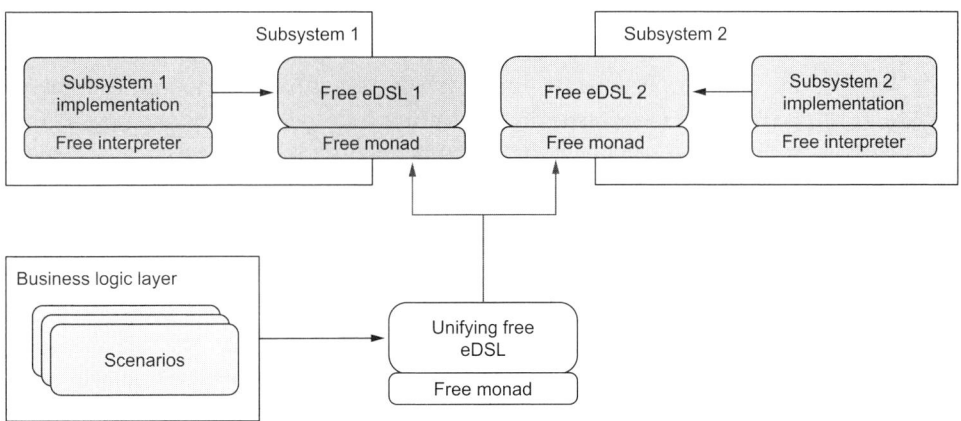

Figure 2.15   Hierarchical free monads

We'll avoid discussing the details of the technique here. We'll come to it in a more natural way by building a spaceship control application. We'll go from simpler concepts to free monads step-by-step, and this will show you the rationale behind HFMs and their place in software design.

Summary

- Functional declarative design is a practical engineering methodology that reiterates object-oriented design in application to functional programming.
- Learn to reason as an engineer. If you are a senior developer or a software architect, your responsibilities now go beyond just coding.
- The engineering approach is educated, systematic, and conscious. It is the opposite of sporadic, blind code hacking with the hope that something will work eventually.
- The engineering approach is intended to ensure the quality of the product and a better lifetime support of the code.
- The engineering approach aims to reduce complexity and risks and allow components to be decoupled and observed by a human mind.
- Software architecture is a complex process that requires careful consideration of goals, requirements, and complexity.
- Making decisions at a lower level can lead to higher costs for mistakes.

- Functional languages have the advantage of combining functions to create powerful abstractions that are easier to use than other language features.

- Leaky abstractions are abstractions that reveal implementation details instead of hiding them, and they can be an obstacle when refactoring code.

- Designing systems means knowing methodologies, practices, patterns, approaches, and high-level ideas. Try to broaden your horizons to have a better foundation when making decisions.

- To work in the functional paradigm effectively, you need to be familiar with its many concepts, idioms, and patterns, just as object-oriented developers need to be fluent in their respective technologies.

- Collecting requirements and talking to the business is also a part of the work. Organizing the requirements model in a systematic way should help you keep things in order.

- Questions and answers, use case diagrams, mind maps, and user scenarios are good for investigating the requirements of the product.

- Mind mapping is a powerful tool for domain analysis that allows users to create diagrams with pictures, numbered and bulleted lists, side notes, links to external resources, and even embedded sounds and movies.

- Software architecture has many levels. You might want to learn all of them, but this book focuses on application architecture.

- Embedded domain-specific languages are ubiquitous in functional programming! Use them to reduce the complexity of the system and keep things decoupled from each other.

Part 2

Minimum viable product

This part explores the strategic development of the initial stages of a software project. Our journey begins with the concept and crafting of a minimum viable product (MVP), a foundational step in the software development lifecycle. An MVP is not just a one-time prototype but a sustainable foundation for future development. The focus is on the importance of a fast feedback loop in these early stages, which is achieved through the creation of an MVP and the implementation of integration tests. Using the case study of Andromeda Control Software, we'll cover some essential aspects such as drafting, module organization, mnemonic analysis, and the use of reactive streams in the MVP process.

Next, we move to the realm of end-to-end design, focusing on establishing clear, final goals and aligning each design decision with these objectives. We discuss the importance of functional services for subsystem decoupling, the critical analysis of dependencies between layers, and the structuring of larger layers into more manageable sublayers. We talk about best practices for interface design, the Service Handle pattern for functional interfaces, the role of mocking in testing, and the utilization of type classes for added functionality. This approach aims to equip you with the knowledge and tools to ensure that your MVP and end-to-end design meet immediate requirements and lay a strong foundation for future scalability and adaptability.

Drafting the MVP
application

This chapter covers

- Clarifying product requirements
- Defining the scope of work
- Designing the application architecture
- Forging a simple implementation of the core
  subsystem

In this chapter, we'll start working on a SCADA-like system that we mentioned in a storytelling format in chapter 1 when describing our interactions with the Space Z corporation. SCADA (supervisory control and data acquisition) systems are software systems that work with complex hardware and allow the staff to control it. Such systems are usually complex and big, and I'm not nearly an expert in any of them. But this will be an interesting real-world task to explore. Let's call our SCADA system Andromeda Control Software. This project aims to develop a spaceship control and simulation software that the engineers from Space Z Corporation can use in their work. It has many parts and components, and all of them have their own requirements and desired properties. But for now, we only need a skeleton implementation with muscles that are enough for a little dancing. This will be our starting point, and we'll call this application a *minimum viable product* (MVP).

However, describing the domain to the extent we can afford is an inevitable step. I can't skip it in my narrative, and it is covered in section 3.1. In section 3.2, we'll talk about designing the architecture of the application. The section includes different diagrams to illustrate the process of reasoning. It very much resembles what we could do at a whiteboard when meeting with our colleagues. Yet, if you want to code, section 3.3 opens a door to the development world. We use mostly Haskell, but many concepts will be applied to other languages, such as F# and Scala.

3.1 Goals, requirements, and plans

We're going to build an application. Where to start? What goals should we pursue in the first place?

Let's try to guess what parts Andromeda Control Software should contain: a database, networking, GUI, application, external DSL for spaceship blueprints, multithreading, and some low-level libraries to connect with hardware.

Imagine we did this. Now imagine we appointed three independent teams to work on these components. This was done with no prior plan and no common guidelines. Later on, we start merging the results and realize that nothing matches up. All the codebases have their own approaches and design ideas. There is no common denominator (architecture) to unify these three contraptions into a working application. It's not Lego blocks like we expected—it's Frankenstein's monster.

This is a risk that can destroy your project, and I've seen it happen many times. People spend weeks developing libraries and microservices only to realize once the deadline arrives that the whole system cannot function properly. They end up having to start over from scratch—the end.

3.1.1 Minimum viable product

To avoid unnecessary risks, we should prove that our subsystems can work together even if the whole application isn't ready. Integration tests can help a lot here. They are used to verify the system as a whole when all parts are integrated and functioning in the real environment. When integration tests pass, this indicates that the circle is now complete—the system is proven to be working. However, there is a better choice: a sample program, a prototype with limited but still sufficient functionality to verify the idea of the product. You can find many articles about this technique using the keywords *minimum viable product*, or MVP. The technique aims to create something real, something you can touch and feel right now, even if not all functionality is finished. This will require a pass-through integration of many application components; the MVP is more presentable than integration tests.

Figure 3.1 introduces an MVP-based workflow.

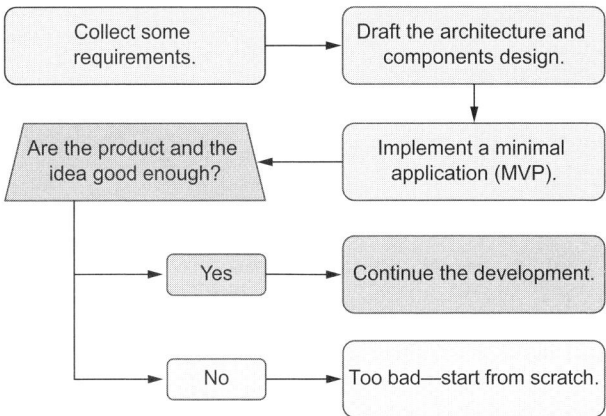

Figure 3.1 MVP-based workflow

The figure shows that MVP is not a one-time prototype. It's a foundation for future development that tries to be usable as soon as possible. This means it's still a good idea to draft an application architecture and some initial design of the components because we're going to proceed further with this code.

Our MVP will be a spaceship simulator program and a draft implementation of the spaceship control software. With the simulator, engineers can test spaceship systems for reliability or check other characteristics before the real spaceship is launched into space. Unfortunately, we can't support many actual SCADA requirements, including a hard real-time environment and minimal latency. Hard real-timeliness implies another set of tools: a system-level language with embedding possibilities (such as C or Rust), some specific operating system, programmable hardware (for example, field-programmable gate arrays [FPGAs] or microcontrollers), and so on. But let's consider our program as a kind of training simulator because we don't need to create a complex, ready-to-use program. We will try, however, to identify as many real requirements as we can to make our development process as close as possible to reality.

3.1.2 *Andromeda software requirements*

What do we know about the product? It's SCADA software, it's a GUI application, it connects to hardware controllers, and it's for astronauts and engineers. Let's collect these high-level requirements into a mind map (figure 3.2).

This map invites us to descend one level for the following components: hardware, logic control, database, and human user interface. We'll be analyzing the notion of "logic control," which is marked with a triangular arrowas, as the central notion of the next chapters.

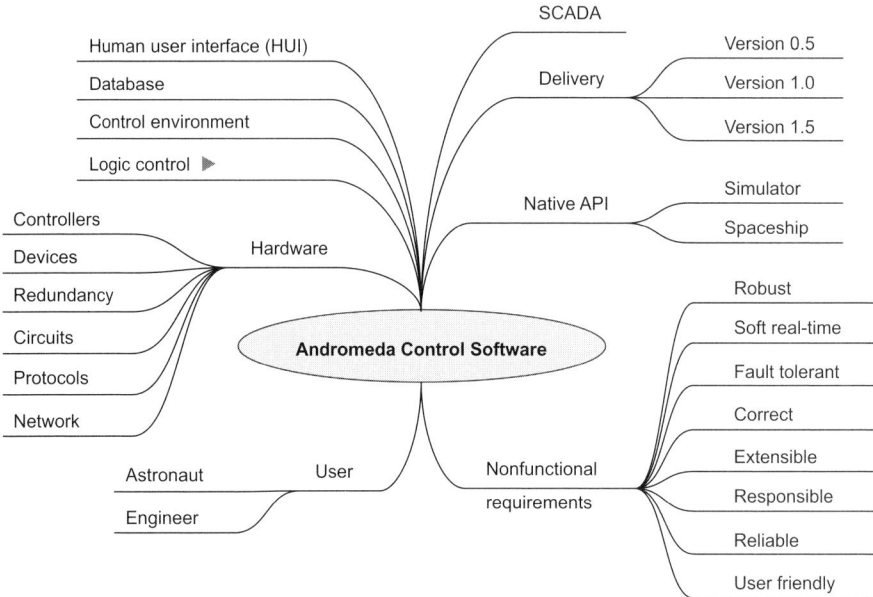

Figure 3.2   Andromeda Control Software mind map

What is logic control? In SCADA, it's a subsystem that evaluates the control of hardware: it sends commands, reads measurements, and calculates parameters. A programmable autonomous logic then utilizes the operational data to continuously correct spaceship orientation and movement. This is an important fact because one of the main responsibilities of engineers is to create this kind of logic during the shipbuilding process. That means we should provide either an interface to an external programming language or a custom DSL (or both). We don't need to think about how we can do this, just note that we should. Figure 3.3 shows the requirements related to logic control. I've collected a lot of them when working on the Andromeda application, so you can learn a bit about the SCADA domain from it.

The most interesting part of this is the "language" branch. Every time we are about to implement a domain model (in this case, the domain model of logic control), we should create a specific language (an *embedded DSL*, or eDSL) as the formal representation of the subsystem. The design of such a language is highly situational because domains are very different, and eDSLs should reflect that. In functional languages, implementing eDSLs is a kind of default design choice because it's so simple and convenient. In particular, Haskell and Scala have algebraic data types and some type-level features, making this task very interesting and beneficial. As for big subsystems, you might want to model a bunch of separate eDSLs and possibly use some advanced language features for that. Once you have an eDSL, you can think about it as formal documentation of your domain, and this opens a lot of interesting possibilities we'll talk about later.

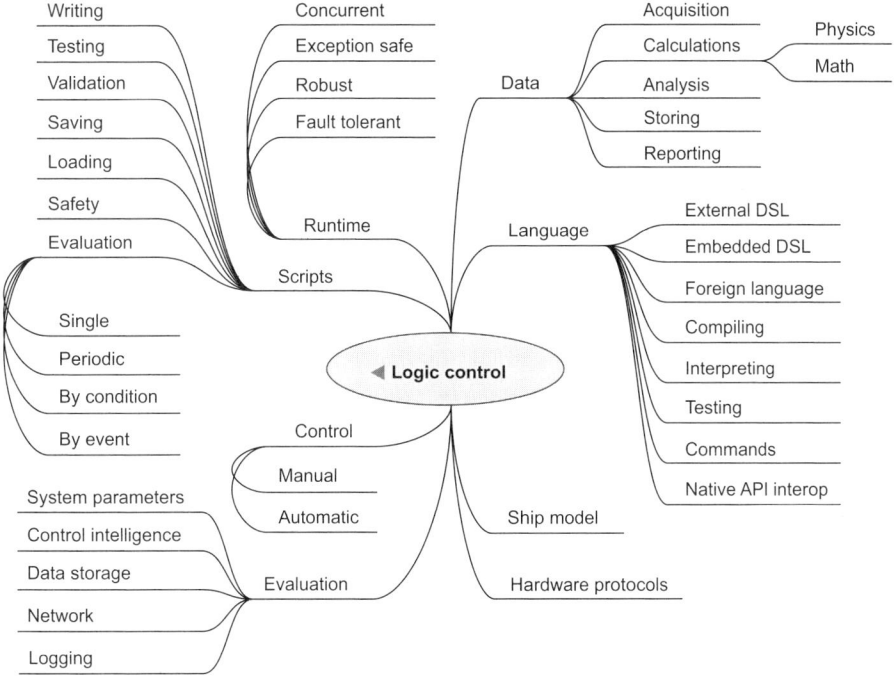

Figure 3.3 Logic control mind map

3.1.3 *The hardware subsystem*

Imagine you're once again in the shoes of the architect from the first chapter. Upon returning to the office, you get a letter: your employer, Space Z Corporation, has proposed a new requirement. They want you to create a language hardware, one from the family known as *hardware description language* (HDL) in the SCADA domain. HDLs come in different forms: standardized and ad hoc, proprietary and free, popular and unknown. Space Z Corporation wants its own. The language should have internal and external representation (meaning embedded DSL and external DSL), should be able to describe a wide set of measuring devices (sensors) and terminal units, should be simple rather than universal, and should abstract the nuts and bolts of native APIs. Maybe a couple of algebraic data types will tell you more about these requirements:

```
data Device
  = Sensor
  | TerminalUnit

data NativeAPI = NativeAPI          ◄─  Not yet defined

data Hdl                            ◄─  There are many devices.
  = Devices [Device]
  | NativeAPIs [NativeAPI]          ◄── There are many APIs.
```

Here, we have defined our HDL, but we are not yet familiar with native APIs. We have simply assumed that it could be incorporated into the language. Similarly, with regard to devices, we would like to gain a better understanding before making any further modifications to the `Device` ADT.

Fortunately, there is documentation available. According to the documentation, every device is accompanied by a passport, which contains a comprehensive set of technical information such as schematics, hardware interface descriptions, installation notes, and more. However, attempting to encode all this information for every engine, solar panel, and fuel tank ever produced would be an insurmountable task. Nevertheless, we can identify common properties and abilities of devices, such as sensors for measuring parameters and terminal units for evaluating commands. Table 3.1 displays a few examples of imaginary devices and components.

Table 3.1   Imaginary devices for the spaceship

Device	Manufacturer's identifier	Components
Temperature sensor	AAA-T-25	None
Pressure sensor	AAA-P-02	None
Controller	AAA-C-86	None
Booster	AAA-BS-1756	Sensor AAA-T-25, "nozzle1-t" Sensor AAA-P-02, "nozzle1-p" Sensor AAA-T-25, "nozzle2-t" Sensor AAA-P-02, "nozzle2-p" Controller AAA-C-86
Rotary engine	AAA-RE-68	Sensor AAA-P-02, "nozzle-p" Sensor AAA-T-25, "nozzle-t" Controller AAA-C-86
Fuel tank	AAA-FT-17	Four propellant-depletion sensors for fuel Four propellant-depletion sensors for oxidizer Controller AAA-C-86

It appears that every device can be incorporated into another device. As we update the code, we will end up with recursively nested types.

Listing 3.1   Recursive device type

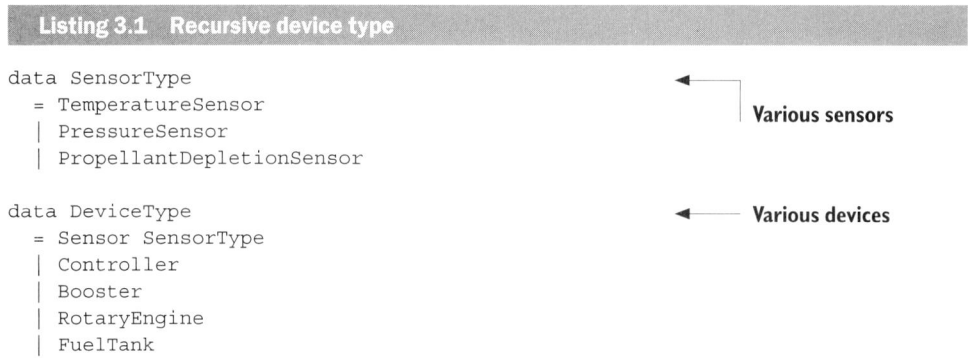

```
data SensorType
  = TemperatureSensor
  | PressureSensor
  | PropellantDepletionSensor

data DeviceType
  = Sensor SensorType
  | Controller
  | Booster
  | RotaryEngine
  | FuelTank
```

Various sensors

Various devices

```
type Name = String
type Components = [Device]

data Device = Device Name DeviceType Components
```

◀─┐ **Components are
  │ a list of devices.**

◀─┘ **Device may be composed
     of other devices.**

This structure does not account for the possibility of unusual devices, such as a self-referencing one or a device that contains a set of components that clearly cannot exist in the physical world:

```
self :: Device
self = Device "Self" Controller [self]

uselessMachine :: Device
uselessMachine = Device "Gadget" RotaryEngine [self]
```

Maybe we can fix this after reading the rest of the documentation:

- *Temperature sensor*—A sensor for measuring temperatures, widely used in space devices; has good measurement characteristics.
- *Pressure sensor*—A sensor widely used in space devices; has good measurement characteristics.
- *Controller*—A simple microcontroller; is suitable for work in space conditions.
- *Rotary engine*—A small engine controlling the rotations of a spaceship. It has one nozzle and two sensors (for temperature and pressure).
- *Booster*—The main engine of a spaceship used for movement in space. This modification has built-in pressure and temperature sensors in each of the two nozzles.
- *Fuel tank*—A fuel-supplying device that has one tank for fuel and another one for the oxidizer.
- *Nozzle*—A chamber or pipe in a rocket engine that expands and accelerates combustion products.

Indeed, if we had information regarding nozzles in the `DeviceType` ADT, we could consider defining a rotary engine as a compound object.

Listing 3.2 Rotary engine device

```
data DeviceType                                    ◀──── Updated device type ADT
  = ...
  | Nozzle

pressureSensor    = Device "P" (Sensor PressureSensor) []   ◀──── Leaf devices
temperatureSensor = Device "T" (Sensor TemperatureSensor) []

rotaryEngine :: Device                             ◀──── Compound device
rotaryEngine = Device "Rot engine" RotaryEngine [nozzle]
  where
    nozzle = Device "Nozzle" Nozzle [pressureSensor, temperatureSensor]
```

Thankfully, the documentation was packed with nice illustrations. The illustration in figure 3.4 introduces a graphical representation.

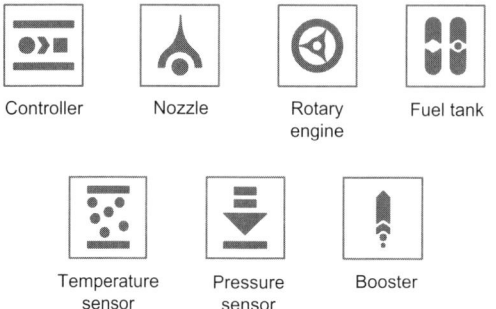

Figure 3.4   Graphical representation of components

The pictures of a booster and a rotary engine contain more hints on how it can be organized (figure 3.5).

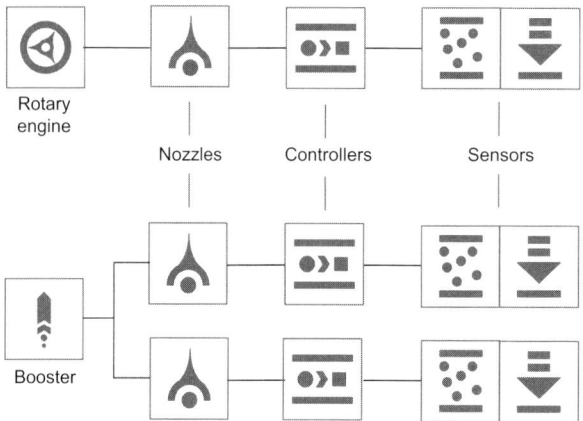

Figure 3.5   Booster and rotary engine devices

Note that there is some tricky business with controllers for each nozzle. We don't know why yet. We have enough understanding of what these things are but not how they work—this should be our next concern.

3.1.4   *Logic control scripts*

The logic control scripts are responsible for the actual work. Once a tool for writing the scripts is available, there may be many scripts needed for a single spacecraft, perhaps even hundreds or thousands. These scripts will need to process every possible situation that a spacecraft may encounter.

The format of the scripts can vary depending on the software, including pseudo-languages or external DSL scripts. To explore this idea further, we will perform a mnemonic analysis, which is a useful technique for determining the internal behavior of a given domain. The analysis involves implementing a scenario in a pseudolanguage and trying to find the most reasonable representation possible that can be turned into an external or internal domain-specific language.

A scenario presented in listing 3.3 investigates what readings of a temperature sensor could look like. It's essentially a sample in the specification of the sensor. This scenario has conditional branches, variables, external API calls, and descriptions. It's how the SpaceZ engineers want to program. The pseudocode should be like literature—readable even for nondevelopers.

Listing 3.3 Temperature sensor readings scenario

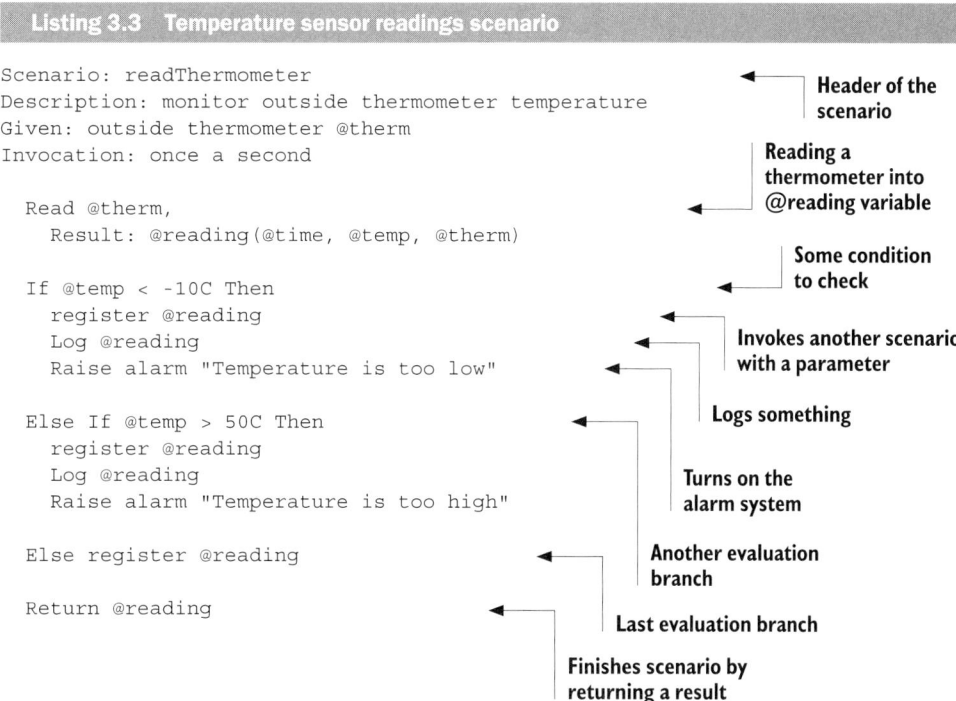

The scenario reads a thermometer once a second and then runs one of the possible subroutines: registering the value in a database if the temperature doesn't cross the bounds and logging the problem or raising an alarm otherwise. The `register` subroutine is defined as

```
Scenario: register
Parameters: (@time, @tempCelsius, @device)
Invocation: on call

  @tempCelsius + 273.15,
    Result: @tempKelvin

  Store (@time, @tempKelvin, @device)
```

It converts the value from Celsius to Kelvin and stores it in the database along with additional information—the timestamp of the measurement and the device from which the value was read.

It seems the scenario is completely imperative. All the parts have some instructions that are clinging to each other. We probably should address this imperative in the future; however, being sequential isn't a must for domain languages. In fact, we started thinking our scenario was imperative because we didn't try any other forms of mnemonic analysis. Let's continue juggling and see what happens. In the next listing, we're making an attempt to try stream-based reasoning. It's now a stream of values that, being given with a thermometer, will produce data once a second.

Listing 3.4   Stream-based scenario

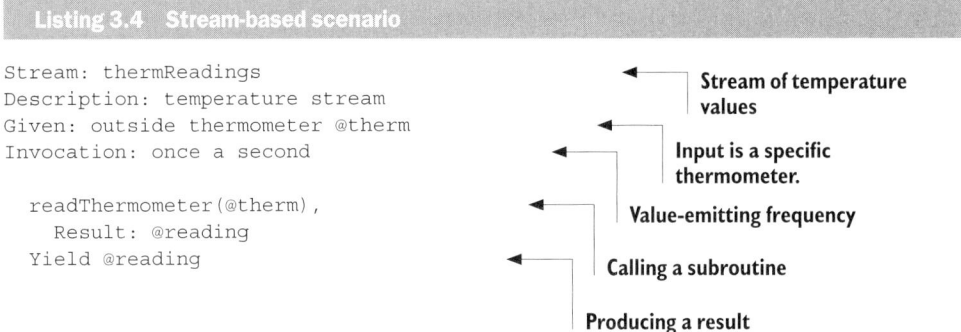

It talks to the thermometer by invoking the `readThermometer` subroutine (see the following listing) and then yields the result.

Listing 3.5   Sequential subroutine for reading a thermometer

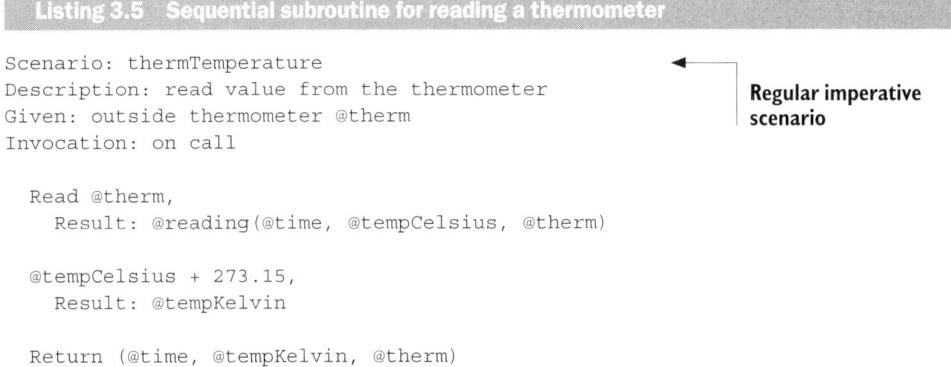

Let's add another stream, which we'll call a `monitor`. This stream can be triggered every time it receives a value from the `thermTemperature` stream. The `monitor` can perform useful actions, such as storing the values in a database and validating them. Once the validation is complete, the `monitor` can yield a result and notify the external world. The following listing shows both the stream and validation subroutine.

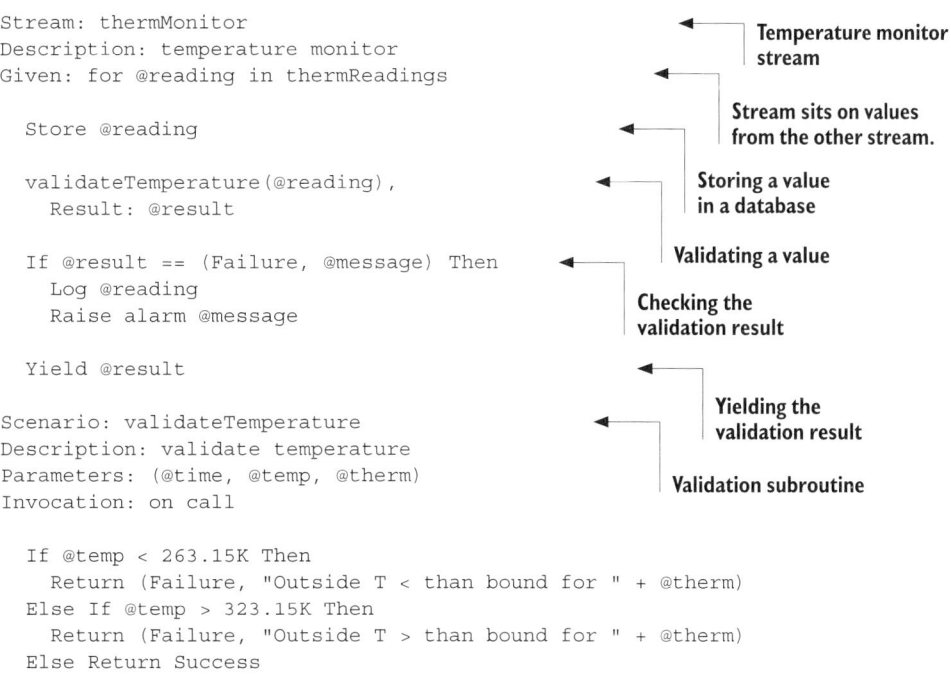

Listing 3.6 Thermometer monitor stream

```
Stream: thermMonitor                              ◄─── Temperature monitor
Description: temperature monitor                        stream
Given: for @reading in thermReadings              ◄─┐
                                                     │ Stream sits on values
  Store @reading                                  ◄─┘ from the other stream.

  validateTemperature(@reading),                  ◄─── Storing a value
    Result: @result                                    in a database

  If @result == (Failure, @message) Then          ◄─── Validating a value
    Log @reading
    Raise alarm @message                          ┌─ Checking the
                                                  │  validation result
  Yield @result                                   ◄─┐
                                                     │ Yielding the
Scenario: validateTemperature                     ◄─┘ validation result
Description: validate temperature
Parameters: (@time, @temp, @therm)                ┌─ Validation subroutine
Invocation: on call                               │

  If @temp < 263.15K Then
    Return (Failure, "Outside T < than bound for " + @therm)
  Else If @temp > 323.15K Then
    Return (Failure, "Outside T > than bound for " + @therm)
  Else Return Success
```

This form of mnemonic scenario opens the door to many functional idioms. The first, which is perhaps obvious, is functional reactive streams. These streams run constantly to produce values you can catch and react to. The functionality of streams means you can compose and transform them in a functional way. Reactive streams are a good abstraction for interoperability code. In our case, it's possible to wrap value reading and transforming processes into the streams and then construct a reactive domain model. The scenario gives a rough view of how it will look in code.

3.2 Designing the architecture

"If one does not know to which port one is sailing, no wind is favorable," said Seneca, a philosopher of ancient Rome. This holds true for us: If we don't have a bird's-eye view of the software that we're going to create, how can we make architectural decisions?

The architecture of an application includes interacting components (also known as *subsystems*), which are independent, programmable units that can be implemented as separate libraries or projects. A component is not a layer, as it can operate on multiple layers, and a layer can encompass multiple components. While a layer is a logical concept, a component is a physical one, defined by its interface and a singular, specific function. A component can be composed of modules, but it itself performs a single, concrete task. While traditionally thought of in an object-oriented context, in a functional context, components are the same; the difference is in their interaction and implementation. Examples of common components include the GUI, network, database, ORM, and logger.

How would we organize the components of our software? And how would we communicate our ideas to our teammates? This chapter introduces a methodology suitable for the top-level design, and not only in functional languages. The diagrams presented here (the necessity, components, and elements maps) are less formal than UML and are only needed for organizing the design process. You're free to invent your own methodology, or you might want to jump to the code directly in your projects.

3.2.1   Defining architecture components

A *necessity map* helps to define big parts of the system. It is essentially a concept map. Concept maps represent diagrams with bars, arrows, and other situational graphical objects. I believe most of the diagrams in this book are concept maps: they contain concepts that are somehow connected to other concepts. Would you agree that my diagrams are simple and illustrative enough? That's the goal of any concept map.

Let's build a necessity map. What components should our spaceship control software have? The requirements in our mind maps can tell us. Here's the list of components extracted from mind maps (figures 3.2 and 3.3):

- Logic control
- Hardware protocols
- Simulator or real spaceship
- Database
- Scripts
- GUI
- Hardware interface
- Network

All the entities in the necessity map are necessary for the application—that's where the diagram's name comes from. From what I discovered about the domain, I could achieve a diagram presented in figure 3.6.

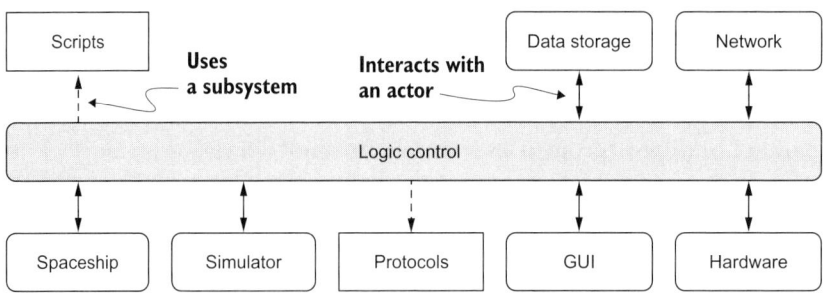

Figure 3.6   Initial necessity diagram of the Andromeda Control Software

This diagram only reflects my initial impression of what to do and establishes some relationships between the blocks. I assumed the actor nature of GUI, spaceship, simulator, and other round components; however, I do not believe it is entirely accurate or functional, which is not my concern at the moment. My goal is to gain a better understanding of the ideas and concepts and possibly illuminate some areas of uncertainty. The diagram is conceptual and not perfect or architectural. It seems to me that logic control is the boss, and it does all those things, but I have no idea how. "How" is a technical question. Making the necessity diagram more technical may lead us to figure 3.7.

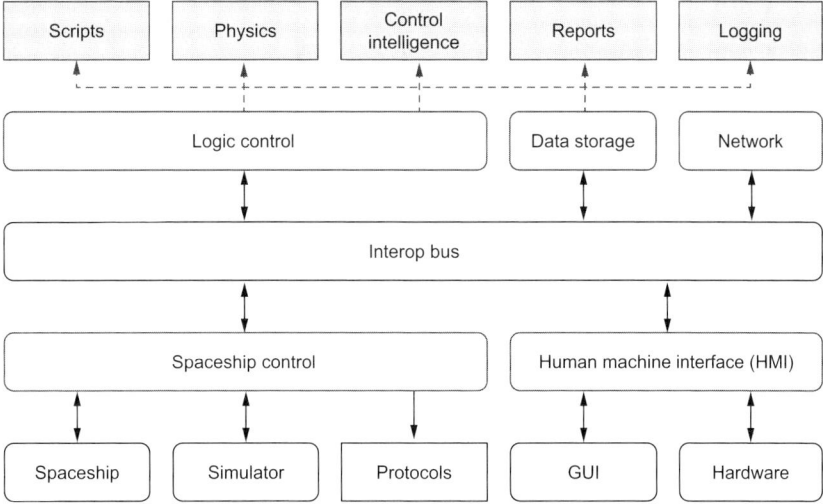

Figure 3.7 Extended necessity diagram

In the center of the diagram, you can see the interop bus. Without the interop bus, the logic control component would have to directly interact with other components, which would greatly increase its responsibility, contrary to the low coupling principle. The interop bus, as it is referred to here, is an abstraction of the interaction logic intended to detach components from each other. Therefore, the interop bus is an architectural solution, and its implementations can vary in philosophy, purpose, scale, and complexity. Most of the implementations are based on the message-passing concept. Some implementations, such as event aggregators, event queues, or message brokers, are mainstream. In functional programming, reactive streams, functional reactive programming approaches (FRP), and actors (the next level of abstraction over the interaction logic) are commonly used.

3.2.2 Defining modules, subsystems, and relations

The next step of defining the architecture follows logically from the previous one. The necessity diagram stores information about what to do, and now it's time to figure out how to do it. Again, we'll use brainstorming to solve this problem. Our goal is to elaborate on one or more elements diagrams as an intermediate step before we form the whole architecture. This is a concept map too, but in this case, it's much closer to a mind map because it doesn't dictate any structure. But unlike with mind maps, in the elements diagram, there is no one central object. All elements are equal. Just place them somewhere and continue thinking. The reasoning is the same: while brainstorming, we shouldn't waste our attention on formalities. It's an exploration of possibilities, and it's pretty chaotic by definition.

As an example, I've taken the notion of logic control and expanded it, as shown in figure 3.8.

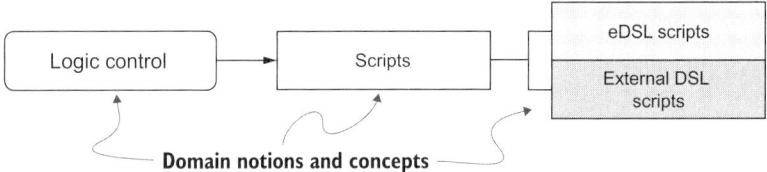

Figure 3.8   Simple elements diagram

What elements can be in the same diagram? There are no specific limitations. If you aren't sure whether a notion is suitable for an elements diagram, the answer is always yes. You are free to refer to any concepts, domain terms, notions, libraries, layers, and objects, even if they have little chance of appearing in the software. There are no rules on how to connect the elements; you may even leave some elements unconnected. It's not important. Focus on the essence. A set of typical relations you may use is presented in, but not limited by, the following list:

- A is part of B.
- A contains B.
- A uses B.
- A implements B.
- A is B.
- A is related to B.
- A is made of B.
- A interacts with B.

For example, scripts use a scripting language, data storage can be implemented as a relational database, and the interoperability layer works with the network, database, and GUI. To illustrate how these might look, consider the following two elements diagrams, both developed out of the necessity diagrams. Figures 3.9 and 3.10 show what we think should be implemented for logic control and interoperability.

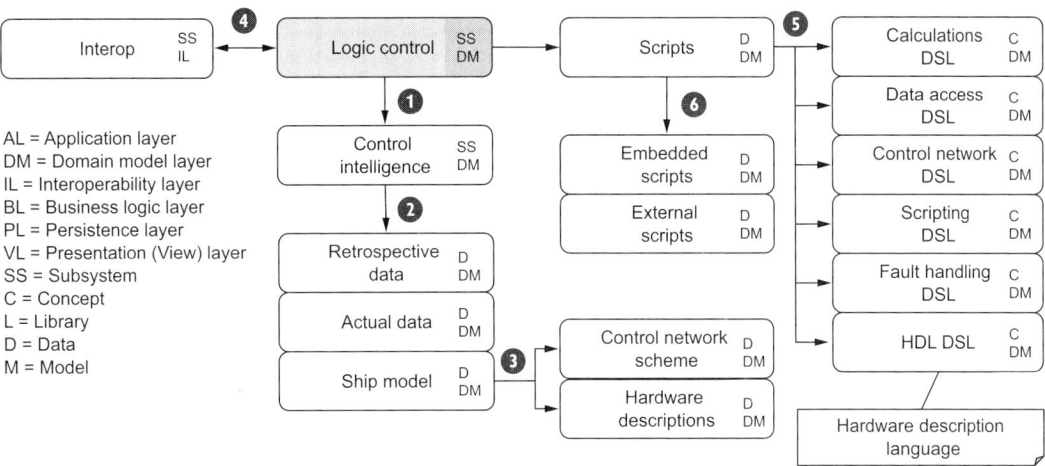

Figure 3.9 Elements diagram: logic control

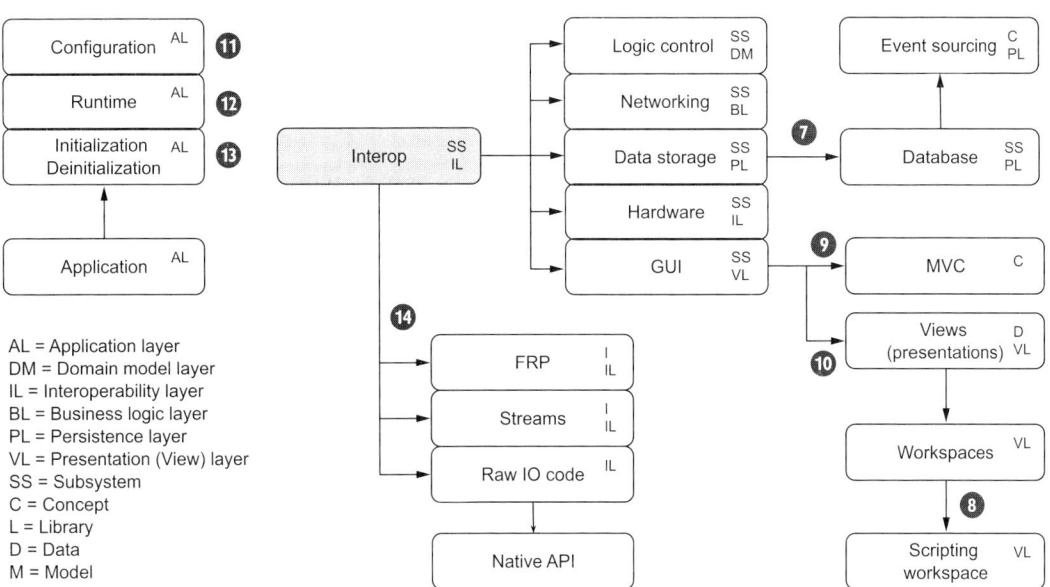

Figure 3.10 Elements diagram: interoperability

Numbers placed on the diagrams indicate the ideas behind the numbered elements. The following list can be considered a part of the requirements discovered during design:

1 Control intelligence is the logic of automatic control of the ship: for example, correction of rotations, control of the life support system, and so on.

   2 Control intelligence uses retrospective data, actual data, and the ship model.

   3 The ship model includes the control network scheme and hardware descriptors.

   4 Logic control interacts with other subsystems through interop.

   5 Scripts are written using many separate DSLs.

   6 Scripts should be embedded and external.

   7 Data storage is an abstraction over some database.

   8 The scripting workspace provides visual tools for writing scripts.

   9 The GUI may be implemented using the MVC pattern.

   10 The GUI consists of many views (presentations).

   11 The application has a runtime.

   12 The application manages configuration.

   13 The application does initializations and deinitializations of subsystems.

   14 Interop includes the following approaches: FRP, streams, and raw IO code.

Additionally, elements may have special labels. Every time you label an element, you ascertain whether the element is in the right place. The labels used in the preceding diagrams are

- *Library (L)*—The element is an external library, or it can be.
- *Subsystem (SS)*—The element is a subsystem, module, or service.
- *Concept (C)*—The element represents some general concept of software engineering.
- *Data (D)*—The element represents some data.
- *Model (M)*—The element is a model of some domain part.

Since these diagrams are informal, feel free to modify them at your own discretion. There is only one thing that matters: adding elements to the diagram should give you new requirements and ideas on upcoming work.

3.2.3 *Defining the application architecture*

The elements diagram certainly doesn't reveal all the secrets of the domain. But we rejected the idea of the waterfall development process and agreed that the iterative process is much better. We can also return to the elements diagram and improve it or create another one. After that, it becomes possible to elaborate on the last architecture diagram suggested by FDD: the *architecture diagram*.

   An architecture diagram is much more formal. It is a concept map with a tree-like structure—no cycles are allowed, and separate elements are prohibited. An architecture diagram should have all the important subsystems and the relations among them. It also describes concrete architectural decisions, such as which libraries, interfaces, modules, and so on are used. An architecture diagram can be made from elements diagrams, but it's not necessary to take all the elements from there.

In the architecture diagram, you show a component and its implementation by a burger block. Figure 3.11 says that the interoperability bus should be implemented using some unnamed FRP library.

NOTE For more information about FRP, see *Functional and Reactive Domain Modeling* by Debasish Ghosh (Manning, 2016; https://mng.bz/7dNg) and *Functional Reactive Programming* by Stephen Blackheath and Anthony Jones (Manning, 2016; https://mng.bz/qOqE).

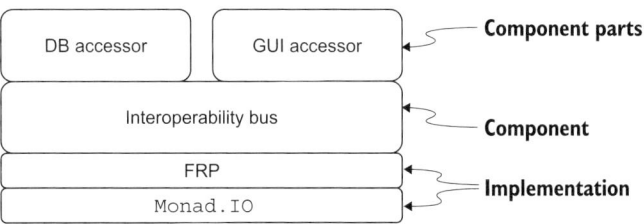

Figure 3.11   Component description block

The bus seems to be impure because its implementation has a `Monad.IO` block and consists of two parts: accessors to the database and the GUI. All components that your application should contain will be connected by relations "interacts with" (bidirectional) or "uses" (one directional).

The whole architecture diagram (figure 3.12) can tell you many important facts about the architectural decisions, but it certainly has limited tools to describe all ideas of the application structure. So consider this diagram as a graphical roadmap for the path you're going to take.

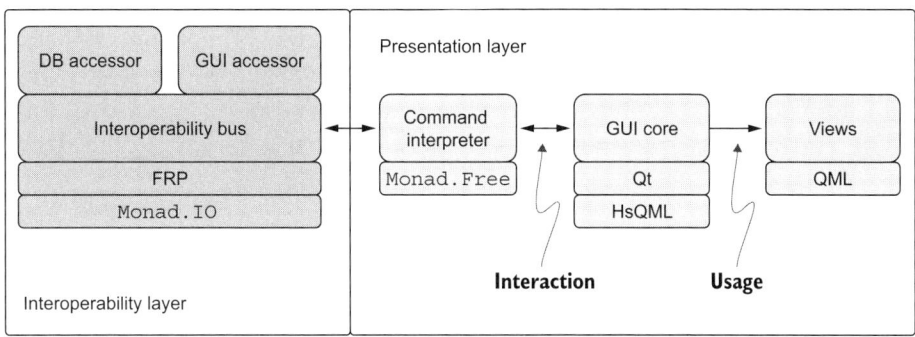

Figure 3.12   Relations between blocks

Let me show you the architecture diagram for the Andromeda Control Software (see figure 3.13).

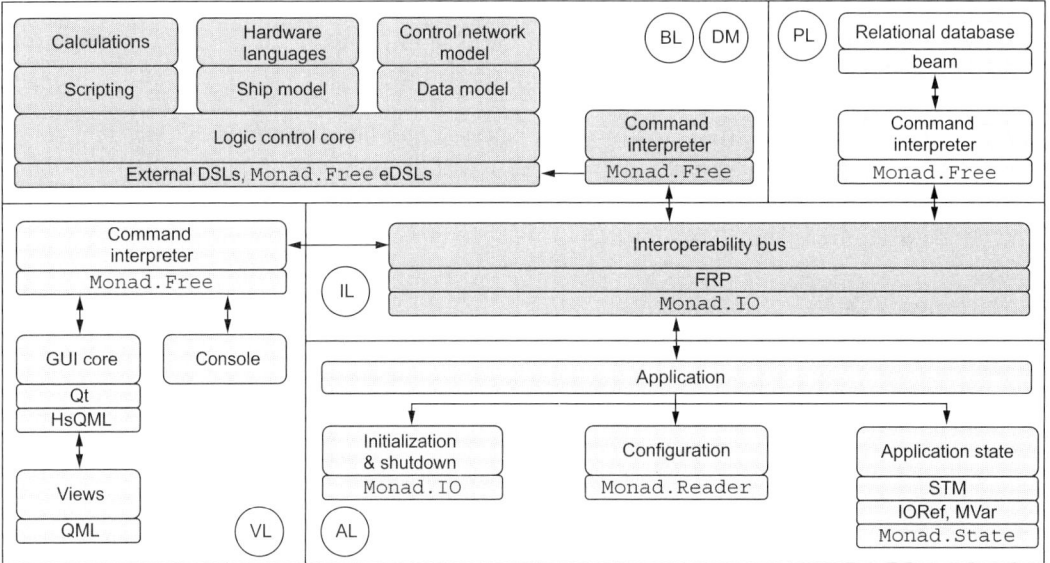

Figure 3.13   Architecture diagram for the Andromeda Control Software

We can conclude the following: there is a central layer that ties all other layers together, there is a presentation (view) layer with Qt as a GUI library, there is some business logic and a relational database, and all of them are abstracted by means of their own free monad interfaces (more about free monad interfaces in chapter 6). We also need some application-level stuff, such as proper initialization and graceful shutdown, configs, and global application state. This is only a draft that will likely evolve in the future. In particular, the need for FRP will be questioned and rethought. It turns out that this decision doesn't pay off its complexity. Being reactive is nice, although this doesn't mean using FRP. After all, Haskell has a great Software Transactional Memory (STM) library for a beautiful and convenient concurrency, and we'll see later how to build custom reactive solutions on top of it.

For now, let's try to modularize our application according to the understanding we have.

3.2.4   *Module organization*

In OOP, the notion of encapsulation plays a leading role. Along with the other three pillars of OOP—abstraction, polymorphism, and inheritance—encapsulation simplifies the interaction between classes by preventing casual access to the internal state. You can't corrupt an object's state in a way unexpected by the interface of a class. But a badly designed or inconsistent interface can be a source of bugs, thus invalidating the internal state. We can roughly say that encapsulation of the internal state is another type of code contract, and once it's been violated, we encounter bugs and instability.

Unsafe mutable code situated in a concurrent environment would be a good example of when the lack of encapsulation causes troubles. In chapter 9, we'll discuss the struggles we might encounter in such cases. What if an openly mutable variable is changed by one thread while someone else believes that the variable will never change? Public mutable variables that are not encapsulated by some objects can suddenly become invalid, but even if they are encapsulated, this might not be enough to prevent occasional unwanted mutations. But putting the variable into an object would at least concentrate the possible changes into one place, and we'll have some options to fix the concurrency problems without many changes in the outside code.

Encapsulation in functional languages often takes the form of modules and is needed to hide the unstable construction of the internals. Consider this code with a simple ADT representing an abstracted value of a given type:

```
data Value = BoolValue Bool
           | IntValue Int
           | FloatValue Float
           | StringValue String
```

Suppose you left the value constructors public: `BoolValue`, `IntValue`, `FloatValue`, and `StringValue`. This means you don't establish any contracts that a code user must comply with. They are free to pattern match over the value constructors, so the client code has a right to depend on the internal structure of `Value`. But then you decide to rename some constructors or add a new one, and all the dependent code immediately gets out of action.

Obviously, there should be a mechanism for encapsulating internal changes and hiding the actual data structure from external users. This is achieved in two steps: by introducing *smart constructors* for your ADT and by making your type *abstract* (*opaque*) and placing it into a module, exposing only the type itself and not the value constructors. Having a built-in feature for this in your favorite language would be a big plus; otherwise, it can only be achieved informally through verbal agreements. Many languages that have modules have an explicit exporting mechanism or a way to simulate it.

DEFINITION A *smart constructor* is a function that constructs a value of any type without revealing the actual nature of the type. Smart constructors may contain some tricky logic to construct complex values when needed. It seems that smart constructors are an analogue of the pattern *Factory Method* from OOP.

DEFINITION A *module* is the unit of encapsulation that unifies a set of related functions and also hides implementation details, providing a public interface.

TIP Modules in Scala are called objects because they have a multipurpose use: as objects in OOP and as modules in functional programming. Modules in Haskell have syntax to control the export of certain things: types, functions, type classes, or ADTs, with or without value constructors.

The next example introduces a widespread pattern of encapsulation —smart constructors for the ADT `Value`:

```
boolValue :: Bool -> Value
boolValue b = BoolValue b

stringValue :: String -> Value
stringValue s = StringValue s

intValue :: Int -> Value
intValue i = IntValue i
```

Let's place the `Value` type into a module `Andromeda.Common.Value` and make it abstract by leaving its value constructors (`BoolValue`, `StringValue`, `IntValue`) private:

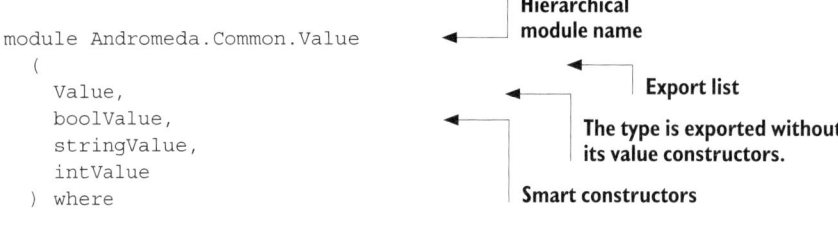

```
module Andromeda.Common.Value
  (
    Value,
    boolValue,
    stringValue,
    intValue
  ) where

...
```

If we wanted to export value constructors, we could write `Value(..)` in the export list, but we don't, so the export record is just `Value`.

So modules represent another incarnation of the interface segregation principle (ISP). We declare the interface to the functionality that a module has. It's easy to see that the single responsibility principle (SRP) is also applicable to modules: a module should have a single theme of content (that is, responsibility).

From the design viewpoint, modules are the main tool for the logical organization of the code. Modules can be arranged hierarchically, and there is no reason to avoid this advantage. You grow your project structure according to your taste to achieve better readability and maintainability—but my design diagrams wouldn't be so useful if they didn't give any hints. By reading the elements diagrams in figures 3.9 and 3.10 and the architecture diagram in figure 3.13, we can elaborate something similar to what the following listing presents. Here, directories are marked by backslashes, while modules are formatted in italics.

Listing 3.7   Structure of the Andromeda project

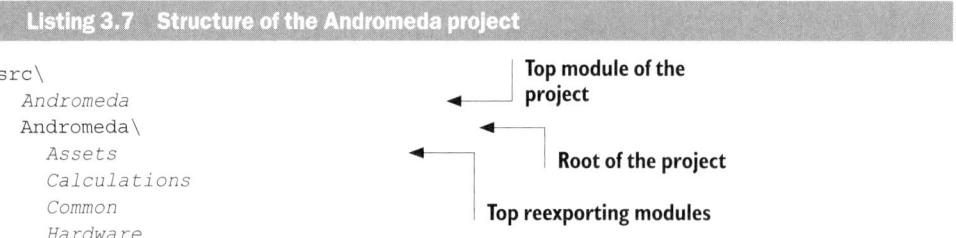

```
src\
  Andromeda
  Andromeda\
    Assets
    Calculations
    Common
    Hardware
```

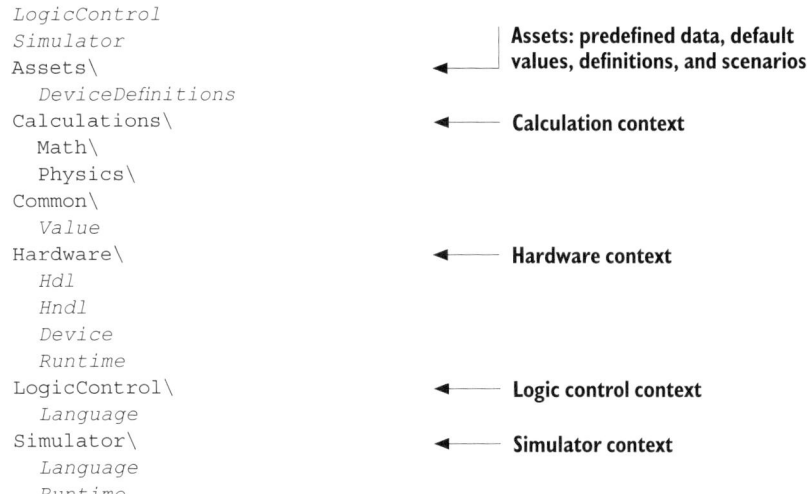

```
LogicControl
Simulator
Assets\                          |  Assets: predefined data, default
   DeviceDefinitions          ◄──┘  values, definitions, and scenarios
Calculations\                 ◄───── Calculation context
   Math\
   Physics\
Common\
   Value
Hardware\                     ◄───── Hardware context
   Hdl
   Hndl
   Device
   Runtime
LogicControl\                 ◄───── Logic control context
   Language
Simulator\                    ◄───── Simulator context
   Language
   Runtime
```

In Haskell, it's common to have reexporting modules on the top of the project structure. They reexport the logic from the like-named contexts, like the top module Simulator and the Simulator context. Generally, top modules only reexport other modules but don't bring any logic. Two sample files with two modules are presented in the following listing.

Listing 3.8 Structure of Andromeda Control Software

```
-- file src\Andromeda.hs:
module Andromeda
  ( module Andromeda.Simulator          ◄───── Reexporting, syntax 1
  , module Andromeda.Common
  ) where

import Andromeda.Simulator              ◄───── Reexported modules
import Andromeda.Common

-- file src\Andromeda\Simulator.hs:
module Andromeda.Simulator             ◄───── Reexporting, syntax 2
  ( module X
  ) where

import Andromeda.Simulator.SimulationModel as X  ◄─── Reexported modules
import Andromeda.Simulator.Simulation       as X
import Andromeda.Simulator.Actions          as X
```

For example, you should import the Andromeda module in tests, or if you want more granularity, you may import any subsystem by referencing its top module:

```
module TestLogicControl where
import Andromeda.LogicControl

testCase = error "Test is not implemented."
```

External code that depends on the module `Andromeda.LogicControl` will never be broken if the internals of the library change. With this approach, we decrease the coupling of modules and provide a kind of facade (a design pattern from OOP) to our subsystem. So all of this is about separation of responsibilities. Functional programming has very nice techniques for it. But we've just gotten started. In the next section, we'll discuss a truly brilliant aspect of functional programming: domain modeling with algebraic data types.

3.3   *Naive implementation of the hardware subsystem*

We've finally come to the implementation part. From here on, we'll be writing code, designing subsystems, outlining interfaces, and doing other things developers usually do. The knowledge we got from the previous chapters will be a reasoning foundation or reasoning framework for us. We're going to write a lot of Haskell code, but keep in mind that many techniques can be applied to Scala and F#.

3.3.1   *The structure of the hardware subsystem*

According to the requirements, two languages should be created (embedded and external HDL):

- *HDL embedded DSL*—The base HDL. These data structures and helper functions are used to define the spaceship's control hardware: engines, fuel tanks, solar panels, remote terminal units, and so on. These devices consist of components such as sensors that read measurements. An HDL script describes a device and its components. Many HDL scripts form a set of available devices. When put together, these devices become an intelligent control network of a spaceship.
- *HDL external DSL*—A special format of HDL existing outside the program code. Engineers will describe devices in separate text files, even possibly within a custom IDE. When loaded into the Andromeda Control Software, these descriptions can be applied and executed. External definitions of hardware will be translated into HDL by parsing and translation services.

The HDL definitions aren't devices themselves but rather stateless declarations of the actual network to be created. There are two better words for this: templates and blueprints. Remember Factorio, a famous crafting and construction game that also happens to be Turing complete? Instead of designating complicated factories for construction one by one, you store your facilities as a blueprint and then stamp this blueprint repeatedly. HDL blueprints would be kind of like this: with one device as a description, many similar devices can be instantiated.

We use our stateless declarations and compile them into the HDL runtime. There can be many internal representations of devices acting within this runtime. For example, you might want to use a simplified representation for tests and another one for real production. The latter will interact with a physical device through some internal, hidden protocol. You don't have to know too much about this protocol when construct-ing a blueprint.

Figure 3.14 shows the initial hardware subsystem design.

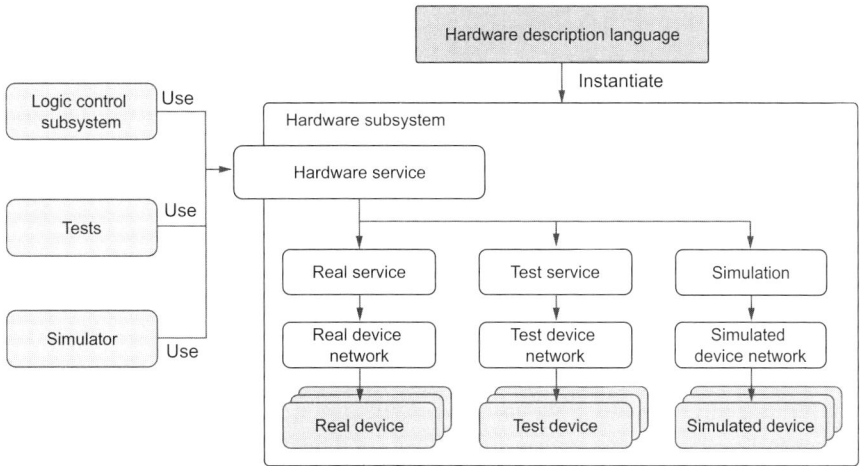

Figure 3.14　Design of the hardware subsystem

3.3.2　Algebraic definition of HDL

Let's make the first design of our HDL simple. Listing 3.9 shows the type `Hdl`, which is just a list of components. Now things start getting serious, so we should model it as closely as possible to the expectations—hence, additional information about components: class, vendor (manufacturer), GUID, and others. We call it `ComponentPassport`. An `Hdl` item would be `ComponentDef` because it's a definition, a template, and a blueprint. In this design, there is some duplication and a little inconsistency. Try to find them yourself.

Listing 3.9　HDL for device definitions

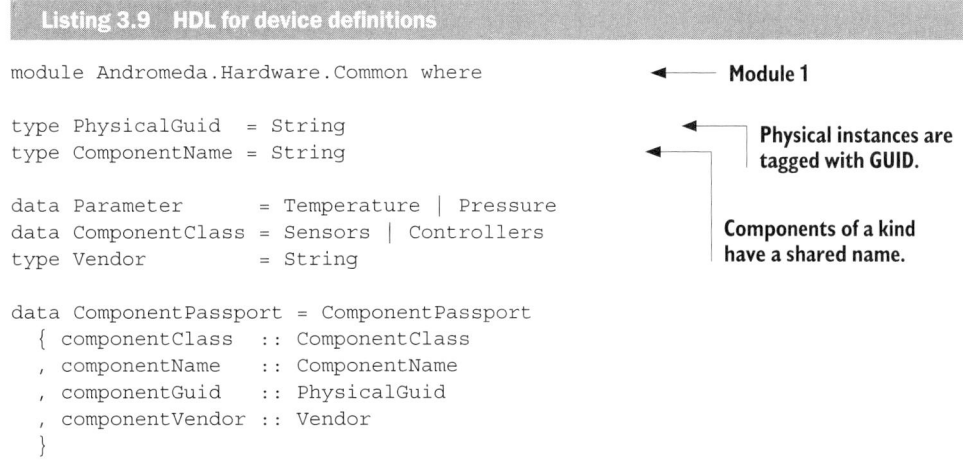

```
module Andromeda.Hardware.Common where            ◄─── Module 1

type PhysicalGuid   = String                      ◄
type ComponentName  = String                            Physical instances are
                                                        tagged with GUID.

data Parameter       = Temperature | Pressure
data ComponentClass  = Sensors | Controllers        Components of a kind
type Vendor          = String                       have a shared name.

data ComponentPassport = ComponentPassport
  { componentClass  :: ComponentClass
  , componentName   :: ComponentName
  , componentGuid   :: PhysicalGuid
  , componentVendor :: Vendor
  }
```

```
module Andromeda.Hardware.Hdl where          ◀──── Module 2

import Andromeda.Hardware.Common             ◀──── Exporting module 1

type ComponentIndex = String

data ComponentDef
  = Sensor     ComponentPassport ComponentIndex Parameter
  | Controller ComponentPassport ComponentIndex
                                                      List of components a
type Hdl = [ComponentDef]                     ◀───── device might have
```

This has gone far from the initial ADTs for devices. Let me remind you where all of this started:

```
type Components = [Device]

data Device = Device Name DeviceType Components
```

This refactoring of the domain model will be one of many as our understanding of the domain improves and new requirements emerge. Here, we've dropped the term device and invented the notion of an `Hdl` specification. I present a typical `Hdl` blueprint for boosters in the following listing.

Listing 3.10   Boosters device described with HDL

```
aaa_t_25 = ComponentPassport Sensors     «AAA-T-25» guid2 «AAA Inc.»
aaa_p_02 = ComponentPassport Sensors     "AAA-P-02" guid1 "AAA Inc."
aaa_c_86 = ComponentPassport Controllers "AAA-C-86" guid3 "AAA Inc."

boostersDef :: Hdl                               The definition of the boosters
boostersDef =                                    device corresponds to the
  [ Sensor aaa_t_25 "nozzle1-t" Temperature      graphical representation.
  , Sensor aaa_p_02 "nozzle1-p" Pressure
  , Sensor aaa_t_25 "nozzle2-t" Temperature
  , Sensor aaa_p_02 "nozzle2-p" Pressure
  , Controller aaa_c_86 "controller"
  ]
```

So we took the data from the Space Z documentation, tables, and figures and compiled them into the `boostersDef` compound device. There is a problem, though. The `ComponentDef` type declares sensors and controllers. The `ComponentPassport` type also has a field for sensors and controllers. It's quite possible to construct an invalid definition:

```
validComponent :: ComponentDef
validComponent = Sensor aaa_t_25 "nozzle1-t" Temperature

invalidComponent :: ComponentDef
invalidComponent = Controller aaa_t_25 "central controller"

--                                 ^ a sensor passed by a mistake
```

What should we do with the inconsistency? We can ignore it and hope our colleagues will never create an invalid definition. We can also fix the model somehow. Maybe removing the `ComponentClass` type will be enough. If reworking the model is not desirable, we can at least create an interface so that the construction of components is only possible through smart constructors and none of them return an invalid definition. This is how we do it.

Listing 3.11 Smart constructors

```
module Andromeda.Hardware.Hdl
  ( module X
  , ComponentDef
  , ComponentIndex
  , sensor
  , controller
  ) where

import Andromeda.Hardware.Common as X
  (PhysicalGuid, Parameter, Vendor, ComponentIndex, ComponentName)

import Andromeda.Hardware.Hdl.Internal
  (ComponentPassport (..), ComponentClass (..))

sensor
  :: PhysicalGuid -> Vendor -> ComponentName
  -> ComponentIndex -> Parameter
  -> ComponentDef
sensor guid vendor name idx param =
  Sensor (ComponentPassport Sensors name guid vendor) idx param

controller
  :: PhysicalGuid -> Vendor -> ComponentName
  -> ComponentIndex
  -> ComponentDef
controller guid vendor name idx =
  Controller (ComponentPassport Controllers name guid vendor) idx
```

Value constructors aren't exported. ◄

Smart constructors ◄

Smart constructor for sensors ◄

There is nothing we can do to prevent engineers from passing incorrect data. It's a logical bug that is beyond our control. However, we can prevent invalid states by hiding types and exposing only smart constructors. Yet this can create a new problem. Sometimes we need to work with these opaque data types, such as when constructing test samples, but they are no longer accessible. The choice of what to do with the types is always up to us. One potential solution is to mark certain functionalities as internal while keeping them public. The marking will simply be the name of the module (`Internal`), serving as a warning to developers to never export it:

```
module Andromeda.Hardware.Hdl.Internal
  ( ComponentClass (..)
  , ComponentPassport (..)
  ) where

data ComponentClass = ...
data ComponentPassport = ...
```

Whenever you need this, you can import the internal module and have full access to the types, but you do so at your own risk. The authors do not guarantee any stability for the internal modules.

Another solution is the abstract data types pattern we introduced earlier. We can export `ComponentClass` and `ComponentPassport` data types but not their internal structure. But then we should provide some functions to operate with those types:

```
module Andromeda.Hardware.HDL
  ( ComponentClass
  , ComponentPassport
  , doSomethingWithComponentClass
  , doSomethingWithComponentPassport
  ) where

doSomethingWithComponentClass = ...
doSomethingWithComponentPassport = ...
```

One solution may be acceptable in one case, but not in another. Keeping everything public is the simplest approach, but its appropriateness depends on how the subsystem is intended to be used and how you plan to develop it. The decision is ultimately yours.

3.3.3   *Functional interface to the hardware subsystem*

Now, as we've freed the notion `Device`, we'll attach it to another meaning. We'll be using it for runtime instances of devices, the instances that we'll be creating according to the `Hdl` list of components. These runtime instances serve a similar purpose to file-handles in an operating system—the instance knows how to connect to a real device, read real measurements, and evaluate real commands:

```
module Andromeda.Hardware.Device where

data Device = ...                        -- to be defined
```

We treat an `Hdl` script as a single device:

```
boostersDef :: Hdl
boostersDef =
  [ Sensor aaa_t_25 "nozzle1-t" Temperature
  , Sensor aaa_p_02 «nozzle1-p» Pressure
  , Sensor aaa_t_25 «nozzle2-t» Temperature
  , Sensor aaa_p_02 "nozzle2-p" Pressure
  , Controller aaa_c_86 "controller"
```

This might be a bit confusing if we remember that HDL stands for *hardware description language*. This sounds like it's something more general than just a device. This is definitely a design flaw, but let's postpone the improvements for later chapters. To produce a `Device` value from the `Hdl` definition, there should be a function with the following signature:

```
makeDevice :: Hdl -> Device
```

The function is actually an interpreter from the `Hdl` type to the `Device` type. We also can say it is a translator. In the following code, you can see a possible implementation:

```
import Andromeda.Hardware.Device
  (Device, blankDevice, addSensor, addController)

makeDevice :: Hdl -> Device
makeDevice hdl = makeDevice' hdl blankDevice
  where
    makeDevice' [] d = d
    makeDevice' (c:cs) d    = makeDevice' cs (add' c d)
    add' (Sensor c idx p)    = addSensor idx p c
    add' (Controller c idx)  = addController idx c
```

Here, we use recursion to traverse the list of component definitions and pattern matching to compose the `Device` type. This code doesn't know much about the `Device` type: we use interface functions only. We made this interpreter more future-proof by facading the `Andromeda.Hardware.Device` module. If the inner module changes, the `makeDevice` function will continue working. As this module exports some types and hides their actual implementation, we call it a functional interface to the `Device`-related part of the subsystem.

> **DEFINITION** A *functional interface* to a subsystem is a set of abstract types accompanied by functions that work with those types without revealing the implementation details.

The next listing demonstrates a possible internal structure of the `Device` data type, along with function declarations. I have omitted the bodies of the functions to avoid being distracted from the functional interface itself.

Listing 3.12 Hardware runtime

```
module Andromeda.Hardware.Device (
    Device,                                      ◄──── Abstract types
    DevicePart,
    makeDevice,                                  ◄──── Interface to the subsystem
    blankDevice,
    addSensor,
    addController,
    getDevicePart,
    updateDevicePart
  ) where

import Andromeda.Hardware.Common
import Andromeda.Hardware.Hdl

data DevicePart                                  ◄──── Implementation of device parts
  = SensorImpl       ComponentPassport
  | ControllerImpl   ComponentPassport
                                                       Implementation of
type DeviceParts = Map ComponentIndex DevicePart  ◄──┘ a list of device parts

data Device = DeviceImpl DeviceParts             ◄──── Implementation of a device

makeDevice :: Hdl -> Device                      ◄──── Interface implementation
```

```
blankDevice :: Device
addSensor :: ComponentIndex -> Parameter
            -> ComponentPassport -> Device -> Device
addController :: ComponentIndex -> ComponentPassport
              -> Device -> Device
getDevicePart :: ComponentIndex -> Device
              -> Maybe DevicePart
updateDevicePart :: ComponentIndex -> DevicePart
                 -> Device -> Maybe Device
```

Exported types and functions are actually a small part of the interface that will be extended as needed. You can meditate on it, guessing what these functions do and how to implement them.

We need to delve into the concept of APIs. Assuming that we can control various sensors, cameras, and actuators through commands in a programming language (such as Python or JavaScript for better safety), we need an API with appropriate methods, types, and data structures.

Physical devices are all the same except for their unique `PhysicalGuid`. However, it would be unreasonable to attach a unique API to each device. Instead, there should be an API version that corresponds to a group of similar devices shared under the same group name. We have a `ComponentName` for a series of devices, and this string will correspond to the native API specific to this component.

Imaginary API handlers could look like this:

```
module Andromeda.Hardware.Components.API where

data SensorAPI = SensorAPI                                ◄─┐ API handle data
  { reset :: IO ()                                          │ structure
  , readMeasurement :: IO Measurement                     ◄─── API methods
  , setCallback :: Period -> IO Measurement -> IO ()
  }

data ControllerAPI = ControllerAPI
  { reboot :: IO ()
  , turnOff :: IO ()
  , eval :: String -> IO ()
  , doSomethingElse :: IO ()
  }
```

These two data types define methods and expose interfaces that hide various implementations. I call them handlers because they follow the service handle pattern for creating functional interfaces. We will explore this pattern in all its glory later. For now, let's focus on how these handlers are used in a real instance of a `Device`. We extend this data type to support API handlers. Namely, we add `SensorAPI` and `ControllerAPI` to the `SensorImpl` and `ControllerImpl` value constructors:

```
- data DevicePart
-   = SensorImpl     ComponentPassport
-   | ControllerImpl ComponentPassport
```

```
+ import Andromeda.Hardware.Components.API (SensorAPI, ControllerAPI)

+ data DevicePart
+   = SensorImpl     ComponentPassport SensorAPI
+   | ControllerImpl ComponentPassport ControllerAPI
```

Then, in the assumption that we are given with a library and module `Andromeda`
`.Vendors.AAA` responsible for AAA vendor's device APIs, we ask for a specific API
when adding a sensor. All of this is shown in the following listing.

Listing 3.13   Connecting the real API

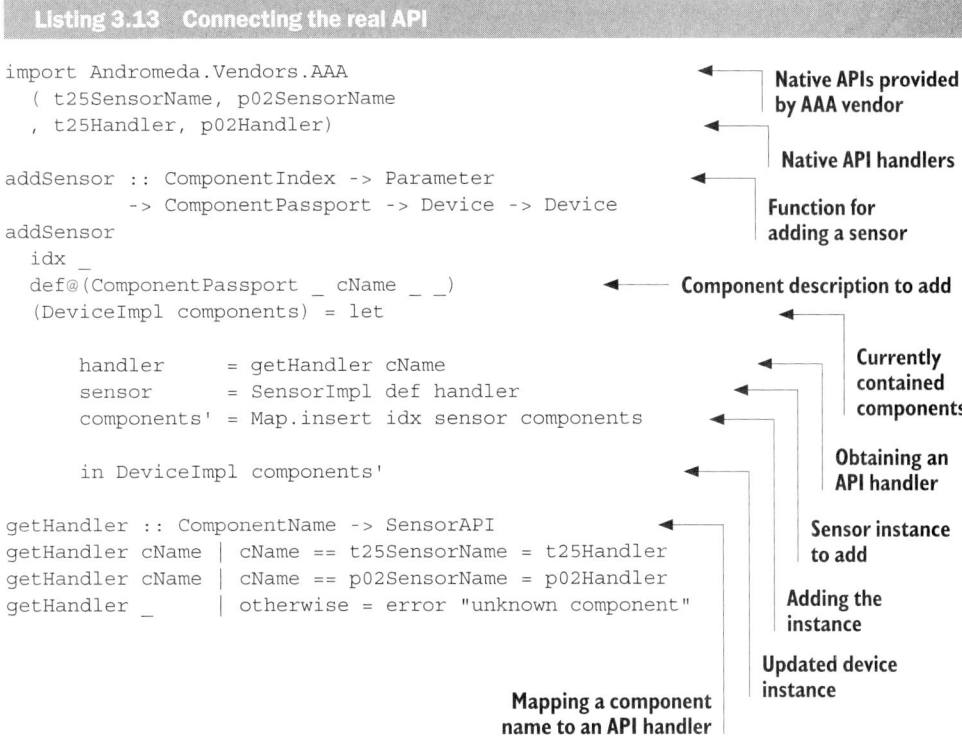

```
import Andromeda.Vendors.AAA                          ◄──    Native APIs provided
  ( t25SensorName, p02SensorName                              by AAA vendor
  , t25Handler, p02Handler)
                                                      ◄──    Native API handlers
addSensor :: ComponentIndex -> Parameter             ◄──
          -> ComponentPassport -> Device -> Device           Function for
addSensor                                                    adding a sensor
  idx _
  def@(ComponentPassport _ cName _ _)                ◄────   Component description to add
  (DeviceImpl components) = let                      ◄──

      handler     = getHandler cName                 ◄──          Currently
      sensor      = SensorImpl def handler           ◄──          contained
      components' = Map.insert idx sensor components ◄──          components

                                                           Obtaining an
      in DeviceImpl components'                      ◄──    API handler

getHandler :: ComponentName -> SensorAPI             ◄──    Sensor instance
getHandler cName | cName == t25SensorName = t25Handler       to add
getHandler cName | cName == p02SensorName = p02Handler
getHandler _     | otherwise = error "unknown component"    Adding the
                                                           instance

                                                           Updated device
                            Mapping a component            instance
                            name to an API handler
```

Now, every time we add a sensor to `Device`, we'll get it with a proper API handler. But
it's clear that we're not finished yet. How would we use this subsystem? Who is the client of the APIs `SensorAPI` and `ControllerAPI`? What code invokes the methods such
as `readMeasurement`, `reboot`, and others? How do we access the handlers while they
are hidden in the opaque (abstracted) `Device` value? Who can initialize and deinitial-
ize those components? Where is all the intelligence of the system displaced?

These are very difficult questions. We've shown a few patterns: abstract data type,
declarative definitions and interpretation, and internal modules. We've designed some
domain models and even discussed functional interfaces a little. But the MVP is not yet
ready. In the next chapter, we'll finish what we started here, and our journey through
the Andromeda Control Software will lead us to a minimally working system.

Summary

- A fast feedback loop at the beginning of the development process can be achieved by creating an MVP and implementing integration tests.

- A minimum viable product (MVP) is a sample program with limited but sufficient functionality to verify the idea of the product.

- MVP is not a one-time prototype but a foundation for future development.

- Integration tests are used to verify that all parts of a system are working together correctly in a real environment.

- The MVP for Andromeda Control Software includes a draft implementation of the spaceship control software and a simulator capable of interacting with this application.

- We can make the whole process of designing an architecture more systematic. Different kinds of diagrams help us reason without touching the code: a necessity diagram for a big picture, an elements diagram for brainstorming, and an architecture diagram as a final artifact of the design.

- Module organization will be your first actual task in the project. You should decide how to lay out your subsystems, interface modules, and implementation.

- Mnemonic analysis is a technique used to determine the internal properties of a domain by taking a scenario and transforming it into a more formal representation.

- We use top reexporting modules to address the internal ones and to prevent too much refactoring if the internals have changed.

- When you need to make an MVP, it makes sense to try the simplest approach to domain-specific languages first. Interpretable algebraic data types and module-based services will help you start.

- Reactive streams are a useful abstraction for writing interoperability code, allowing for the composition and transformation of values in a functional way.

- An MVP may consist of rudimentary implementations of subsystems, but this does not mean that interfaces should be ignored. On the contrary, interfaces can aid in better organizing subsystem code and defining its key properties.

End-to-end design

4

This chapter covers

- Improving the structure of an application
- Finding and fixing design flaws
- Designing the frame of an application from end to end
- Implementing functional services using the Service Handle pattern
- Writing simple tests with and without mocks

Determining the final goals of a design is a very helpful technique. I'm speaking from experience. There have been many times when I've missed flaws in my design that I could have easily avoided if I had had my system used somehow. It would have been more future proof had there been code that called my system somehow and highlighted blind spots and potential problems. The subsystem can still be under construction, and it doesn't have to provide full functionality, but once you manage to connect all the parts into a consistent story, you'll immediately know whether everything fits well. You'll be sure that there are no critical problems in the architecture, interfaces, and implementation. We call the approach of tying all the knots of the system *end-to-end design*.

The code for the spaceship control software we developed in the previous chapter doesn't follow this idea. We've just implemented a tiny, isolated subsystem and no more than that. We obviously can't find and connect a real spaceship to our system, and I believe neither of us has spaceship components in our garages. The only two possibilities we have for providing a final client are a simulator and tests. We'll implement both to some degree, starting with tests. By doing so, we'll prove that our MVP application is not fake.

This chapter will also introduce you to a very important design pattern: Service Handle. We'll replace the module-based interface with it for the hardware subsystem and see what the benefits are. This pattern can be an architectural foundation for the whole application, and as long as it's very simple, it will soon be a foundation for more impressive solutions.

But first, we should revisit the code. We drafted the application, and now we have to talk about what we really did. The initial design of the Andromeda application has several significant flaws, some inconsistencies, and unclear parts. Let's find and eliminate those problems.

4.1   *Finding the place for the end-to-end design*

I labeled the design of the hardware subsystem naive even if I tried to follow the interface segregation and single responsibility principles. The module-based interface (module `Device`) and the `Hdl` language as a blueprint for device instances helped us to shape out the subsystem and cut only one entrance to this scope:

```
data Device = DeviceImpl DeviceParts

data DevicePart
  = SensorImpl     ComponentPassport SensorAPI
  | ControllerImpl ComponentPassport ControllerAPI

makeDevice :: Hdl -> Device
```

There are functions for creating a device from the HDL definition, functions for working with sensors and controllers, and functions for obtaining device parts:

```
blankDevice :: Device
addSensor :: ComponentIndex
          -> Parameter -> ComponentPassport -> Device -> Device
addController :: ComponentIndex -> ComponentPassport -> Device -> Device
getDevicePart :: ComponentIndex -> Device -> Maybe DevicePart
```

Where should this go? Who is the client of this subsystem? What use cases does the hardware functionality cover? Are we on the light side of the Force?

The design of types, domain models, and subsystem interfaces could be imperfect. It's an open-world game and definitely not a corridor-narrowed one. You might realize that the proposed plan doesn't fit into some new requirements, which happens sometimes. Of course, reiterating the architecture will have a high cost, but sometimes, there can be no other choice. Our modules aren't organized well—they have wrong dependencies and inappropriate responsibilities. The naming scheme could also be better. We should fix the inconsistencies in the HDL language and the related types before we reach the client code that consumes our subsystems. In other words, it's time for some code refactoring.

4.1.1 Identifying and fixing wrong dependencies

The module `Andromeda.Hardware.Device` is supposed to be a target for compiling our `Hdl` script. Yes, this operation fits into the compiling concept. Maybe "translating" would be a better term, but still. The main compiler function `makeDevice` depends on the internal `addSensor` and `addController` functions:

```
makeDevice :: Hdl -> Device
makeDevice hdl = makeDevice' hdl blankDevice
  where
    makeDevice' [] d = d
    makeDevice' (c:cs) d    = makeDevice' cs (add' c d)
    add' (Sensor c idx p)   = addSensor idx p c
    add' (Controller c idx) = addController idx c
```

◄─┐ **makeDevice depends on addSensor.**

◄── **makeDevice depends on addController.**

In turn, the two "add a component" functions depend on the specific functionality from the `Andromeda.Vendors.AAA` module (see the `getHandler` function in the following listing).

Listing 4.1   Dependency from the assets-like module

```
import Andromeda.Vendors.AAA as AAA

addSensor idx _
  def@(ComponentPassport _ cName _ _)
  (DeviceImpl components) = let

    handler     = getHandler cName
    sensor      = SensorImpl def handler
    components' = Map.insert idx sensor components

    in DeviceImpl components'

getHandler cName
  | cName == AAA.t25SensorName = AAA.t25Handler
```

◄─┐ **Getting an API handler**

◄─┐ **Dependency from the AAA asset module**

The `Device` module knows too much about a real vendor `AAA`, which is the mixing of the layers (implementation and domain) and a high coupling of the two. The problem goes even deeper because a functionality related to concrete titles like the AAA vendor is actually an asset that should not occur in the implementation. Take a look at figure 4.1.

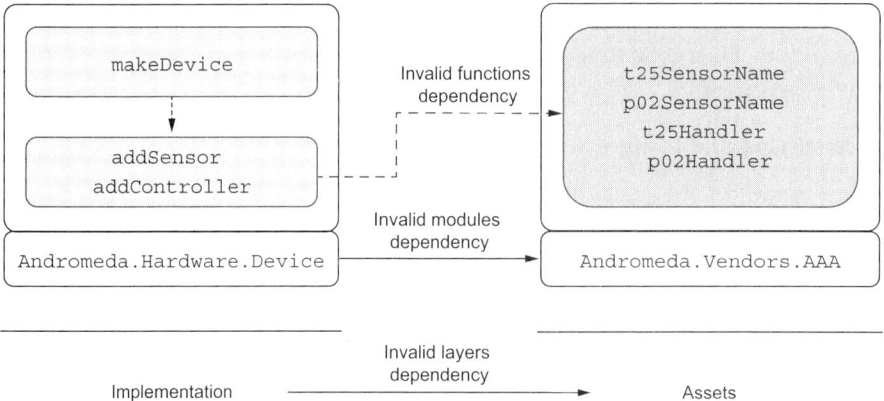

Figure 4.1   Implementation depends on assets.

Wrong dependencies in the design will become a significant problem sooner or later. The business domain should never know the details of the implementation. The implementation should only address general properties and behavior of the business domain and not specificities such as assets. The assets should be considered a configuration, a concrete instance of the domain notions, and this should come in the form of data. Everything should be separated.

In our case, how would we add more vendors? By fixing the Device module and other functions? Perhaps we could use

```
import Andromeda.Vendors.AAA as AAA
import Andromeda.Vendors.BBB as BBB
import Andromeda.Vendors.CCC as CCC

getHandler :: ComponentName -> SensorAPI
getHandler cName | cName == AAA.t25SensorName = AAA.t25Handler
getHandler cName | cName == BBB.bbbSensorName = BBB.t25Handler
getHandler cName | cName == CCC.cccSensorName = CCC.t25Handler
```

This is not a scalable practice; it is a bad practice. The makeDevice method and the company should ideally stay untouched once written. Domain-specific vendors such as AAA and BBB and their components live on a completely different level of abstraction and should not be included in the Device module. We also have a top-level scope for it: the Assets subfolder. Table 4.1 describes the main modules and their purpose.

Table 4.1 Modules and their purposes

Module	Description
Andromeda.Hardware modules	Hardware subsystem
`.Common`	Contains common types that can be used in all the layers: domain, languages, implementation, and assets
`.Language.Hdl`	Definitions, eDSLs, and interfaces for defining a declarative model of the control software and spaceship configuration
`.Impl.Component`	Low-level interfaces and related types to operate with native components. It's a draft of API, and we don't yet have much info about what API will be needed in the future.
`.Impl.Device`	Runtime-acting devices and parts of the control network; a stateful implementation of the HDL definitions that talks to the real devices
Assets modules	The actual description of devices, components, and network. We can say this is a part of the domain-related business logic.
`.DeviceDefinitions`	Contains declarative definitions of the devices
`Assets.Vendors modules`	Modules with device passports and APIs provided by specific vendors
`.AAA.Common`	Common data types specific to this vendor
`.AAA.Components`	Definitions of AAA's components
`.AAA.ComponentsAPI`	AAA's components API implementation and bindings

Now modules can be connected without producing wrong dependencies, as figure 4.2 shows.

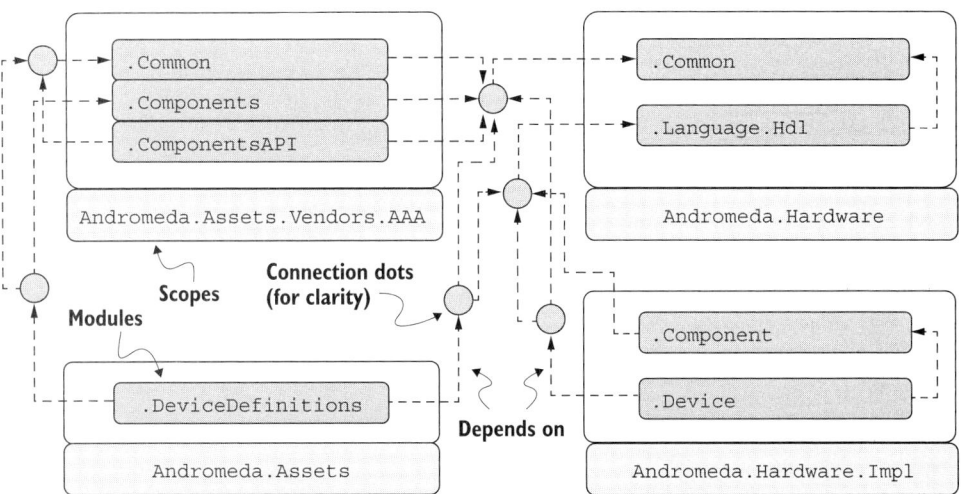

Figure 4.2   Correct dependencies between modules

These dependencies between modules imply dependencies between scopes and, as a result, dependencies between layers. Now the dependencies are correct: nothing depends on `Impl`. Only `Assets` depend on `AAA`, and the `Andromeda.Hardware` scope that hosts the interface doesn't depend on anything. With this clarification of responsibilities, the code will become more maintainable, less confusing, and more consistent. A better naming scheme is also welcomed. Working on these samples, I experienced a big struggle with the best possible design that could be suitable both for the code and the book. Let me present the results.

4.1.2   *Improving models and naming*

I doubt the naming scheme for this domain is optimal; maybe a domain expert will say there are better namings out there. Fortunately, statically typed languages with a good type system, such as Haskell or Scala, combined with functional approaches, make refactoring very safe and simple. And we're going to change a lot!

The `Parameter` property (values are `Temperature` and `Pressure`) was situated in the `ComponentDef` ADT as part of the `Hdl`:

```
data ComponentDef
   = Sensor ComponentPassport ComponentIndex Parameter      ◀──┐ Physical units of
   | Controller ComponentPassport ComponentIndex               │ measurement are here.

type Hdl = [ComponentDef]
```

This design is inconsistent: passport may indicate one component, while `ComponentDef` is something different. For example, a thermometer that measures pressure is

```
aaa_t_25 = ComponentPassport Sensors "AAA-T-25" guid2 "AAA Inc."

myThermometer = Sensor aaa_t_25 «nozzle1-t» Pressure
```

Or it's a controller that has a pressure sensor passport:

```
aaa_p_02 = ComponentPassport Sensors "AAA-P-02" guid1 "AAA Inc."

myController = Controller aaa_p_02 "nozzle1-p"
```

Two minor problems can be found in the definitions of devices we developed previously.

Listing 4.2   Boosters device described with HDL

```
aaa_t_25 = ComponentPassport Sensors     "AAA-T-25" guid2 "AAA Inc."
aaa_p_02 = ComponentPassport Sensors     "AAA-P-02" guid1 "AAA Inc."
aaa_c_86 = ComponentPassport Controllers "AAA-C-86" guid3 "AAA Inc."

boostersDef :: Hdl
boostersDef =
  [ Sensor aaa_t_25 «nozzle1-t» Pressure
  , Sensor aaa_p_02 «nozzle1-p» Pressure
  , Sensor aaa_t_25 «nozzle2-t» Temperature
```

```
, Sensor aaa_p_02 "nozzle2-p" Pressure
, Controller aaa_p_02 "nozzle1-p"
]
```

This code has the following problems:

- *Magic constants*—"AAA-T-25", "AAA Inc".
- *Inconsistent naming*—Unexpected underscores and unclear abbreviations (aaa_t_25, aaa_c_86).
- *Invalid components*—These are caused by inconsistencies in the domain model.

Fixing constants and naming is easy, but the last problem with the design will affect a lot of code, including the code that depends on the HDL domain model. If we move the measurement unit type into ComponentClass, a part of the device passport, this should make sense, although it will force the vendors to specify it on their side. We, the clients, will get it as correct as a vendor can be:

```
-- module Andromeda.Hardware.Common:
data ComponentClass
  = Sensors Parameter                        ◀── Physical units of
  | Controllers                                   measurement are here.

data ComponentPassport = ComponentPassport
  { componentClass  :: ComponentClass
    ...
  }
```

This means a definition of a sensor will look like the following code:

```
-- provided by the AAA vendor:
aaa_t_25 = ComponentPassport (Sensors Temperature) «AAA-T-25» guid «AAA Inc.»

-- client code:
nozzleSensor = Sensor aaa_t_25 «nozzle1-t»
```

Now let's clarify the naming and modules' structure. We'll mandate that every vendor should have a namespace within the Assets.Vendors folder. The data of the AAA vendor will also land here. As there is no real AAA company I could ask to read my book and provide the passports of the components, I'll make its modules myself. There will be several constants, some common definitions, and declarations. The following listing contains two modules with constants, common definitions, and declarations.

Listing 4.3   Refactored declarations

```
-- module Andromeda.Assets.Vendors.AAA.Common:

aaaInc :: Vendor
aaaInc = "AAA Inc."

-- module Andromeda.Assets.Vendors.AAA.Components:

aaaTemperature25Name :: ComponentName
```

```
aaaTemperature25Name = "AAA-T-25"

aaaPressure02Name :: ComponentName
aaaPressure02Name = "AAA-3-02"

aaaController86Name :: ComponentName
aaaController86Name = "AAA-C-86"

guid1 = "some_guid1"
guid2 = "some_guid2"
guid3 = "some_guid3"

aaaTemperature25Passport :: ComponentPassport
aaaTemperature25Passport =
  ComponentPassport (Sensors Temperature) aaaTemperature25Name guid2 aaaInc

aaaPressure02Passport :: ComponentPassport
aaaPressure02Passport =
  ComponentPassport (Sensors Pressure) aaaPressure02Name guid1 aaaInc

aaaController86Passport :: ComponentPassport
aaaController86Passport =
   ComponentPassport Controllers aaaController86Name guid3 aaaInc
```

You've certainly noticed those aaa prefixes. An alternative scheme would suppose that the AAA modules should be imported qualified, and then those prefixes won't be necessary:

```
import qualified Andromeda.Assets.Vendors.AAA as AAA
aaaComponents :: [ComponentPassport]
aaaComponents =
  [ AAA.temperature25Passport
  , AAA.pressure02Passport
  , AAA.controller86Passport
  ]
```

This is not a bad naming scheme, but the prefixes look too archaic—hello, Hungarian notation! But we'll stick with prefixes to save one symbol place and avoid importing modules as qualified.

4.1.3   *Improving the Hdl language and interpreter*

The next obstacle that prevents us from moving further is the Hdl language:

```
data ComponentDef
  = Sensor ComponentPassport ComponentIndex Parameter
  | Controller ComponentPassport ComponentIndex

type Hdl = [ComponentDef]
```

As soon as we move Parameter into the ComponentClass data type, there is no point in keeping it in ComponentDef, and there is no point in having Sensor and Controller value constructors there. It's all in the passport now. By the way, this Def postfix is the best thing I could think of to indicate that it's a declarative definition. This type is a part of the language and not of the domain model because it's highly coupled with `Hdl`. They should go together:

```
-- module Andromeda.Hardware.Language.Hdl:

data ComponentDef = ComponentDef ComponentIndex ComponentPassport

type Hdl = [ComponentDef]
```

This is now an affected boosters definition:

```
-- module Andromeda.Assets.DeviceDefinitions:

boostersDef :: Hdl
boostersDef =
  [ ComponentDef "nozzle1-t"  aaaTemperature25Passport
  , ComponentDef "nozzle1-p"  aaaPressure02Passport
  , ComponentDef "nozzle2-t"  aaaTemperature25Passport
  , ComponentDef "nozzle2-p"  aaaPressure02Passport
  , ComponentDef "controller" aaaController86Passport
  ]
```

The target data model and the code itself simplify a lot. The `Device` type is still a dictionary of separate components, and we're still using string keys (`"nozzle1-t"`, `"nozzle1-p"`) for addressing every component:

```
data DevicePart = DevicePart VendorComponent
data Device = Device (Map ComponentIndex DevicePart)
```

Due to the refactoring, there is no inconsistency here. The `DevicePart` does encode a kind of component. Whether it's a sensor, a controller, or something else, this information is only presented in the domain type `ComponentClass` and in the special implementation type `VendorComponent`. The latter comes from the `Hardware.Impl.Component` module. It's simple:

```
-- module Andromeda.Hardware.Impl.Component:

data VendorComponent
  = VendoredSensor       ComponentPassport SensorAPI
  | VendoredController ComponentPassport ControllerAPI

type VendorComponents = Map ComponentName VendorComponent
```

These two types are needed to decouple the actual implementations from the `Device` machinery. When we create a device, we should provide a real context for the sensors and controllers. This might include established network connections, internal state, or even some actor that interacts with this device from a separate thread. If it was an OOP language, we could create a `VendorComponent` class and make it implement an interface `IDevice`. A regular, stateful object of `VendorComponent` could keep its state, connections, and whatever else was needed. But in functional programming, the state works differently. We provide the state from outside in the form of variables, possibly immutable ones. We can't and shouldn't use domain types for this. They only have a descriptive purpose, hence `VendorComponent`. It doesn't carry that much state for now because we haven't designed it yet. We'll return to this question in future chapters explicitly dedicated to organizing stateful applications.

Let's dismantle the interpreter and learn how it works. The `makeDevice` method is the entry point into the interpreter. Notice how we're injecting the `VendorComponents` map into it:

```
makeDevice                                              Real context
  :: VendorComponents                          provided by vendors
  -> Hdl                                        Device definitions
  -> Device
makeDevice vc hdl                               Helper function that starts
  = makeDevice' vc hdl blankDevice              from an empty device
```

Given that `Hdl` is a list, we should traverse it and instantiate components for all items. The helper function does it recursively:

```
makeDevice' :: VendorComponents -> Hdl -> Device -> Device
makeDevice' _ []        device = device
makeDevice' vc (c:cs) device = makeDevice' vc cs (add' vc c device)
```

The `add'` function validates the passport, and if found in the vendors' map, it appends a new component to the device:

```
add' :: VendorComponents -> ComponentDef -> Device -> Device       Validating the
add' vc (ComponentDef idx passp) device =                          passport
  case validateComponent vc passp of
    Right part -> addComponent idx part device          Adding a new component
    Left err   -> error err

                                                    Exception on error
                                                    (bad practice)
```

Validation means looking into the map and returning an instantiated device part on success:

```
validateComponent
  :: VendorComponents
  -> ComponentPassport
  -> Either String DevicePart
validateComponent vc (ComponentPassport _ cName _ _) =
  case Map.lookup cName vc of
    Nothing        -> Left  ("Not found: " <> cName)
    Just component -> Right (DevicePart component)
```

Finally, the `Device` value can be updated and returned:

```
addComponent :: ComponentIndex -> DevicePart -> Device -> Device
addComponent idx part (Device parts) = Device (Map.insert idx part parts)
```

The interpreter doesn't do anything magical. It just obtains some bits from here and there, and it composes a value of `Device`. This code is relatively simple, yet it has a design problem: instead of processing an error gracefully, we call the `error` function right in the pure world. It's so easy to break this code: just pass an empty `VendorComponents` map, and this vessel will drown. Fixing this problem is easy. Try doing it as an exercise. I'll leave it as is for a while, at least until we discuss the opposite edge of this story: the end of the end-to-end design.

4.1.4 Tests as a final consumer

Tests are a final consumer. They are also a cheap design validator. I can't estimate the number of cases where tests have saved me from wrong decisions and design flaws. Even if there is no significant functionality implemented yet, writing tests helps shape the interfaces and communication types. Yes, it's a test-driven development (TDD) philosophy, and I highly recommend giving it a chance. I don't mean the purest TDD, though, because following its rigid algorithm can be too limiting. I do TDD in a more relaxed form while keeping this idea in mind: tests should strengthen the design process and prevent the code from going in the wrong direction. We'll return to this question in the future. For more information, see Kent Beck's *Test-Driven Development: By Example* (Addison-Wesley Professional, 2002; https://mng.bz/maqM).

Let's write our first test. It will check a device's equipment after its construction. Does it contain what it should contain? Are all the parts correct and in the right places? See the following listing for the test. I use the `hspec` Haskell library, where `describe` opens a bunch of test cases grouped by a topic, and `it` represents a single test case.

Listing 4.4 Test as a final consumer

```
import Andromeda.Assets.Vendors.AAA.ComponentsAPI as AAA      ◄──── Vendor's data

spec :: Spec                                                  ◄──── Test with hspec
spec =
  describe "Hardware tests" $ do                              ◄──── Group of hardware tests

    it "Hardware device components check" $ do                ◄──── Test case

      let boosters = makeDevice aaaVendorComponents boostersDef  ◄──┐ Making a
                                                                    │ device
      let mbThermometer = getDevicePart "nozzle1-t" boosters ◄──┐
      case mbThermometer of                                     │ Validating
        Nothing -> fail "There is no such component"            │ the device
        Just _  -> putStrLn "Component found."    ◄──┐
                                                     │ The part
                                                     │ should exist.
```

Luckily, the AAA vendor has provided all the bindings and wrappers around their components. Unluckily, we realize it's all trash because the APIs do not implement anything real. For the `AAA-T-25` thermometer, the binding does not interact with it; it does nothing or returns a dummy value.

Listing 4.5   Fake APIs provided by aaa

```
aaaTemperature25Handler :: SensorAPI
aaaTemperature25Handler = SensorAPI
  { reset = pure ()
  , readMeasurement
      = pure (Measurement Temperature 100.0)
  , setCallback = \_ _ -> pure ()
  }

aaaVendorComponents :: VendorComponents
aaaVendorComponents = Map.fromList
  [ (aaaTemperature25Name, t25VSensor)
  , (aaaPressure02Name,    p02Sensor)
  , (aaaController86Name,   c86Controller)
  ]

t25VSensor :: VendoredSensor
t25VSensor =
  VendoredSensor
    aaaTemperature25Passport
    aaaTemperature25Handler
```

Fake API

Does nothing

Returns a dummy temperature

Does nothing

Some vendored temperature sensor

Other vendored devices

Temperature sensor utilizes the faked handler

What a pity—it's a fake. No worries. The initial stages of design are all full of fakes and dummy implementations. It's much wiser to shape a form, fill it with dummies, and proceed than to try to push every separate part to the production level and then meet insurmountable obstacles when it's impossible to assemble the whole system. A straight-through design is all about avoiding risks on the edges and building a better understanding of the task. This is so important that I would call it a design principle.

Designing systems should be done against shapes but not against the content. Fake the content until it's truly required. We can at least run the test and make it pass because the VendorComponents map contains everything to compose a boosters device.

As long as we made the Device type abstract and opaque, the test can't just unroll the internal dictionary of components. There should be an accessor, a function that knows how to deal with Device values. The getDevicePart function and the public interface of the Device module are shown in the following listing.

Listing 4.6   Module-based Device interface

```
module Andromeda.Hardware.Impl.Device (
    Device,
    DevicePart,
    makeDevice,
    blankDevice,
    getDevicePart
  ) where

getDevicePart :: ComponentIndex -> Device -> Maybe DevicePart
getDevicePart idx (Device parts) = Map.lookup idx parts
```

The test will pass, although it doesn't do anything with `DevicePart`. It makes sense to check the whole structure of the `Device` value, because what if the interpreter missed something? Or instead of five parts, it only created two? Or 10 of them with a lot of duplications? Feel free to write these tests as an exercise. (You'll probably need some additional functions exposed from the `Device` module.)

It that it? To be honest, I'm not fully satisfied. I feel that the topic requires more elaboration. Verifying what device we got is fine—this must be checked anyway. Still, it doesn't seem representative enough. Nothing interacts with the device, and we don't really know whether it works. We have a thermometer instance in the test, so why not trigger its main function measuring the temperature? There is the corresponding method in the `SensorAPI` structure, after all. Well, yes, a great plan, I would say, but I'll postpone it for a moment. This functionality requires some additional mechanisms, and it will be wiser to do it as an additional exercise at the end of the chapter.

Tests are not intended for searching for bugs exclusively. In fact, tests cover functional and nonfunctional requirements when reducing the risk of bugs is just one of them. This book revolves around testable code and architecture and talks about many useful test approaches. My personal opinion is that every software engineer should be aware of them. We're moving on to the next big themes of software design in functional languages, and we'll be using tests to demonstrate our design decisions as if they were real consumers and clients of our system.

4.2 Functional services

I would like to begin with an apology. This section does not discuss authentic services, as you might expect, such as service-oriented architectures, CORBA, microservices, services with HTTP API, and so on. This all relates to a broader notion of service or even to a number of such notions. We're not interested in this side of software architecture, at least until we're comfortable with the application design. We'll be talking about functional services—a way to decouple subsystems from each other and make architectural layers more explicit.

> **DEFINITION** A *functional service* is a single-responsibility behavior hidden by a public functional interface that allows us to substitute the code at runtime transparently to the client code.

This definition doesn't say anything about the remoteness of a functional service, so it doesn't matter whether the service works in the same process or is forked into a separate one. The definition only requires that the functional service has a functional interface: one of the previously used (module based and ADT based) or another that we haven't touched on yet. We had an intuitive understanding of functional services and interfaces before, and now we'll put everything on the table.

4.2.1   *Layers and sublayers*

It is true that the `Hdl` language represents a functional interface, and it divides the application into bigger layers: business logic (`Hdl` definitions) and implementation (all the `Device` machinery). These two layers, with the `Hdl` language in between, make our architecture three layered. This architecture is very natural for functional languages such as Haskell, and most of the code I have written in my Haskell career falls into this category.

However, the services we'll be developing are all about dividing the implementation layer into smaller sublayers. We'll try both the Service Handle pattern and a type-class–based service for decoupling parts of the hardware subsystem from each other. After all, we can reason about each of the big layers as a separate world and apply the same principles of software design, such as single responsibility, interface segregation, low coupling, and high cohesion. The mechanisms we'll introduce here won't affect the whole architecture, but they will make the code better. Figure 4.3 illustrates this idea.

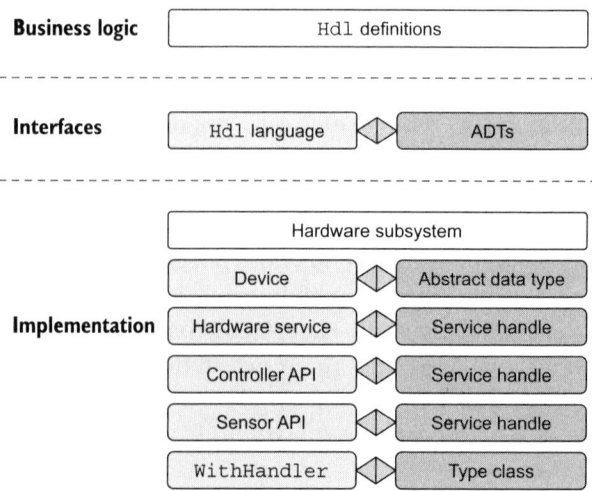

Figure 4.3   Layers and sublayers

You can use the two approaches on a bigger scale as architectural design patterns and have a three-layered architecture, but I would argue that it's not a good place for them. Instead, I'm proposing interpretable languages such as free monads for that role, and I'll show you why. For now, we'll stay on the implementation layer and try to make it less coupled.

4.2.2   *The Service Handle pattern*

The story takes off from one of the most popular design patterns in Haskell: the Service Handle pattern. With this pattern, we want to achieve the following goals:

- *Low coupling*—We can easily observe the ways of communication with a subsystem if it has fewer relations with the outside environment.
- *Better maintainability*—Changing requirements leads to code modification. We prefer modular code rather than spaghetti code because it can be modified more easily.
- *Wise responsibility distribution*—The SRP says that each part of the code should have only one responsibility, only one idea to implement. Why? Because we want to know what this part does and what it will never do, but we don't want to have to examine the code to check. When each part does a single thing, the whole system stays coherent and focused, which makes it easily explorable.
- *Abstractions over implementations*—Abstractions hide implementation details from the client code. This is good because the client code sees only a high-level interface to a subsystem, and the knowledge about the internals is guarded by this interface. Ideally, an interface to a subsystem should be small and clear to simplify its usage. Moreover, an abstraction makes it possible to modify (or even completely replace) an implementation without breaking the client code. Finally, correct abstractions give additional power and expression, which leads to less code and more functionality.
- *Testability*—We'll design a subsystem that can be tested well. Sometimes we need mocks for this, and we'll learn how to organize the code to support this with the Service Handle pattern.

What's so special about the Service Handle pattern? This is the simplest functional interface available to a developer if the language has first-class functions. We've seen this before: remember `SensorAPI` and `ControllerAPI` data structures. Let me explain.

Service Pattern should have this kind of handle containing a couple of methods, for example:

```
type Name = String                                          Service handle

data GreetingsHandle = GreetingsHandle                       Pure method
  { sayHiPurely   :: Name -> String
  , sayHiImpurely :: Name -> IO String                       Impure method
  }
```

Implementations of this interface would need to fill a value of this data type by specific functions doing the real work.

Listing 4.7 Two implementations (handle values)

```
handle1 :: GreetingsHandle                                  Implementation 1
handle1 = GreetingsHandle
  { sayHiPurely   = \name -> "Hello, " <> name <> "!"
  , sayHiImpurely = \name -> pure ("Hello, " <> name <> "!")
  }
```

```
handle2 :: GreetingsHandle                          ◀─── Implementation 2
handle2 = GreetingsHandle
  { sayHiPurely   = \name -> name <> "! What a surprise!"
  , sayHiImpurely = \name -> do
        let greetings = name <> "! What a surprise!"
        putStrLn greetings
        pure greetings
  }
```

Notice that the first handle composes some data and returns it, while the second handle prints the string to the console. Side effects are allowed by the sayHiImpurely method, which is explicitly stated in the method's declaration. Business logic code should consider this somehow. The following code just calls the methods of the handle and doesn't bother about problems with impurity.

Listing 4.8   Injecting the dependency with service handle

```
helloUser :: GreetingsHandle -> IO ()                  ◀──────── Function accepts
helloUser (GreetingsHandle _ sayHi) = do                         a handle
  putStrLn "What is your name?"
  name <- getLine
  _ <- sayHi name                        ◀──────── Injected impure method;
  pure ()                                          result is dropped

main :: IO ()
main = do                                         Injecting
  helloUser handle1              ◀──────────────── dependency 1
  helloUser handle2             ◀────────────────
                                                  Injecting dependency 2
```

As you can see, we pass a handle as an argument. This is nothing but dependency injection with the Service Handle pattern. Everything has a place here—interface, implementation, client code that should select the implementation, and business logic code that works against the interface without knowing what implementation is injected. Dependency injection is, therefore, a mechanism, or a practice, for bringing some external functionality into a client code so that the client code can see only the interface of that functionality without knowing much about its actual inner workings. It makes the code independent from much knowledge and also has a good effect on the project structure. Dependency injection as a practice relates to the Dependency Inversion principle from SOLID, which marks a design as good when the subsystems depend on the abstract interface and not on the specific implementation details.

The best part of this pattern is that it is extremely simple—no need to do any type-level magic or anything too mind-bending. The pattern looks pretty much like an OOP interface passed as an argument into a function. Haskell developers love this pattern and use it quite often. With that being said, the Service Handle pattern has some drawbacks. I'll name one: when the number of handles becomes too big, managing them can be very unpleasant. You would definitely want to group your interfaces somehow, and this would cause other difficulties. I'll name the second drawback as well: once you want to make an interface to a subsystem that involves some type-level magic (like many Haskell and Scala libraries), this will immediately transform your handle type to a monster with type-level hacks.

To understand this pattern better, we should take a closer look at it in the wild. Let's apply it to our domain task.

4.2.3 Hardware service

Suppose we know that the Hardware subsystem will be replaced by an improved version in the future, but today, we can't do this easily because it has too many external relations. For now, it's supposed to be used as shown in figure 4.4.

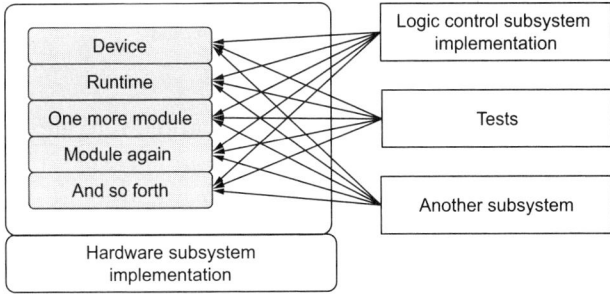

Figure 4.4 Complex relations between subsystems

Some other subsystems depend on the Hardware subsystem, and we don't want this dependency to be strong. The more relations there are, the more difficult the refactoring will be if or when updating of the subsystem becomes required. We might want a simple lever that just does the whole task of replacing an old version with a new one. In other words, we want an additional chain between the two worlds, as shown in figure 4.5.

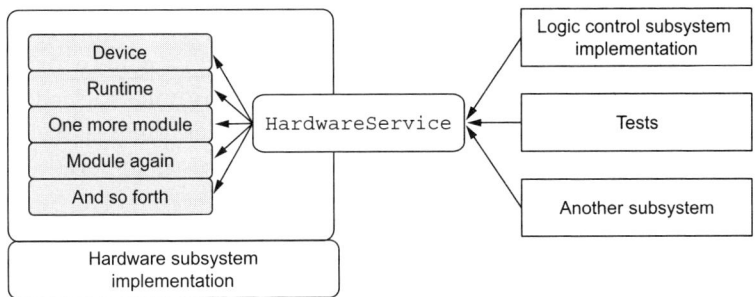

Figure 4.5 Simple relations between subsystems

To make this possible, we add one more layer of abstraction in the form of the Service Handle pattern. Take a look at the definition in the following listing.

Listing 4.9   A service handle for the hardware subsystem

```
module Andromeda.Hardware.Impl.Service
  ( HardwareService (..)                              ◄───── Exposing the
  ) where                                                    interface

import Andromeda.Hardware.Language.Hdl (Hdl, ComponentIndex)
import Andromeda.Hardware.Impl.Device.Types (Device, DevicePart)

data HardwareService = HardwareService
  { makeDevice     :: Hdl -> Device              ◄─────┐  Pure method for
  , getBlankDevice :: Device                     ◄─────┤  making devices
  , getDevicePart
      :: ComponentIndex                             Pure accessor
      -> Device                                     method
      -> Maybe DevicePart
  }
```

Notice that the `Device` and `DevicePart` types have been moved into another name-space. Again, this was done because previously, we violated an important rule of good form: keep types separated from the behavior. This will make the structure of the application more consistent. Yet this means that we can't make those types abstract—the details should be exposed from those modules so that the `Device` module can have full access:

```
module Andromeda.Hardware.Impl.Device.Types (
    Device (..),
    DevicePart (..),
  ) where
```

Will it be a Java-world antipattern *Public Morozov*—the one having all the internal bits shamelessly exhibited? (This name comes from the history of the ancient USSR and is probably not understood outside Russia.) It's debatable. But as long as there is the namespace `Impl`, we can at least mandate that the developers of the business logic avoid touching this module.

For now, the handle contains only pure methods like before. We just repeated them without any change. However, common applications of this pattern that you might encounter will have impure methods only because we mostly abstract side effects and hide the complexities of the real world behind handlers. This brings Haskell code closer to any other imperative language, and to some degree, this is an imperative approach.

Hence, this is the impure service with all the methods acting within the `IO` environment:

```
data HardwareService = HardwareService
  { makeDevice     :: Hdl -> IO Device           ◄──── Impure methods
  , getBlankDevice :: IO Device
  , getDevicePart
      :: ComponentIndex
      -> Device
      -> IO (Maybe DevicePart)
  }
```

Next, where should we keep implementations of this interface? We have one in the `Device` module, and we can easily put those (pure) methods into this handle, except we don't have `VendorComponents` map, so the handler creation function should obtain it from the caller:

```
include qualified Andromeda.Hardware.Impl.Device as D

createHardwareService :: VendorComponents -> HardwareService
createHardwareService vComponents = HardwareService
  { makeDevice     = \hdl -> pure (D.makeDevice vComponents hdl)
  , getBlankDevice = pure D.blankDevice
  , getDevicePart  = \idx device -> pure (D.getDevicePart idx device)
  }
```

If you check out the book samples, however, you'll see that I moved this responsibility closer to the AAA vendor assets—namely, into the following module.

Listing 4.10 Service implementation provided by a vendor

```
module Andromeda.Assets.Vendors.AAA.HardwareService where

import Andromeda.Hardware (HardwareService(..))
import qualified Andromeda.Hardware.Impl.Device as D
import Andromeda.Assets.Vendors.AAA.ComponentsAPI (aaaVendorComponents)

aaaHardwareService :: HardwareService
aaaHardwareService = HardwareService
  { makeDevice     = \hdl -> pure (D.makeDevice aaaVendorComponents hdl)
  , getBlankDevice = pure D.blankDevice
  , getDevicePart  = \idx device -> pure (D.getDevicePart idx device)
  }
```

I'm sure I'll be moving things across the project once more, but for now, I want to hide the AAA details and not think about them in my tests:

```
it "Hardware device components check" $ do
  boosters      <- makeDevice aaaHardwareService boostersDef
  mbThermometer <- getDevicePart aaaHardwareService "nozzle1-t" boosters

  case mbThermometer of
    Nothing -> fail "There is no such component"
    Just _  -> putStrLn "Component found."
```

Calling the makeDevice method from the handle

My architect's sense allows me to see that I can even integrate the BBB vendor and join the two on the upper level.

Listing 4.11 Multiple vendor components

```
include qualified Andromeda.Hardware.Impl.Device as D

allComponents :: VendorComponents
allComponents =
  Map.union
    aaaVendorComponents
```

Joining two dictionaries

```
    bbbVendorComponents
```

```
genHardwareService :: HardwareService
genHardwareService = HardwareService
  { makeDevice     = \hdl -> D.makeDevice allComponents hdl
  , getBlankDevice = pure D.blankDevice
  , getDevicePart  = \idx device -> pure (D.getDevicePart idx device)
  }
```

◄─┐ **Returns a unified
  │ service handle**

Another way of combining the two is by making a service of services and redirecting the calls to the nested AAA or BBB service. If one `AAA.makeDevice` fails, try `BBB.makeDevice`. However, this idea reveals a problem: we don't have proper error handling for the `makeDevice` method. Remember that the interpreter dives into the vendor's dictionary, and once the real component is not found, the interpreter throws an exception:

```
testDef :: Hdl
testDef = [ ComponentDef "t1" testPassport ]

-- throws an exception
testDevice :: IO Device
testDevice = makeDevice genHardwareService testDef
```

We've found a design flaw. The `makeDevice` method must process possible errors, and it should manifest what errors it supports. Yes, this is the place for the `Either` data type, which is a popular way to have either an error as a value or a valid result.

```
data DeviceCreationError
  = ComponentImplementationNotFound

makeDevice :: Hdl -> IO (Either DeviceCreationError Device)
```

I encourage you to revisit the implementation and make all the methods safer. Later in this book, we'll talk about error-handling strategies more closely and see how difficult this theme is.

4.2.4   *Mocking with the Service Handle pattern*

The two implementations that came from the depths of AAA and BBB offices could behave strangely, and we don't have any control over them. If something unpredictable happens in a spaceship because of that, astronauts will have a lot of trouble, likely critical to the mission and lives. This is a huge risk. Of course, it's the vendor's responsibility to provide good-quality hardware with all the needed certificates and licenses, but still, this happens. We can't get rid of this risk completely. All we can do is reduce it by using better testing. But we can't take either of the two implementations as a baseline; in reality, those bindings will require connecting physical devices, which is a serious obstacle to testing.

There is no other way: we should mock the Hardware subsystem. Mocking means using a fake implementation (mock) without the need to call real ones and being able to configure this mock to emulate various problems and cases. Putting the mock into the mechanism will allow us to reveal its weak spots. I can give you an analogy:

speleologists color a water source in caverns to see what path the flow takes under the ground. This is pretty much what we'll do with the code.

Have a look at the `HardwareService` structure. A peculiar feature of this design is that we can't change the final product: the `Device` type and its constituents. Its shape is given already; it's fixed and nonchangeable. It distinguishes our functional design from an object-oriented one. In the object-oriented world, we substitute interfaces with custom objects that can have an arbitrary internal structure. In statically typed functional languages, we mostly operate with functions. Later we'll talk about type-level design, where substituting of types is also possible.

Let's substitute both `makeDevice` and `getDevicePart`. The test will create a fake device, and when we try to get a part from it, the mocked service will return a fake device part. The template of the device will have two components only, while we'll be requesting three. The `getDevicePart` function shouldn't crash and should return `Nothing` if there is no such fake component in this fake device.

Listing 4.12   A test that uses a mocked hardware service

```
it "Getting absent device part" $ do

  let testDef =
       [ ComponentDef "t1" thermometer1Passp          Using a mocked
       , ComponentDef "p1" pressure1Passp              service handle
       ]
                                                          Part is available
  device   <- makeDevice mockedHardwareService testDef  ◄──┘

                                                          Part is available
  mpPart1 <- getDevicePart mockedHardwareService "t1" device  ◄──┘
  mpPart2 <- getDevicePart mockedHardwareService "p1" device  ◄── Part is not
  mpPart3 <- getDevicePart mockedHardwareService "t2" device  ◄── available

  case (mpPart1, mpPart2, mpPart3) of                    ◄──┐
    (Just _, Just _, Nothing) -> pure ()                    Success test condition
    _ -> fail "Device is assembled incorrectly."    ◄──┐
                                                        Failed test condition
```

The test is pretty straightforward. It's more interesting to see what the mocked handle looks like, as shown in the following listing. (I don't present passports and API handlers for components; there is nothing special there. You can look for those in the book's samples.)

Listing 4.13   A mocked hardware service handle

```
module Andromeda.Test.HardwareService where

import Andromeda.Hardware
import qualified Andromeda.Hardware.Impl.Device.Types as D

import Andromeda.TestData.Components
  (thermometer1Passp, thermometer1Handler
```

```
  , pressure1Passp, pressure1Handler)

mockedThermometer1 :: D.DevicePart                    ◄───── Fake device part 1
mockedThermometer1 = D.DevicePart
  (VendoredSensor thermometer1Passp thermometer1Handler)

mockedPressure1 :: D.DevicePart                       ◄───── Fake device part 2
mockedPressure1 = D.DevicePart
  (VendoredSensor pressure1Passp pressure1Handler)

mockedHardwareService :: HardwareService             ◄───── Mocked service
mockedHardwareService = HardwareService                     implementation
  { makeDevice      = mockedMakeDevice
  , getDevicePart   = mockedGetDevicePart
  , getBlankDevice = error "getBlankDevice not supported"
  }

mockedMakeDevice :: Hdl -> IO Device                 ◄───── Mocked functions
mockedMakeDevice _ = pure (Device mempty)

mockedGetDevicePart
  :: ComponentIndex -> Device -> IO (Maybe DevicePart)
mockedGetDevicePart idx _ =
  case idx of
    "t1" -> pure (Just mockedThermometer1)           ◄───── Returning fake parts
    "p1" -> pure (Just mockedPressure1)
    _        -> pure Nothing
```

As you can see, the mockedGetDevicePart function knows about some possible components and their indexes in HDL: "t1" and "p1". When it recognizes the index (with pattern matching), the corresponding fake part will be returned. Otherwise, Nothing.

This testing infrastructure doesn't check to see what device is coming, assuming it will always be a faked one. In more complex tests, you might want to distinguish devices. Assigning names or GUIDs to them would be quite sufficient, but this will require improving the Device type so that DeviceName will hold a unique name:

```
data Device = Device DeviceName (Map ComponentIndex DevicePart)
```

Now you manufacture multiple mocks and address them separately:

```
mockedMakeDevice :: DeviceName -> Hdl -> IO Device
mockedMakeDevice name _ = pure (Device name Map.empty)

mockedGetDevicePart idx device =
  case (idx, device) of
    ("t1", Device "fake1" _) -> pure (Just mockedThermometer1)
    ("t2", Device "fake2" _) -> pure (Just mockedThermometer2)
    _        -> pure Nothing
```

So we have two devices here ("fake1" and "fake2") and can choose any of them from the tests.

Mocks wouldn't be so useful if we could not configure them somehow. In particular, we can check how many times a method is called by having a counter. The hardware service methods are all impure, so it's possible to use `IORef`, a Haskell mutable variable, for this. It has an IO-based interface and works as a regular mutable variable.

Listing 4.14 Mutable method invocation counter

```
mockedHardwareService :: IORef Int -> HardwareService
mockedHardwareService counterRef = HardwareService
  { getDevicePart = mockedGetDevicePart counterRef }
```
◄—— The counter is used when constructing the service.

```
mockedGetDevicePart
  :: IORef Int
  -> ComponentIndex
  -> Device
  -> IO (Maybe DevicePart)
```
◄—— The counter is used in the mocked function.

```
mockedGetDevicePart counterRef idx device = do
  modifyIORef' counterRef (+1)
  ...
```
◄—— Increases the counter when the method is hit

We can do even more interesting things in tests, if you don't mind me calling these well-known mainstream techniques interesting. But we're getting too far away from our theme. There will be more about mocking, tests, and state latter in the book.

4.2.5 *Type class-powered service handle*

This section is here because the story with the end-to-end design can be finished in a more convincing manner. The code I'll show you here relies on the advanced type-level feature—type classes. This concept exists in many languages, not only in Haskell. In Scala and Rust, type classes can be emulated with traits. C++ has a port of type classes called concepts. Generics in C# have some functionality that repeats a small subset of properties of type classes.

Our task will be reading measurements from a thermometer that we know is contained in the boosters device. Reading pressure from a pressure sensor would be exactly the same because there is only one interface per sensor for now—the `SensorAPI` handle:

```
data SensorAPI = SensorAPI
  { reset           :: IO ()
  , readMeasurement :: IO Measurement
  , setCallback     :: Period -> IO Measurement -> IO ()
  }
```

This is another application of the Service Handle pattern. `SensorAPI` declares an interface for dealing with native devices. It contains three methods, and we're not quite sure how they behave. We drafted this interface too roughly, we made a proof of concept, and we didn't think about whether it was good or bad. Both `SensorAPI` and `ControllerAPI` will be redesigned to reflect the domain better, but not here, of course.

The only method we need is `readMeasurement`. How should we invoke it?

Let's take a look. `Device` contains a map of `DevicePart` items. Each of them has a `VendorComponent` value, either `VendoredSensor` or `VendoredController`:

```
data Device = Device DeviceName (Map ComponentIndex DevicePart)
data DevicePart = DevicePart VendorComponent

data VendorComponent
  = VendoredSensor      ComponentPassport SensorAPI
  | VendoredController ComponentPassport ControllerAPI
```

And here we have a `SensorAPI` handler put into the second field of `VendoredSensor`. In our current design, this handler comes from a particular vendor (for example, AAA). As you might remember, we faked the handlers because the AAA vendor doesn't exist. This was listing 4.5, and here is an excerpt from it:

```
aaaTemperature25Handler :: SensorAPI
aaaTemperature25Handler = SensorAPI
  { reset = pure ()
  , readMeasurement = pure (Measurement Temperature 100.0)
  , setCallback = \_ _ -> pure ()
  }

t25VSensor :: VendoredSensor
t25VSensor = VendoredSensor aaaTemperature25Passport aaaTemperature25Handler
```

The `readMeasurement` method returns a single value each time: `100.0` units of temperature. It would be very natural to obtain this value in tests, which would prove that the system can be used for this by the client code. In the previous tests, we successfully requested a part of the device by its index, for example, `"nozzle1-t"`. As developers, we know this must be a thermometer sensor, and we could even violate the rule "don't interact with internals directly" to extract a handler from it.

Listing 4.15 Bypassing interfaces to access the internals

```
let service = aaaHardwareService

boosters       <- makeDevice service boostersDef
mbThermometer <- getDevicePart service "nozzle1-t" boosters

case mbThermometer of                                    Extracting
                                                         the handler
  Just (DevicePart (VendoredSensor _ handler)) -> do
    measurement <- readMeasurement handler
    measurement `shouldBe` (Measurement Temperature 100.0)   Using the handler

  _ -> error "Invalid operation"
```

Revealing details of `DevicePart` in the code means increasing coupling between this client code and the implementation of the Hardware subsystem. We should avoid doing this as much as possible. The client code has to be done against interfaces, not implementations.

So let's create an interface for this. Take a look at this type class with the method withHandler:

```
-- module Andromeda.Hardware.Impl.Device.Types:

class WithHandler handlerAPI where
  withHandler :: DevicePart
              -> (handlerAPI -> IO ())
              -> IO ()
```

Part to work with

Callback for handler

Type classes tie some additional functionality to the user-defined types. When a user-defined type supports a type class, client code may be sure that methods from the type class exist somewhere in the scope. We'll make an instance of WithHandler for SensorAPI so we can rewrite listing 4.15:

```
let service = aaaHardwareService

boosters      <- makeDevice service boostersDef
mbThermometer <- getDevicePart service "nozzle1-t" boosters

case mbThermometer of
  Just thermometer -> withHandler thermometer verifyTemperature
  Nothing          -> error "Component not found"
```

No direct access to handler

We removed an explicit pattern matching and used the thermometer value instead. We then pass this value into the withHandler method, as well as the verifyTemperature callback:

```
verifyTemperature :: SensorAPI -> IO ()
verifyTemperature handler = do
  measurement <- readMeasurement handler
  measurement `shouldBe` (Measurement Temperature 100.0)
```

When the compiler sees what callback we passed to withHandler, it tries to find an instance of the WithHandler type class in the scope for this type. In our case, all the available instances are defined in the Impl.Device.Types module, as well as the type class itself:

```
-- module Andromeda.Hardware.Impl.Device.Types:

instance WithHandler SensorAPI where
  withHandler (DevicePart (VendoredSensor _ h)) f = f h
  withHandler _ _ = error "Invalid part API handler"

instance WithHandler ControllerAPI where
  withHandler (DevicePart (VendoredController _ h)) f = f h
  withHandler _ _ = error "Invalid part API handler"
```

We migrated pattern matching there and hid it with a type-class–based service. We still need to do something with those ugly errors, but at least our client code won't be broken if we decide to rework the DevicePart data type. There is no high coupling between the two anymore.

We thus learned two approaches to functional interfaces. We implemented a complete hardware subsystem from end to end but left many places faked. In the next part, I'll talk about domain-driven design and its refraction in the light of functional languages. I'll show you more ways of organizing functional code and introduce more functional interfaces—in particular, free monads. Stay positive, and keep learning!

Summary

- Establishing final goals for the design is a beneficial technique that can help identify flaws and potential problems.
- End-to-end design is preferred when you want to be sure your design choices will not compromise the final goal.
- Functional services can be used to decouple subsystems from each other and make architectural layers more explicit.
- Carefully analyze dependencies between layers. Detect and rework invalid dependencies in the early design stages.
- Bigger layers (functional interfaces, implementation, and business logic) can be split into smaller sublayers.
- Subsystems should have a clear, concise, accurate, and minimal interface. Every external code should interact with this interface only. Bypassing it would be a bad design practice.
- The Service Handle pattern is the simplest approach to functional interfaces.
- Mocking helps remove the need for real implementations in tests.
- Being an interface, the Service Handle pattern allows for mocking and making fakes.
- A good design is often defined as one that allows the code to be tested in isolation from the external subsystems.
- Type classes provide additional functionality to user-defined types. When a type supports a type class, the client code can be sure that the methods from the type class are available.

Part 3

Domain-driven design

This part takes us to the land of domain modeling with embedded domain-specific languages. We start by exploring the pivotal role of abstractions in DSLs, which not only prevent software bugs but also facilitate a deeper understanding of the domain by allowing only correct operations. This section emphasizes the significance of statically typed languages with robust type systems in developing safe, robust programs, positioning domain-specific languages as a core component in domain-driven design. We dive deep into the complexities of designing effective DSLs, the importance of algebraic data types (ADTs) in creating clear, reliable domain-specific languages, and the effective organization of embedded DSLs to enhance application design.

While exploring domain modeling, we will focus on free monads, highlighting them as the most idiomatic functional interface with interesting parallels to object-oriented programming interfaces. The Free Monad pattern is highlighted as a powerful method for designing eDSLs, offering advantages such as the nesting of languages and chaining of different types of scripts. This approach simplifies complex domain models, making them more accessible and easier to manage. We discuss the importance of a thorough investigation of the domain, defining its properties, components, and laws, and emphasize the role of free monads in designing domain languages suitable for expressing user scenarios, especially in contexts that require imperative-like operations.

Embedded domain-specific languages

5

Software development is a difficult job. Developers do make wrong decisions, and this happens more often than it should. Developers do write incorrect code, and most likely, it happens against their will. Developers do feel lost in complex business domains, broad and contradictory requirements, and mind-bending technologies, each of which is able to make anyone depressed when something goes wrong. Nothing is perfect; nobody is superhuman.

While it's certainly fine to demand software correctness, it's not so obvious why unnecessary complex abstractions lead to bugs. One of the major reasons is that we lose the focus of the domain we're implementing. If we treat an abstraction as a universal hammer that can solve all our problems at once, we risk straying far from the actual task, which is creating working code that solves a business problem. Many abstractions and approaches are intended to make our code more correct, but correctness is mostly about meaning (the domain) rather than technique (an abstraction).

You probably know what happens when a project suddenly falls into the abstraction hell, and not one piece of domain becomes visible through it. How can you be sure all the requirements are handled? The domain is blurred and shattered into thousands of pieces, and reasoning about it becomes hard. In this situation, you'll likely run into many bugs that you could have avoided by having a fine-readable and simple, but still adequate, business logic. The abstractions shouldn't be too abstract; otherwise, they tend to skyrocket into the wild, unpopulated space, and nothing about your real domain would be appropriate in this escapism.

This chapter discusses domain modeling as a great tool for building simple, clear, and maintainable software. We'll see the abstractions available for this and how to use them for greater benefits. We'll learn a domain-first approach that is a part of domain-driven design, a methodology introduced by Eric Evans in his *Domain-Driven Design: Tackling Complexity in the Heart of Software* (Addison-Wesley Professional, 2003). I highly recommend learning from this ground-breaking masterpiece of engineering.

> **NOTE**   I shouldn't forget to mention some recent books on domain modeling. You can find a lot of interesting ideas in *Domain Modeling Made Functional: Tackle Software Complexity with Domain-Driven Design and F#* by Scott Wlaschin (Pragmatic Bookshelf, 2018; https://mng.bz/67E6) and *Functional and Reactive Domain Modeling* by Debasish Ghosh (Manning, 2016; https://mng.bz/7dNg).

Are embedded domain-specific languages (eDSLs) so special from the developer's perspective that the whole chapter is dedicated to them? I truly believe one chapter isn't enough, and it's very insufficient to introduce the subject properly. There are many different books on DSLs, so why not get familiar with the work of Martin Fowler? You can check out his book *Domain-Specific Languages* (Addison-Wesley Professional, 2010; https://martinfowler.com/books/dsl.html).

I've organically come to the same ideas during my career and while writing the first edition of *Functional Design and Architecture*, and this makes me feel that everything is interconnected if done correctly. So let's talk about my favorite topic: domain-specific languages.

5.1   *Approaching embedded DSLs*

The history of development has many dark chapters in which using the wrong abstractions ruined great projects. Did you know there was a satellite called the Mars Climate Orbiter that burned up in that planet's atmosphere because of a software bug? The problem was a measurement unit mismatch in which the program returned a pound-second measurement, but it should have been newton-second. This bug could have been eliminated by testing or having better logic powered by a static type system. It seems the developers missed something important when programming this behavior.

Abstractions can save us from bugs in two ways:

- *By making it simple to reason about the domain*—This means decreasing accidental complexity so we can easily see the problems. Simplifying the code, making it more domain oriented, and freeing it from nonrelated implementation details make observing the domain easier and help developers focus on the business tasks.

- *By making it impossible to push the program into an invalid state*—This means encoding a domain so that only correct operations are allowed. Domains can be encoded in many ways, and there are techniques enabling a safer, clearer encoding so the design of the domain directs the developers to do things correctly. This approach, also known as making invalid states irrepresentable, is a great principle of design, and we'll discuss the tools at our disposal to follow it.

It's not surprising that statically typed languages with a good type system are considered to be the best choice for developing safe and robust programs. Type-level language features such as (generalized) algebraic data types, type classes, and higher-kind types have become the norm in modern programming languages. Hopefully, we'll sell the increased popularity of languages such Scala, Haskell, PureScript, and Rust.

Let me confess: I'm a big fan of domain-specific languages—a technique that follows both of the points listed. In my opinion, designing DSLs should be a central idea of domain-driven design.

5.1.1 *Everything is an eDSL*

The DSL approach addresses one main problem: the smooth translation of the domain's essence into the code without increasing accidental complexity. Done right, a DSL can replace tons of messy code, but of course, there's a risk that it will restrict and annoy the user too much if designed badly. And this is not something rare. There are programming languages that are designed badly (we won't point fingers [it's C++]). Designing a DSL was an equally challenging task for a long time, especially if it was an external DSL. But designing an internal, embedded DSL can be easy. And moreover, we do it all the time.

From a certain standpoint, everything in the code that we clearly relate to a particular domain can be called an eDSL. Obviously, domain types form an eDSL about this business field. Business logic often tells a story about processes happening in that business. This code operates through small actions from the domain and combines them to achieve a worthy effect.

That's all understandable. But why is a networking library not an eDSL in the domain of networking? See the following code:

```
-- network library:

connect :: Socket -> SockAddr -> IO ()
bind    :: Socket -> SockAddr -> IO ()
listen  :: Socket -> Int -> IO ()
accept  :: Socket -> IO (Socket, SockAddr)
close   :: Socket -> IO ()
```

It may be a bit imperative and impure because everything is in IO, but the notions are clearly from networking: sockets, addresses, and so on. In functional languages, we deal with eDSLs all the time.

What about the Control.Monad module in Haskell? It's a rich toolbox for working with monadic code. Additional power is achieved by its genericity. Functions from this module are monad-agnostic, and they are universally applicable to any monad—no exclusions:

```
mapM :: (Traversable t, Monad m) => (a -> m b) -> t a -> m (t b)
sequence :: (Traversable t, Monad m) => t (m a) -> m (t a)
replicateM :: Applicative m => Int -> m a -> m [a]
```

The lens library is an eDSL for manipulating data structures in a combinatorial way:

```
to :: (Profunctor p, Contravariant f)
   => (s -> a) -> Optic' p f s a
sets :: (Profunctor p, Profunctor q, Settable f)
    => (p a b -> q s t) -> Optical p q f s t a b
(^.) :: s -> Getting a s a -> a
```

Okay, the lens library and the generic monadic functions look like extraterrestrial writings because they are built on top of category theory and abstract algebra, two other specific domains you'd need to know if you were looking for ways to overengineer your code. Being merged in tricky ways, these two disciplines make the code a toughie, but if you ask me, this is the purest and most idiomatic possible sample of functional eDSL existing in Haskell today.

> **DEFINITION**   *A functional eDSL* is an embedded DSL that uses functional idioms and patterns for expressing domain notions and behavior. A functional eDSL should contain a concise set of precise combinators that do one small thing and can be composed in a functional manner.

Fortunately, on the basic level of "functional programming Jediism," you don't even need to know any advanced concepts coming from mathematical theories. These concepts serve the purpose of unifying code patterns to abstract behavior and make the code much more generic, safe, expressive, and powerful. But the possibility of just writing functions over functions is still there.

Designing data types and writing their transformations is just enough to solve many programming problems. We did this already in the previous chapters, and I'm going to do it again as part of domain-driven design. Encoding business domains in algebraic data types seems to be a must-have skill for a functional developer, and there is a huge advantage to understanding how functional design works.

5.1.2 Domain specific vs. domain centric

There are at least two approaches to designing eDSLs, and each can be considered a domain-driven design but with a different granularity of domain notions. I called them domain specific and domain centric. All the languages we've worked on before belong to the class of domain-specific languages. What would be a domain-centric language in this case?

Domain-centric languages, as I define them, are rigid, direct, and straightforward languages that treat the domain naively without trying to rely on its essential properties or true nature. Domain-centric languages (let's abbreviate them as DCLs) are the least programmable and the most literate languages of all embedded languages. DCLs encode domain notions directly, without any idea of orthogonality or composability behind them.

> **TIP** Orthogonality of a set of notions means that these notions are independent yet complimentary to each other.

Here is an example of DCL that reiterates a domain notion of a *boosters device*. Previously, we've encoded it indirectly by composing it with components. There were no *boosters* or *engine* right in `Hdl`, and rightly so: by having component definitions, component passports, and other domain notions, we could not only manufacture boosters but do much more. In domain-centric design, the boosters device would be rigidly encoded as is, ignoring its internal structure and all the properties that could normally emerge from the composition of some notions. The same is true for the actions of the domain: they would be represented directly, encoded naively, and would not be compound by any means. For example, if it were a language for launching rockets into the earth's orbit, it could look as shown in the following listing.

Listing 5.1 Domain-centric eDSL for rockets launching

```
type ThrustDx = Float
type Name = String

newtype SolidFuelBoosters = SolidFuelBoosters Name        ◀── Direct representation
newtype MainEngine = MainEngine Name                          of a domain notion
newtype RotaryEngine = RotaryEngine Name

data FlightProcedure                                      ◀── Direct domain actions
  = Delay Time
  | InitSolidFuelBoosters SolidFuelBoosters
  | InitMainEngine MainEngine
  | InitRotaryEngine RotaryEngine
  | DecoupleSolidFuelBoosters SolidFuelBoosters
  | ChangeMainEngineThrust MainEngine ThrustDx Time
  | ChangeRotaryEngineThrust RotaryEngine ThrustDx Time

type FlightControl = [FlightProcedure]
```

Notice that this time, boosters are nothing but a solid-fuel engine used to accelerate rockets during the first stages of flight. We don't allow any other meanings, and there is no possibility of reading this language the wrong way. The scripts in this procedural language are also pretty straightforward.

Listing 5.2   Domain-centric eDSL script

```
rocketOrbitalLaunch :: FlightControl
rocketOrbitalLaunch =
  [ InitSolidFuelBoosters boosters                          ◄─── Phase 1: launch
  , InitMainEngine mainEngine
  , InitRotaryEngine rotaryEngine                           Phase 2: lift off,
                                                            first 30 seconds
  , ChangeMainEngineThrust mainEngine 100.0 (seconds 30) ◄─ of launch
  , Delay (seconds 30)

  , ChangeRotaryEngineThrust rotaryEngine 10.0 (seconds 20) ◄─ Phase 3:
  , Delay (seconds 20)                                      powered ascent

  , DecoupleSolidFuelBoosters boosters                      ◄─── Phase 4: staging
  , ChangeRotaryEngineThrust rotaryEngine 20.0 (seconds 20)
  , Delay (seconds 20)

  , ChangeRotaryEngineThrust rotaryEngine 0.0 (seconds 20) ◄─ Phase 5: upper
  , Delay (seconds 20)                                      stage burn
  ]
```

You can't really use this language for anything else—it's not generic, universal, or composable. It's too specific and dedicated. This script reflects the very description of the flight, and not by chance, we can relate it to the graphic image (figure 5.1).

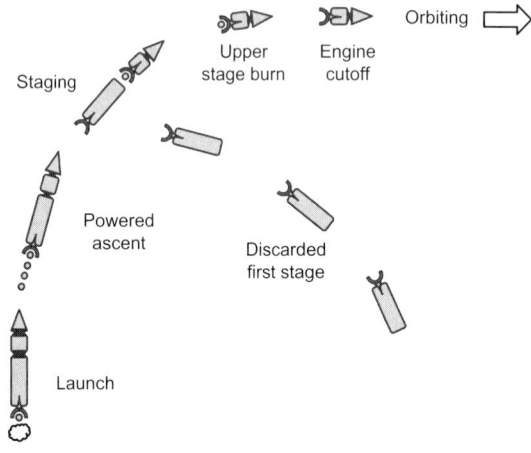

Figure 5.1   Rocket flight stages

Every flight procedure is just a command to be sent to the system (interpreter) that will be able to evaluate it. The language doesn't care about the validity of the order in which these procedures follow each other. We just hope that the interpreter will evaluate it somehow. Here is some sample interpreting code:

```
interpretFlightProcedure :: FlightProcedure -> IO ()
interpretFlightProcedure (Delay t) = delay t
interpretFlightProcedure (InitSolidFuelBoosters name) = ...
interpretFlightProcedure ...       -- other procedures

runFlightControl :: FlightControl -> IO ()
runFlightControl [] = pure ()
runFlightControl (p:ps) = do
  interpretFlightProcedure p
  runFlightControl ps
```

Domain-centric languages do not provide any validity control through their design. It's possible for domain-centric languages to evolve so much that they turn into domain-specific ones. There is no strict distinction between them, except that domain-centric languages are extremely focused and very narrow. They are simpler, as well. However, the more requirements come from a domain, the more problematic this approach becomes.

There is nothing to add—we'll be developing mostly domain-specific languages here. We want to talk about different tricks and mechanisms to encode domain notions in a more general way.

5.2 *Modeling eDSLs with algebraic data types*

Algebraic data types shouldn't necessarily be exclusive features of a functional language. I personally see no excuse for avoiding ADTs and not adding them into all programming languages. ADTs cover most of your needs when you want a complex data structure—a tree, graph, dictionary, and so forth—but they're also suitable for modeling. In OOP, you may choose UML. Or you may start constructing classes that encode your domain. But once you've mastered ADTs, you won't need those two ancient and clumsy tools. ADTs are very handy, and one doesn't even need to be proficient in programming to understand those models.

I like weaving eDSLs based on ADTs when thinking about my business tasks—this is a great way to reason about the domain. I find it very satisfying. This is pure creativity. You can take any path or design you want, so you can choose the design you think will work best. That should make your job as a developer easier, thus making your work also safer and quicker. I hope this introduction will not only teach you practical approaches but also help me share my love of DSLs.

5.2.1 *Clarifying the requirements*

Earlier, we developed an HDL machinery. The `Hdl` ADT is no doubt an eDSL. It contains a set of pieces for describing devices as compound objects:

```
data ComponentDef = ComponentDef ComponentIndex ComponentPassport

type Hdl = [ComponentDef]
```

With `Hdl`, we define a sensor, a controller, a mechanical arm, and a solar panel, which is just enough to build a spaceship! But we aren't that close to the working prototype of a spaceship model yet. There are also many other requirements, which we developed in chapter 3. There are mind maps with requirements and elements diagrams we used to brainstorm the domain. Figure 5.2 is a small reiteration of the elements diagram for logic control.

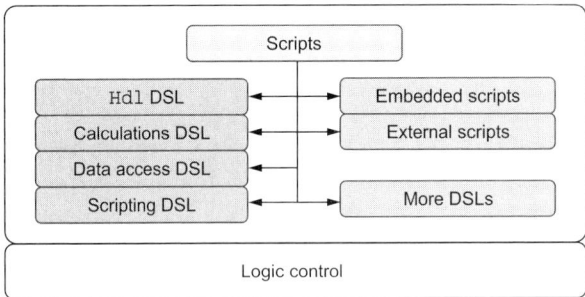

Figure 5.2   Logic Control subsystem

The Logic Control subsystem encapsulates code that covers a relatively large part of the spaceship domain. The subsystem provides a set of tools (functional services, eDSLs, and so on) for the following functionality:

- Defining the hardware schema of a spaceship (`Hdl` and `Hndl` languages).
- Accessing different hardware by interacting with remote control units (mostly digital controllers mounted into devices).
- Reading actual data from sensors.
- Accessing archive data and parameters of the hardware under control.
- Handling events from other subsystems and hardware.
- Running control scripts and programs. Scripts can be run according to different conditions:
  - Boolean condition
  - Exact time or by hitting a time interval
  - Event
  - Demand from other subsystems
  - Periodically, with a time interval
- Monitoring of spaceship state and properties.
- Autonomously correcting spaceship parameters according to predefined behavioral programs.
- Logging and managing security logs.
- Evaluating mathematical calculations.

- Handling hardware errors and failures.
- Testing scenarios before pushing them into a real environment.
- Abstracting different hardware protocols and devices.

Typically, the Logic Control subsystem should not interact with sensors, manipulators, and other components directly. From the logic control point of view, there is a network of devices acting independently, and each device has a representation in the network in the form of a controller. We can rely on the fact that each device has at least one controller, and these controllers are compatible with the central Logic Control intelligence system.Figure 5.3 illustrates these relations.

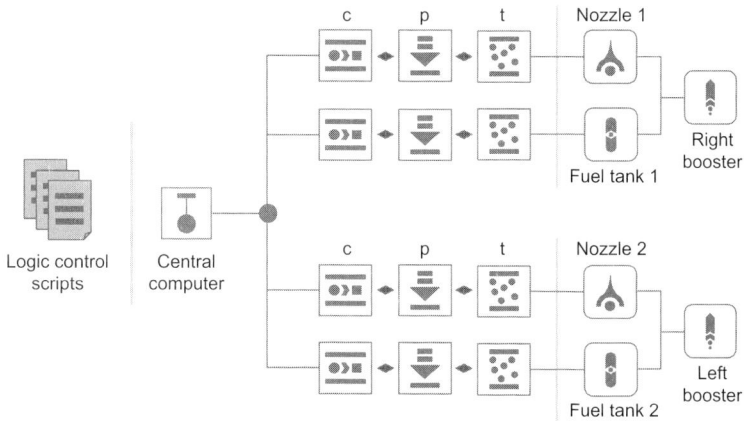

Figure 5.3 Logic control, hardware network, and devices

We deliberately simplify the domain, and I'm sure it won't make us proficient space engineers, but the main ideas seem valid. The central computer and the controllers (denoted by the letter c) participate in the common network, and they communicate and share the information. Earlier, our booster was quite a dumb device. From this scheme, we can conclude that it's essentially a compound mechanism having two separate instances of a single booster, and each of them has its own nozzles and fuel tanks. In turn, the electronics fitted to the nozzles and fuel tanks can perform some intellectual commands and provide a stream of data about temperature and pressure.

In our languages, we'd want to disallow fragile interfaces, such as interaction protocols between controllers. This becomes even more important when designing DSLs of any kind: there are tricks and techniques for raising the correctness of (not even written yet) business logic to the next level. Let's learn some of them while revisiting the `Hdl` language and allies. Later on, we will be moving more toward good practices and correctness based on what comes next.

5.2.2   *Modeling eDSLs with ADTs*

Take a look at the following two listings. The first one is familiar to you because we've been declaring a device this way for a very long time:

```
boostersDef :: Hdl
boostersDef =
  [ ComponentDef "nozzle1-t"  aaaTemperature25Passport
  , ComponentDef "nozzle1-p"  aaaPressure02Passport
  , ComponentDef "nozzle2-t"  aaaTemperature25Passport
  , ComponentDef "nozzle2-p"  aaaPressure02Passport
  , ComponentDef "controller" aaaController86Passport
  ]
```

If we remember the discussion about Space Z engineers, imperative and statement-based languages are more familiar to them. The engineers would rather organize their Andromeda control programs as steps: do this, do that. For now, they seem to be very skeptical about the feasibility of declarative languages such as `Hdl` in the previous code. They think this approach is a bit limiting and won't allow them to implement everything from the space domain.

Fortunately, we can introduce a procedural language that is nearly the same as the previous `Hdl` language. Take a look at the next listing with a modern script that does the same with a brand-new, fancy `Hdl`:

```
boostersDef :: Hdl
boostersDef =
  [ SetupController "left booster" "left b ctrl" aaaController86Passport
  , RegisterComponent "left b ctrl" "nozzle1-t" aaaTemperature25Passport
  , RegisterComponent "left b ctrl" "nozzle1-p" aaaPressure02Passport

  , SetupController "right booster" "right b ctrl" aaaController86Passport
  , RegisterComponent "right b ctrl" "nozzle2-t" aaaTemperature25Passport
  , RegisterComponent "right b ctrl" "nozzle2-p" aaaPressure02Passport
  ]
```

It's now less declarative and more imperative if we consider the verbs `SetupController` and `RegisterComponent` to be statements. However, it's still declarative: the list of actions doesn't do anything by itself; it just describes what to do to set up a device. We now have to set up a controller, and then we'll be able to register components for it. Notice that controllers are referenced by a string key: `"left b ctrl"`, `"right b ctrl"`. The `RegisterComponent` method should also know what controller the component belongs to. The language itself is a simple ADT:

```
type Hdl = [HdlMethod]

data HdlMethod
  = SetupController DeviceName ControllerName ComponentPassport
  | RegisterComponent ControllerName ComponentIndex ComponentPassport
```

Although this eDSL enables cases in figure 5.3 (boosters is a compound device with multiple sets of controllers onboard), it has obvious problems from the start. Placing the `RegisterComponent` line before any controller is set up will lead to undefined behavior. Neither the `HdlMethod` ADT nor the documentation says what the program should do when meeting this kind of script:

```
invalid1 :: Hdl
invalid1 =
  [ RegisterComponent "left b ctrl" "nozzle1-t" aaaTemperature25Passport
  , SetupController "left booster" "left b ctrl" aaaController86Passport
  ]
```

Or when there is no controller at all:

```
invalid2 :: Hdl
invalid2 =
  [ RegisterComponent "left b ctrl" "nozzle1-t" aaaTemperature25Passport
  ]
```

They also don't say what the program should do when the name has a mistake, which is equivalent to not having such a controller, or when the developer specified two identical components.

On a positive note, I can easily write a non-strict and relaxed interpreter for this badly designed eDSL. Thus, the interpreter may tolerate orphan occurrences of `RegisterComponent`, drop the repeating actions, and expect the corresponding `SetupComponent` action to be defined later. This will make you feel your `Hdl` scripts are more friendly, like Haskell: the order of declarations in a module doesn't matter. There is no difference—you can move them around freely. Adopting the same reasoning for the eDSL will make it convenient but will complicate the interpreter.

You might want to do an exercise here: refactor the code from chapters 3 and 4, and implement those relaxed interpreters. Stepping down from the design of systems to the local code design, we can also mitigate the problem of bare string keys. Constants will help, but they won't prevent occasional copy–paste errors:

```
leftControllerName :: String
leftControllerName = "left b ctrl"

invalid4 :: Hdl
invalid4 =
  [ SetupController "left booster" leftControllerName aaaController86Passport

    -- invalid controller specified:
  , RegisterComponent "right b ctrl" "nozzle1-t" aaaTemperature25Passport
  ]
```

Additionally, we could utilize newtypes for a safer code:

```
newtype ControllerName = ControllerName String
newtype ComponentIndex = ComponentIndex String
```

Newtypes prevent specifying wrong arguments by making them explicitly typed. `ControllerName` is no longer a bare string, and it's not the same as `ComponentIndex`— neither for the developer nor for the compiler. Many errors can suddenly go away if you do the wrapping of all your bare types into newtypes. I'm avoiding this in my examples for clarity, but in production, I would use newtypes more often.

Yet, we're interested in a more rigorous design. What can we do with the language? How can we make invalid scripts irrepresentable? The pattern I show in the following code is very common in functional programming. The pattern makes two methods dependent via some value. It utilizes continuations—a way to compose computations into a single one-directed chain. When used with interpretable languages, continuations can enable a safer, more typed, and more type-safe code. You'll see that this pattern is deeply rooted in the free monads we'll be talking about very soon.

The `Hdl` language will be updated as follows. We make the two methods (`Setup-Controller` and `RegisterComponent`) chained and dependent through a value. This value, which has the type `Controller`, will be produced by the `SetupController` method and should be specified for the `RegisterComponent` method. Not having this value means we won't be able to fully declare `RegisterComponent`, so the developer will not have a chance to forget `SetupController` before calling `RegisterComponent`. To indicate that `SetupController` should return something, we put a continuation of the type (`Controller -> Hdl`) into it as a field.

Listing 5.3   Hdl language with the continuation pattern

```
newtype Controller = Controller ControllerName         ◀──── Type for representing
                                                               controllers
type Hdl = [HdlMethod]

data HdlMethod
  = SetupController
        DeviceName
        ControllerName                                 ◀──── Regular
        ComponentPassport                                    fields—arguments
        (Controller -> Hdl)                            ◀──── Continuation field that
  | RegisterComponent                                        produces a value
        Controller                                     ◀──── Controller value is
        ComponentIndex                                       utilized here
        ComponentPassport
```

The new value `Controller` will be our representation of an actual instantiated controller. I call such values avatars, as they are only indexes—pointers to the actual runtime instances. As you can see, the `Controller` value only contains the name and nothing more. We were addressing controllers with constants, and now we'll do it with `Controller` values. There are more methods that work with this device, and all of them should now accept the avatar as a parameter. Take a look at the three methods I added to the `Hdl` language:

```
data Status = StatusOk | StatusFail String
type Message = String

data HdlMethod
  = ...
  | ReadSensor Controller ComponentIndex (Either String Measurement -> Hdl)
  | GetStatus Controller (Either String Status -> Hdl)
  | Report Message
```

The `Report` method doesn't need `Controller`, while the two other methods expect a `Controller` value and thus depend on `SetupController`. `ReadSensor` needs a controller and an index of a sensor component for reading measurements. `GetStatus` just asks the controller about its health. Both methods have their own continuation fields denoting the idea of "values to return." In scenarios, we should read

```
myScript :: Controller -> Hdl
myScript ctrl = [ GetStatus ctrl (\eStatus -> [ Report (show eStatus) ]) ]
```

as "get a status of this controller, return as an `Either` value, and then report the value." This continuation nesting can be made more readable by dividing it into functions:

```
reportStatus :: Either String Status -> Hdl
reportStatus eStatus = [ Report (show eStatus) ]

myScript :: Controller -> Hdl
myScript ctrl = [ GetStatus ctrl reportStatus ]
```

In the following listing, you can see a more detailed script. It creates a controller for the left booster, registers some components for it, creates another controller for the right booster, gives it some components, and then makes a measurement of a temperature.

Listing 5.4 A tree-like script

```
script :: Hdl
script =
  [ SetupController "left booster" "left b ctrl" aaaController86Passport

    ( \lCtrl ->
      [ RegisterComponent lCtrl "nozzle1-t" aaaTemperature25Passport
      , RegisterComponent lCtrl "nozzle1-p" aaaPressure02Passport
      , SetupController "right booster" "right b ctrl"
aaaController86Passport

          ( \rCtrl ->
            [ RegisterComponent rCtrl "nozzle2-t" aaaTemperature25Passport
            , RegisterComponent rCtrl "nozzle2-p" aaaPressure02Passport
            , ReadSensor lCtrl "nozzle1-t"

              ( \eMeasurement -> [ Report (show eMeasurement) ] )
            ]
          )
      ]
    )
  ]
```

All the methods are self-descriptive except `Report`. It's not clear where the message goes. The `Hdl` language doesn't define that. The interpreter of this method will decide what to do: to print the message to the console, store it in a database, or push it to some external service. But these three methods—`ReadSensor`, `GetStatus`, and `Report`—don't fall under the "hardware description" nature of the `Hdl` language. They don't describe the devices but some actions over the devices and in general. The Single

Responsibility principle (SRP) says these methods shouldn't be here, and the Interface Segregation principle (ISP) recommends putting them in their own interfaces. We'll do that later.

I understand if you are concerned that this code is awkward. Readable? Kind of. Simple? Absolutely. Ugly? No doubt. No worries; functional languages such as Haskell and Scala offer good tools for reducing the clumsy boilerplate. And by the way, Lisp developers may find this code more or less familiar. Compare it with a Clojure variant.

Listing 5.5   A Lisp-style tree-like script

```
(def aaaController86Passport "aaaController86Passport")
(def aaaTemperature25Passport "aaaTemperature25Passport")
(def aaaPressure02Passport "aaaPressure02Passport")

(defn setup-controller [device-name controller-name passp next] ())
(defn register-component [controller component-idx passp] ())

(def script [
    (setup-controller "left booster" "left b ctrl" aaaController86Passport
        (fn [controller] ([
            (register-component
                controller
                "nozzle1-t"
                aaaTemperature25Passport)
            (register-component
                controller
                "nozzle1-p"
                aaaPressure02Passport)
            ]
            )))
    ])
```

It isn't complete, it isn't well-composed, and it may not be idiomatic enough. It's just a sample of similarities between our languages. Essentially, we're doing the same: we're writing the logic declaratively, and its tree-like structure with lists is intended to imitate sequential actions. The logic may seem a little imperative, and this is not a disaster. Every capable paradigm can mimic some other paradigm. I see this as very encouraging because the most interesting things are lying on the edge in between.

Continuations are very important. We deal with them all the time, but merging continuations, interpretable languages, and avatars opens new design possibilities for DSLs. With this pattern, we are now able to encode two semantics: *sequencing actions* and *returning values*. The following code is a scheme of the pattern:

```
MethodName ParamType1 ParamType2 ... (ReturnType -> nextScript)
```

This is actually the deepest idea in functional programming, and it leads to many interesting applications, including monads. We've just scratched the surface. There is much more below, including more layers of matter and more things to learn, especially about interpretable domain-specific languages.

How about using the continuation pattern as a trampoline and jumping higher? Let's do more domain-driven design to learn more advanced mechanisms such as parametrized ADTs.

5.2.3 *Modeling multiple interacting eDSLs*

`Hdl` was a god-like domain-specific language, and `script` was a verbose business logic scenario. I would not keep the `Hdl` language in its current form. It violates the SRP and does too much. Shall we add more languages and distribute the responsibilities across them? Yes, of course. We're mandated to do so by our design principles. Let's get started refactoring, and (spoiler alert!) this will bring even more mess instead of removing it.

Before that, I should clarify why we're paying so much attention to the design of such eDSLs. There are two key points:

- You'll see the same approach in building ASTs (abstract syntax trees), including ASTs constructed by a typical compiler after parsing a code and ASTs we'd like to implement for an external domain-specific language for the Andromeda control software.

- This is a basis for more advanced and more convenient approaches. Thus, free monads are based on continuations, but instead of exhibiting this magic to the developer, they wrap it into a very convenient, very clean form.

Besides that, it seems a good idea to try various design techniques and discuss their pros and cons. Now, when we've clarified all this, let's jump in.

Breaking the `HdlMethod` will give us three responsibilities:

- *Defining a device (*`SetupController` *and* `RegisterComponent` *)*—This will be the `Hdl` language.

- *Interacting with a device (*`ReadSensor` *and* `GetStatus` *)*—A new `DeviceControl` language will do that.

- *Report something with* `Report`—Let this be in `LogicControl`.

If you try to put them into three languages, you'll face a big problem. Can you spot it in the next listing?

Listing 5.6   Highly entangled languages

```
type Hdl = [HdlMethod]                                    ◄───┐ Hardware description
                                                              │ language
data HdlMethod
  = SetupController
      DeviceName
      ControllerName
      ComponentPassport
      (Controller -> LogicControl)                        ◄───┐ Continuation with a
  | RegisterComponent                                          │ LogicControl script
```

```
          Controller
          ComponentIndex
          ComponentPassport

type DeviceControl = [DeviceControlMethod]        ◄───  Language for interacting
                                                        with devices
data DeviceControlMethod
  = GetStatus
       Controller
       (Either String Status -> LogicControl)     ◄───  Continuation with a
  | ReadSensor                                           LogicControl script again
       Controller
       ComponentIndex
       (Either String Measurement -> LogicControl) ◄──  Continuation with a
                                                        LogicControl script
type LogicControl = [LogicControlMethod]          ◄───  once more

data LogicControlMethod                                 Unifying language for
  = EvalHdl Hdl                                         controlling a spaceship
  | EvalDeviceControl DeviceControl   ◄──────
  | Report Message                                 Recursive roundtrip back to
                                                   the two other languages
```

The problem is that we now have languages depending on each other in a cycle:

```
Hdl -> LogicControl -> Hdl
DeviceControl -> LogicControl -> DeviceControl
```

Figure 5.4 illustrates this cyclic dependency.

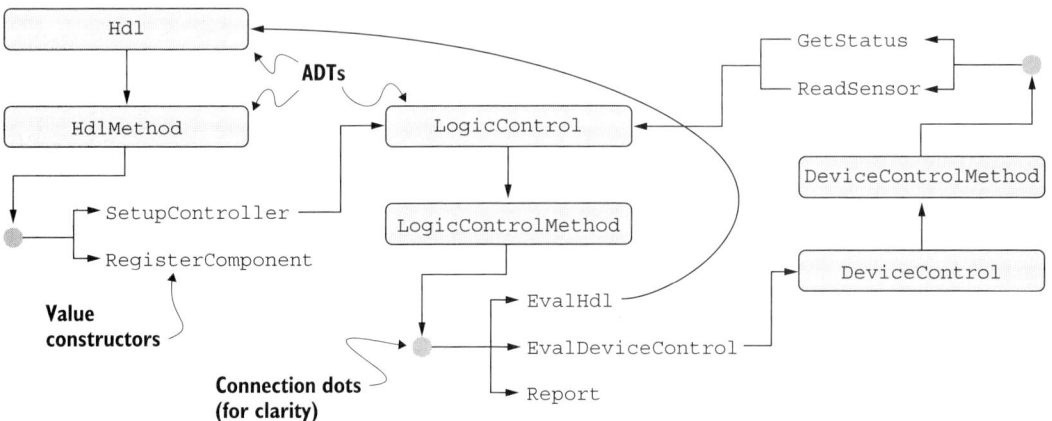

Figure 5.4   Highly entangled languages

The SetupController method produces a Controller that we pass into the internal LogicControl script. We want to call RegisterComponent with it, so we do a recursive nesting of another Hdl script with EvalHdl. When we finish preparing a device, Read-Sensor may be invoked, so we need to pass through LogicControl again and jump into `DeviceControl` using `EvalDeviceControl`, and so forth. The following listing shows this scenario in a nutshell.

Listing 5.7 Not a plain `LogicControl` script

```haskell
script :: LogicControl                              LogicControlMethod
script =
  [ EvalHdl
    [ SetupController "device" "ctrl" passp1 (\ctrl ->
      [ EvalHdl                                      HdlMethod
        [ RegisterComponent ctrl "therm" passp2 ]
        , EvalDeviceControl (readAndReport ctrl)     LogicControlMethod
        ]
      )]
  ]                                                  HdlMethod
  where                                        LogicControlMethod
    readAndReport :: Controller -> DeviceControl
    readAndReport ctrl =
      [ ReadSensor ctrl "therm" (\eMeasurement ->
        [ Report (show eMeasurement) ])
      ]
```

This design becomes problematic in our task with the internal domain-oriented and imperative language. The coupling between the languages is catastrophic. It violates so many design principles, including *low coupling–high cohesion*, that the benefits of introducing the eDSLs become questionable. It's the strongest design smell, an obvious design mistake that we had better fix.

Another problem is that we have to keep these languages in a single Haskell module. Haskell allows for an arbitrary order of notions, so this cyclic ADT stuff will work. But trying to put those three languages into three separate modules as the Single Responsibility principle mandates will lead to cyclic dependencies between modules. Cyclic modules are prohibited in most languages, including Haskell. Our three eDSLs are entangled like three quarks in a nucleon, and they can only come together. This either forces us to have a god-like module or to think about the careful separation of concerns and about adopting proper techniques.

5.2.4 Decoupling languages with parameterized ADTs

In OOP, we would like to go with OOP interfaces to decouple something from something. OOP interfaces are mostly dynamic polymorphism. Statically typed solutions do exist as well, and they often involve plenty of type-level magic. The Haskell world is densely packed with such things so that type-level polymorphism dominates the codebases. Type families and type classes inhabit any more-or-less complicated library, so decoupling essentially becomes genericity.

This is why the task of decoupling our eDSLs has multiple solutions in Haskell, but perhaps we'll be fully satisfied with a simple one. For now, parameterization of algebraic data types would be sufficient and will prepare us for better solutions in the future.

Given that the `LogicControl` language is the main language, and a top-level one, we'll let it know about the other two languages. `Hdl` and `DeviceControl` eDSLs will be subordinate. The hierarchical structure of the languages remains the same, but the two underlying ones won't know what they nest. Consider the following listing. Both `Hdl` and `HdlMethod` ADTs now have a type parameter `next` that we may vary for different usage contexts. The `DeviceControl` is reworked similarly, so I'll omit it.

Listing 5.8   Parametrized `Hdl` language

```
module Andromeda.Hardware.Language.Hdl where

import Andromeda.Hardware.Common (ComponentPassport)
import Andromeda.Hardware.Domain (DeviceName, ControllerName,
  ComponentIndex, Controller)

type Hdl next = [HdlMethod next]          ◀──── Parametrized ADT

data HdlMethod next                        ◀──── Parametrized ADT
  = SetupController
      DeviceName
      ControllerName                              Type variable is
      ComponentPassport                           used here
      (Controller -> next)           ◀──────┘
  | RegisterComponent Controller ComponentIndex ComponentPassport
```

The language is the same except for the `next` type parameter and an abstracted continuation. Let's say `LogicControl` would want to nest `Hdl` and would require that after some `Hdl` script, a `LogicControl` script will be called again. We do this by making the `next` type variable of `Hdl` specific as `LogicControl`:

```
data LogicControlMethod
  = EvalHdl (Hdl LogicControl)
```

See the following listing for a full definition of the language.

Listing 5.9   `LogicControl` specifying inner languages

```
module Andromeda.LogicControl.Language where

import Andromeda.Common (Key, Value, Message)
import Andromeda.Hardware.Language.Hdl (Hdl)
import Andromeda.Hardware.Language.DeviceControl (DeviceControl)

data LogicControlMethod
  = EvalHdl (Hdl LogicControl)                          ◀──── Nesting an Hdl script
  | EvalDeviceControl (DeviceControl LogicControl)      ◀──┐   with a LogicControl
  | Report Message                                          │   continuation
  | Store Key Value

type LogicControl = [LogicControlMethod]
```

Nesting a DeviceControl
script with a LogicControl
continuation

Neither option influences the design but just alters it a little. Let's update figure 5.4 and show this decoupling by dashed lines (figure 5.5).

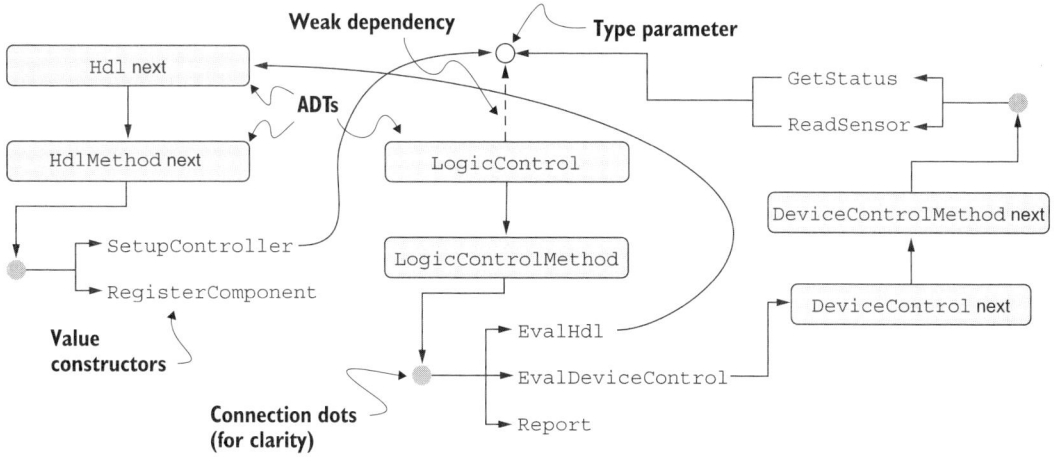

Figure 5.5 Decoupled languages

This trick does its job: modules become less coupled and better concentrated, and interestingly, the developer's experience of the languages remained the same. The script from listing 5.5 didn't change. So what's the point?

Hopefully, this reasoning will help you in some cases; it's an easy way to get started with generics and parameterized ADTs. Sometimes, we want our domain models and domain-specific languages to be customized, and sometimes, extracting subparts of a language into separate modules makes sense on its own, for example, when the inner language is supposed to have a slightly different lifetime, or when it's required in other projects as a library. You'll need to do a little refactoring of your languages, and there is a chance that the business logic won't be affected that much.

Yet, I'm not very satisfied. Writing such scripts is too tedious. The root cause that leads to this design isn't that obvious. The cause is that our methods are dissimilar to normal functions. Normal functions return values as they do in all programming languages. Instead, our methods must push result values deeper into the nested scripts, which in turn continue this plunging to access the outer ones. The continuation-passing style of encoding things doesn't look nice here. Or at least, it's an implementation detail, an internal mechanism that leaks to the business logic and makes things too wordy. And you know what? We'll fix this problem with free monads in the next chapter. Our languages will be decoupled, correctly organized, and monadic, and as usual, a familiar style of coding will be allowed.

I'm intriguing you to motivate you to read further. But before we jump to the next topic, we should pay some attention to the dirty underworld of the interpretable languages—interpreters.

5.3   *Implementation of eDSLs*

Interpreting isn't something new to us. It's been discussed many times before, in many contexts, with many samples. Conceptually, interpreters for the languages we've just developed are pretty much the same. You take your ADT structure, pattern-match over it, and connect the steps to the real actions. We've even created a light testing infrastructure with mocking interpreters that can fake things and let us check our business scripts in isolation.

I won't keep looping around the same theme again and again, but there is a topic to discuss more thoroughly: maintaining an internal state of interpreters. Interestingly, our languages don't explicitly expose something for stateful applications, but what are the result values of eDSL methods if not a state? Immutable, localized, yet a state. For example, the `ctrl` variable in listing 5.5 holds an instance of a controller—well, some reference to it:

```
newtype Controller = Controller ControllerName
```

A logical question emerges here: Where is the instance? Don't we think the controller name is everything we need to interact with the actual controllers? Of course, it's a bit more complicated. The instance exists, and it only exists in the runtime and not in the scenarios. It's time to talk about runtime objects and their lifetimes.

5.3.1   *Runtime objects and lifetimes*

The `Controller` type is just a reference. The instance it points to can't occur in scripts because it only lives at the implementation level. Instances connect a concrete `Controller` reference to some real controller. We did it before, just not for controllers. What is `SensorAPI` from the previous chapter if not a low-level interface to sensors? And what is the `Device` type if not a runtime instance?

Here, the meaning of the controller has changed: it's not just a device part but something more important and significant. The languages have evolved as well, and now we can talk about the path of `Controller` values through the scripts. Consider the `ctrl` variable from listing 5.5 again. Do you see how long it should live? It's only accessible to the methods at the same level or at the deeper levels. What should the corresponding instance look like, then? How long should it live? Take a look at figure 5.6 first.

This is essentially a sequence diagram that shows the flow of the scenario from listing 5.5. The lifetime of `ctrl` corresponds to the lifetime of its runtime instance. The `ctrl` value will be disposed of automatically when the interpreter leaves the scope of the `SetupController` method (the second dashed line). Now we have a choice: either let the instance live after the script is finished (a dashed continuation of its lifetime on the picture) or destroy it right after the `ctrl` becomes inaccessible.

Earlier, a `Device` value could live longer than the script itself. We've been utilizing it in the tests:

```
-- hdl script run
device  <- makeDevice aaaHardwareService hdl

-- device utilization
mbTherm <- getDevicePart aaaHardwareService "therm" device
```

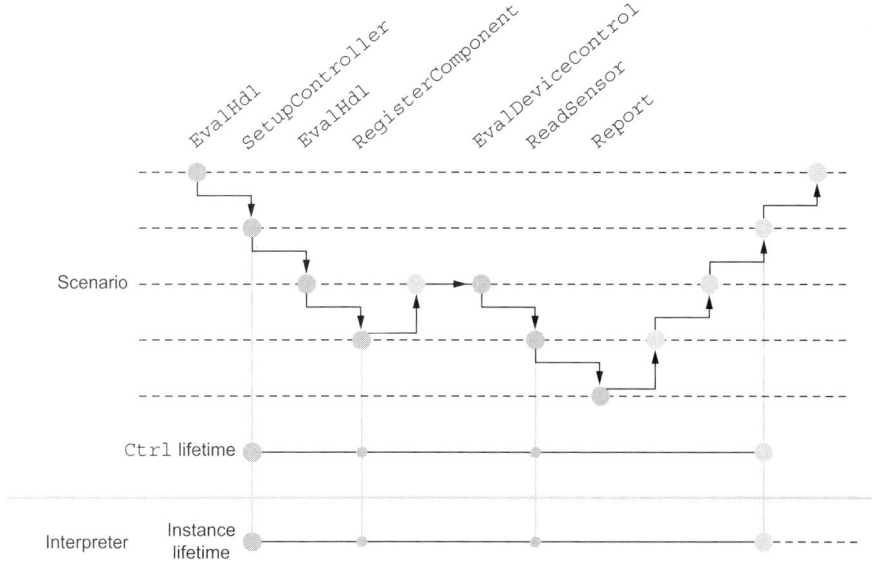

Figure 5.6 Script flow and lifetimes of instances

`Device` was a state created by the `makeDevice` interpreting function. However, the assumption that an `Hdl` script describes a single device is not quite accurate and doesn't work with the new languages where a controller is a boss and is what determines a device itself. No controller means no device is visible to the central computer. We should rework this part of the implementation accordingly.

What follows is the type for controller instances called `ControllerImpl`. It has two fields, a name and vendor-related data, and it doesn't hold any controller-specific possibly mutable state for now:

```
data ControllerImpl = ControllerImpl ControllerName VendorComponent
```

Let's update the `Device` machinery. To remove unnecessary obstacles when accessing the controller, we put `ControllerImpl` right into `Device`:

```
data Device = Device DeviceName ControllerImpl DeviceParts
```

A controller instance, or maybe other device parts, should actually have a state. A lot of things can happen to devices in the network. Controller instances may be seen as individual actors, forming the actor model, behaving somehow, managing their state, and making queries to the real controllers. Hopefully, our current design will not interfere with this topic in chapter 7, where we will develop the simulator.

As long as it's possible to produce many devices, our new runtime state will be a map of devices addressed by a controller. And for the clarity of the interpreters, we'll put devices into the `Runtime` structure:

```
type Devices = Map Controller (ControllerImpl, Device)

data Runtime = Runtime
  { _devices         :: Devices
  , _hardwareService :: HardwareService
  }
```

This is actually it. This `Runtime` structure will exist only at the implementation level, and the interpreters will do their job by interacting with it.

The last thing to discuss in this chapter is interpreters.

5.3.2   *Impure stateful interpreters*

The `makeDevice` function was our interpreter, but this is not enough. The languages have been improved a lot. We have three of them organized hierarchically (see figure 5.5), so there should be a proper naming for the interpreters. Each language will get an interpreter, namely a pair of functions such as `runLanguage` and `interpretLanguageMethod`. We'll start with one for `LogicControl`. This is the entry point to interpret all the scripts:

```
runLogicControl :: Runtime -> LogicControl -> IO Runtime
runLogicControl runtime [] = pure runtime
runLogicControl runtime (m:ms) = do
  devices' <- interpretLogicControlMethod runtime m
  runLogicControl runtime ms
```

Notice that we treat `Runtime` as an argument-passing state. The function takes it, traverses the methods recursively, and returns the modified state.

The method interpreting function shown in the following listing does a couple of interesting things. First, it calls the other two interpreters (`runHdl` and `runDeviceControl`), and second, it passes this interpreter into them as an argument.

Listing 5.10   Intepreter for `LogicControlMethod`

```
interpretLogicControlMethod :: Runtime -> LogicControlMethod  -> IO Runtime

interpretLogicControlMethod runtime (EvalHdl hdl) =
  runHdl runtime runLogicControl hdl

interpretLogicControlMethod runtime (EvalDeviceControl dc) =
  runDeviceControl runtime runLogicControl dc

interpretLogicControlMethod runtime (Report msg) = do
  putStrLn msg
  pure runtime

interpretLogicControlMethod runtime (Store k v) = do
  error "not implemented"
```

Run a script, pass the interpreter deeper

Run a script, pass the interpreter deeper

It's not hard to guess why those two interpreters need this one. Our languages are nested, and moreover, they are parametrized by `LogicControl`. The internal interpreters should know how to run the nested `LogicControl` scripts; therefore, we're passing `runLogicControl` to them.

There is no need to investigate the code of the interpreters because it doesn't give us any new ideas. You can always consult with the code samples. But I think you'd want to take a look at the function signatures. They are almost the same. As the languages are parametrized by something, so are the interpreters, and this is why they take a generalized external interpreter.

Listing 5.11   Runner for `Hdl`

```
runHdl
  :: Runtime
  -> (Runtime -> next -> IO Runtime)          ◄──────── Input state
  -> Hdl next                                  ◄
  -> IO Runtime                                ◄
                                                   │    External interpreter
runDeviceControl
  :: Runtime                                        Script
  -> (Runtime -> next -> IO Runtime)
  -> DeviceControl next
  -> IO Runtime
```

See this repetitive `Runtime` entry? This might be a problem, and handling a clearly mutable state as an argument-passing state isn't that convenient. We can rely on the fact that we're at the implementation level after all, and everything happens in `IO`, so why not just use a mutable reference? Either put the very `Runtime` structure into `IORef`, or do this with its fields separately. The second option is better:

```
data Runtime = Runtime
  { _devicesRef         :: IORef Devices
  , _hardwareServiceRef :: IORef HardwareService
  }
```

The interpreters will change slightly—it's a good thing that their signatures become shorter and clearer.

Listing 5.12   `LogicControl` interpreter with mutable `Runtime`

```
interpretLogicControlMethod
  :: Runtime -> LogicControlMethod  -> IO ()

runLogicControl :: Runtime -> LogicControl -> IO ()

runHdl
  :: Runtime
  -> (next -> IO ())                ◄──┐   No need to pass
  -> Hdl next                            │  Runtime anymore
  -> IO Runtime

runDeviceControl
```

```
:: Runtime
-> (next -> IO ())                    ◄——— Same here
-> DeviceControl next
-> IO Runtime
```

This is not the only win we get. In fact, we'll find this very useful when implementing concurrent and multithreaded systems. Organizing the runtime structures into concurrent mutable primitives such as `MVar` and `STM TVar` instead of thread-unsafe `IORef` will make a lot of sense when the time comes. We are not done with domain-driven design, so we can't really develop runtime and implementation yet. In the next chapter, the full power of free monads will come to serve our needs.

Summary

- Abstractions can prevent software bugs by making it easier to reason about the domain and encoding it so that only correct operations are allowed.
- Everything that is unified in programming by a single domain can be considered a DSL.
- Statically typed languages with a good type system are the best choice for developing safe and robust programs.
- Using domain-specific languages is a great technique for achieving both safety and robustness, and they should be a central idea of domain-driven design.
- Poorly designed DSLs can be restrictive and annoying, and they may produce excessively high accidental complexity.
- Domain-driven design is a useful skill for functional developers, as it involves encoding business domains in algebraic data types.
- Domain-centric DSLs are more straightforward than domain-specific ones, but with more requirements coming from a domain, they become more difficult to use.
- Domain modeling with algebraic data types helps us build clear, reliable, and understandable domain-specific languages.
- Embedded DSLs are a great tool for analyzing and modeling business domains.
- Algebraic data types are a powerful tool for creating complex data structures, modeling, and creating DSLs.
- Use interpretable embedded DSLs to tame the complexity of your difficult domain and its notions.
- Keep your embedded DSLs properly organized: group methods by their meaning and scope, separate responsibilities carefully, and put the eDSLs into hierarchies. This will have a good effect on the application design.
- Runtime objects can have their own lifetimes. This helps keep the notions of the domain separate from domain implementations.
- OOP interfaces are used for decoupling, and type-level polymorphism is used in the Haskell world to achieve this.

Domain modeling
with free monads

This chapter covers

- Free monads and how to use them in domain modeling
- How to apply the functor abstraction
- Some advanced functional concepts

Imagine you're building a robot from a bunch of preprogrammed modules. Each module can do something specific, like move something forward, turn on the lights, or make a sound. To make the robot do something interesting, you need to create a sequence of actions using these blocks. For different behaviors, you'd rearrange the sequence. Obviously, being able to create and arrange these sequences will make the robot easier to control.

That's the basic idea behind a free monad. A free monad is a data structure that organizes domain-related actions into interpretable sequences (interpretable scenarios), making it possible to alter those sequences more easily as values. In this chapter, we'll take a closer look at this concept from functional programming and see how free monads make domain modeling and eDSL design even more powerful and convenient. Free monads play the central role in the rest of the book, serving as

147

functional interfaces that will enhance our programs with good design qualities, such as low coupling, proper subsystems design, and testability.

6.1   *Introducing free monads*

Interface-like abstractions (such as the free monad) can be distinguished from genericity-like abstractions (such as functors, monoids, and categories) through the concept of lifetime (see figure 6.1). Genericity-like abstractions, mostly achieved with generics (or templates in C++), don't possess the dimension of lifetime because they are just timeless expressions over data structures. They focus on some properties and ignore others. They declare the mathematical nature of a structure, but they don't work in a common way. They exist during the design time and the compile time and mostly disappear after the program is compiled.

However, interface-like abstractions help us handle complexity. Unlike generalizations, interfaces carry some meaning from a business domain and give us the minimum information needed for the tasks—no implementation details, nothing unrelated, nothing too abstract. Interfaces communicate the essence of that domain and often serve as documentation. Knowing your interface means knowing a part of your business domain—at least its public representation.

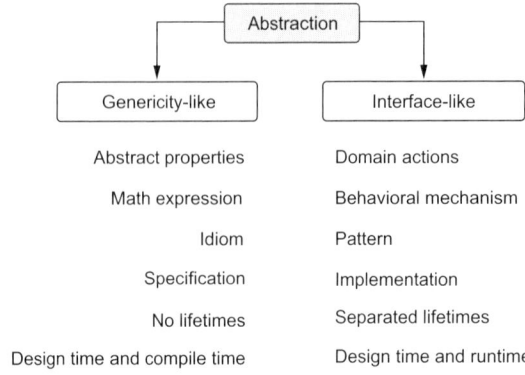

Figure 6.1   Two sorts of abstractions

> **TIP**   You can get more insights about this dualism from the talk "The Clear Path to Haskell Complexities" by Vitaly Bragilevsky (https://youtu.be/n3H_YipBDrY).

Interfaces are very domain specific. We've already seen how interpretable eDSLs can be functional interfaces, and we've discussed some other approaches as well (service handle and type classes). Now we should ask this question: What is the closest analog of OOP interfaces in FP? The answer is *free monads*. At first, they seem tricky because they take everything we know about interpretable parametrized recursive ADTs, spice it up with the concept of monads, and combine it with the concept of functors. But if used as a design pattern, free monads aren't really that difficult in practice. They're a very powerful tool, though, and they demand a thorough discussion.

6.2 *Free monads as a functional interface*

I consider free monads the most idiomatic functional interface of all. I've found that they have many interesting parallels with OOP interfaces, and this discovery allowed me to utilize the same reasoning I gathered from object-oriented design with C#. Of course, when comparing OOP and FP at the programming language level, we see it's rather a dissimilar story, but on the design level, both functional and OOP interfaces have the same purpose.

When I realized this, everything I knew from mainstream software design fit into place: design principles, code quality metrics, and project organization ideas. By the way, the functional declarative design (FDD) methodology offers free monads as a key design pattern. You may certainly use other things instead, such as final tagless, effect systems, or the ReaderT pattern), but I'm very confident that free monads are better.

As you continue reading this book, you'll program a framework using free monads and the FDD methodology. Much of what we encounter in real-world projects can be seen here: relational and key–value databases, logging, concurrency, the REST applications' structure, and so forth. Free monads will be used as an architectural design pattern to achieve testability, separation of concerns, clarity, and other desirable software properties that normal, full-power interfaces should be able to provide.

6.2.1 *Decoupling of computation and interpretation*

As stated earlier, a free monad is a data structure that organizes domain-related actions into interpretable sequences (interpretable scenarios), making it possible to alter them more easily as values. While being only declarative descriptions written in a free monadic language, scenarios can later be interpreted against real actions to do the actual stuff.

The free monad mechanism allows these actions to be seen as monadic chains, so scenarios may feel imperative. Nevertheless, free monadic scenarios are pure values that represent a clean interface to the domain, and interpreters of these scenarios can be seen as an interface implementation. This separation gives a lot of flexibility in structuring the architecture of applications.

Consider the following benefits:

- *Decoupling of computation and interpretation*—You can define your program's structure and logic in a pure, declarative way using the free monad and decide separately on the interpretation of effects. This is especially beneficial in complex applications where you want to maintain flexibility regarding how actions (now called effects) are executed (e.g., for testing or changing requirements).
- *Compositionality*—Because effects are described abstractly and combined using monadic operations, it's easy to compose large, complex operations from smaller ones. This promotes code reuse and modularity.

- *Testability*—Because the interpretation of effects is separated from their description, you can easily swap out real effects for mocked ones in tests, thus improving testability.

- *Interpretability*—You can interpret the same free monad structure differently, which allows multiple interpretations of the same program. This, for example, enables running the same logic in different environments or with different effect implementations.

- *Controlling side effects*—It provides a structured way to manage side effects in your application, making it easier to reason about and maintain code that deals with external systems or operations that are not purely functional.

The free monad is particularly useful in applications where the flexibility of changing how effects are interpreted is important, such as when you need to run the same logic in different contexts (e.g., testing versus production) or when building highly modular systems that require clear separation between logic and effects.

Now we should expand on what was said here and discuss various technical nuances of this concept.

6.2.2 *The Free Monad pattern*

The free monad, which comes from the depths of category theory, is used to wrap some (but not all) types into a monad. Applications of the free monad usually live in the academic part of functional programming, but using it as an architectural pattern can really help the development. There are three key points regarding this pattern:

- *Interface*—Declarative interpretable free monad eDSL related to a business domain

- *Implementation*—One or more interpreters of the eDSL

- *Business logic*—Scenarios formed with the free monad interface

All the points will be discussed after the following scheme of the pattern (figure 6.2).

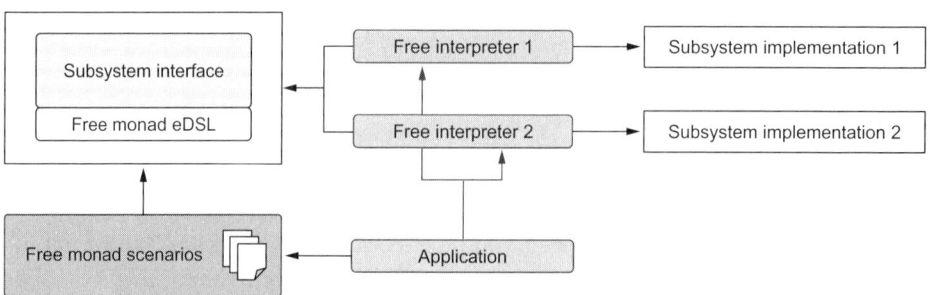

Figure 6.2   The Free Monad pattern

On its own, the free monadic mechanism doesn't express anything about particular domains. It's rather a template to wrap around your eDSLs. Putting them into the free monad will make them monadic, sequential, and composable, and it will enable a number of interesting tricks that make the code more convenient to work with. Free monadic eDSLs are the next step of the list-based eDSLs that we've seen in the previous chapter.

Being monadic is much better than being list based. Remember the returning problem? We could not just return a result from a domain action, so we had to supply the action with a continuation. The idea was that the domain action, once evaluated, feeds the lambda with its result, and the evaluation continues for the nested actions. In the following example, we encode a usual terminal interaction with the user. We ask them to type a string and then echo this string back to the console:

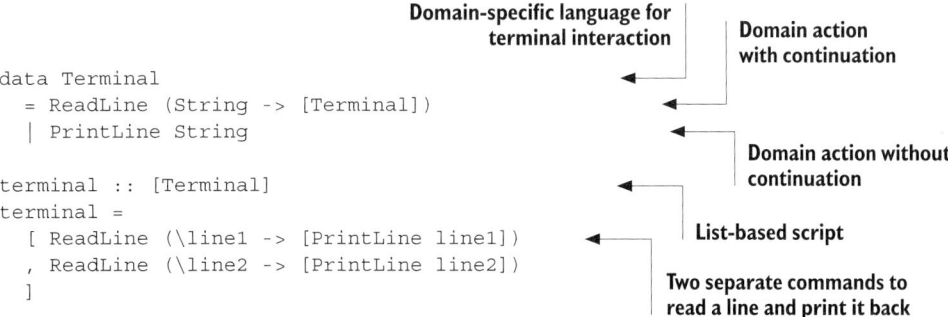

```
data Terminal
  = ReadLine (String -> [Terminal])
  | PrintLine String

terminal :: [Terminal]
terminal =
  [ ReadLine (\line1 -> [PrintLine line1])
  , ReadLine (\line2 -> [PrintLine line2])
  ]
```

We don't call functions here—it's all just values of the `Terminal` ADT. We construct a scenario and must deal with its inconvenient syntax. In Python, for example, we could just write the following:

```
def terminal():
    line1 = input()
    print(line1)

    line2 = input()
    print(line2)
```

Arguably, this is the form we'd like to have for our functional eDSLs as well, although it looks imperative. Luckily, we can have it with the Free Monad pattern and yet stay completely functional. In Haskell and Scala, monadic means that the do-notation (for-comprehension) becomes available to your scenarios, and tons of boilerplate will just go away. Once freemonadized, the `terminal` script becomes

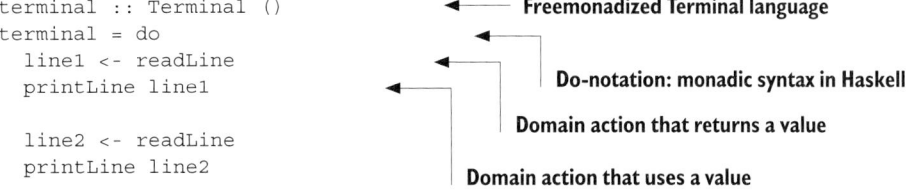

```
terminal :: Terminal ()
terminal = do
  line1 <- readLine
  printLine line1

  line2 <- readLine
  printLine line2
```

Or in Scala, we have

```
def terminal: Unit = {
  for {
    line1 <- readLine
    _ <- printLine(line1)

    line2 <- readLine
    _ <- printLine(line2)
  } yield ()
}
```

For-comprehension in Scala

The snippets look very similar, except the Python's script runs direct commands, while our scripts are values that should be interpreted against real actions. We can craft an interpreter that evaluates Haskell's `readLn` on `ReadLine` and `print` on `PrintLine`, or we can have an interpreter that, for example, interacts with us via a web UI.

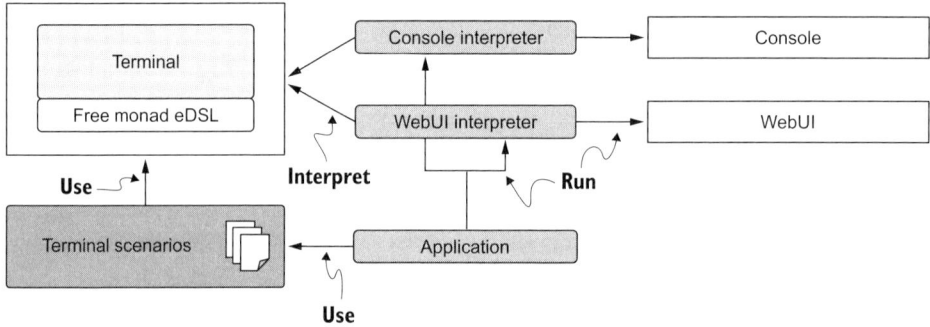

Figure 6.3   Terminal free monadic subsystem

As figure 6.3 illustrates, it's even possible to have both within the same application and to switch between them when needed. We'll learn all of this soon and even see that the Free Monad pattern works nicely both as a mechanism for dependency injection and as a basis for various domain-specific languages.

6.2.3   *Advantages and disadvantages*

What else should we know about the Free Monad pattern? The following list summarizes the pattern's advantages:

- *It is monadic.* A monadic interface to an embedded language is much more convenient than just a functional one, especially for sequential and mutually dependent actions. In addition, you gain the power of standard monadic libraries, the functions of which will considerably enhance your monadic language.
- *It is readable and clean.* A language that has a free monad interface is usually self-descriptive. Monadic actions that the language is turned to will be obvious in usage.

- *It is safely composable and type-safe.* Two monadic actions can be monadically composed; they have the same free monad type. The base bricks of this monadic language are defined by your free language. This will add more static checking of the correctness of your free scripts.

- *It is abstract.* A free monad interface abstracts the underlying language. Scripts don't depend on the implementation details. It's even possible to completely replace the implementation of a language, and all code contracts and invariants will be saved. The free monad mechanism is an analog of the OOP interface in this sense.

- *It is interpretable.* The Free Monad pattern provides an easy way to interpret declarative definitions of domain entities into evaluable actions or another language. Different interpreters serve different needs. For example, we'll have interpreters for tests and for real production, for concurrent run time and for sequential-only run time, for connecting to different external subsystems such as SQL DBs while having the same interface, and so on.

- *It has small adopting costs.* To "free monadize" your language, which is probably an ADT, you make your language a functor and wrap it in the `Free` type. Unless you examine what's inside a free monad library, it stays simple.

- *It has low maintenance costs.* Modifying both a language and a monadic interface isn't a big deal. You also need to keep the interpreters consistent, which can break some external code if the monadic interface isn't stable, but this is a common interface problem, regardless of whether they are object oriented or functional.

There are several implementations of free monads to choose from: regular free monad (in Haskell, it's `Free` type from the `free` library), Church-encoded free monad (the `F` type from `free`), "no remorse free monad," and probably some others. Regular free has a quadratic evaluation complexity $O(n^2)$ on binding, and Church-encoded is closer to $O(n)$.

> **TIP** The "no remorse" free monad from PureScript has a fairly fast implementation. It is thus called because it's based on the paper "Reflection without remorse" (http://okmij.org/ftp/Haskell/zseq.pdf). The `free` Haskell library by Edward Kmett contains both the usual free monad (the `Free` type) and the Church-encoded free monad (the `F` type). The last one is fast enough.

They differ in their internal functioning, and this slightly affects how we write the interpreters, but the user scenarios remain the same. My Hydra framework (https://github .com/graninas/Hydra) demonstrates two identical engines based on both normal free and Chuch-encoded free. I created several demo applications for you to compare between the engines. Check out, for example, `astro`, `labyrinth`, or `PerfTestApp` applications. All of them are shipped with the framework.

We should also consider its disadvantages:

- Because it's a monad, the developer should be familiar with this concept in order to use your language smoothly.
- The free monad requires the language to be a functor. Although it's an easy transformation for your language, you need to understand what it's for. However, other free monads, such as Church-encoded free monads, do not have this restriction but possibly have their own, so the topic is a bit wider than described in this introductory chapter.
- The theory behind the free monad is complex. For example, the free type has a recursive value constructor that's a kind of fixpoint notion (the mathematical concept of recursive operation). Also, converting a language into the free monad form looks like a magical hack. But it's not magic—it's science. The good thing is that you can use the free monad in practice without knowing the theory at all.
- It's hard (sometimes impossible) to convert your language into the free monad form when it's made of advanced functional concepts: generalized algebraic data types (GADTs), phantom types, type-level logic, and so on. This probably means you need another approach.

Now let's deep dive into the topic.

6.3 How free monads work

I find it beneficial to have a thorough lesson on the functional programming concepts coming with the free monad approach. This is a step down from the design level to the implementation level, and the tutorial here contains many details about the internal, usually hidden, mechanisms. I hope it will give you enough understanding so that we can talk more about free monads in further sections.

6.3.1 Wrapping languages into the free monad

A running sample will be an eDSL for making sandwiches. We all love snacking on sandwiches! Why not memorize our favorite recipes? My sandwich is quite simple:

```
mySandwich :: SandwichRecipe Sandwich
mySandwich = do
  body1 <- startNewSandwich Toast Tomato
  body2 <- addComponent Cheese body1
  body3 <- addComponent Salt body2
  finishSandwich (Just Toast) body3
```

I'm sure you can read this script because it's self-descriptive. My recipe has three layers and is made of toast, cheese, tomato, and salt. You don't even need to see the definition of types for `Toast`, `Tomato`, `Cheese`, and `Salt` to get the meaning. Still, you'll need those types to construct your own sandwiches, so here they are, shortened to save space:

```
data BreadType = Baguette | Toast
data Component = Bread BreadType | Tomato | Salt | Cheese
```

The `Sandwich` type represents the final product:

```
data Sandwich = Sandwich
                  BreadType
                  (Maybe BreadType)
                  [Component]
```

- ← **Final product**
- ← **Base bread piece**
- ← **Optional last bread piece**
- **Ingredients**

What about the body variables? They all express the fact that the sandwich is not yet completed. We need a special type for this case that we'll update during the script. As it accepts more ingredients, its `Component` list grows:

```
data SandwichBody = SandwichBody BreadType [Component]
```

Given the monadic nature of the script, we can write it in a different way, using the explicit bind operator (`>>=`) and nested lambdas:

```
mySandwich2 :: SandwichRecipe Sandwich
mySandwich2
    = startNewSandwich Toast Tomato
   >>= (\body1 -> addComponent Cheese body1
       >>= (\body2 -> addComponent Salt body2
           >>= (\body3 -> finishSandwich (Just Toast) body3
               )
           )
       )
```

The recipe is sequential, but in reality, it becomes a chain of calls (continuations) until the resulting `Sandwich` is formed and returned. The bind operator here (`>>=`) replaces the left arrow of the do-notation (`<-`). Explicit writing demonstrates that nested continuations play a significant role in the monadic code.

> **TIP** What if we incidentally misplace `body1`, `body2`, or `body3`? What if we don't like those bulky lambdas all over the script? Another form of the same code would free us from these two problems. It relies on the partial application of `addComponent`, and `finishSandwich` functions lambdas just disappear:
>
> ```
> mySandwich3 :: SandwichRecipe Sandwich
> mySandwich3
>     = startNewSandwich Toast Tomato
>  >>= addComponent Cheese
>  >>= addComponent Salt
>  >>= finishSandwich (Just Toast)
> ```

Self-descriptiveness of the eDSL methods doesn't free us from examining how to get them. Obviously, we need an ADT, sometimes called an algebra, related to the sandwich construction domain. The following listing contains the full definition.

Listing 6.1   The `SandwichRecipe` free monad language

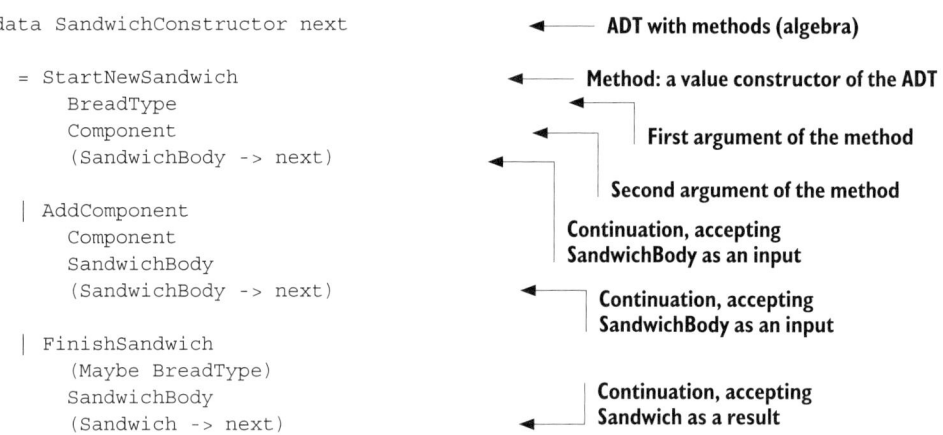

```
data SandwichConstructor next                    ◄──── ADT with methods (algebra)

    = StartNewSandwich                       ◄──── Method: a value constructor of the ADT
        BreadType                          ◄┐
        Component                          ◄─┤  First argument of the method
        (SandwichBody -> next)          ◄──┘
                                                Second argument of the method

    | AddComponent                           Continuation, accepting
        Component                            SandwichBody as an input
        SandwichBody
        (SandwichBody -> next)          ◄┐   Continuation, accepting
                                         │   SandwichBody as an input
    | FinishSandwich
        (Maybe BreadType)
        SandwichBody                          Continuation, accepting
        (Sandwich -> next)            ◄──────  Sandwich as a result
```

Naming the only type parameter as `next` is a common convention referring to the fact that (`result -> next`) will inhabit each method as a continuation. In the previous chapter, we've already seen how continuation and parametrization help embed the languages into each other. Free monads exploit this idea even further and encrust their own mechanisms to glue the scripts together. Here is how we put our `Sandwich-Constructor` algebra into the free monad:

```
import Control.Monad.Free

type SandwichRecipe a = Free SandwichConstructor a
```

Notice that while being a parametrized type, `SandwichConstructor` is partially applied here. Once you wrapped your algebra, you'd want to provide smart constructors for a better developer experience. The following listing presents them, and I recommend paying specific attention to the use of the `Free` and `Pure` value constructors.

Listing 6.2   Smart constructors

```
startNewSandwich
    :: BreadType                                   SandwichRecipe is a
    -> Component                                   monad; the function
    -> SandwichRecipe SandwichBody           ◄──── returns SandwichBody.
startNewSandwich breadType component
    = Free (StartNewSandwich breadType component Pure)   ◄─── Wrapping the
                                                             StartNewSandwich
                                                             constructor into a
addComponent                                                 free monad
    :: Component
    -> SandwichBody
    -> SandwichRecipe SandwichBody
addComponent component sandwichBody
    = Free (AddComponent component sandwichBody Pure)

finishSandwich
    :: Maybe BreadType     -- the last piece of bread is optional
```

```
      -> SandwichBody
      -> SandwichRecipe Sandwich
finishSandwich mbBreadType sandwichBody
    = Free (FinishSandwich mbBreadType sandwichBody Pure)
```

Upon closer analysis, the `Free` value constructor (don't confuse it with the `Free` type) has one field that we're filling with one of the three methods, which are fully specified with the arguments:

```
Free (StartNewSandwich breadType component Pure)
```

The `Pure` value constructor goes to the continuation field as a temporary placeholder. Essentially, `Pure` in this context means "end of the chain, and whatever the result is, it should be returned." Let me explain this in more detail.

6.3.2   *The Free type*

`Pure` and `Free` value constructors operate as adapters between our algebra and the free monad. We must wrap the value constructors of our language into the `Free` value constructor to adapt to the monadic chaining (nesting of lambdas). The nesting is recursive and layered: a layer of free, a layer of the eDSL, a layer of free, and so on, until the `Pure` terminator is met.

Not by chance, the `Free` type is a recursive ADT with two value constructors:

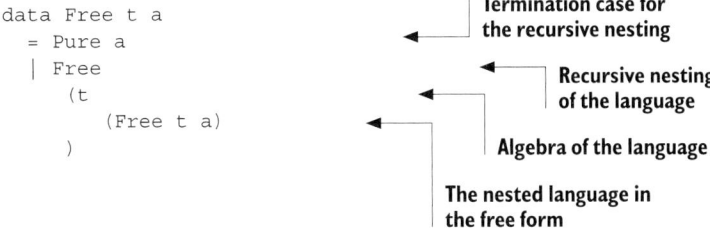

Let's disassemble these notions:

- `Free`—This value constructor stores a monadic action that should be able to keep another action of type `Free a` inside. We call the other action a continuation because when the outer action is interpreted, the interpretation process should be continued with the inner action.
- `Pure`—This value constructor finalizes the chain of computations. It also keeps some value of type `a` to be returned after the interpretation is over. We can see this value constructor used as a function: `Pure :: a -> Free t a` in the expressions like `FinishSandwich a b Pure` where it behaves as a placeholder. There should be a continuation, but we don't have any, so we use `Pure` to say we'd like to finish this chain with some value that `Pure` will hold for us.

The correct manual wrapping should look like this:

```
mySandwich4 :: SandwichRecipe Sandwich
mySandwich4 = do
```

```
incomplete <- Free (StartNewSandwich Toast Tomato Pure)
Free (FinishSandwich (Just Toast) incomplete Pure)
```

Still, manual wrapping doesn't look as clean as the smart constructors:

```
mySandwich4 :: SandwichRecipe Sandwich
mySandwich4 = do
  incomplete <- startNewSandwich Toast Tomato
  finishSandwich (Just Toast) incomplete
```

These `Pure` placeholders look strange, but they are necessary. Once we have two separate monadic `SandwichRecipe` functions, we can chain them. For this to happen, the second function should be nested into the depths of the first one by replacing the `Pure` placeholder. Consequently, there will be only one chain with only one `Pure` chain terminator. This all happens behind the scenes, thanks to the monadic binding mechanism of the free monad and the functor instance that we're about to write and investigate.

6.3.3 The functor instance

We're not finished with our ADT yet. We should also craft a functor instance for it. This requirement comes with the free monad because this functor instance will be used to nest continuations into each other.

If you are not familiar with this functional idiom, I would recommend another excellent and fun book: *Learn You a Haskell for Great Good!* by Miran Lipovača (No Starch Press, 2011; http://learnyouahaskell.com/). It has a nice narrative free from unnecessary academicism, which makes this book approachable and easy to read. In particular, the section on functors, applicative functors, and monads is awesome even today, so many years after it was written. The book is available online.

First, take a look at the instance in the next listing, and then we'll discuss what it means for a type to be a `Functor`.

Listing 6.3 Functor instance for the free monad

```
instance Functor SandwichConstructor where          ◀── Functor instance

  fmap f (StartNewSandwich breadType component next)   ◀──┐ Repacking a value
    = StartNewSandwich breadType component (f . next)     │ constructor

  fmap f (AddComponent component sandwichBody next)
    = AddComponent component sandwichBody (f . next)

  fmap f (FinishSandwich mbBreadType sandwichBody next)
    = FinishSandwich mbBreadType sandwichBody (f . next)
```

Type is a `Functor` when you can map some function `f` over its internals without changing the data structure. A plain list is a `Functor` because you can map various functions over its stored items and alter the type of the items while the structure of the list remains the same. For example:

```
oldList :: [Int]
oldList = [1, 2, 3, 4]

newList :: [String]
newList = map show oldList

-- newList: ["1", "2", "3", "4"]
```

We stringify each integer item with the `show` function (`show :: Int -> String`) while the structure is preserved. There are still four items in each list.

When you call the `map` function, you actually use the list type as a `Functor`. You may use the `fmap` function instead—the only method of the `Functor` type class:

```
newList = fmap show list
```

This is the same. Consider the type class `Functor` and its instance for the list type:

```
class Functor f where
  fmap :: (a -> b) -> f a -> f b

instance Functor [] where
  fmap = map
```

Here, f is [] (list), the a type variable is `Int`, and the b type variable is `String`:

```
fmap :: (Int -> String) -> [Int] -> [String]
```

Certainly, any other function may be used instead of `show` if we need to get a list of something. We can double the numbers or replicate them, for example:

```
fmap (\n -> n * 2) oldList        -- [2, 4, 6, 8]
fmap (\n -> replicate n n) oldList   -- [[1],[2,2],[3,3,3],[4,4,4,4]]
```

Effectively, the `Functor` replaces a simple `for` loop and makes it very convenient to work with data structures in a functional way.

Now we can declare the `Functor` instance for the `SandwichConstructor` type. The `fmap` function will be specified like this:

```
fmap
  :: (a -> b)
  -> SandwichConstructor a
  -> SandwichConstructor b
```

Consequently, our type should have a type parameter for some purpose. Why? The type `SandwichConstructor a` has three value constructors: `StartNewSandwich`, `AddComponent`, and `FinishSandwich`. All of them have fields with parameter type a, and all of them are mappable. From listing 6.3, you can see that the methods are being repacked, with the continuation reiterated:

```
fmap f (AddComponent component sandwichBody next) =
       AddComponent component sandwichBody (f . next)
```

◀── **Repacking and reiterating the continuation**

The new continuation does what the old one was doing, but the result of the old one will be transformed with the f function. Alternatively, we might want to avoid the point-free notation and replace the continuation by a lambda:

```
- (f . next)
+ (\a -> f (next a))
```

The Functor is needed to alter the internals without changing the shape. In the case of free monads, the fmap function will be altering the type of continuations when it comes to merging two free monadic scripts. By the way, the procedure of replacing continuations looks very similar to how two ordinary lists concatenate. The free monad traverses a script from the top outer action to the inner one. Then, the free monad replaces the innermost continuation with the second script.

Listing 6.4   Scripts nesting

```
script1 :: SandwichRecipe SandwichBody
script1 = startNewSandwich Toast Tomato

script2 :: SandwichRecipe SandwichBody
script2 =
  script1
  >>=                                    Traversing script1 and
  addComponent Salt                      repacking the continuation

script3 :: SandwichRecipe Sandwich
script3 = do
  b <- script2                           Traversing a longer chain and
  finishSandwich (Just Toast) b          repacking the continuation
```

Because this traversing happens every time we call the bind (>>=) function, the usual free monad has an $O(n^2)$ complexity of joining two monadic chains (monadic binding). Yes, quadratic, exactly the way it is for list concatenation. So the longer your scripts, the slower they work. But don't worry: this is true for the base free monad. There are more efficient implementations. There are various free monads that don't exhibit this problem of quadratic complexity—for example, Church-encoded free monad. Moving from free to Church-encoded free won't take much time. You need to change a few lines in your code, and wow, it works better now. It doesn't matter what the internals are or how the bind function is implemented in both free monads—just treat them as a black box, a good tool to create monadic eDSLs.

6.3.4   *Learning the recursive free type*

A better intuition for free monads may come from comprehending why this type is recursive and what problem it solves. What happens when we parametrize it?

```
data Free t a
  = Pure a
  | Free (t (Free t a))

type SandwichRecipe a = Free SandwichConstructor a
```

Substituting the t parameter manually in the Free ADT gives

```
Free SandwichConstructor a
  = Pure a
  | Free (SandwichConstructor (Free SandwichConstructor a))
```

The bind function (`>>=`) uses `fmap` to nest values and push the bottom `Pure` value deeper in the recursive chain. This is how it's implemented:

```
instance Functor t => Monad (Free t) where
  return = pure
  Pure a >>= f = f a
  Free m >>= f = Free (fmap (>>= f) m)
```

I'll leave it to your consideration. What I want to tell you instead is how this recursive `Free` type eliminates the uncontrolled growth of type signatures. With a naive nesting of scripts, you'd get something like this:

```
SandwichConstructor (SandwichConstructor (SandwichConstructor SandwichBody)))
```

The `Free` type doesn't have this problem. All the scripts are of the same type `SandwichRecipe a`, no matter how deep they are. Let's elaborate on this.

Putting `SandwichConstructor` a into itself gives

```
val'  = \b -> AddComponent Cheese b (\b' -> ())
val'' = \b -> AddComponent Salt b val'
val = StartNewSandwich Toast Tomato val''
```

or

```
val = StartNewSandwich Toast Tomato
        (\b1 -> AddComponent Salt b1
           (\b2 -> AddComponent Cheese b2 (\b3 -> ())))
        )
```

The more actions we insert, the bigger the type of the action becomes:

```
val' :: SandwichBody -> SandwichConstructor ()
val'' :: SandwichBody -> SandwichConstructor (SandwichConstructor ())
val :: SandwichConstructor (SandwichConstructor (SandwichConstructor ()))
```

That is, all three variables, `val'`, `val''`, and `val`, have different types (ignoring the `SandwichBody` argument), and we can't use them uniformly. The `Free` type solves this problem by wrapping our enhanced type with its own recursive structures. Because of this, the nesting of values of type `Free SandwichConstructor` a instead of just `SandwichConstructor` a gives a unified type for the whole chain regardless of its length:

```
val' :: SandwichRecipe SandwichBody
val' = Free (StartNewSandwich Toast Tomato Pure)

val'' :: SandwichBody -> SandwichRecipe SandwichBody
val'' = \body -> Free (AddComponent Salt body Pure)

val :: SandwichRecipe SandwichBody
val = val' >>= val''
```

The real work of the binding mechanism can be illustrated in pseudocode. The record

```
val = val' >>= val''
```

becomes

```
(Free (StartNewSandwich Toast Tomato Pure))
  >>=
    (\body -> Free (AddComponent Salt body Pure))
```

And now it takes this form:

```
val = (Free (StartNewSandwich Toast Tomato
              (\body -> Free (AddComponent Salt body Pure))
          )
        )
```

It's a bit more difficult to explain why the crafty recursive `Free` type reduces everything to a single type. But it really does. It acts as a Russian nesting doll and does so at both levels—at the value level and at the level of types.

It's worth noting that *recursion* is the only fundamental way to chain computations in functional programming upon which all other concepts are based. Not continuations. Not monads. Recursion. It doesn't matter whether we mean recursive functions or types, continuations, or another thing that has a self-repeating property. Essentially, the `Free` type represents the fixed point combinator. In turn, the fixed point combinator is a fundamental representation of recursion in lambda calculus.

But don't pay that much attention to this theoretical fact because there is a more important thing to talk about. To give the free monad even more sense, we should talk about the interpreters.

6.3.5 *Interpretation of free monadic scripts*

There will be no information conceptually new to us here because we're familiar with interpretation. But looking through the prism of the `Free` type described previously, we can suppose that free interpreters are a bit trickier. Frankly, I don't think they are because there is a single common template for all the free interpreters that you can just copy–paste for all your eDSLs. One can say the code of those interpreters is boilerplate because its structure doesn't change that much from one eDSL to another. I'd rather call it a pattern, not a boilerplate.

In some sense, free monad interpreters are more straightforward than the ones we've created for custom mutually recursive eDSLs in the previous chapter. As illustrated in figure 6.4, we must unroll both the `Free` type and our domain-specific type and match all the methods with real actions.

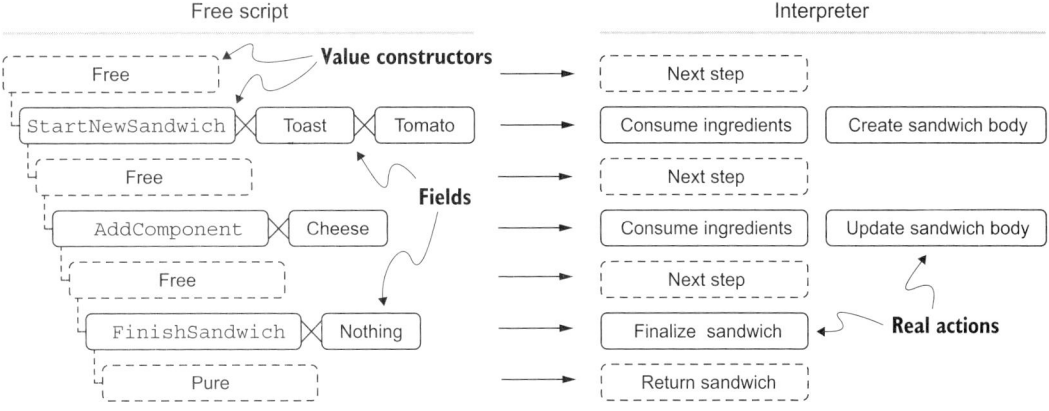

Figure 6.4 Unrolling a free script

Unrolling here effectively means pattern matching the `Free` value constructor, descending into its continuation field, pattern-matching a domain-specific constructor, then descending into its continuation field, and repeating those steps again until the end—the `Pure` value constructor—is reached. Let's dismantle two functions of the interpreter, `interpretRecipe` and `interpretStep`, and see how they work. The function `interpretRecipe` is an entry point and a recursive processor of the `SandwichRecipe` language. See the following listing.

Listing 6.5 Free interpreter for `SandwichRecipe`

You see a manual unfolding of the free structure here. Interestingly, the invocation of `interpretStep` must return the next script for `interpretRecipe` to continue the interpretation. Sounds logical—the next script is embedded into `Sandwich-Constructor`'s continuations, and it can't just be extracted here. In contrast, `interpretStep` visits every value constructor of `SandwichConstructor`, performs something useful, and prepares the next step for further interpretation. This is a general shape of the function. Let's talk about it in detail:

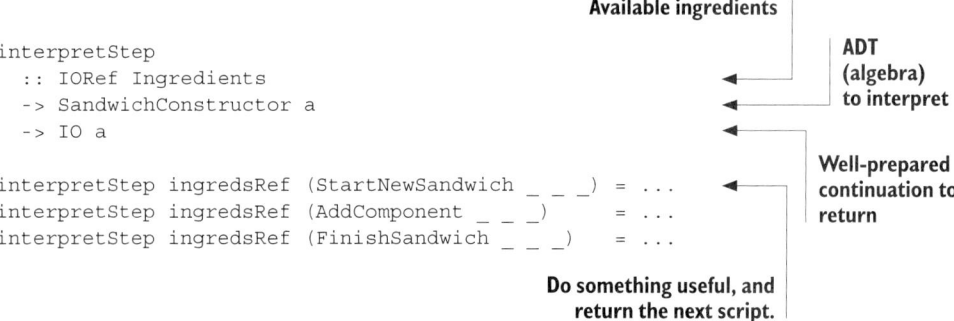

For the sake of simplicity, this interpreter is made stateful: it tracks the available ingredients within a mutable variable `IORef Ingredients`. The `Ingredients` type will only exist at the interpretation layer. It's an implementation detail and should not occur in the business logic. This type denotes an actual stock of ingredients in the kitchen:

```
type Ingredients = Map Component Int
```

The `interpretStep` function does all the things needed to bookkeep the ingredients and to construct a sandwich. It doesn't do any other effects except reading and writing `IORef`. For example, the `AddComponent` method reserves an ingredient, reconstructs the sandwich, fills the `next` continuation with it, and gets a new sandwich. As long as the continuation wants the results of this step, we feed it the new sandwich and get the next script back. This script should be returned to the parent function `interpret-Recipe` for further interpretation:

```
interpretStep ingredsRef (AddComponent component body next) = do

  withdrawIngredient ingredsRef component

  let SandwichBody bread components = body
  let body' = SandwichBody bread (component : components)

  let nextScript = next body'
  pure nextScript
```

Updates the ingredients

Reconstructs the snack

Passes the snack to the continuation

Returns the next script

The `withdrawIngredient` utility function is presented in the following snippet. It searches for the ingredient, decreases its count, and considers it consumed. If no ingredients are available, it throws an exception:

```
withdrawIngredient :: IORef Ingredients -> Component -> IO ()
withdrawIngredient ingredsRef component = do
  ingreds <- readIORef ingredsRef
  case Map.lookup component ingreds of
    Nothing -> error ("Ingredient not found: " <> show component)
    Just count | count <= 0 -> error ("No ingredient: " <> show component)
               | otherwise  -> do
      let ingreds' = Map.insert component (count - 1) ingreds
      writeIORef ingredsRef ingreds'
```

The `interpretStep` function doesn't go deeper into the recursion: it returns the continuation back to the caller. It's an interesting mechanic that is not obvious immediately. It also makes it possible for the `interpretStep` function to return a polymorphic type `IO` a regardless of what it is. It can't be everything, though, and this type variable a is defined for each domain method of the `SandwichConstructor` type. For `AddComponent`, a continuation field `next` expects `SandwichBody`. We feed this next field by a new sandwich body and exit the `interpretStep` function. If you put together everything you know about continuation fields and the `Free` type, you'll see that, for this case, the type becomes

```
interpretStep
  :: IORef Ingredients
  -> SandwichConstructor (SandwichRecipe SandwichBody)
  -> IO (SandwichRecipe SandwichBody)
```

I could make this particular interpreter pure (not IO) by just reconstructing the `Ingredients` dictionary on every step, without any mutable references; however, the code will be much wordier compared to `IORef`. I could make the interpreter much safer and process errors in a better way. For now, it throws an exception if some ingredient is lacking, but this isn't how real systems should be designed. In Haskell, the `error` function is mostly a tool for debugging and should be avoided if possible. Starting in the next chapter, we'll learn a lot about stateful interpreters and error-processing strategies. State in functional programs becomes a very important object to think about, and we have to design it carefully.

6.4 Free monadic eDSLs

We have covered many topics already—requirements analysis; domain-specific versus domain-agnostic languages; ADTs for domain modeling, layering, continuations, declarative scripts, and simulating imperativity by means of interpretable eDSLs; distancing from the impure world; and the benefits of being pure. We definitely missed even more topics.

This talk on free monadic eDSLs will be our last conversation on domain modeling. We'll implement a better version of the scripting languages and try to chart the way to the rest of the spaceship control system—namely, spaceship schema, network, and environment. My goal is to show how convenient monadic scripting can be and how much benefit it gives to business logic programmers.

6.4.1 Improving eDSLs with the free monad

Earlier in chapter 5, I promised that we'd fix several problems of the `Hdl` list-based language by freemonadizing it. This is what we had before:

```
type Hdl next = [HdlMethod next]

data HdlMethod next
  = SetupController
      DeviceName ControllerName ComponentPassport (Controller -> next)
  | RegisterComponent Controller ComponentIndex ComponentPassport
```

In principle, we could write sequential scripts of any depth, as shown in the following listing.

Listing 6.6   A continuation-powered and list-based `Hdl` script

```
boostersDef :: Hdl (Hdl ())
boostersDef =
  [ SetupController "left booster" "left b ctrl" aaaController86Passport
    ( \lCtrl ->
      [ RegisterComponent lCtrl "nozzle1-t" aaaTemperature25Passport
      , RegisterComponent lCtrl "nozzle1-p" aaaPressure02Passport
      ]
    )
  , SetupController "right booster" "right b ctrl" aaaController86Passport
    ( \rCtrl ->
      [ RegisterComponent rCtrl "nozzle2-t" aaaTemperature25Passport
      , RegisterComponent rCtrl "nozzle2-p" aaaPressure02Passport
      ]
    )
  ]
```

Here, I'm setting up two controllers for two booster devices and utilizing them immediately. Nesting another `SetupController` call would mean increasing the syntax noise and making the type `Hdl (Hdl ...)` even longer:

```
boostersDef :: Hdl (Hdl (Hdl ()))        ◄───── The type is growing.
boostersDef =
  [ SetupController "a" "a" passport      ◄───── Layer 1
    ( \aCtrl ->
      [ SetupController "b" "b" passport   ◄───── Layer 2
        ( \aCtrl -> []
      ]
    )
  ]
```

This growth doesn't make much sense. Also, the script is highly coupled because there is no possibility of creating a device and then returning it to the caller. We're obligated to utilize the controller instance right after its creation in the subsequent lambda. If we're asked why the syntax is so ugly, we could answer that it's simple, and after all, there are even less convenient eDSLs out there. But this argument is silly if we can do better.

Listing 6.7   A free-monad-based monadic `Hdl` script

```
createBoosters :: Hdl (Controller, Controller)
createBoosters = do
  lCtrl <- setupController "left booster" "left b ctrl"
                          aaaController86Passport
  registerComponent lCtrl "nozzle1-t" aaaTemperature25Passport
  registerComponent lCtrl "nozzle1-p" aaaPressure02Passport
```

```
rCtrl <- setupController "right booster" "right b ctrl"
                            aaaController86Passport
registerComponent rCtrl "nozzle2-t" aaaTemperature25Passport
registerComponent rCtrl "nozzle2-p" aaaPressure02Passport
pure (lCtrl, rCtrl)
```

The second script reads naturally. It's plain and not polluted by unnecessary list brackets. At least, we see it as plain, although we already know it has the same continuations and chains as the original code, but it is better organized with the free monad. Let me show you the free-prepared `Hdl` ADT.

Listing 6.8 The `Hdl` algebra

```
data HdlMethod next

= SetupController
    DeviceName                          ◄──── Method argument 1
    ControllerName                      ◄──── Method argument 2
    ComponentPassport                   ◄──── Method argument 3
    (Controller -> next)

| RegisterComponent                     Continuation 1
    Controller
    ComponentIndex
    ComponentPassport
    (() -> next)                        ◄──── Continuation 2
```

It's almost the same ADT, but please don't be confused by that strange continuation `(() -> next)` in the `RegisterComponent` method. In the previous scenarios, `RegisterComponent` appears to be a void method. It's the C++ terminology for functions that don't return anything, so they return `void`. By analogy, the semantics of `RegisterComponent` doesn't imply anything to return—it's just an imperative-like procedure. We put a unit continuation to indicate this and to make this value constructor suitable for freemonadizing.

We now need a `Functor` instance for the `HdlMethod`. All the continuations of `HdlMethod` should be transformed by the `fmap` function and repacked with the same arguments:

```
instance Functor HdlMethod where

  fmap f (SetupController deviceName ctrlName passp next) =
    SetupController deviceName ctrlName passp (f . next)

  fmap f (RegisterComponent controller idx passp next) =
    RegisterComponent controller idx passp (f . next)
```

When this preparation is done, the `HdlMethod` ADT is ready to be wrapped by the `Free` type, plus smart constructors for a better developer experience.

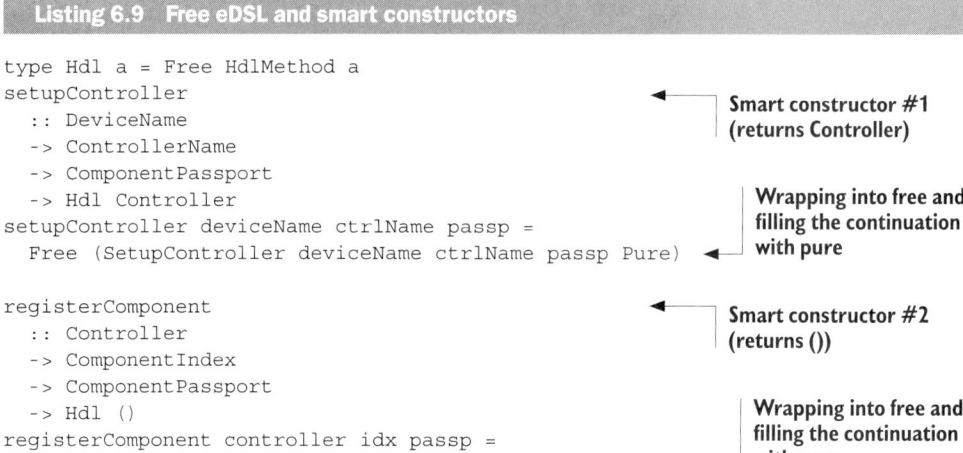

Listing 6.9   **Free eDSL and smart constructors**

```
type Hdl a = Free HdlMethod a
setupController                          ◄─┐ Smart constructor #1
  :: DeviceName                            │ (returns Controller)
  -> ControllerName
  -> ComponentPassport                     ┐ Wrapping into free and
  -> Hdl Controller                        │ filling the continuation
setupController deviceName ctrlName passp =│ with pure
  Free (SetupController deviceName ctrlName passp Pure) ◄─┘

registerComponent                       ◄─┐ Smart constructor #2
  :: Controller                            │ (returns ())
  -> ComponentIndex
  -> ComponentPassport                     ┐ Wrapping into free and
  -> Hdl ()                                │ filling the continuation
registerComponent controller idx passp =   │ with pure
  Free (RegisterComponent controller idx passp Pure) ◄─┘
```

Take a look at figure 6.5 for more insights about this trickery.

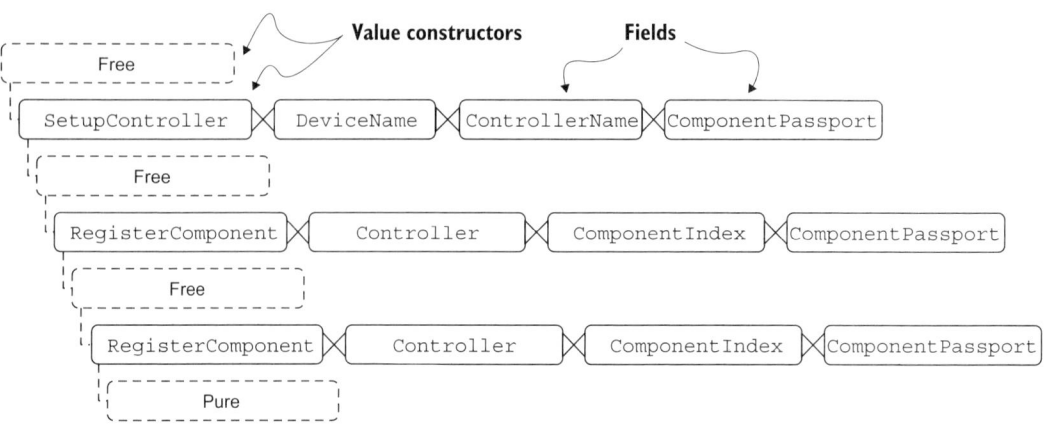

Figure 6.5   Nesting a user-defined ADT and the free type

Now the script in listing 6.7 becomes operational. We're finally freed from monolithic list-like structures and can describe our domain in terms of normal functions. This also allows us to apply all the design principles to the scripting. For example, having only one responsibility for creating a device would please the single responsibility (SRP) principle:

```
createSomeDevice :: Hdl Controller
createSomeDevice = do
  lCtrl <- setupController "some device" "ctrl" aaaController86Passport
  registerComponent lCtrl "thermometer" aaaTemperature25Passport
  pure lCtrl
```

Moreover, as long as these scripts form a business logic layer, we would have it properly organized: loosely coupled, highly consistent, and as readable as possible. We would even design its architecture properly, with its own sublayers and isolated parts. This is what we couldn't fully achieve with the list-based nested languages. Let's see how free monads—especially my hierarchical free monads approach—help here.

6.4.2 Hierarchical free eDSLs

Technically, we don't yet have anything beyond the basic functionality of defining the model of a spaceship. Our `Hdl`, `LogicControl`, and `DeviceControl` languages allow us to declare devices, read sensors, and work with some storage. According to the requirements elaborated earlier, we miss a lot of stuff: calculations, physics, automation, and so on. We just can't implement the whole domain in the book, and that's not our particular goal. We want to establish the principles and practices of design that we then apply to the actual development. And one of these practices will be the approach I call *hierarchical free monads* (HFMs).

Hierarchical free monads help to organize free monadic languages hierarchically. This is a simple idea that reveals its power to keep the subsystems loosely dependent and enables various smart tricks to achieve the effects in code with less complexity and more safety. Later, I'll teach you how to utilize the approach in building application frameworks, and here we'll take a look at how HFM works for domain modeling.

The `Hdl` language is supposed to be a low-level eDSL that only exposes the device definition interface and doesn't do anything related to controlling the ship. To control the ship, we have `LogicControl` and other languages. The structure of the languages is shown in figure 6.6.

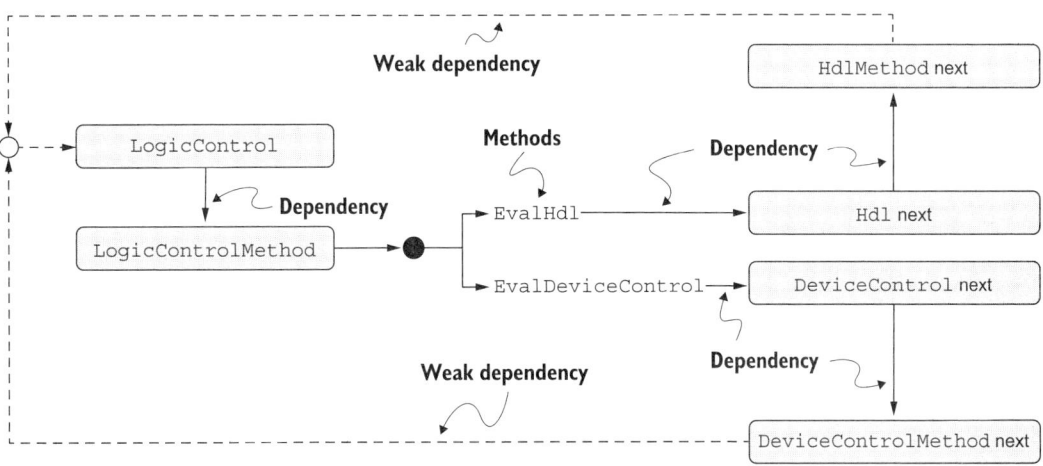

Figure 6.6 Structure of domain-specific languages

It's hierarchical already, although we had to propagate the external language, `Logic-Control`, as a type parameter of the internal languages. We did this without letting them know what they depend on, but it still was a circular dependency that was only needed for making the scripts infinite. We could write a method of `LogicControl`, then call a method of Hdl, then again call a method of LogicControl, and so on. This resulted in a clumsy nesting of lambdas and lists, but it at least worked.

Listing 6.10   List-based script

```
script :: LogicControl
script =
  [ EvalHdl
    [ SetupController "device" "ctrl" aaaController86Passport (\ctrl ->
      [ EvalHdl
        [ RegisterComponent ctrl "therm" aaaTemperature25Passport ]
      , EvalDeviceControl (readAndReport ctrl)
      ]
    )]
  ]
  where
    readAndReport :: Controller -> DeviceControl LogicControl
    readAndReport ctrl =
      [ ReadSensor ctrl "therm" (\eMeasurement ->
        [ Report (show eMeasurement) ])
      ]
```

This script initializes a device, registers a thermometer, reads it, and then reports the measurement to somewhere. And this script is difficult to observe due to its list-based ADT nature. While keeping the overall hierarchy of the languages the same, we'll now freemonadize them and make them truly decoupled, without compromises. Figure 6.7 explains the new design.

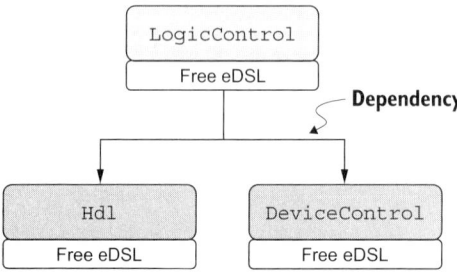

Figure 6.7   Hierarchical structure free eDSLs

Yes, it's that simple. Let's see how.

The LogicControl language should be free monadic too. Reworking its old ADT will be quite straightforward for the two methods Report and Store. The old ADT was

```
data LogicControlMethod
  = Report Message
  | Store Key Value
  ...
```

Neither of the two actions returns a value currently, and we don't even wait for these methods to indicate success or failure. They will just implicitly return () — a void value.

Consequently, freemonadized methods will get continuation fields that only make this void value explicit. Also, some other boilerplate is needed, such as the functor instance and the smart constructors.

```
data LogicControlMethod next                          ◄──┐
  = Report Message   (() -> next)                         │  Language algebra
  | Store Key Value (() -> next)                          │  with methods

instance Functor LogicControlMethod where         ◄──── Functor instance
  fmap f (Report msg next)     = Report msg      (f . next)
  fmap f (Store key value next) = Store key value (f . next)

type LogicControl a = Free LogicControlMethod a   ◄──── Free monadic eDSL

report :: Message -> LogicControl ()              ◄──── Smart constructors
report msg = Free (Report msg Pure)

store :: Key -> Value -> LogicControl ()
store key value = Free (Store key value Pure)
```

Scripts feel good now. You read them normally as if they are imperative procedures:

```
storeJohnDoe :: LogicControl ()
storeJohnDoe = do
  store "First Name" "John"
  store "Last Name" "Doe"
  report "John Doe is written into KV DB."
```

Yet, there is a question of what to do with the `EvalHdl` that we had in the previous design. Remember this construction?

```
data LogicControlMethod
  = EvalHdl (Hdl LogicControl)
```

The parametrization with `LogicControl` is no longer needed. The `Hdl` type remains parametrized, but this parametrization has a very different nature: a free monadic nature. With this nature, `Hdl result` is a script returning `result`, or something specific, when seen in concrete business logic scripts such as

```
createBoosters :: Hdl (Controller, Controller)
```

Can we just put `Hdl result` into that `EvalHdl` constructor? For example:

```
data LogicControlMethod next
  = EvalHdl (Hdl result)
```

Do not forget about a continuation field! Our intuition should now hint that the continuation is a function that wants that `result` from the `Hdl` script:

```
data LogicControlMethod next
  = EvalHdl (Hdl result) (result -> next)
```

Otherwise, where should this value go? This is the idea: we enclose the script, its returning value, and the continuation within the single `EvalHdl` method. This will work, except that in Haskell, another extra feature is required, namely, generalized algebraic data types:

```
{-# LANGUAGE GADTs #-}

data LogicControlMethod next
  = forall result. EvalHdl (Hdl result) (result -> next)
```

Now the two fields of the value constructor are related; they share the same type. This is what the `forall` keyword does for `result`. The `result` type variable can't escape the `EvalHdl` method; it's localized there and should only be accessed with the method itself. Since `forall` is there, `LogicControlMethod` is no longer a regular ADT; it's a bit of an advanced type now. I believe that in other languages, this can be done using some tricks. At least, I did this in PureScript, a Haskell-like language that lacks GADTs and type families. I even managed to do this in C++, a language that would seem to be quite far from Haskell. As a matter of fact, modern C++ developers know that C++ and Haskell are closely related, and learning Haskell improves your knowledge of C++ almost magically.

Interestingly, if we add another type variable—`result`—the whole type will get a different meaning:

```
data LogicControlMethod result next
  = EvalHdl (Hdl result) (result -> next)

type LogicControl result a = Free (LogicControlMethod result) a
```

No GADTs are required now, but look—the `result` type variable is one for the whole ADT, and it propagates up into `LogicControl`. This means that whenever we call a `LogicControl` script, all the `Hdl` insertings are obligated to return the same type `result`. This will not compile:

```
myScript :: LogicControl ??? ()
myScript = do
  evalHdl createBoosters        -- Hdl (Controller, Controller)
  evalHdl createBoostersTwice   -- Hdl ()
```

Also, this global type variable prevents having different return types if we want to call `Hdl` and `DeviceControl` scripts from `LogicControl`. So the `forall` keyword allows each occurrence to have its own return types. The complete definition is shown in the following listing, and variables are shortened to save space.

Listing 6.12 Complete `LogicControl` type

```
{-# LANGUAGE GADTs #-}

data LogicControlMethod next
  = forall a. EvalHdl (Hdl a) (a -> next)
  | forall a. EvalDeviceControlMethod (DeviceControlMethod a) (a -> next)
```

```
| Report Message (() -> next)
| Store Key Value (() -> next)
```

As a side note, I made `DeviceControlMethod` be GADT as well. I've been trying to create some extensible type for commands, but this didn't end well. So I stopped with a design that is okay for this chapter, but I'd recommend thinking more about the task and creating something better instead. For now, the `DeviceControlMethod` contains two actions, but distinct from the old design, the type is GADT (and utilizes a slightly different syntax).

Listing 6.13 `DeviceControl` **type**

```
{-# LANGUAGE GADTs #-}

data DeviceControlMethod a where          ◄───── GADT type with
                                                 GADT syntax
  GetStatus
    :: Controller
    -> DeviceControlMethod (Either HardwareFailure ControllerStatus)

  ReadSensor
    :: Controller
    -> ComponentIndex
    -> DeviceControlMethod (Either HardwareFailure Measurement)
```

GADTs are a genericity-like abstraction. This is why some extra stuff happens to that generic type variable a of the ADT when it reaches its value constructors. Here's a short explanation for curious readers. Every value constructor (either `GetStatus` or `ReadSensor`) corresponds to some action. Both have some arguments, as functions usually do. You can even see the same syntax with double colons and right arrows. Both actions happen to be returning results. In contrast to the free monad mechanism, they utilize GADT to describe the fact of returning. Hence, we have this instead of `DeviceControlMethod a`:

```
not:
  GetStatus  :: ... -> DeviceControlMethod a
  ReadSensor :: ... -> DeviceControlMethod a

but rather:
  GetStatus  :: ... ->
            DeviceControlMethod (Either HardwareFailure ControllerStatus)
  ReadSensor :: ... ->
            DeviceControlMethod (Either HardwareFailure Measurement)
```

The GADT syntax requires this kind of ending for each value constructor, and the type itself should be parametrized. When pattern-matching, we can rely on the compiler and be sure that if our action is `ReadSensor`, the return value must be `Either Hardware-Failure Measurement`.

Listing 6.14   `DeviceControl` **interpretation**

```
interpretDeviceControlMethod :: DeviceControlMethod a -> IO a

-- must return (Either HardwareFailure ControllerStatus)
interpretDeviceControlMethod (GetStatus _)
  = pure (Right ControllerOk)

-- must return (Either HardwareFailure Measurement)
interpretDeviceControlMethod (ReadSensor _ _)
  = pure (Right (Measurement Pressure 111.0))
```

Interestingly, we don't need an extra type. It was `HdlMethod` (a bunch of actions) and `Hdl` (a free monadic type), but now it's only `DeviceControlMethod` (a GADT type), and it's included in `LogicControlMethod` (as listing 6.12 shows). I would rather avoid using value constructors directly, though, because why not create convenient smart constructors? There will be two sets of them: low- and high-level. "Low-level" means they wrap data into `DeviceControlMethod`:

```
getStatus'
  :: Controller
  -> DeviceControlMethod (Either HardwareFailure ControllerStatus)
getStatus' controller = GetStatus controller

readSensor'
  :: Controller
  -> ComponentIndex
  -> DeviceControlMethod (Either HardwareFailure Measurement)
readSensor' controller idx = ReadSensor controller idx
```

They can't be called monadically because `DeviceControlMethod` isn't a monad. However, high-level functions wrap low-level ones into the `LogicControl` monad, so they are now full citizens of this world.

Listing 6.15   `DeviceControl` **smart constructors**

```
import qualified Andromeda.Hardware.Language.DeviceControl as DC

evalDeviceControl :: DC.DeviceControlMethod a -> LogicControl a
evalDeviceControl dc = Free (EvalDeviceControlMethod dc Pure)

getStatus
  :: Controller
  -> LogicControl (Either HardwareFailure ControllerStatus)
getStatus ctrl = evalDeviceControl (DC.getStatus' ctrl)

readSensor
  :: Controller
  -> ComponentIndex
  -> LogicControl (Either HardwareFailure Measurement)
readSensor ctrl idx = evalDeviceControl (DC.readSensor' ctrl idx)
```

Just look at the scripts we're able to write now! The next listing creates two booster devices and immediately requests their statuses. The status request procedures may fail as their types indicate, so we must verify the results via pattern matching.

Listing 6.16 Sample `LogicControl` script

```
import qualified Andromeda.LogicControl.Language as L

data LogicFailure = LogicFailure String

getBoostersStatus
  :: LogicControl (Either LogicFailure (ControllerStatus, ControllerStatus))
getBoostersStatus = do
  (lCtrl, rCtrl) <- L.evalHdl createBoosters        ◄──── Creates the boosters device
  eLStatus <- L.getStatus ctrl lCtrl                ◄──── Gets the status
  eRStatus <- L.getStatus ctrl rCtrl                       of the left nozzle
  let res = case (eLStatus, eRStatus) of            ◄──── Gets the status
        (Right s1, Right s2) -> Right (s1, s2)              of the right nozzle
        (Left e, _) -> Left (LogicFailure (show e))  ◄──── Validates the statuses
        (_, Left e) -> Left (LogicFailure (show e))
  pure res
```

Some device has failed: log an error.

Statuses are okay: return them.

This is not an easy topic, though, and definitely not the first time we've used the advanced programming in Haskell. I just hope that I successfully explained the overall idea of having domain-specific languages with HFMs. As we progress, your understanding of the concept should improve by going through more use cases and applications. If not, please consider consulting other resources on this topic.

Keep learning!

Summary

- Interfaces are used to handle complexity and communicate the essence of a business domain.
- Free monads are the most idiomatic functional interface and share interesting parallels with OOP interfaces.
- The Free Monad pattern is a powerful and convenient way of designing eDSLs.
- The free monad is a template for wrapping eDSLs to make them monadic and sequential, which is better than being list based.
- Free monads allow the nesting of languages and chaining of scripts of different types while resolving the "returning" problem, making the code more usual and easier to compare.
- It's better to design domain-specific languages so that the scenarios can feel more natural from the domain experts' point of view.

- If your domain is supposed to have some imperative-like operations or if you'd like to design your domain in a such a way, consider wrapping your eDSLs into free monads.
- GADTs are a weaker design pattern than free monads for making domain-specific languages.
- GADTs are a genericity-like abstraction, while free monads are an interface-like abstraction.

Part 4

Stateful and reactive applications

This part examines the realms of managing state in functional programming and the dynamics of reactive application design. We begin by demystifying the concept of state in functional programming, emphasizing that it not only accommodates state but also introduces innovative approaches for creating safe, well-designed stateful applications. Furthermore, we study the nuances of pure and impure states, the singular approach of argument-passing state, and how state monads facilitate the handling of the immutable state in a manner that mimics imperative programming while remaining functional and combinatorial. The discussion extends to the internal workings of state monads, their role in structuring monadic applications, and their evolution into state monad transformers, highlighting strategies for managing multiple state contexts and dealing with impure mutable states in industrial functional languages.

Next, our focus shifts to reactive applications, examining the application of reactive programming in creating environments where formulas dynamically respond to new data. We find a place for the actor model as a framework for organizing stateful applications, addressing the challenges of ensuring safe and reliable interactions between actors. The concept of an abstracted communication protocol as a binding contract among actors is discussed, along with the practical use of MVars for thread-safe shared variable access. We explore advanced architectures, such as the adaptability of free monadic architecture in providing multiple implementations for the same business logic. The section concludes with insights into the limitations of MVar-based concurrency models and the potential benefits of transitioning to software transactional memory (STM) for managing complex concurrent data models.

Stateful applications

7

This chapter covers

- Organizing stateful functional applications
- Creating pure and impure states
- Using state monads

Some people argue against functional programming by saying that it doesn't work for real tasks because it lacks mutable variables. There are no mutable variables, and therefore, no state can change, so interaction with the program is impossible. You might even be hearing that a functional program is really a math formula without effects, and consequently, it doesn't work with memory, network, standard input and output, and whatever else the impure world has. But when it does, it's not functional programming anymore. There are even more emotional opinions and questions. For example, "Is it cheating in Haskell when an IO monad just masks the imperative paradigm?" The use of impure code in Haskell's IO monad may even lead to questioning how it is functional when it's clearly imperative.

Functional programming doesn't mean there should be no state or side effects. In fact, functional programming is friendly to these concepts, but it does the job differently, preventing state and side effects from vandalizing our code.

This chapter deals with an important topic from the design standpoint—state in functional programs. Is it something special? In what manner should we develop state and yet maintain the benefits of immutability? Are there any best practices for organizing stateful code? I want to give you a comprehensive answer to these questions. While being quite basic, the discussion about state leads to significant consequences in software design that we'll discover in the next chapters.

7.1   *Stateful functional programming*

As with most things in programming, a closer look into the topic of state reveals a vast world of interesting structures, such as immutable state, argument-passing state, state monad, and concurrent state in the form of software transactional memory (STM). The concept of state is much wider than just some variable to change. State is not about mutable or immutable values of data in our code. Values are a coding category, whereas state is a design category and should be treated accordingly, with a full spectrum of design considerations.

So what characterizes state as a design category? The first criterion will be lifetime—that is, when and in what conditions the state is operating in the program. These lifetimes are

- *Local or auxiliary state*—State that exists during a single calculation. This kind of state isn't visible from the outside. The state variable will be created at the beginning and destroyed at the end of the calculation (note that with garbage collection, this may be true in a conceptual sense, but it isn't how it truly is). The variable can mutate freely without breaking the code purity until the mutation is strictly deterministic.
- *Operational state*—State with a lifetime comparable to that of the application. This kind of state is used to drive the application's business logic and keep important user-defined data.
- *External state*—State with a lifetime exceeding that of the application. This state lives in external storage (databases) that provides long-term data processing.

The second division concerns a purity question. State can be

- *Pure*—Pure state isn't really some mutable imperative variable bound to a particular memory cell. Rather, it's a functional imitation of mutability. We can also say that pure state doesn't destroy the previous value when assigning a new one. Pure state is always bounded by some pure calculation. In Haskell, there are two forms of pure state: argument-passing state and the state monad.
- *Impure*—Impure state always operates by dealing with impure side effects, such as writing memory, files, databases, or imperative mutable variables. While an impure state is much more dangerous than a pure one, there are techniques that help secure impure stateful calculations. Functional code that works with impure state can still be deterministic in its behavior. In Haskell, there are a variety of impure mutable variables: `IORef`, `MVar`, and STM primitives such as `TVar`.

From imperative programming, we learned the habit of handling mutable variables as if they are the most fundamental primitives possible. Learning how to deal with variables happens in the first lecture for every programming language. But in functional languages, mutability has never been welcomed. Lambda calculus and all the combinator calculi (such as SKI) prove that the essence of state isn't in mutability of a distinct cell of memory. However, in practice, we'd like to step away from purism and allow a real, destructive mutability, even in functional programs. Avoiding the impure state is possible, although the price will be blatantly wordy code. Furthermore, mutable imperative variables show better performance compared to nonmutable state transformations.

7.1.1 Simple stateful application

Remember the example with sandwiches from the previous chapter? We had

```
mySandwich :: SandwichRecipe Sandwich
mySandwich = do
  body1 <- startNewSandwich Toast Tomato
  body2 <- addComponent Cheese body1
  body3 <- addComponent Salt body2
  finishSandwich Nothing body3
```

We'll convert it into a finished stateful application and learn a specific architectural pattern from it. We have everything for that—figuratively speaking, we've collected all the ingredients for this sandwich application (figure 7.1).

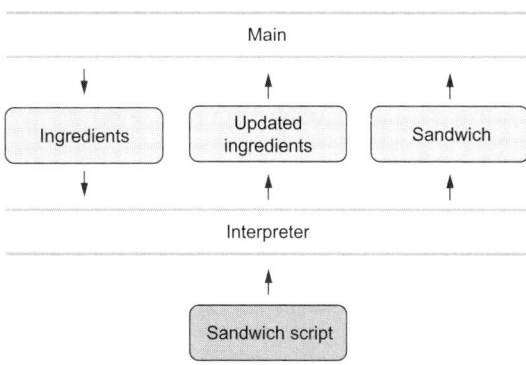

Figure 7.1 Simple stateful application

So we define the initial ingredients and then utilize them in the interpreter according to the recipe we provided. As a result, we get a new sandwich, and the fridge loses some weight.

The interpreter has two inputs: script and ingredients. During the process, some ingredients should be consumed, and others should stay untouched. The picture doesn't show us how the changes are handled by the interpreter. What kind of state is this? We're free to choose. It can be an impure state in the form of `IORefs`. It can also be a pure immutable argument-passing state that is so common in functional programs.

The simplest stateful application that makes a sandwich and prints the result will have the `main` function to start from and some data to operate with. Let's bring all the pieces together. In the following listing, note that a call is made to the `interpret-Recipe` interpreter.

Listing 7.1   A simple stateful application

```
ingredients :: Ingredients                              ◀─── Operational data
ingredients = Map.fromList
  [ (Tomato, 10), (Bread Toast, 6)
  , (Salt, 4), (Cheese, 5) ]
                                                              Application
main :: IO ()                                           ◀─── entry point
main = do
  -- sudo make me a sandwich                                 Using predefined
  ingredientsRef <- newIORef ingredients                ◀─── ingredients
  sandwich <- interpretRecipe ingredientsRef mySandwich ◀──┐ Interpreting
  print sandwich                                            │ the script
```

Don't devalue the program, though—it does a good job of demonstrating different layers. First, business logic goes to the `mySandwich` free monad script. This script relies solely on eDSL interfaces. Second, you can recognize the `interpretRecipe` function corresponding to the implementation of those interfaces. The operational state is also here, and it's represented by the `ingredientsRef` variable. All the layers have definite boundaries—they play definite roles and are not allowed to interfere with other layers. But they can't just coexist in isolation. There should be a place such as this `main` function where everything is tied together. We call this specific place the application layer.

Figure 7.2 demonstrates the primary layers and makes the pun about sandwich application even funnier because the free monadic architecture is essentially a sandwich itself.

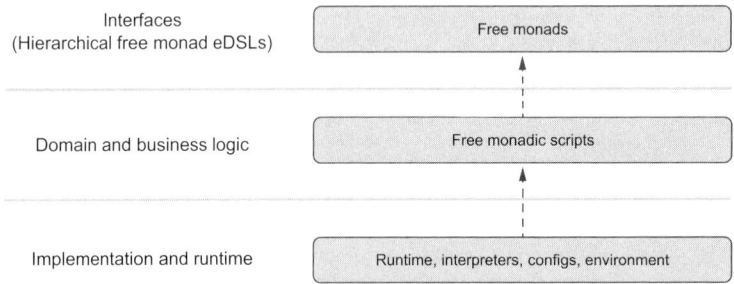

Figure 7.2   A layered free monadic architecture

There are certainly other layers, such as the persistence, interoperability, view layer, and so forth. You can refresh your memory about layers by reading chapter 2. Some of them have an application-wide significance, while others occur episodically. In the Haskell community, there are different approaches to combining the layers. Choosing between them is an architectural decision, although it's not always clear what the long-term consequences will be. This is why it's important to have some fundamental principles, such as KISS and SOLID, which help us evaluate the decisions and better satisfy the requirements.

7.1.2 Purity, layering, state, and design

Business logic, interfaces, and implementation layers play a central role in such an architecture. However, as we know from the previous chapters, there are two unavoidable, essential, intrinsic layers in every application. These are pure and impure layers. Explicitly separating them is a modern idea in software design (for example, with the IO environment in Haskell, but this hasn't always been so). Impurity hasn't always been a software design topic, and it was normal to write impure code without realizing this fact. If you like, impurity is the prose of software development, while purity is poetry.

Given this, state can be considered with respect to those layers—there is a definite dependency here. Table 7.1 describes the relationship between state and purity layers.

Table 7.1 Purity layers and state

	Pure state	**Impure state**
Pure layer	Allowed	Disallowed
Impure layer	Allowed	Allowed

What does this mean in the context of architecture? Take a look at figure 7.3, in which the arrows mean *uses* or *knows about*.

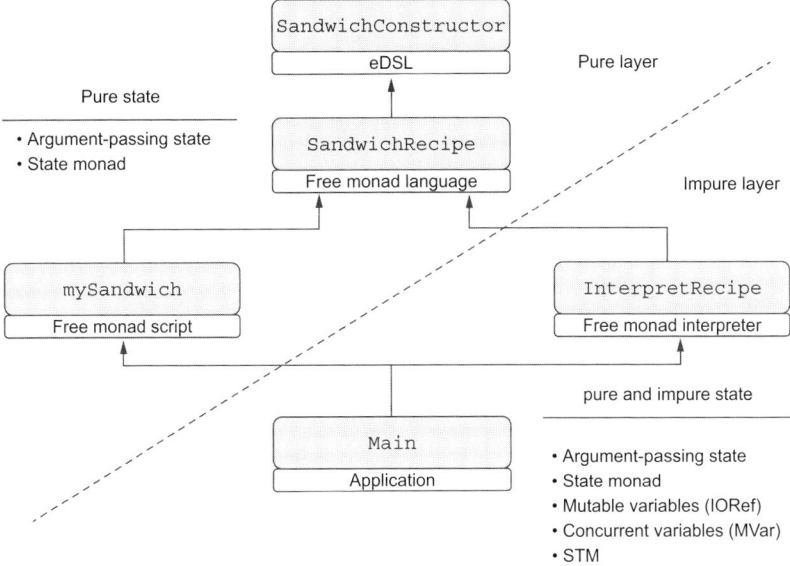

Figure 7.3 Pure and impure layers

Here, both functions, `mySandwich` and `interpterRecipe`, can work with state, but only `interpretRecipe` is allowed to be impure if required. The only possibility of being pure for free monadic scripts leads to a specific consequence of the whole design: none of the implementation details on the upper-left side of this figure are welcomed. And suddenly, everything becomes organized well.

Once you start following this pattern, you realize that developing becomes simpler and more conscious. It's no longer blind hacking—it's engineering. Your reasoning changes from "How do I shove some code into an unstructured project, and what is the most appropriate place for it?" to "What is the interface of this thing? Should it be a subsystem with its own eDSL representation, or can it just be a domain part where the current eDSL capabilities are sufficient?" In other words, your attention to the business part becomes less suppressed by unrelated matters, and you have more time to solve real problems instead of artificially created ones.

Take logging as an example. Logging is quite necessary in our programs. It's the primary tool for collecting diagnostic info from the working application. Logging itself can be an intimidating and difficult subject worth discussing in a separate book. I'm sure you are already aware of this.

Why not add some logging into our primitive sandwiches program and see what happens? Do you think we can hammer down some logging calls into the script itself?

Listing 7.2   Embedding impure logging into free script

```
import Logger (LoggerConfig, LvlInfo, logMessage)        ◄──── External logging library

logInfo :: LoggerConfig -> String -> IO ()               ◄──┐ Custom wrapper
logInfo cfg msg = logMessage LvlInfo cfg msg                 │ for logging

mySandwich :: LoggerConfig -> SandwichRecipe Sandwich    ◄──── Business logic
mySandwich loggerCfg = do
  body1 <- startNewSandwich Toast Tomato

  logInfo loggerCfg "Sandwich started! Will be ready soon."   ◄──── IO call here

  body2 <- addComponent Cheese body1
  body3 <- addComponent Salt body2
  finishSandwich Nothing body3
```

This code will not even compile. Those logging functions are impure, and the free monad `SandwichRecipe` just won't allow those invocations. Also, passing `Logger-Config` into `mySandwich` feels so weird.

Do you think our `SandwichConstructor` eDSL will be happy with more logging possibilities? Let's take a look:

```
data SandwichConstructor next
  = StartNewSandwich BreadType Component (SandwichBody -> next)
  | AddComponent Component SandwichBody (SandwichBody -> next)
  | FinishSandwich (Maybe BreadType) SandwichBody (Sandwich -> next)

  | LogInfo Message (() -> next)                          ◄──── A new logging method
```

Definitely not. It doesn't fit all other methods, which are about the domain, not about some auxiliary subsystem. It screams "Why am I here?" so loudly that it is possible to hear it. This feeling is actually a design smell. We just committed a sin of software design. We mixed different levels of abstraction and thus violated the general principle of divide and conquer.

So the only place left for logging is the interpreter, the impure one. I see some value in logging the errors before throwing exceptions from their depths, namely from the `withdrawIngredient` function. I could also log every step of sandwich creation when interpreting the script. If that makes sense, then okay, but I doubt it. Nevertheless, for the sake of education, I present a part of such an interpreter in the following listing.

Listing 7.3   Impure interpreter with logging

```haskell
withdrawIngredient :: IORef Ingredients -> Component -> IO ()
withdrawIngredient ingredsRef component = do
  ingreds <- readIORef ingredsRef                              ◀─── Gets ingredients

  case Map.lookup component ingreds of
    Just count | count > 0 -> do
      let ingreds' = Map.insert component (count - 1) ingreds
      writeIORef ingredsRef ingreds'                           ◀─── Consumes ingredients
    Nothing -> do
      logError ("No ingredient: " <> show component)           ◀─── Logs an error
      error ("No ingredient: " <> show component)

interpretStep :: IORef Ingredients -> SandwichConstructor a -> IO a
interpretStep ingredsRef (StartNewSandwich bread component next) = do
  logInfo ("Starting new sandwich: "                           ◀─── Logs an info
    <> show bread <> " "
    <> show component)

  withdrawIngredient ingredsRef component                      ◀─── Consumes ingredients
  withdrawIngredient ingredsRef (Bread bread)

  let body = SandwichBody bread [component]
  pure (next body)                                             ◀─── Returns the updated
                                                                    sandwich
```

This is how we do a hidden, occasional logging solely on the implementation layer. The business logic stays unaware of this, but every step is being protocoled anyway.

You can reasonably say that we usually do need logging in more complicated domains. You're completely right. We'll be working on the more real-world tasks in the rest of the book. We'll discover ways to produce interfaces for such subsystems. We'll introduce the appropriate eDSL design, and it won't violate those principles. It also won't sacrifice purity and abstraction, and the beautiful scheme from figure 7.4 will not be distorted.

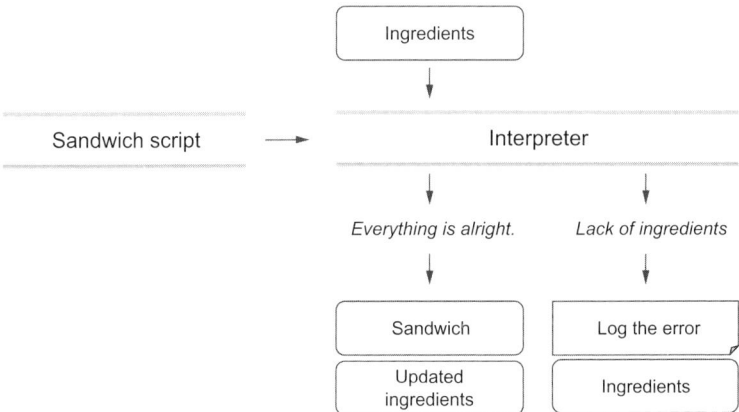

Figure 7.4   Success and failure paths for sandwich creation

7.2   State-handling approaches

That was the reasoning behind making decisions about state and layering. Now I believe it makes sense to briefly discuss state approaches and examine concrete samples—not the sandwich application, though. It's too simple and barely representative. We will return to our Andromeda software and develop several different scripts and interpreters, all with their own state-handling mechanisms.

7.2.1   Argument-passing state

Do you remember the main idea of the `LogicControl` eDSL and its components? Let me remind you: it's the main programming environment for writing spaceship control scripts, including calculations on how to move the ship in space and which engines should be enabled at what power for what amount of time to achieve what momentum along which axis. This task requires a certain amount of math and physics. Those calculations may be quite unobvious and difficult, as they depend on thousands of spaceship characteristics (for example, mass and component properties).

The following script is an example of what a piece of code for angular impulse calculation for a specific thruster may look like:

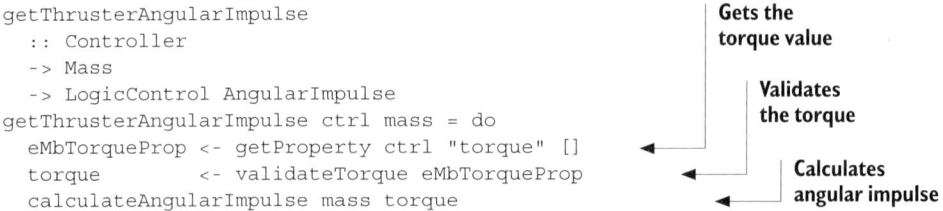

We need two spaceship properties: torque of the thruster and mass of the spaceship. Torque is an inherent property of thrusters, and we believe we can obtain it from the thruster controller. The validation function ensures that the value we got is correct and suitable for the calculations that follow.

This code is imaginable, but it's not yet clear where the functions `getProperty`, `validateTorque`, and `calculateAngularImpulse` came from. I can tell that `getProperty` is a new member of the `DeviceControl` eDSL (and is therefore callable from `LogicControl`) that allows you to request different properties of devices in a generic yet loosely typed way:

```
getProperty
  :: Controller
  -> PropertyName
  -> [Param]
  -> LogicControl (Either LogicControlFailure (Maybe Property))
```

A property may not make any sense to a device, so the function returns a `Maybe` value. Also, there can be some error in reading the controller (for example, it was crashed by space junk and doesn't respond anymore), so the function returns `Either LogicControlFailure`.

This function might look too generic and untyped because we're not guaranteed to get a torque property. Instead, we can be surprised by something else from these options.

Listing 7.4   Generic loosely typed properties

```
data PhysicalUnit
 = UnitTemperature Temperature
 | UnitPressure Pressure
 | UnitMass Mass
 | UnitVelocity Velocity
 | UnitThrust Thrust
 | UnitTorque Torque
 | UnitAngle Angle

data Property
 = ValueProperty PropertyName Value
 | PhysicalUnitProperty PropertyName PhysicalUnit
```

This design violates a good rule we've discussed before: make invalid states irrepresentable. In my defense, I can tell that it's nearly impossible to design a well-typed domain for all the peculiarities of the various spaceship hardware. I'm almost sure there are attempts to build a statically verifiable, massively type-level, and fully correctness-proven SCADA software, but I hardly believe those attempts are successful.

We can think of `Controller` and `Mass` parameters as an immutable state passed in arguments. However, I honestly don't think that spaceships have a constant mass all the time. After all, they burn fuel and emit combustion products into space. This is why we want to update the value of mass during the flight. As an example, here I'll put another script, `performRotation`, that utilizes the previous one to calculate angular impulses. The general idea of this logic is that you need two opposite burns separated by a time interval to rotate the ship at a certain degree. The first burn starts the rotation of the ship. And once the ship has achieved the needed angle, the rotation should stop; hence, the second opposite burn.

The logic in the following listing does these two burns and also recalculates the mass during the process.

Listing 7.5 Performing the rotation script

```
data SpaceshipProperties = SpaceshipProperties          All possible spaceship
  { spMass :: Mass                                      characteristics
  }

data SpaceshipModel = SpaceshipModel                    Spaceship with
  { smSpaceshipProperties :: SpaceshipProperties        all its devices
  , smMainEngine          :: Controller
  , smRotationThruster    :: Controller
  }

performRotation                                         Rotates the ship
  :: SpaceshipModel
  -> Angle
  -> LogicControl SpaceshipModel                        Gets the thruster
performRotation model angle = do
  let thrusterCtrl = smRotationThruster model           Gets the mass
  let shipMass1    = spMass (smSpaceshipProperties model)
                                                        Calculates
  impulse1 <- getThrusterAngularImpulse thrusterCtrl shipMass1   the impulse
  shipMass2 <- recalcMass shipMass1 impulse1
  impulse2 <- getThrusterAngularImpulse thrusterCtrl shipMass2   Recalculates
  shipMass3 <- recalcMass shipMass2 impulse2            the mass

  (burnStart, burnStop, time) <- calcBurn impulse1 impulse2 angle   Calculates
                                                                    two burns
  performBurn thrusterCtrl burnStart                   Performs
  wait time                                            the burns
  performBurn thrusterCtrl burnStop

  pure (model { smSpaceshipProperties = SpaceshipProperties shipMass3 })
```

Given the angle, the script finds an appropriate engine, performs various calculations, and then communicates with the thruster's controller to do the actual burns. In the end, the script returns an updated spaceship model with a new mass. There are several state variables here, but what is interesting to us is the mass parameter that we recalculate with the `recalcMass` function:

```
recalcMass :: Mass -> AngularImpulse -> LogicControl Mass
recalcMass shipMass impulse = ...
```

This function uses the argument-passing state technique. It has the following shape:

```
value -> use value -> updated value
```

This state-handling approach is simple and essential unless it's not—namely, when the data structure is complex and deep, which is, in other words, almost always. For example, spaceship properties might contain not only mass but also coordinates and orientation, current orbital speed, and many other characteristics:

```
data SpaceshipProperties = SpaceshipProperties
  { spMass                    :: Mass
  , spOrbitalCoordinates      :: OrbitalCoordinates
  , spOrientation             :: Orientation
  , spOrbitalSpeed            :: Speed
  , spManyOtherCharacteristics :: ManyOtherCharachteristics
  }
```

Imagine the wordiness of updating constructions in the code:

```
func :: SpaceshipModel -> LogicControl SpaceshipModel
func model1 = do
  newProps1 <- doSomething model1
  let model2 = model1 {smSpaceshipProperties = newProps1}
  newProps2 <- doSomething model2
  let model3 = model2 {smSpaceshipProperties = newProps2}
  model4 <- doManyOtherThings model3
  pure model4
```

I assumed that all those functions return bare value types `SpaceshipModel`:

```
doSomething       :: SpaceshipModel -> LogicControl SpaceshipProperties
doManyOtherThings :: SpaceshipModel -> LogicControl SpaceshipModel
```

However, the more realistic codebase will have many methods encrusted with error-handling mechanisms such as the `Either` and `Maybe` types. The code will grow tremendously in this case. Check it out:

```
doSomething
  :: SpaceshipModel
  -> LogicControl (Either LogicControlFailure SpaceshipProperties)   ◄──────┐

func :: SpaceshipModel -> LogicControl SpaceshipModel                        Advanced type
func model1 = do                                                             to return
  eNewProps1 <- doSomething model1
  case eNewProps1 of
    Left err -> error err
    Right newProps1 -> …
```

Haskell developers don't really like such boilerplate, and they've found alternatives. Have you heard about the state monad? You can expect to meet it in a regular Haskell codebase, although other languages experience less invasion because of the inherent mutability available to developers. Undoubtedly, the state monad approach should be put on the table due to the specific role it plays in the design of our stateful programs.

7.2.2 *Pure state with the state monad*

Rockets can't lift off from green grass and jump straight to orbit. There must be a reliable launchpad equipped with all the important subsystems: fuel supply, crane system, testing devices, and a solid launch silo. In the same way, the introduction to state monads can't start without understanding the origins of monads, their history, the corresponding math, and what's so special about the category theory here.

Oh, come on, of course, that's sarcasm. There is no need for the category theory in this book, and there is no need to know what a monad is. I've already introduced IO and free monads, so our discussion of the state monad will rely on this prior knowledge.

The state monad is cunning. The code will pretend that the state is mutable, while it isn't. The state variable will be available to all your monadic functions in the monadic do-environment so that you can either read or update the state whenever you need to. Those reading and writing functions (get and put) are all implemented for you already. You get them instantly once you say that your function works within this monad:

```
import Control.Monad.State (State, get, put)          ◀── State monad library

type Age = Int
                                                      State monad that
gettingOlder :: State Age String              ◀──     stores Age
gettingOlder = do
  age <- get                                  ◀──     Getting the Age variable
  let newAge = age + 1                                from the state context
  put newAge
  pure ("You're now older for 1 year: " <> show newAge)    ◀── Putting the updated
                                                                Age back
```

As you can see, the state monad comes with the type parameter that denotes the state you want to maintain. The other type parameter denotes the return type as is usual for all the monads:

```
someFunc :: State someState someOutput
```

Certainly, calling the identically monadized functions from each other means that the state will be the one and only, as if there was a shared mutable variable somewhere in the context of those functions:

```
bornAndGettingOlderTwice :: State Age [String]
bornAndGettingOlderTwice = do
  put 0                        -- born

  msg1 <- gettingOlder         -- Age == 1
  msg2 <- gettingOlder         -- Age == 2

  age  <- get                  -- should be 2 now

  pure [msg1, msg2, "Your age now: " <> show age]
```

After running the script, you're right to expect that two sequential invocations of gettingOlder will change the Age state they have in common to 2.

I say, "They have in common," while knowing that the internal mechanism doesn't actually do any state sharing. It doesn't do any mutation, and there is no common context as it may seem from the script. In fact, the internal mechanism operates as an argument-passing state that is smartly wrapped into the monad machinery. If you start digging deeper, you'll see how the bind operator (>>=) makes it possible to pass the state from one monadic function to another (see figure 7.5). It's amazing that this behavior is monadic, and consequently, it becomes quite handy in the do-notation form.

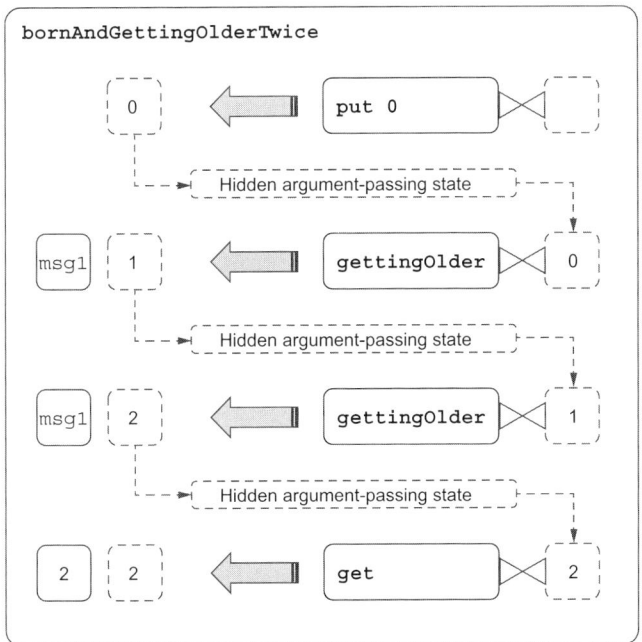

Figure 7.5 Schematic behavior of the state monad

Should I talk more about the implementation of state monads? I don't think so. As users, we can completely ignore it and enjoy the clearness of the code. Knowing the details might be important in the production setting (for example, from the performance point of view), but otherwise, it's an abstraction, and like any other abstraction, it can be only observed as is, without opening this Pandora's box.

Here, I avoid teaching you functional programming per se. I don't teach lambdas, continuations, or high-order functions. I even refuse to reveal the hidden mechanisms of state monads or other concepts abundantly scattered through here. Those things are too low-level nuts and bolts, and they are explained sufficiently in other materials. For those of you who need a lesson on monad stacks and monad transformers, I recommend the great Haskell books *Get Programming With Haskell* by Will Kurt (Manning, 2018; www.manning.com/books/get-programming-with-haskell) and *Haskell in Depth* by Vitaly Bragilevsky (Manning, 2021; www.manning.com/books/haskell-in-depth).

Running a state monadic script, however, should be demonstrated. Many monads have this notion of running, including the state monad, the free monad, and, for example, the STM (software transactional memory) monad. For the state monad, it's a no-brainer, really. You just need to specify the initial state (for example, the Age variable set to 111) and the script itself. The runState function will then consume those two arguments and produce the final state among the values the script wants to return:

```
runState
  :: State state returnValue
  -> state
  -> (state, returnValue)
```

Consider the test that passes:

```
import Control.Monad.State (runState)

spec :: Spec
spec =
  it "Age script" $ do
    let (msgs, s) = runState bornAndGettingOlderTwice 111

    s `shouldBe` 2
    msgs `shouldBe` [ "You're now older for 1 year: 1"
                    , "You're now older for 1 year: 2"
                    , "Your age now: 2"
                    ]
```

We simply ensure that the return value s is 2 and the log is what we expect it to be.

Alright! It's cool, brilliant, amazing, exciting—learning state monads with such toy programs—definitely the level of maturity we deserve!

But I'm sure you'll expect that if I start talking about some concept, I have a plan to utilize it for our main tasks. Greatly appreciated in code bases, the state monad has many faces and forms, some of which can be joined with other monads to achieve similar state-like behavior. I'm talking about the StateT monad transformer, which can wrap around any other monad and make its scripts purely stateful. Our custom-crafted monads LogicControl and Hdl can also be empowered by StateT. With almost no additional effort, we'll get stateful scripts with less boilerplate than with argument-passing state. Are you ready to talk about it?

7.2.3 *Bringing pure state into your monadic eDSLs*

From the developer's perspective, monad transformers such as StateT do the same thing as their counterpart monads such as State. StateT brings a pseudo-mutable pure state into monadic chains with the same functions to deal with it: get and put. The difference is that apart from this StateT, another monad of your choice will be fully available, with only a little bit of ceremony. Technically speaking, the StateT monad transformer wraps another monad and thus forms a two-layer monadic stack:

```
someFunc :: StateT someState internalMonad someOutput
```

> **TIP** I certainly want to help you understand monad transformers, and this is why I wrote two appendixes (B and C) about monad transformers.

Let me introduce you to a very common monadic stack with StateT on the top and IO on the bottom (figure 7.6).

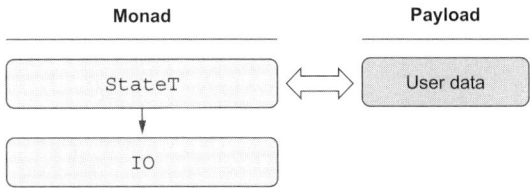

Figure 7.6 `StateT` and `IO` **monadic stack**

I'm sure I've seen two or three monad tutorials with this stack helping people in game development. For example, if we wanted to implement a Minesweeper game with it, we could go with the following definitions.

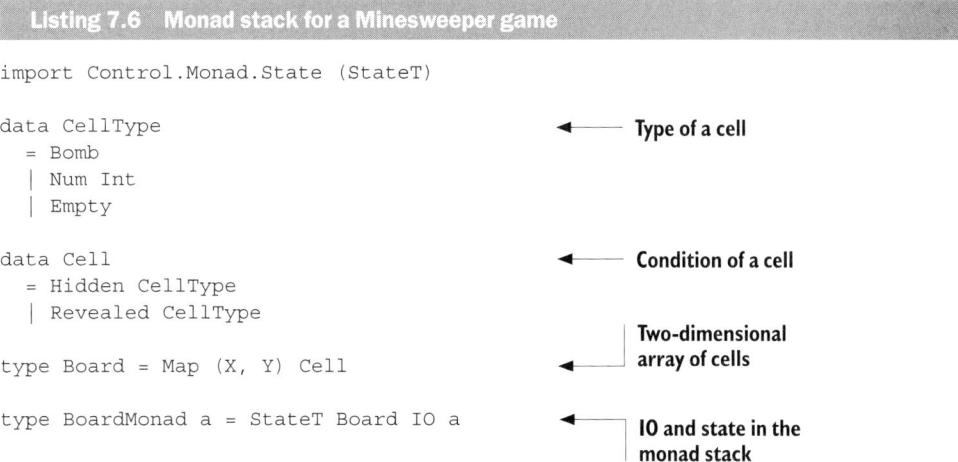

Listing 7.6 Monad stack for a Minesweeper game

```
import Control.Monad.State (StateT)

data CellType                          ◄──── Type of a cell
  = Bomb
  | Num Int
  | Empty

data Cell                              ◄──── Condition of a cell
  = Hidden CellType
  | Revealed CellType

type Board = Map (X, Y) Cell           ◄──── Two-dimensional
                                             array of cells

type BoardMonad a = StateT Board IO a  ◄──── IO and state in the
                                             monad stack
```

This `BoardMonad` will have some state (a value of `Board`) and will also be able to do `IO` calls. Figure 7.7 corresponds to this type.

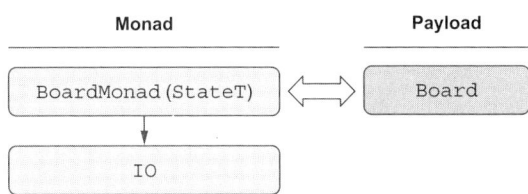

Figure 7.7 A board monad stack

To reveal a cell and update cell state, we could write a script that asks the board for the context, checks the cell, updates it, and puts the new board back into the context. During this process, we may print something about the cell to the console with an impure invocation of `putStrLn`.

Listing 7.7   Lifting of IO actions

```
import Control.Monad.State (get, put, lift)

revealCell :: (X, Y) -> BoardMonad ()
revealCell (x, y) = do
  board <- get

  lift (putStrLn ("Trying cell " <> show (x, y)))          ◄─── Lifts the IO action

  case Map.lookup (x, y) board of
    Nothing            -> lift (putStrLn "No such cell.")
    Just (Revealed _)  -> lift (putStrLn "Already revealed.")
    Just (Hidden Bomb) -> lift (putStrLn "It's bomb! You loose!")
    Just (Hidden c)    -> do
      let newBoard = Map.insert (x, y) (Revealed c) board
      put newBoard
      lift (putStrLn "Cell revealed.")
```

There are two things to note in this script. First, StateT is a monad itself, so the do-notation works as usual. Second, we must wrap IO calls with the lift function because the monad of the do block is StateT, not IO. Therefore, the lift function plays the role of an adapter between the monads in the stack:

```
lift :: IO a -> StateT Board IO a

-- the same:
lift :: IO a -> BoardMonad a
```

Or course, other monad stacks will have their own lift function. If you decide to build a longer monad stack, you'll be doing more liftings in a row. Take a look at figure 7.8 for an advanced monadic state with two state monads in a row.

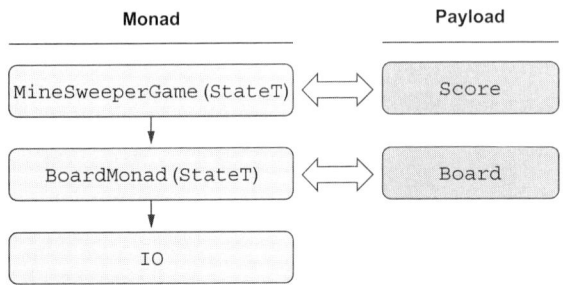

Figure 7.8   A three-layer monadic stack

It shows that we now have two distinct StateT contexts, each of which has its own user data to maintain: board in the middle and game score on top of the stack. This is the new type that nests the previously crafted BoardMonad, so it adds its own dimension above it:

```
type Score = Int
type MinesweeperGame a = StateT Score BoardMonad a
```

To me, this looks strange. Why not just join the two state types into a single one and keep only the `StateT` monad?

```
type SomeGame a = StateT (Score, Board) IO a
```

That's totally valid and is probably better for many reasons, such as simplicity, convenience, and clarity. However, I want to show you how to do double lifting, so I prepared a `printGame` function for you.

Listing 7.8 Two state monads

```
printGame :: MinesweeperGame ()
printGame = do

  score <- get                          ← No lifting
  board <- lift get                     ← Lifts once

  lift (lift (putStrLn (               ← Lifts twice
    "Score: " <> show score
    <> ", board: " <> show board
    )))
```

To access the top `Score` context, no lifting is required. But the `Board` context is one layer down, so we do lifting once. For IO actions, we must do double lifting, like in the previous code snippet. So it seems that this concept of monad transformers and long monad stacks is a clever trick that doesn't have a direct analog in OOP.

Another thing we should discuss about the state monad stacks is running. When we had just one state monad, running once would be enough to enroll the stack. You could do this with any of the three following functions:

```
runState  :: State st a -> st -> (st, a)   ← Returns the final state and the result
execState :: State st a -> st -> st         ← Returns the final state
evalState :: State st a -> st -> a           ← Returns the result
```

You pick one depending on what result you need: the final state, the final value, or both. Obviously, the same functions should exist for `StateT`, and they really do. These functions don't bother with the inner monad, but when the `StateT` layer is run, you get an action in this inner monad instead of just a value:

```
runStateT  :: Monad m => StateT s m a -> s -> m (a, s)
execStateT :: Monad m => StateT s m a -> s -> m s
evalStateT :: Monad m => StateT s m a -> s -> m a
```

This makes running a `StateT` script trickier. Every time you run `StateT`, you do not get a pure value but rather an action of the next monad in the stack. Then you must repeat the procedure for every monad in the stack.

Let's study `execStateT`. Running a `MinesweeperGame a` script, such as `printGame`, with it twice would give you the following types:

```
execStateT :: MinesweeperGame a -> Score -> BoardMonad Score
execStateT :: BoardMonad a       -> Board -> IO Board
```

The first execution returns a `BoardMonad` script, and the second execution returns an `IO` script. And you know exactly what to do with the `IO` script now. To demonstrate the calls, I wrote two tests that pass.

Listing 7.9   Running the monad stack in tests

```
board1 :: Board
board1 = Map.fromList
  [ ( (1, 1), Hidden Empty )
  , ( (2, 2), Hidden Bomb  )
  ]

board2 :: Board
board2 = Map.fromList
  [ ( (1, 1), Revealed Empty )
  , ( (2, 2), Hidden Bomb  )
  ]

spec :: Spec                                              Runs StateT
spec =
  describe "StateT monad tests" $ do
    it "BoardMonad stack" $ do                            Runs IO
      let runBoard = runStateT (revealCell (1, 1)) board1
      (_, board') <- runBoard
      board' `shouldBe` board2
                                                          Runs StateT
    it "MinesweeperGame stack" $ do
      let runGame  :: BoardMonad Score = execStateT printGame 0
      let runBoard :: IO Board = execStateT runGame board1
                                                          Runs StateT
      board' <- runBoard
      board' `shouldBe` board1                            Runs IO
```

You can see here that we start running from the `printGame` stateful computation. This gives us the first layer of the monad stack skinned out and another computation to run (`runGame`). We execute the state monad once more and get an IO computation `runBoard` as a result. Then we evaluate it, which finally kicks off all the effects of the `printGame` script.

A brief note—for some Haskell-specific reason, the `BoardMonad` data type is defined a bit differently in the sources as

```
type BoardMonad = StateT Board IO
```

instead of

```
type BoardMonad a = StateT Board IO a
```

This shrinking of the return type parameter seems strange, but due to limitations of Haskell's type system, this is the only form that will allow us to define the `Minesweeper-Game` data type:

```
type MinesweeperGame a = StateT Score BoardMonad a
```

This topic is irrelevant to us, but I hope you won't be surprised when playing with the code.

Now, after those preparations, it should not be difficult to construct a stateful `Logic-Control` scenario and remove that ugly boilerplate. Although our `LogicControl` is a free eDSL, it's a monad and therefore will work fine with `StateT`. A new monad stack called `ShipControl` will look like

```
import Control.Monad.State (StateT, put, get, lift)

type ShipControl a = StateT SpaceshipModel LogicControl a
```

You can see it in figure 7.9.

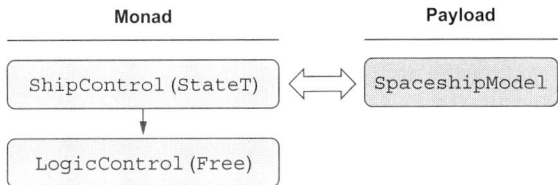

Figure 7.9 Monad stack for stateful ship control scripting

Now we're able to write a stateful logic for ship control. Let me repeat a part of the `performRotation` function here:

```
performRotation :: SpaceshipModel -> Angle -> LogicControl SpaceshipModel
performRotation model angle = do
  let thrusterCtrl = smRotationThruster model
  let shipMass1   = spMass (smSpaceshipProperties model)

  ...
```

The `model` variable is no longer needed, as it went into the context of the state monad. Liberating the interface of this function from one argument makes it more direct and clear:

```
performRotation :: Angle -> ShipControl ()          ◄─── New monad
performRotation angle = do
  model :: SpaceshipModel <- get                    ◄─── Accessing the state

  let thrusterCtrl = smRotationThruster model
  let shipMass1   = spMass (smSpaceshipProperties model)
```

Some other changes relate to the fact that we've replaced the monad. Specifically, we must lift all the functions operating in the `LogicControl` monad. We have two of them—`getProperty` and `validateTorque`:

```
eMbTorqueProp <- lift (getProperty thrusterCtrl "torque" [])
torque        <- lift (validateTorque eMbTorqueProp)
```

These two functions didn't change, so we can reuse the whole set of functions developed earlier if we want to. Backward compatibility is somewhat preserved.

The following listing contains a complete `performRotation` script.

Listing 7.10 The stateful script for performing rotation

```
performRotation :: Angle -> ShipControl ()             ◀——— Stateful script
performRotation angle = do

  model :: SpaceshipModel <- get                       ◀——— Getting the state

  let thrusterCtrl = smRotationThruster model
  let shipMass1 = spMass (smSpaceshipProperties model)

  eMbTorqueProp <- lift (getProperty thrusterCtrl "torque" [])   ◀——— Lifting
  torque        <- lift (validateTorque eMbTorqueProp)

  let impulse1  = calcAngularImpulse shipMass1 torque
  let shipMass2 = recalcMass shipMass1 impulse1
  let impulse2  = calcAngularImpulse shipMass1 torque
  let shipMass3 = recalcMass shipMass2 impulse2
  let (burnStart, burnStop, time) = calcBurn impulse1 impulse2 angle

  performBurn thrusterCtrl burnStart               -- mass changes
  lift (wait time)
  performBurn thrusterCtrl burnStop                -- mass changes
```

Notice that I invoked `performBurn` as it was in the `ShipControl` monad. Because of this, we expect that this function will update the `SpaceshipModel` state once it burns some fuel. At least, its type allows it:

```
performBurn :: Controller -> Burn -> ShipControl ()
```

Internally, it should interact with various sublanguages to force up the engine. No matter how, let's just assume it does.

Now what if you have a `LogicControl` script and you need to run `ShipControl` from it? Intuitively, this looks like a violation of the monadic stack hierarchy. `ShipControl` is the boss of `LogicControl`, not vice versa. But nothing can stop us from running a `ShipControl` script and getting some internal `LogicControl` action that we can then run within the initial `LogicControl` script:

```
someShipControl :: ShipControl ()

myShipModel :: SpaceshipModel

someLogicControl :: LogicControl ()
someLogicControl = do
  let internal :: LogicControl () = evalStateT someShipControl myShipModel
  internal
```

For this, we certainly need an initial state for `evalStateT`, which is `myShipModel` here. The following listing demonstrates the use of the idea to first create a spaceship and then rotate it while staying in the `LogicControl` environment.

Listing 7.11 The stateful script for performing rotation

```
import Control.Monad.State (execStateT)

spaceshipRotation :: LogicControl SpaceshipModel
spaceshipRotation = do

  mainEngineCtrl <- evalHdl createMainEngine
  thrusterCtrl   <- evalHdl createRotaryThruster

  let shipProps  = SpaceshipProperties (Kilogram 100000.0)
  let shipModel1 = SpaceshipModel shipProps mainEngineCtrl thrusterCtrl

  shipModel2 <- execStateT (performRotation (Radian 100.0)) shipModel1

  pure shipModel2
```

In this case, state becomes localized, defined for only a part of business logic, namely for the `performRotation` function. It's only a virtual state—nothing actually mutates during its evaluation. You could achieve the same with argument passing, but sometimes introducing `StateT` makes your scripts more convenient and concise.

At this point, we transformed our business logic into a stateful application without adding new features, without sacrificing purity, and without bringing that much complexity. It's really good stuff. Congratulations!

I wish I could say that wrapping `LogicControl` into `StateT` doesn't affect the framework we've built. Unfortunately, this is untrue. This won't compile in Haskell:

```
type LogicControl a = Free LogicControlMethod a
type ShipControl a = StateT SpaceshipModel LogicControl a

> Compilation error: The type synonym 'LogicControl' should have 1 argument,
but has been given none
```

We must convert `LogicControl` to a newtype and redefine all the instances of `Functor`, `Applicative`, and `Monad` we had previously defined from the free monadic type. After that, we'll be able to put `LogicControl` into `StateT`. If you're not familiar with those concepts, it's okay. I'll show you how to derive the instances with the `GeneralizedNewtypeDeriving` feature:

```
{-# LANGUAGE GeneralizedNewtypeDeriving #-}
newtype LogicControl a = LogicControl (Free LogicControlMethod a)
  deriving (Functor, Applicative, Monad)
type ShipControl a = StateT SpaceshipModel LogicControl a
```

Fortunately, not a single word of business logic code is affected. We must fix interpreters, though. Some unwrapping will be necessary for this `newtype`, and hopefully, it's not a big deal:

```
runLogicControl :: LogicControl a -> IO a
runLogicControl (LogicControl lControl) = ...
```

I'm certainly not giving you all the explanations for this logic because it will lead us into the depths of Haskell. A curious reader may want to look for materials on partial type synonyms and undecidability.

7.2.4   *Impure mutable state*

While our business logic should stay pure, the implementation behind the eDLSs is free from such limitations. Interpreters are impure by default; hence, they can deal with mutable values and collections. Of course, you could keep some of your free interpreters pure if that makes sense for a specific language, but I'd expect them all to be in the IO environment.

This makes even more sense if we bring the question of performance to the table. Sometimes, you can be pleased with pure persistent data structures, which are efficient enough for many cases. However, C-like arrays, which are guaranteed to be continuous, fast, and efficient, are also impure and destructively mutable. Impure mutable data structures can do all the stuff we like in imperative languages, are less demanding to memory, can be mutated in place, and can even be marshaled to low-level code in C. This is what your interpreters may do behind the interpretable eDSLs, and I find it very similar to what OOP interfaces and implementation classes do.

Scala, Haskell, F#, PureScript—all of these languages have their own tools for that. There is some intersection between them, though. You may or may not find the following Haskell things in your language, but they're worth learning anyway:

- Haskell's `IORef` variable has the same semantics as regular variables in other languages. It can be mutated in place, making potential problems (nondeterminism, race conditions, and so on) the developer's responsibility. The `IORef a` type represents a reference type over some type a. In Scala, there are various mutable references from various libraries, not to mention the actual mutability Scala provides.

- `MVar` is a concept of thread-safe mutable variables. Unlike the `IORef`, this reference type guarantees atomic reading and writing. `MVar` can be used for communication between threads or managing simple use cases with data structures. Still, it's susceptible to the same problems: race conditions, deadlocks, and nondeterminism. Scala also has `MVar`s with a similar interface.

- `TVar`, `TMVar`, `TQueue`, `TArray`, and other STM primitives can be considered further steps in the development of the `MVar` concept. STM primitives are thread safe and imperatively mutable, but unlike `MVar`, STM introduces transactions. Every mutation is performed in a transaction. When two threads compete to access the variable, one of two transactions will be performed, while the other can be safely delayed (be retried) or even rolled back. STM operations are isolated from each other, which reduces the possibility of deadlock. With the advanced combinatorial implementation of STM, two separate transactional operations can be combined into a bigger transactional operation that's also an STM combinator. STM is considered a suitable approach for maintaining complex state in Haskell programs; that said, STM has many characteristics and properties one should know in order to use it effectively.

In chapters 4, 5, and 6, we've already introduced `IORef`s in the code. It wasn't a thorough discussion, though. I just demonstrated a couple of design options and promised to talk about them later. In chapter 4, we talked about services and the Service Handle pattern. We found a way to mock services, which in turn helped us write unit tests. A mocked service could report its internal state to the outside by writing into the corresponding `IORef` variable. There was the hardware service and a counter that counts the invocations of `getDevicePart`.

Listing 7.12 An `IORef` application example

```
mockedHardwareService :: IORef Int -> HardwareService
mockedHardwareService counterRef = HardwareService
  { getDevicePart = mockedGetDevicePart counterRef
  }

mockedGetDevicePart
  :: IORef Int
  -> ComponentIndex
  -> Device
  -> IO (Maybe DevicePart)
mockedGetDevicePart counterRef idx device = do
  modifyIORef' counterRef (+1)
  ...
```

In chapter 5, the interpreters of the various eDSLs were done statefully. All we needed for that was a specific, implementation-layer–only data structure called `Runtime`. This structure contains everything for the interpreters to operate, including the internal state, temporary values, configs, database or network connections, thread pools, and threads themselves. This all should be hidden from the business logic, but at the same time, not one application can work without this mutable, operational data:

```
data Runtime = Runtime
  { _devicesRef         :: IORef Devices
  , _hardwareServiceRef :: IORef HardwareService
  }

interpretLogicControlMethod :: Runtime -> LogicControlMethod  -> IO ()

runLogicControl :: Runtime -> LogicControl -> IO ()
```

I can easily imagine an interpretable eDSL for a Turing-complete programming language that will be doing its work with the runtime. Let's say it's Brainfuck. Do you remember what programs look like in this language?

Listing 7.13   Brainfuck actions and a program

```
incPointer    = ">"                                    ◄──── Available language terms
decPointer    = "<"
incVal        = "+"
decVal        = "-"
input         = ","
output        = "."
jumpForward   = "["
jumpBackward  = "]"


type BFProgram = String                                ◄──── Program is just a string.


helloWorld :: BFProgram
helloWorld =
    "++++++++[>++++[>++>+++>+++>+<<<<-]>+>+>->>        ◄──── Multiline string
    +[<]<-]>>.>---.+++++++..+++.>>.<-.<.+++.--
    ----.--------.>>+.>++."
```

And while being declarative and interpretable, those single-symbol commands mandate that the interpreter does mutable actions over a set of mutable cells. We can naturally place these cells into the runtime of the interpreter. The following listing outlines this idea in a simple form.

Listing 7.14   Brainfuck language definition

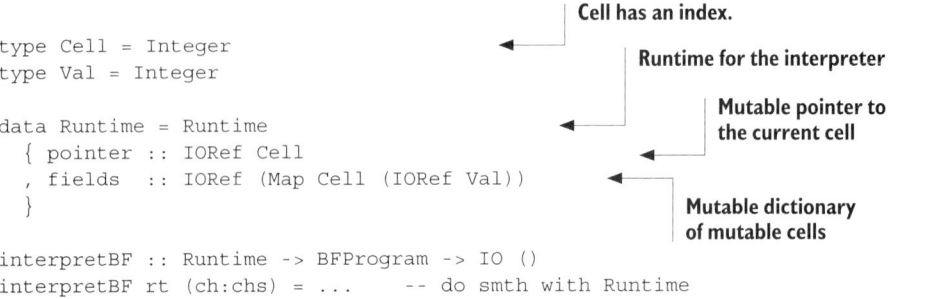

```
type Cell = Integer                          Cell has an index.
type Val = Integer
                                             Runtime for the interpreter
data Runtime = Runtime
  { pointer :: IORef Cell                    Mutable pointer to
  , fields  :: IORef (Map Cell (IORef Val))  the current cell
  }
                                             Mutable dictionary
interpretBF :: Runtime -> BFProgram -> IO () of mutable cells
interpretBF rt (ch:chs) = ...      -- do smth with Runtime
```

The type of the interpreter function says this for itself: by having an operational state (Runtime), we pop symbols of the program one by one and do something mutable over the cells we have. There is something deep about the idea of interpretable programming languages and DSLs. Compare the interpretBF function with interpret-Recipe from chapter 6:

```
interpretRecipe :: IORef Ingredients -> SandwichRecipe Sandwich
                -> IO Sandwich
interpretBF     :: Runtime           -> BFProgram
                -> IO ()
```

There is an operational state, a script to run, and a result. It feels so natural to implement programming languages this way, and it looks like the name "domain-specific languages" is really justified, in contrast to many other software engineering terms.

Of course, real software today gets more complicated than our toy examples. The fact that we mostly deal with concurrency makes IORefs an unfortunate tool for keeping internal data. In such a concrete application as an HTTP backend, a RESTful server should be able to respond to parallel, concurrent requests and not mess things up in the operational state. This means that data in runtimes should be designed as thread-safe, with the help of corresponding data structures (MVars or STM):

```
data Runtime = Runtime
  { _devicesRef         :: MVar Devices
  , _hardwareServiceRef :: MVar HardwareService
  }
```

Approaches to concurrency can be difficult and intimidating to someone with a limited background in multithreading. We absolutely need this knowledge in our everyday practice, but we don't have to learn the whole subject. Instead, we'll learn some very convenient approaches, such as concurrent MVars and STM, and we'll see that even this accidental complexity can be beaten and controlled.

Summary

- Functional programming doesn't prohibit state. It does the opposite—it provides new ideas for building safe and carefully designed stateful applications.

- State can be pure and impure. Pure business logic may deal with pure state, while implementation can deal with an impure, mutable one.

- There is only one immutable state handling approach: the argument-passing state. Everything else is built on top of it.

- State monads help handle immutable state in a convenient monadic form when dealing with state; it feels like it's imperative, although it's functional and combinatorial.

- State in state monads is kept in the context of this monad and can be updated during a monadic computation.

- Internally, state monads utilize an argument-passing state.

- State monads can empower the way we structure our monadic applications by separating state from regular function arguments.

- State monad transformers are the next development stage of state monads.

- You can maintain several state contexts with a stack of state monads, or you can put all your data into a single state monad context.

- An impure mutable state exists in all industrial functional languages. In Haskell, it's IORefs, MVars, vectors, and STM.

- Sometimes, impure state works better in terms of performance or convenience. It's important to organize the program so that controlling the impure state is easy and safe.

Reactive applications

This chapter covers

- The actor model and how to design it
- The MVar Request–Response pattern
- How to create a stateful concurrent simulator
- More information on reactive architectures

Looking back at the work we have done so far, we can be proud of ourselves. We have learned a lot, discussed many interesting ideas in software design, and tackled a variety of engineering problems. The solutions and approaches we've explored are all part of functional declarative design—a methodology for building applications from end to end in functional languages. This chapter provides the final proof that the methodology really works. We're going to assemble many parts of our Andromeda software and produce its final result—the simulator. I promised we'd do it, and here we are!

This is a good time to talk about reactive applications. Our simulator is an application with individual parts that are able to react to something. "Individual" here means that the parts will have their own threads, and they will act as small, separate applications. In other words, this chapter will slightly touch on a specific reactive model of interactions—namely, the actor model.

204

This also means that we should talk about concurrency. Actors can be implemented even in a single-threaded environment, and they will have all the properties of a concurrent system. You won't be able to tell this system apart from a truly multithreaded one without additional scrutiny. Regardless, a single-threaded concurrency is rarely a go-to system for production codebases. Our actor model will be characteristically multithreaded, with concurrent behavior and state. And by the way, the knowledge about state handling obtained from the previous chapter will be significantly improved.

8.1 Actor model

Most of the physical characteristics of a flight are dynamic and time dependent. The mass of a ship changes while the engines are burning and fuel is being consumed. The ship coordinates change in relation to pivotal objects, such as stars and planets. The ship may rotate along some axis, and this is also a variable characteristic to consider.

The math of this process isn't simple—it's differential equations all down the road. Given some inputs, a formula will expectedly return a single result. For example, there is Tsiolkovsky's formula for a rocket-like motion required to calculate the mass of fuel and the ship so that it is possible to launch it into the orbit. For a vessel in space, there are many formulas that describe the dynamic life of all the interconnected systems. Having a good equation for motion means having an efficient, safe flight. But it's hardly possible to have everything precalculated. Survival of an expedition often depends on how well those formulas react to new data coming from the environment. The same formulas should then be alive and be fed by data to produce new results constantly.

This all sounds like a good task for reactive programming. Actors, reactive streams, custom-crafted event-driven models, or other exotic reactive models—all of these approaches may help to organize the environment for your spaceship's formulas to live in. And we should learn some of them to explore this area of software design.

8.1.1 Simulation of actors

With a sampling period, sensors can produce measurements and push them to whatever the consumer wants to consume. Controllers may sit on top of the data flow and evaluate calculations on the fly, thus making decisions on the commands that should be propagated to the devices. The navigation system can make small corrections to the route according to the program established by a central computer. All the systems and devices act like musicians in a symphony of a spaceship flight.

Conceptually, devices can be seen as actors, all of them having a state, lifetime, public interface, and a specified behavior. Each device will then represent a separate process, thread, or even machine. It doesn't really matter what implementation is selected for the actor model. To make it work, there should also be a certain medium, an environment for the devices to communicate through. Again, the options are various: message brokers, a database, an event bus, or something else. This really depends on your high-level requirements and the constraints you have to comply with. Two of the options are presented in figure 8.1. The left picture treats a network displaced system as separate actors with the TCP/IP communication channel between them. It may not be a true message broker, but you can put Kafka between the computers, and you'll get it. The right side of the figure supposes that there is a queue in between (perhaps Kafka, RabbitMQ, or something like that).

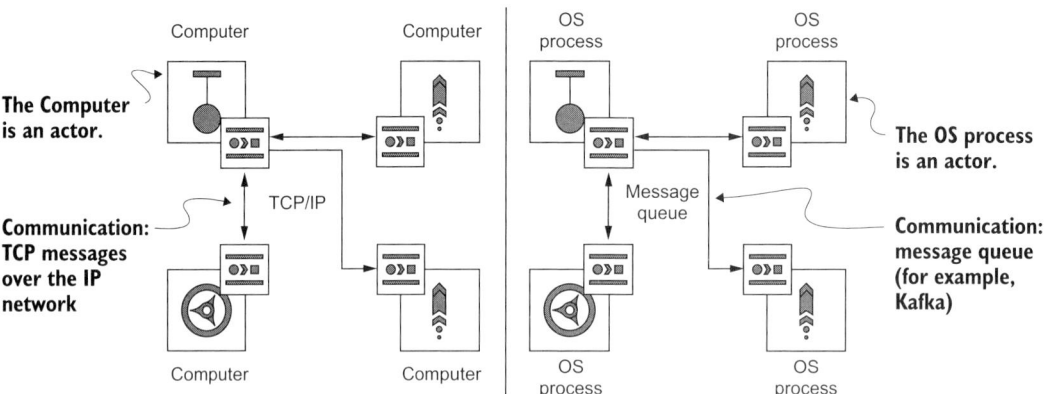

Figure 8.1   Two-actor model implementations

In our case, the environment will only be limited by a single application—the simulator. The parts of a spaceship will act independently, being individual green (lightweight) threads. The simulator will then be responsible for the orchestration of their lifetimes and interactions, but it should not be visible to them. All the actors should be unaware of the environment they are evaluated in. The ship model therefore becomes a virtual reality, and we can expect it to behave similarly to the real spaceship. See figure 8.2 for more hints.

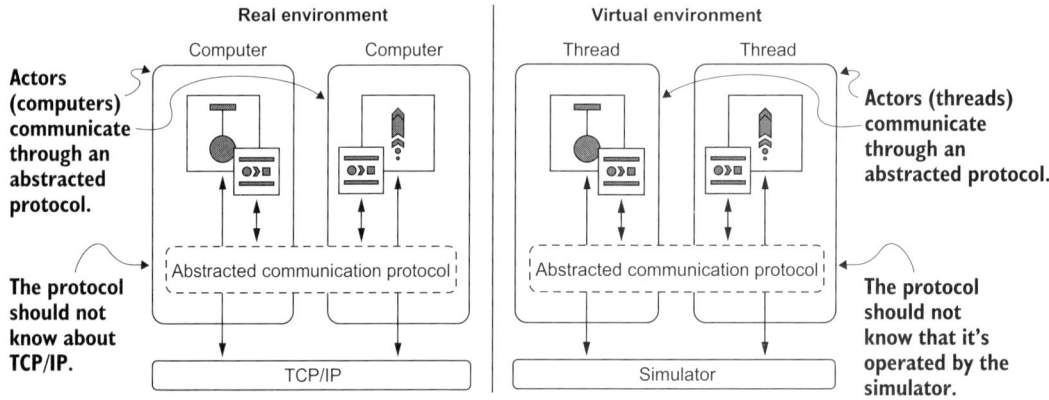

Figure 8.2   Real environment and virtual environment

As you can see, we rely on an abstracted communication protocol that hides the underlying world. The protocol described in terms of requests and responses will be a contract, an interface, or an agreement all the actors should be comfortable with. So we can say the protocol is a part of our domain or even a glue for the agents in our simulation model.

Obviously, we'll obtain the simulation model from our logic control scripts, because what else could play this role for us? They will be exactly the scripts we've been developing using the domain-driven design approach—nothing extra is needed, and no changes are expected. Embedded domain-specific languages such as `Hdl` are therefore appropriate for both worlds. They are interfaces to real subsystems, so a spaceship engineer assumes they can program a real spaceship using them. Simultaneously, the scripts will define all the properties of the simulated actors. This transformation from scripts to a simulator model can be called *compilation* (figure 8.3).

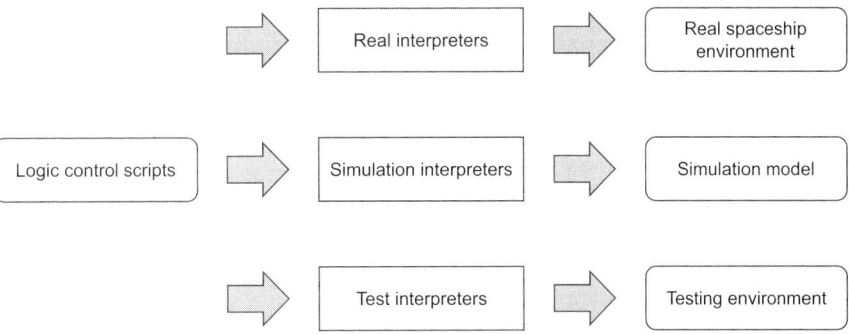

Figure 8.3   Compilation from logic control scripts to specific environments

Again, it's another proof that interpreting can do powerful things. This is certainly a conceptual idea we'll be implementing. But before that, we should discuss specific technical details about the simulator.

8.1.2   *The architecture of the simulator*

The compilation of the simulation model is about traversing our interpretable eDSLs and scripts. We'll write new interpreters for that, and they will be quite the same structurally but will mind their own business. New interpreters should not know about the real ones and should not interfere with them, and in general, the code of the simulator can be (and ideally should be) placed into a separate project or repository. We'll keep it simple and put the simulator close to the real code. This is a selected list of simulator modules:

```
./src/Andromeda/Simulator
./src/Andromeda/Simulator/Hardware/Interpreters/DeviceControl.hs
./src/Andromeda/Simulator/Hardware/Interpreters/Hdl.hs
./src/Andromeda/Simulator/Hardware/Device.hs
./src/Andromeda/Simulator/LogicControl/Interpreter.hs
./src/Andromeda/Simulator/Control.hs
./src/Andromeda/Simulator/Runtime.hs
```

This structure is already familiar to us. Free monadic architecture comes with this best practice. We again see the `Runtime` module, the `Device` module, and some interpreters. The uniformity of the simulator and the real code eases the navigation across the projects. Following this best practice is highly recommended, although it might not be the perfect way to organize the code. We don't say other big frameworks, such as Ruby on Rails, are perfect, but once you join an RoR project, you can expect that your experience is finally applicable. So "the best" here means pragmatic, time saving, and well spread. We want to help developers focus their efforts on important things, such as business logic, edge cases, and tests, so we do not spend much time inventing new ways of doing things. Let me demonstrate the simulator architecture (figure 8.4).

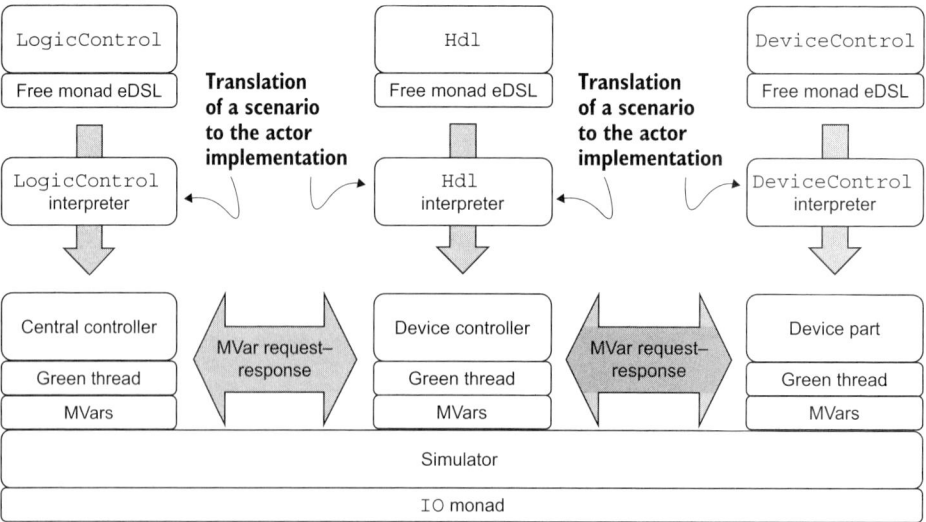

Figure 8.4   Architecture of the simulator

This is the same three-layered architecture with a new implementation layer. Having three distinct implementations for the same interface ("real" for the simulator tests) confirms that the free monadic architecture does indeed have power similar to interfaces in other languages.

Now we have many architectural questions about the simulator to answer before we can jump into the code. Check out a short list of definitions here:

- *What is an actor?* Every device in the network that has a controller is an actor. All the communication will go through the controller, and there will be no way to directly access the internal components of a device.
- *What are actors technically?* They are green threads with their own behavior, mutable state, and lifetime.
- *Are the actors independent?* Generally, actors should be isolated and should not know about each other. However, we'll implement a hierarchy of actors while

following our logic control scripts. You can consult figure 5.3: it shows a central computer that keeps track of the four subordinate controller devices.

- *How do the actors exchange data and communicate?* We'll adopt a certain design pattern for that—it's called the *MVar Request–Response pattern*. Our environment is multithreaded, so we should do it carefully. This pattern makes it easy for several distinct threads to talk without race conditions and deadlocks. For this to happen, we'll need to utilize concurrent mutable variables (MVars) in a certain way. We'll learn more about this pattern in the next section. Also, we could take STM (software transactional memory) instead of MVars. Although a better choice for this task, STM is beyond the scope of this chapter. We'll learn about it in future chapters.

- *How do the actors manage their internal state?* When necessary, actor workers will keep their data in MVars.

There is one more consideration about the actor model. I highly recommend expanding your horizons and reading more about Alan Kay's OOP (https://mng.bz/QZd1)!

8.1.3 *The MVar Request–Response pattern*

The idea behind a concurrently *mutable variable* (MVar) is pretty simple. The variable of the `MVar a` type may hold one value of type `a` or hold nothing. The MVar mutation is a real mutation in the sense of imperative programming, but what's important is that it's thread safe. As the notion of the MVar involves mutation, it works on the `IO` layer. The MVar interface consists of the creation functions

```
newEmptyMVar :: IO (MVar a)
newMVar      :: a -> IO (MVar a)
```

and the blocking functions for reading and writing contents:

```
takeMVar :: MVar a -> IO a
putMVar  :: MVar a -> a -> IO ()
```

A value of type `MVar a` comes in two states: either empty or full. When empty, every thread that calls `takeMVar` will wait until it's full. Conversely, when the MVar is full, a thread that calls `putMVar` will wait until it's empty. Concurrency means that threads can't access the MVar simultaneously; they must wait their turn (first in, first out), and that's why the MVar can't have an invalid state. But classic deadlocks are still possible. Each taking of an MVar with `takeMVar` should be paired by `putMVar` sooner or later. A badly organized branching in the code may lead to no `putMVar` called. While this specific thread continues doing its job, the variable is still owned, and other threads will just hang forever.

> **TIP** MVars have other problems you might want to know about. To learn more about these, consider reading *Parallel and Concurrent Programming in Haskell* by Simon Marlow (O'Reilly, 2013).

With MVars, it's possible to construct a remote service that works in a separate thread, waits until a request is pushed, processes it, and pushes the result back. This is known as the MVar Request–Response pattern. Let's take a look at its structure.

The MVar Request–Response pattern operates with two MVars: one for the request and one for the response. These MVars together represent a communication channel that can abstract any kind of interaction between two threads, namely a requester and a respondent. The basic idea and workflow are shown in figure 8.5.

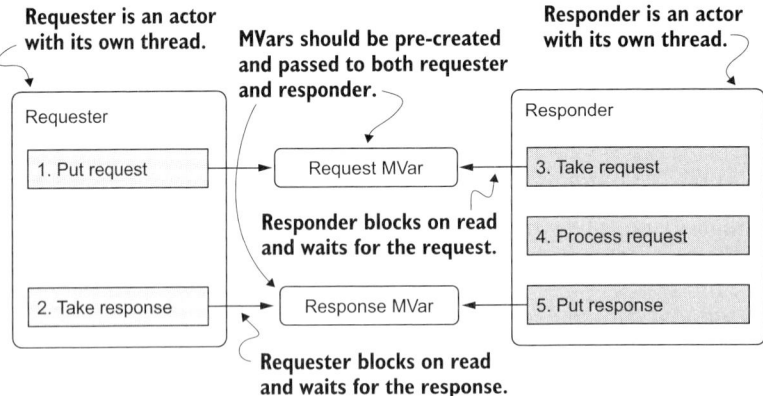

Figure 8.5   The MVar Request–Response pattern flow

The requester performs two steps:

1 Puts a value into the request MVar
2 Takes the result from the response MVar

If the responder isn't ready to accept the request, step 1 will make the requester wait. Step 2 will block the requester if the processor is busy processing the previous request.

The responder does the opposite. It performs the following three steps:

3 Takes the request value from the request MVar
4 Processes the request to get the response
5 Puts the response into the response MVar

If a request hasn't been placed yet, step 3 will block the responder until this is done. Step 5 can block the responder if the requester hasn't had time to extract the previous response.

This is the description. Now let's demonstrate this pattern in an example. We'll create a separate thread that receives a number and converts it to a FizzBuzz word. We'll also create the number generator thread that puts requests, waits for results, and prints them. Let's start by defining the `Pipe` type, the `createPipe` function, and the generic function `sendRequest`.

Listing 8.1 A simple Request–Response pattern

```
type Request a   = MVar a
type Response b  = MVar b
type Pipe a b    = (Request a, Response b)

createPipe :: IO (Pipe a b)
createPipe = do
  request  <- newEmptyMVar
  response <- newEmptyMVar
  pure (request, response)

sendRequest :: Pipe a b -> a -> IO b
sendRequest (request, response) a = do
  putMVar request a
  takeMVar response
```

◄ ── **Request channel**

◄ ── **Response channel**

◄ ── **Bidirectional channel (pipe)**

◄ ── **Initializes the channel**

◄ ── **Sends a request and waits for a response**

Next, we create a worker function that will listen to the channel forever and process requests when they occur. It returns nothing useful to the client code:

```
worker :: Pipe a b -> (a -> b) -> IO ()
worker (request, response) f = forever $ do
  a <- takeMVar request
  putMVar response (f a)
```

> **TIP**   I used `forever` from the `Control.Monad` module to make the do-block loop indefinitely. I could do that with an explicit recursion, but why not save a line of code here? Nothing changes between the iterations, so this function should fit just fine.

Then we parameterize this worker using our `fizzBuzz` function:

```
fizzBuzz x | isDivided x 15 = "FizzBuzz"
           | isDivided x 5  = "Buzz"
           | isDivided x 3  = "Fizz"
           | otherwise      = show x

isDivided x n = (x `mod` n) == 0

fizzBuzzProcessor :: Pipe Int String -> IO ()
fizzBuzzProcessor pipe = worker pipe fizzBuzz
```

Next, we create the `generator` function that will feed the remote worker forever (now with the explicit recursion):

```
generator :: Pipe Int String -> Int -> IO ()
generator pipe i = do
  result <- sendRequest pipe i
  putStrLn ("[" ++ show i ++ "]: " ++ result)
  generator pipe (i + 1)
```

Almost done! The last step is to fork two threads and see what happens:

```
main = do
  pipe <- createPipe
  forkIO (fizzBuzzProcessor pipe)
  forkIO (generator pipe 0)
  threadDelay 10000000
```

We'll see an infinite request–response session with the FizzBuzz words printed:

```
...
[112370]: Buzz
[112371]: Fizz
[112372]: 112372
[112373]: 112373
...
```

The connection is now established, and two threads play ping-pong flawlessly. When organized carefully, this concurrent interaction won't have any problems, and it wll be straightforward. Still, with such a simple approach, we aren't protected from constructing protocols that allow invalid communication. What is `Pipe a b`, after all? Those types `a` and `b` don't seem to be dependent— they are only related by appearing in the `Pipe` type. Nothing stops us from defining two ADTs for multiple requests and responses and hoping they will be processed correctly. Let me define an abstract protocol for you and demonstrate the problem.

Suppose the requester wants some calculations to be done by the responder and the result transferred back. Only two methods are available: squaring an integer and reversing a string. The protocol may look like this:

```
data Request
  = Square Int
  | Reverse String

data Response
  = Squared Int
  | Reversed String

type CalculationPipe = Pipe Request Response
```

Now a requester risks getting a wrong response back. It wants to `Square 10`, but for some reason, the response is `Reversed "enola em evael"`, which is definitely not what we would expect (`Squared 100`). Certainly, this is not only the problem of the pattern we're discussing here, but it's a common problem specific to any communication protocols—generic HTTP and TCP protocols, custom domain-specific protocols, data exchange between processes, and so on. What reaction a requester should have in front of invalid responses can only be determined case by case, accounting for the requirements for that system and other additional considerations.

An interesting property of our interthread protocol through the MVar Request pattern is that we don't have to risk a possible miscommunication, and we can make it

100% reliable and type safe by design. The pattern will change a little, but only a little, and you'll see how this version empowers the simulator.

8.2 Implementing the simulator

We need to wrap up some things we've learned so far. This is a huge toolbox full of ideas, approaches, and design patterns. However, if you get into the Andromeda project, which is is the pillar of this book, you'll realize there are not that many lines in it. We've tried to keep things easily expressible (domain-specific languages and scripts), carefully separated (the SOLID principles and the "low coupling, high cohesion" principle, pure and impure layers), well-built (the free monad architecture), testable (again, the free monad architecture), modular (all the code bits are nicely organized in the project), concurrently safe (pure immutable state or MVars), and of course, simple (the KISS principle). We've achieved simplicity not because we wanted to make things primitive at any cost but because we followed all those principles and ideas and obtained simplicity as a result. This wasn't easy because we had to learn many new tricks, but it was worth it.

Now we'll craft the last phrase in this long and rich story of Andromeda Control Software implementation. Figure 8.4 outlines nicely the work to be done. We should implement the simulator itself and make it an actor. We also should cast a network of devices that are also actors by design. And we should make them communicate better in a safe, concurrent manner.

8.2.1 Simulator as an actor

Our simulator is an environment in which simulation models can evolve and be tested. Simultaneously, the simulator itself can be a specific actor separated from the application and interfaced with the MVar Request–Response pattern. It will be single user for now, but introducing this protocol between the application and the simulator may help in the future if we want to make it multi-user. The simulator will therefore be placed into its own process driven by a dedicated server, and the MVar request–response protocol will be converted into something like HTTP or gRPC.

Figure 8.6 illustrates the idea of a simulator as an actor.

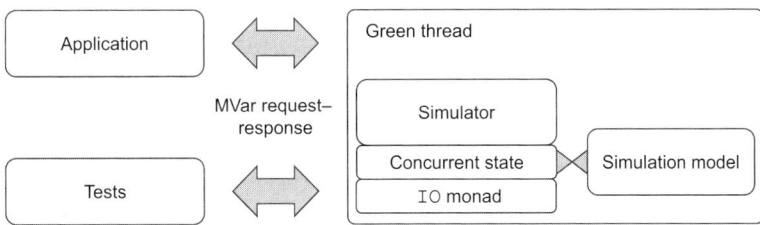

Figure 8.6 Simulator as an actor

Now let's develop a protocol for it. What exact methods should it support? Three of them will be enough: run a simulation, start a simulation, and shut the simulator down. But wait—how is this redundancy in the protocol not a mistake? Why run and start as if they are not synonyms?

In my mind, they are not synonymous. If I needed a simulation model spinning indefinitely inside the simulator, I would start it and would not expect any results. But if my simulation is about to perform a finite number of actions and finish soon, I would rather run it. So *start* implies *no end*, and *run* can be seen as a one-time action.

The request type in the next listing follows this consideration by having two methods with different arguments. Pay attention to the return values of `LogicControl` arguments in `RunSimulation` and `StartSimulation`.

Listing 8.2   Simulator request

```
data SimulatorRequest
  = forall a. RunSimulation (LogicControl a) (RunResult a)
      -- ^ Run the simulation, get the result back

  | StartSimulation (LogicControl ())
      -- ^ start spinning the simulation

  | ShutdownSimulator ShutdownResult
      -- ^ stop the simulation model and finish
```

Two result types in the request are simple and yet interesting because this is essentially the improvement of the MVar Request–Response pattern:

```
newtype RunResult a      = RunResult (MVar a)
newtype ShutdownResult = ShutdownResult (MVar ())
```

What's the idea? We've fused requests and responses into a single data structure and tied a response MVar to its request method. Now the only possible way to properly process the `RunSimulation` method will be to run the simulation, get some result of type a, and fill the MVar from the `RunResult` value. As you can see, the MVar will also be of type a, which is the unavoidable condition provided by the design of the `RunSimulation` method. The a type can be arbitrary, but it should match between the script, its result, and the MVar. What about the `ShutdownResult`, which declares an MVar of unit (())? We don't bother with getting results from the responder in this case. This is not the best design because we might want to know about any problems if termination goes wrong. Consider improving this part of the protocol yourself and see what options there are to indicate problems to the requester.

The scheme of the improved MVar Request–Response pattern is presented in figure 8.7.

We shouldn't count the case when the responder refuses to fill the response MVar because it's a bug and not an acceptable behavior. Apart from that, it is not possible for the responder to send an invalid response.

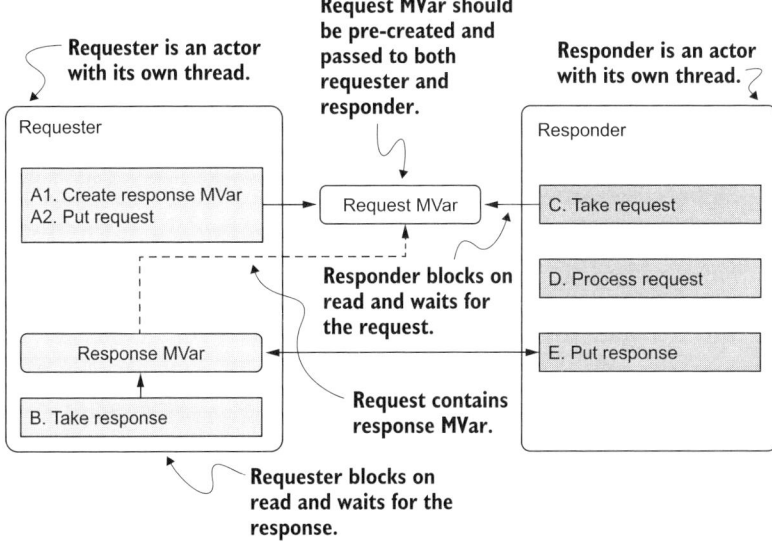

Request MVar should be pre-created and passed to both requester and responder.

Requester is an actor with its own thread.

Responder is an actor with its own thread.

Figure 8.7   Improved MVar Request–Response pattern

TIP   We can also design protocols with sequences of requests, not just separate ones. Try to figure out how to build such a protocol as an exercise.

TIP   The `SimulationRequest` protocol can be easily updated if we want to run multiple simulations within a single simulator. What design would you use to support this requirement?

We've elaborated the protocol, and now it's time to implement the simulator itself. There should be a separate thread for it and a worker function (`simulatorWorker`) that will act forever unless the corresponding request is received. Also, the simulator actor should have its own state, which we call `SimulatorRuntime`. Let's take a look at it.

Listing 8.3   Simulator implementation

```
data SimulatorRuntime = SimulatorRuntime
  { simRtControllerSimsVar
     :: MVar (Map Controller ControllerSim)
  , simRtMessagesVar        :: MVar [String]
  , simRtErrorsVar          :: MVar [String]
  , simSimulationsVar       :: MVar [ThreadId]
  }

simulatorWorker :: SimulatorRuntime -> MVar SimulatorRequest -> IO ()
simulatorWorker runtime requestVar = do
```

Controls structures for actors of the simulation model

Messages to collect by the simulator

Errors to collect by the simulator

Threads of detached simulations

```
    mbRequest <- tryReadMVar requestVar

    case mbRequest of
      Just (RunSimulation lc (RunResult resultVar)) -> do
        result <- runLogicControl runtime lc          ◄──── Calls the
        putMVar resultVar result                              interpreter for the
        threadDelay 1000                                      LogicControl script
        simulatorWorker runtime requestVar
                                                       Forks a separate
      Just (StartSimulation lc) -> do          ◄────── thread for a detached
        simThreadId <- forkIO $ runLogicControl runtime lc   simulation
        sims <- takeMVar $ simSimulationsVar runtime
        putMVar (simSimulationsVar runtime) (simThreadId : sims)
        threadDelay 1000
        simulatorWorker runtime requestVar

      Just (ShutdownSimulator (ShutdownResult resultVar)) -> do
        stopSimulation runtime                  ◄──────
        putMVar resultVar ()                             Stops the simulation
                                                         model
      Nothing -> do                       ◄──────  Does nothing and just waits for the
        threadDelay 1000                            next request after some delay
        simulatorWorker runtime requestVar
```

This code is simple. It just follows the scheme for the responder: get a request, pattern-match it, evaluate the appropriate action, fill the response variable, delay, and fall down with the recursion if needed or terminate. This is our first actor, but we should prepare some data for it. Not a problem! Let's do that. The next function is like taming an animal: you feed it with `SimulationRuntime`, and it obediently returns with a leash in the form of `SimulationControl`:

```
data SimulatorControl = SimulatorControl
  { simulatorThreadId   :: ThreadId
  , simulatorRequestVar :: MVar SimulatorRequest
  }

startSimulator :: SimulatorRuntime -> IO SimulatorControl
startSimulator runtime = do
  simRequestVar <- newEmptyMVar
  simThreadId <- forkIO $ simulatorWorker runtime simRequestVar
  pure $ SimulatorControl simThreadId simRequestVar
```

We'll see this idea of a control structure again in the future because it's a convenient design pattern to have a representation of something that you can interact with. In my tests, for example, I do the following (notice that all the functions here are self-explanatory):

```
it "Some test" $ do
  simRt <- createSimulatorRuntime

  simControl <- startSimulator simRt

  runSimulation simControl logicControlScript
```

```
    simControl <- stopSimulator simRt simControl

    -- do some checks of the SimulatorRuntime state
```

The `runSimulation` function helps to make a proper request:

```
runSimulation :: SimulatorControl -> LogicControl a -> IO a
runSimulation control lc = do
  let SimulatorControl {simulatorRequestVar} = control
  resultVar <- newEmptyMVar
  let runResult = RunResult resultVar
  putMVar simulatorRequestVar $ RunSimulation lc runResult
  takeMVar resultVar
```

I definitely argue that this design of an actor-like simulator is super simple and easy to grasp. With some help from the two design patterns and a strong adherence to a good low-coupled architecture, we've achieved this nice code.

What's next? We should examine the interconnection between our domain-specific scripts and the simulation model: how one becomes another, how we maintain state, what we should do with concurrency, and so on.

8.2.2 *Stateful simulation model*

The latest edition of the `LogicControl` eDSL had four methods:

```
data LogicControlMethod next
  = forall a. EvalHdl (Hdl a) (a -> next)
  | forall a. EvalDeviceControlMethod (DeviceControlMethod a) (a -> next)
  | Report Message (() -> next)
  | Store Key Value (() -> next)
```

The first two methods each nest another eDSL, thus making a hierarchical structure and empowering the `LogicControl` eDSL with more functionality. The `Report` method was intended to communicate some message to the caller. The idea of this method probably isn't the best one because we can't tell if it's about logging or another mechanism of broadcasting the message. And what message it can be in particular cannot be seen from the definition. I would say that this method is not designed well because it's not obvious.

Let's focus on the last one, though: `Store`. It's something about working with key–value storage. But where is the `Load` method? Our interface is clearly incomplete. Let's fix this.

Listing 8.4 A primitive key–value database interface

```
data LogicControlMethod next
  = Store Key Value (() -> next)
  | Load Key (Maybe Value -> next)

-- | Stores a value with a key into Redis
store :: Key -> Value -> LogicControl ()

-- | Load a value with a key into Redis
load :: Key -> LogicControl (Maybe Value)
```

A sample script would look like this:

```
reupload :: LogicControl ()
reupload = do
  mbVal <- load "key"
  case mbVal of
    Just val -> store "another key" val
    Nothing -> pure ()     -- do nothing
```

We correctly look at this as a mutable state accessible from the business logic. This implies that our simulation model (that is, a reflection of the whole `LogicControl` ecosystem) should be stateful.

But how do we know exactly what state this is? Is it in-memory state? Or an external key–value database? Or maybe not even a key–value one? And what about thread safety? The only source of clarification that we see is some documentation for the methods (see the previous code), but it can't guarantee that all the implementations will comply. The simulator does it differently. Instead of going to Redis, it will place all the values into the internal in-memory dictionary. And you already know where to keep this dictionary:

```
data SimulatorRuntime = SimulatorRuntime
  { ... other fields
  , simKeyValueDBVar :: MVar (Map Key (MVar Value))
  }
```

Notice the type: it's an MVar of a map of `MVar`-ed values. It's so special that I am going to illustrate it, as shown in figure 8.8.

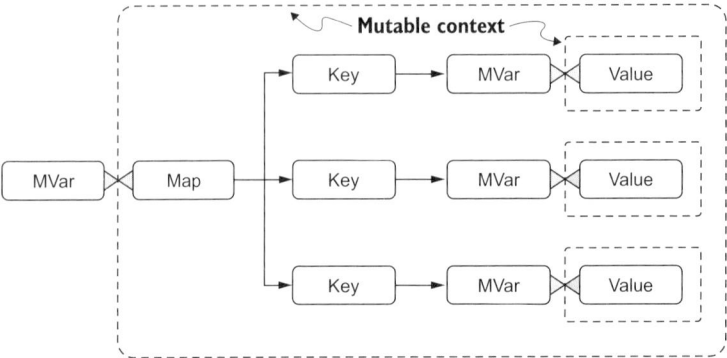

Figure 8.8   Data structure with two layers of concurrent mutability

Can you determine the characteristics of this data model design? What makes it special is called *granularity*. The dashed lines denote a separately mutable, independent cluster of data. You don't have to update the whole structure if you only need to change the internal value. And the control over those values can be distributed across many threads with no harm to concurrency. Compare it with the following snippet:

```
type CoarseGrainedMap = MVar (Map Key Value)
```

With `CoarseGrainedMap`, you must re-upload new values into the map, thus making pure rearrangements all the time. Given multiple updates of the same key, you'll be constructing many new maps, hence updating the MVar many times. This can be less efficient than just looking up an internal `MVar Value` once and altering MVar without the need to alter the outer MVar.

We've just discussed a small part of a bigger problem called "coarse grained versus fine grained" in connection to the data design. Can we talk about it in depth? We should, actually, because it becomes significant when dealing with STM-based concurrent models. We'll cover this topic in the next few chapters.

What else is needed for the rest of the simulation model? I categorize all the devices as a part of it, irrespective of the fact that they are separate actors. The reason is that they are being created during the `LogicControl` script evaluation due to the `Hdl` scripts. The `Hdl` actors will be organized hierarchically. The topmost actor is a controller that has a responsibility to interact with the outer world. There will be no way to bypass the controller to access its internal devices (like sensors). Everything should go through the interaction protocol the controller supports. I create a thread for such a controller when interpreting over `Hdl`. Conveniently, we have the `SetupController` method for this:

```
interpretHdlMethod :: SimulatorRuntime -> HdlMethod a -> IO a

interpretHdlMethod
    runtime
    (SetupController deviceName ctrlName passp next) = do
  -- fork a thread for the controller
  eCtrlSim <- makeControllerSim ctrlName passp
  ...      -- do the rest of initialization
```

I initialize the state for the actor in the form of `ControllerSim`:

```
data ControllerSim = ControllerSim
  { ctrlSimThreadId :: ThreadId
  , ctrlSimDef :: (ControllerName, ComponentPassport)
  , ctrlSimDevicePartsVar :: MVar DevicePartSims
  , ctrlSimRequestVar :: MVar ControllerSimRequest
  }
```

Controller worker thread
Definition of the controller
Submissive actors representing devices
MVar request-response–based protocol

I create other actors during the interpretation of the `Hdl` script, namely, the `RegisterComponent` method:

```
interpretHdlMethod :: SimulatorRuntime -> HdlMethod a -> IO a
interpretHdlMethod runtime (RegisterComponent ctrl idx passp next) = do
  ... -- a lot of code here,
      --including threads forking and bookkeeping of new actors
```

Finally, the `Hdl` script finishes interpreting, and we have the ready simulation model accessible from the `LogicControl` scripts. For example, you can ask for the needed measurements from certain domain-level devices:

```
reportBoostersTemperature :: LogicControl ()
reportBoostersTemperature = do
  (lBoosterCtrl, rBoosterCtrl) <- evalHdl createBoosters  ◀──── Creates a device

  eTemperature  <- readSensor lBoosterCtrl nozzle1t       ◀──── Reads a sensor
  case eTemperature of
    Left err      -> report err
    Right (v1, v2) -> do
      report ("T1 = " <> show v1 <> ", T2 = " <> show v2) ◀──── Reports some info
      report "Temperature values are okay."
```

On the implementation level, this will be interpreted as an MVar request to the specific actor through the entire hierarchy of actors. This is how the whole simulator works, and this is how we utilized the Free Monad pattern to provide another implementation for the same high-level business-specific language. Feel free to play with the Andromeda simulator application to get more hints and investigate the ideas in detail.

We put a big period here but then immediately change it to a big comma because there is so much to talk about, just in another context. Our next effort will involve building more common applications: backends, command-line applications, and services. We were following the domain-first approach. Let's now turn it inside out and try to do something different. Let's create a domain-agnostic concurrent full-fledged framework, suitable for typical business tasks.

Summary

- Reactive programming can be used to create an environment for formulas to live in and react to new data to produce new results.
- The actor model helps to organize stateful applications, but there is a definite cost of making interactions between actors safe and reliable.
- The abstracted communication protocol hides the underlying world and acts as a contract, interface, and agreement between all actors.
- MVars are a type of concurrency tool that allows threads to access a shared variable in a safe and orderly manner.
- A specific communication protocol between actors can be implemented with the MVar Request–Response pattern.
- The MVar Request–Response pattern is a way of using MVars to construct a remote service that works in a separate thread, waits for a request, processes it, and pushes the result back.
- The MVar request pattern can be used to make communication between threads 100% reliable and type safe.
- More advanced architectures may require implementing a message queue (message bus).
- Free monadic architecture lets us provide the third implementation for the same business logic, in addition to the real implementation and test environment.

- MVars are generally capable of maintaining concurrency, but they may be limited in expressiveness, difficult to use properly, and a bit awkward when the concurrent data model is big and sophisticated.
- Large MVar-based concurrent models tend to become overcomplicated.
- Switching to STM is a nice idea when dealing with MVars is too difficult.

Part 5

Designing
real-world software

The final part of the book embarks on a comprehensive exploration of advanced topics crucial for the development of robust, functional software systems. We learn about the complexities of multithreading and concurrency, unraveling the challenges and strategies for designing reliable concurrent code. Our focus includes understanding the nuances of `IORefs`, `MVars`, and software transactional memory (STM) `TVars` and their appropriate use in a concurrent environment. This part also explores the potential of free monads as an architectural pattern for constructing versatile application frameworks, with an emphasis on the role of transactional data structures and transactions in behavior modeling.

We expand our scope by examining the intricacies of foundational subsystems, the significance of resource handling in concurrent and exception-prone environments, and the application of type-level programming for enhanced safety. The discussion includes the design and abstraction of subsystems such as logging and state management, highlighting the critical role of interfaces in software design and the practicality of patterns such as the typed-untyped design. We tackle the challenges of error handling, differentiating between errors and exceptions, and the importance of domain-specific error handling strategies. Our exploration covers various functional interfaces, including the free monad, GADT, Service Handle, and ReaderT patterns and final tagless, offering insights into their applications and benefits. The final segment underscores the essence of testing, not as a bug-free guarantee but as a means to reduce risks and ensure that critical requirements are met, specifically emphasizing the testability offered by free monadic architectures.

Concurrent
application framework

This chapter covers

- How to build a general-purpose concurrent
  application framework
- Why multithreading and complexity are hard yet
  very important
- Why we abstract threads and how to do this in a
  thread-safe manner
- How to incorporate software transactional
  memory into a framework

This chapter opens the final part of this book. Going forward, we will discuss more common matters of software design as they relate to real-world tasks we may encounter in a regular software company. In the remaining chapters, we'll be constructing an application framework suitable for building multithreaded, concurrent web servers and command-line applications. We'll talk about free monads as a way to organize a testable, simple, and maintainable foundation for business logic code. Of course, we can't ignore the important themes such as SQL and key–value (KV) database support, logging, state handling, concurrency and reactive programming, error handling, and so forth. We'll also learn new design patterns and architecture approaches, such as final tagless/mtl, the ReaderT pattern, and others, so we can navigate between the solutions with confidence.

The reference project for this final part of the book will be the Hydra application framework (https://github.com/graninas/Hydra). This project includes several frameworks built specifically for this book. They provide the same functionality but are based on different approaches to compare them more easily. Hydra is a showcase project, but I've designed even more technologies for commercial companies using ideas presented in previous chapters. We'll see what other interesting solutions can help us create real-world software, and the Hydra framework will be a nice source of inspiration.

You might want to investigate some demo applications shipped with Hydra:

- *The Labyrinth game*—This is an interactive command-line application that demonstrates Hydra's CLI subsystem, the layering of business logic, and working with SQL and KV databases (https://mng.bz/gvOG).

- *The astro application*—This is a web server and HTTP client powered by a famous Haskell library, `Servant`. The astro application is a tool that lets astronomers track cosmic activities such as meteors, supernova events, comets, and other things. The client application also demonstrates how to do dependency injection with final tagless, free monads, the ReaderT pattern, bare `IO`, and the Service Handle pattern (https://mng.bz/5l68).

- *The MeteorCounter application*—The application demonstrates working with processes, threads, and concurrency (https://mng.bz/67op).

This chapter establishes a foundation for our brand-new free monadic framework and talks about software transactional memory (STM)–based concurrency. However, these tiny pages don't allow me to cover all possible questions. Consider reading the excellent book by Simon Marlow, *Parallel and Concurrent Programming in Haskell* (O'Reilly, 2013). It's entirely dedicated to explaining the many different aspects of this topic.

A tool for astronomers seems to be a good choice for this chapter. As usual, we start by defining a domain of astronomical observations. We'll create a centralized catalog of meteorites falling on earth. It will be a server that accepts reports about sky events detected by astronomers. Using the client application, a scientist can report the region, the mass, and the time of a meteor. The client will be interacting with the server over some channel (e.g., TCP, UDP, HTTP, or WebSockets). The server will be a multithreaded, concurrent application with a database. And yes, I love the space domain!

This section will briefly cover bare threads and multithreading code—why it's hard, what problems we might run into, and what problems we will run into. In the following sections, we'll start solving some of these problems and continue searching for a better approach until the end of the book.

9.1 *Multithreaded applications*

Multithreading and concurrency remain two of the most difficult themes in programming despite the decades of research in this field. Yes, we've used bare threads in our programs for a long time, we know how to organize our systems as separate processes, and we've even collected broad experience in the wider theme of distributed calculations. But this was never an easy field of practice. We won't go too deep into multithreading—essentially, we can't. Whole books have been dedicated to explaining a huge number of pitfalls and approaches, and they're still not enough to cover them all. We have another goal—to see how multithreading fits into the application architecture. We'll try the most viable techniques to keep our multithreaded code readable and maintainable. Fortunately, the functional programming world has given us such a thing as composable STM. This technology deserves much more attention because it can drastically reduce the complexity of multithreaded applications. Composable STM provides a relatively new reasoning that has produced several useful application-structuring patterns. The STM addresses the main problems of multithreading so neatly that there's no real reason to avoid this technology except perhaps in cases where it is necessary to maximize performance and confidence in how the code evaluates under the hood. In this chapter, we'll take a look at the boundaries of STM and bare threads.

9.1.1 *Why is multithreading hard?*

There are several reasons why creating multithreaded applications is difficult. Some are technical, and others are cognitive. Our brains aren't good at comprehending parallel processes, and our intuition may easily fool us. We probably can't do anything about that, but we at least can and should provide a better design for our programs.

Technical difficulties are mostly coming from interactions among threads in a concurrent, mutable environment. With the greater number of operations that a thread performs over a shared mutable state, there will be more cases in which another thread can change this shared state unexpectedly. Even a single concurrent bug can break all the logic and put the program into undefined behavior. The following problems can occur:

- *Race condition*—Two threads compete for the same shared resource in an unexpected way. In a bad situation, data may be corrupted or turned into the invalid state.
- *Deadlock*—Two threads are stuck waiting for each other. The program just hangs.
- *Livelock*—Two threads are stuck playing ping-pong with data. Nothing advances, and the program doesn't do anything useful, but CPU resources are heavily utilized.
- *Thread starvation*—Threads are underloaded. They could be useful, but an unfair job distribution leaves them uninvolved.

- *Unclear resource management*—Resource management gets really complicated in a concurrent environment. The code may easily turn into a mess that has tricky evaluation paths and possibly wrong resource lifetimes.
- *Resource leakage*—Whenever there is resource allocation, there should be resource disposal as well. Sometimes deallocation of resources doesn't happen due to bugs and incorrect resource management, leading to resource leakages.
- *Resource overflow*—Flooding a system with data is not a good idea. The system should be capable of processing everything it gets. The load should be balanced and carefully distributed to avoid unnecessary jamming on the edges between subsystems.
- *Incorrect exceptions handling*—Exceptions are hard. There's no proper way to organize exception safety in the application. Exceptions are another dimension orthogonal to other code, so we must think about a multiplied number of cases when we write a program.

Concurrent bugs are subtle and hard to search for, test, and fix, and their presence can be spotted well after the code is deployed. This is why constructing concurrent multithreaded applications should be done carefully. Hopefully, we have immutability, MVars, and STM. These concepts eliminate different problems—not only bugs but also the ridiculous complexity of multithreaded code writing.

9.1.2   Bare threads

There are many reasons why we'd want to introduce multithreading in our program:

- We know it will be evaluated on a more or less standard CPU, and we want to utilize the resources effectively.
- Our application is a service that will process irregular external requests, which could come at random moments in time and possibly in parallel.
- Our application is an active member of some bigger system and can produce results and send them to other members.

Let's proceed with our domain and create a code that simulates the two active members of the system:

- An astronomer who is watching for meteorites and reporting about events to the remote tracking center
- The remote tracking center that's accepting astronomers' reports

Given that we already have some experience with threads and actors, we'll try to design the application in the same way. Simulating the astronomer would allow us to feed the system with some data—it's just a subsystem that produces meteors. We'll make the astronomer actor and the tracking center actor communicate through a mutable shared state. No Request–Response patterns, just bare threads and IORefs (figure 9.1).

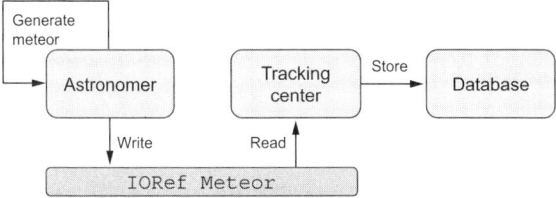

Figure 9.1   Tracking meteors

This is the `Meteor` data type itself and the function to generate random ones:

```
data Meteor = Meteor
  { size :: Int
  , mass :: Int
  }

getRandomMeteor :: IO Meteor
getRandomMeteor = do
  rndSize <- randomRIO (1, 100)
  rndMass <- randomRIO (rndSize, rndSize * 10)
  pure (Meteor rndSize rndMass)
```

Bare IO function for now

A random number from 1 to 100

A random number from rndSize to 1000

Now we propose a way to report newly detected meteors. Essentially, it's an `IORef` without thread-safety facilities. It holds a list and gets updated once the reporting function is triggered. I called the variable a "channel" to highlight its transportation role in the application:

```
type ReportingChannel = IORef [Meteor]

reportMeteor :: ReportingChannel -> Meteor -> IO ()
reportMeteor ch meteor = do
  reported <- readIORef ch
  writeIORef ch (meteor : reported)
```

Reads reported meteors

Appends another meteor to the list

An astronomer will be a simulated actor who detects meteorites by generating random ones. Following the idea of reactive actors, we'll fork a separate thread for the astronomer and make it interact with others via the channel `IORef` variable. This function is a worker for as many astronomer threads as we want:

```
astronomer :: ReportingChannel -> IO ()
astronomer ch = do
  rndMeteor <- getRandomMeteor
  rndDelay  <- randomRIO (1000, 10000)
  reportMeteor ch rndMeteor
  threadDelay rndDelay
```

Generates a meteor

Chooses a delay

Finally, the tracking center must be simulated. This actor polls the channel and waits for new meteorites to be reported. Currently, it does nothing with the space objects but print them, but we might eventually decide to store them in a catalog:

```
trackingCenter :: ReportingChannel -> IO ()
trackingCenter ch = do
```

```
reportedMeteors <- readIORef ch
```

> ◄ — Utilizes the reported meteors by printing them

```
print reportedMeteors
```

```
writeIORef ch []
```

> ◄ — Blanks the channel

```
threadDelay 10000
```

We still must roll `astronomer` and `trackingCenter` inside the threads as if they were hamsters in wheels. One extra thread for the astronomer actor and the main thread for the tracking center will be enough for now:

```
app :: IO ()
app = do
  ch <- newIORef []
  forkIO (forever (astronomer ch))
  forever (trackingCenter ch)
```

> ◄ — Forks a separate infinite thread
>
> ◄ — Spins the main thread forever

While this program is deadly simple, it's also deadly wrong. It won't crash but will produce a lot of invalid data. It can lose meteorites, it can track meteorites multiple times, or astronomers can report more meteorites than the `trackingCenter` is able to process. In other words, this program has destructive concurrency issues: race conditions, invalid balance of production and consumption, and occasional memory overuse.

Finding such problems can be a frustrating experience because it's never obvious where the bug is in a more or less nontrivial program. Here, however, the problem is easy to find but not easy to fix. We have the two processes happening simultaneously (figure 9.2).

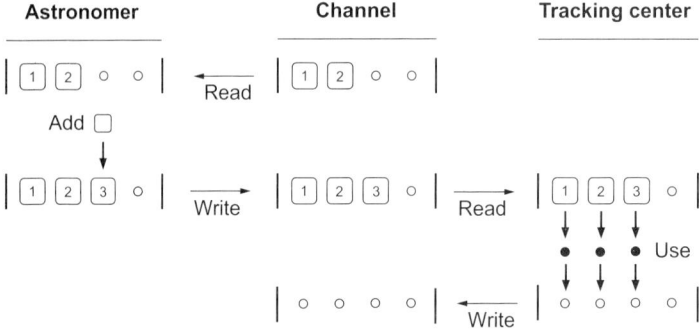

Figure 9.2   Accessing a shared state

`Astronomer` first reads the channel, adds the third meteorite to the list, and writes the list back. `Tracking center` then reads the updated channel, uses what it found there, and clears the channel. But this is the ideal situation. The astronomers and the center don't wait for each other, which is why operations with channels can sequence in an invalid order, causing data loss or double usage. Consider figure 9.3, which shows a situation where meteorites 1 and 2 are used twice.

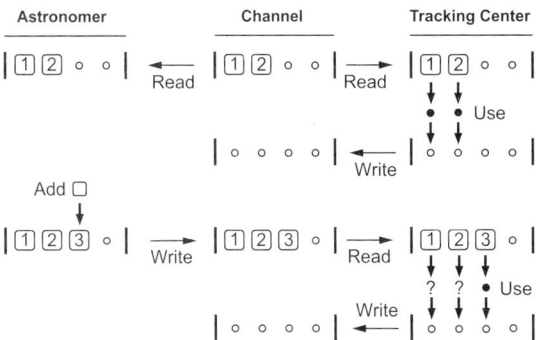

Figure 9.3   Race condition in accessing a shared resource and double-usage error

This is clearly the race condition. We should somehow organize access to the channel in a thread-safe manner. It can be a mutex, which prevents a thread from operating on the channel if another thread still does its work, or it can be a concurrent data structure, such as ConcurrentQueue in C#. Sometimes we can say, "OK, we're fine with data loss and double usage. It's not critical for our task, so let it be." However, it would be better to consider these operations dangerous. In most languages, accessing a shared mutable data structure in the middle of the write procedure will introduce another problem: a partial change of new data might be observed along with a piece of old data. The data we read from an unprotected shared resource can occasionally vanish, leaving an undefined memory cell, and the program will crash. So handling these situations is a default best practice to follow.

9.1.3   *Separating and abstracting the threads*

Uncontrolled imperativity causes most bugs in a concurrent environment. Hardly anyone can predict what will happen in the absence of proper thread management. Consider this short program:

```
astronomer :: ReportingChannel -> IO ()
astronomer ch = do
  someRef <- newIORef [1..10]
  forever $ forkIO $ do                    ◀──── Infinite threads forking
    val <- readIORef someRef
    print val
```

It will run out of memory in seconds by spawning a billion threads. Who would write code like this? Well, this is just a metaphoric exaggeration, but the less structured the code, the easier it is to mess things up.

We need thread safety, and we have to control resources somehow. We already know how to restrict bare IO with interpretable languages, and this technique will help us again. We'll also implement an unavoidable resource pool so that it is impossible to exceed the predefined number of threads.

The key idea is to allow only a certain set of operations in the business logic. At the top level, it will be a logic with the ability to fork threads—let's call them processes. Every process will be restricted so that it won't be allowed to fork child processes or threads. We'll only allow a process to get random numbers, operate with shared state, delay the execution, and maybe perform other useful business logic actions (logging, database access, and so on). Basically, it is everything you need except for forking child threads.

A layered design of such an application framework is shown in figure 9.4.

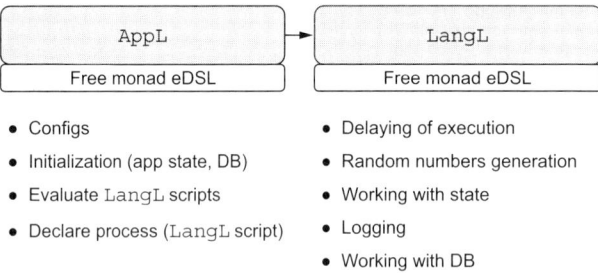

* Configs
* Initialization (app state, DB)
* Evaluate LangL scripts
* Declare process (LangL script)

* Delaying of execution
* Random numbers generation
* Working with state
* Logging
* Working with DB

Figure 9.4   Separation of responsibilities with two free monadic languages

This separation of concerns will not only make some bad things irrepresentable (such as forking threads infinitely from inside other threads) but will also structure the business logic in a layered manner. We did this earlier with languages for the Andromeda Control Software, and we've been organizing them hierarchically (see figure 9.5).

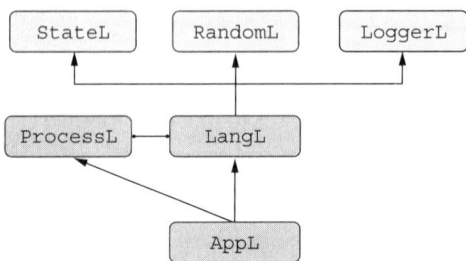

Figure 9.5   Free monadic languages organized hierarchically

These languages aren't raw IO anymore. The AppL scripts will be responsible for initializing the app state, the declarative description of processes and relations between them, config management, and so on. Let's agree that we don't want to keep some specific domain logic here; rather, we must prepare an environment for this domain logic in which it will be run. In turn, the LangL scripts should describe this logic, or at least its parts. We can still call any LangL script and methods from the AppL directly. In fact, all the logic can be written in AppL scripts, unless we consider multithreading. Once it's introduced, as shown in figure 9.5, the scripts evaluating in additional processes can only be `LangL` scripts.

> **NOTE** This is how I recommend arranging the real code. There's no point in smashing everything together. Plain structures are chaotic. Hierarchical structures are essential. However, this is only a showcase, and having several layers of free monadic languages might not be suitable for all cases.

Effect systems vs. subsystems

It makes sense to avoid calling my approach with hierarchical free monads an effect system. In Haskell and Scala, effect systems are mostly connected to a mechanism for tracking effects, typically at the level of types, where "effect" can be any extra responsibility in the code. I've seen a codebase in which the authors claimed they had a database, configuration, and concurrency effects; they also declared domain notion to be an effect. All these things existed together in the plain type-level list and had no proper separation between them. The things called "effects" represented different levels of abstraction, all at once.

The code I saw was violating SRP, ISP, and other principles. It was flawed and badly designed from the beginning when the authors decided everything was an effect. I don't see this as a good approach and genuinely think that effect systems (in the form of effect tracking) are pushing the architectures in the wrong direction.

This is why I use the terms "components" and "subsystems" instead. They work better and are already defined in the mainstream.

> **NOTE** Mainstream developers may find many similarities in how they structure applications in object-oriented and imperative languages. Have you noticed how a Java interface can have a method accepting an argument of another interface? This looks very similar to what I do with HFM.

Figure 9.4 presented a very simple and straightforward design. The corresponding eDSLs will look like the following listing.

Listing 9.1 Two languages for the business logic layer

```
data LangF next where
  Delay        :: Int -> (() -> next)          -> LangF next      Interfaces for
  GetRandomInt :: (Int, Int) -> (Int -> next)  -> LangF next      business logic
  NewVar       :: a -> (IORef a -> next)       -> LangF next
  ReadVar      :: IORef a -> (a -> next)        -> LangF next
  WriteVar     :: IORef a -> a -> (() -> next) -> LangF next

type LangL = Free LangF                                           Bottom language

delay        :: Int            -> LangL ()                        Smart constructors
```

```
getRandomInt :: (Int, Int)    -> LangL Int
newVar       :: a             -> LangL (IORef a)
readVar      :: IORef a       -> LangL a
writeVar     :: IORef a -> a -> LangL ()

data AppF next where                                              ◄──── Top language
  EvalLang    :: LangL a  -> (a -> next)  -> AppF next
  ForkProcess :: LangL () -> (() -> next) -> AppF next

type AppL = Free AppF

forkProcess :: LangL () -> AppL ()                                ◄──── Smart constructors
evalLang    :: LangL a  -> AppL a
```

Listing 9.2 introduces some demo business logic. What does it do? It starts as an app
script, forks a process for the astronomer behavior, and then starts accepting the meteors like it's the tracking center. The listing contains functions to generate a meteor
and report it via a channel (getRandomMeteor and reportMeteor), both in the LangL
context. The two worker functions, namely astronomer and trackingCenter, communicate with each other using the shared reporting channel variable. Notice the
monads of these methods: it's only an app that works in AppL, while other functions are
situated as LangL.

Listing 9.2 Business logic with process

```
getRandomMeteor :: LangL Meteor
getRandomMeteor = do
  rndSize <- getRandomInt (1, 100)
  rndMass <- getRandomInt (rndSize, rndSize * 10)
  pure (Meteor rndSize rndMass)

reportMeteor :: ReportingChannel -> Meteor -> LangL ()
reportMeteor ch meteor = do
  reported <- readVar ch                          ◄─┐  The astronomer mutates
  writeVar ch (meteor : reported)                   │  the shared variable.

astronomer :: ReportingChannel -> LangL ()
astronomer ch = do
  rndMeteor <- getRandomMeteor
  rndDelay  <- getRandomInt (1000, 10000)
  reportMeteor ch rndMeteor
  delay rndDelay              -- random pause between observations

trackingCenter :: ReportingChannel -> LangL ()
trackingCenter ch = do
  -- do something with the reported meteors
  reported <- readVar ch                          ◄─┐  The tracking center mutates
  writeVar ch []                                    │  the shared variable.
  delay 10000

app :: AppL ()
app = do
  ch <- evalLang (newVar [])
```

```
forkProcess (forever (astronomer ch))
evalLang (forever (trackingCenter ch))
```

← Separates thread for the astronomer

← The tracking center is operating in the main thread.

I believe the app script feels too imperative. Although it's true it evaluates another script and forks a thread, we can consider it a declarative definition of the app. Actually, it's better to think of it as a declaration, which will allow more design freedom. Here, we don't fork processes but define a process. We don't call scenarios but define a logic to be evaluated in the main thread. So let's just define two aliases for the forkProcess and evalLang functions:

```
process :: LangL () -> AppL ()
process = forkProcess

scenario :: LangL a -> AppL a
scenario = evalLang

app :: AppL ()
app = do
  ch <- evalLang (newVar [])
  process (forever (astronomer ch))
  scenario (forever (trackingCenter ch))
```

It's just a little tweak that makes us think about the AppL script differently. In FDD, we should seek opportunities for declarative descriptions of our intents. In the future, we could add more declarative definitions, for example, starting some network server:

```
app :: AppL ()
app = do
  serving TCP $ do
    handler someHandler1
    handler someHandler1

  process logic1
  process logic2
```

What do you think—is it better now? Will this abstraction even work? It's only a free monadic eDSL, after all, and it yet lacks the interpreters. What if our design cannot be properly implemented? This might lead to redoing the languages in a certain way. I'm a big fan of designing eDSLs, and given my developer's intuition, I typically manage to get my languages working. However, sometimes I have to try several options until I find a satisfactory one. To be more confident in my design process, I usually follow these steps:

1 Imagine an eDSL from a usage point of view. Don't worry if it's not compiling.

2 Use it to implement some business logic to ensure it looks good and the developer experience is the best. Don't worry if it's not compiling.

3 Make it compile.

4 Make it work.

Our next goal is to make it work. One question: What if someone wrote the following code again with an infinite forking of processes?

```
app :: AppL ()
app = do
  ch <- evalLang (newVar [])

  forever (process (forever (astronomer ch)))
```

| Infinite process forking

Yes, this is the same problem. Let's think about how we can enhance our abstraction here and introduce a thread pool so that the app script is unable to fork more threads than the pool has free slots.

9.1.4   *Threads bookkeeping*

Different methods can be invented to limit the number of threads acting in the system. There are at least two solutions we'll discuss. I call them explicit and implicit.

Having an explicit way means there will be dedicated methods to control the threads. The current and the maximum number of threads will be held in the `ProcessLimits` structure:

```
-- Token for accessing the process forked
data ProcessLimits = ProcessLimits
  { currentCount :: Int
  , maximumCount :: Int
  }
```

Given that, we could end up with a language design as follows.

Listing 9.3   Business logic with process

```
data ProcessToken a = ProcessToken Int

data ProcessF next where
  GetProcessLimits
    :: (ProcessLimits -> next)
    -> ProcessF next
  TryForkProcess
    :: LangL a
    -> (Maybe (ProcessToken a) -> next)
    -> ProcessF next
  AwaitResult
    :: ProcessToken a
    -> (a -> next)
    -> ProcessF next

type ProcessL = Free ProcessF
```

◄—— Gets the limits

◄—| Tries to fork a process and returns a token on success

◄—| Awaits the results (a blocking operation)

Here is `ProcessL` fitted to the `AppL` like we usually do:

```
data AppF next where
  EvalLang :: LangL a -> (a -> next)   -> AppF next
  EvalProcess :: ProcessL a -> (a -> next) -> AppF next

type AppL = Free AppF
```

We also want to have smart constructors for `ProcessF` methods, except we'll lift them higher in the `AppL` context:

```
getProcessLimits :: AppL ProcessLimits
tryForkProcess   :: LangL a -> AppL (Maybe (ProcessToken a))
awaitResult      :: ProcessToken a -> AppL a
```

Suppose a client uses `tryForkProcess` to get a process running. The limit might be exhausted, and the function will return `Nothing` (or another result with more info provided). The next chunk of code shows the usage:

```
getMeteorsInParallel :: Int -> AppL [Meteor]
getMeteorsInParallel count = do
  let f = tryForkProcess getRandomMeteor

  mbTokens :: [Maybe ProcessToken] <- replicateM count f

  let actualTokens :: [ProcessToken[ = catMaybes mbTokens

  mapM awaitResult actualTokens
```

Tries to make a count number of identical AppL calls

Cuts all unsuccessful results and keeps only successful ones

Awaits the forked processes one by one

Once a fraction of the requested threads is forked, the client will await them one by one using the list of tokens.

> **NOTE** What we did here closely resembles the `join` operation in many other languages (for example, C++ or C#). When the join operation is hit from the current thread, it will be blocked and will await the thread it joins.

It might seem like this design is good enough, but there are several flaws. The language doesn't look like a thread pool—it's rather more like a traditional way of working with threads. This similarity itself might or might not be a problem, but it drags another problem along with it: it's possible to run `awaitResult` for a process already finished and destroyed. It's not very clear what to do in this situation. In principle, we could return an `Either` value having an error or a result:

```
data ProcessF next where
  AwaitResult
    :: ProcessToken a
    -> ((Either Error a) -> next) -> ProcessF next

awaitResult :: ProcessToken a -> ProcessL (Either Error a)
```

The `awaitResult` method is still blocking, though. It will stop the evaluation until some results from the specified process are observed. If the process is absent, failed, or made an exception, the error is returned. But what do we do if the process doesn't do anything—wait forever, or at least wait for an eventual timeout?

The language also doesn't allow us to set up new limits. They are predefined at the start of the program, exist at the implementation level, and can only be observed without modification. If we imagine we have a method for changing the limits, we immediately get the possibility of a race condition by design:

```
data ProcessF next where
  GetProcessLimits :: (ProcessLimits -> next) -> ProcessF next
  SetMaxCount :: Int -> (() -> next) -> ProcessF next
```

What if the first actor got the max count already, and the second one decreased it? The first actor would get invalid data without knowing it. Or what if we decreased the max count, but there was a thread pool occupied to its maximum? It's likely that nothing extremely bad would happen, except that there would be more processes evaluating than the limits allowed. Other race conditions are possible with this mutability involved, so we have to be careful. Ideally, our languages shouldn't introduce problems. This is even more important in a multithreaded situation.

To be clear, we didn't plan to run either the `ProcessL` or `AppL` methods from different threads. In fact, we're trying to avoid this. According to eDSL design and semantics, the `ProcessL` and `AppL` scripts will be evaluated sequentially in a single thread. The `LangL` scripts are also sequential. The difference is that the `LangL` scripts can be evaluated in parallel, which brings real multithreading into the whole problem. From the `AppL` point of view, these processes represent asynchronous actions. With no mutability involved, this approach is thread-safe. But the problems of multithreading environments occur immediately if we introduce mutable methods in the `ProcessL` or add a shared mutable state to the `LangL` layer. And we already did it: we have methods to work with `IORef` in `LangL`, which becomes very dangerous. What's the right way to handle this concurrency?

Let's examine how to control the limits implicitly. We're now descending to the language runtime (the implementation layer). All the important activities will be there: checking limits, obtaining a resource, and awaiting the resources to be released. For the client code, the interface will be the same as in listing 9.1:

```
data AppF next where
  EvalLang    :: LangL a  -> (a -> next)  -> AppF next
  ForkProcess :: LangL () -> (() -> next) -> AppF next

type AppL = Free AppF

-- | Evaluate a LangL script.
evalLang :: LangL a -> AppL a

-- | Fork a process. Block if the pool is full.
forkProcess :: LangL () -> AppL ()
```

If the hidden process pool is exhausted, the `forkProcess` method should block the execution and wait for it. In the implementation layer, we'll simply be counting the number of active processes. The following data type shows the runtime structure behind the scenes:

```
data Runtime = Runtime
  { _maxThreadsCount :: Int
  , _curThreadsCount :: MVar Int
  }
```

An interesting moment pops up here. We must use a synchronized `MVar` to store the number of active threads. If the limit is fine, the two actions have to be done in a single shot: increasing the counter and forking a thread. We cannot increase without forking or fork without increasing. These actions should never desync. How can we do this correctly? We want the following: once a worker function finishes and the thread is about to terminate, we should update the counter. Do we need a supervisor to monitor when this happens? Apparently not. The solution is simpler than that. In Haskell, we can tie a finishing action to any other `IO` action so that calling the finishing action is unavoidable. This is what `forkFinally` will do for us: fork a thread with a finishing action to call at the end.

But having `IO` means we should do that at the implementation level. It's now the right time to take a look at the interpreter.

Listing 9.4 Interpreter for `LangL`

```
interpretAppF :: Runtime -> AppF a -> IO a

interpretAppF rt (EvalLang act next) = do
  result <- runLangL rt act
  pure (next result)

interpretAppF rt (ForkProcess act next) =
  pure (next result)
  where
    result = go 1
    go factor = do
      let psVar = _curThreadsCount rt
      let maxPs = _maxThreadsCount rt

      ps <- takeMVar psVar

      when (ps == maxPs) $ do
        putMVar psVar ps
        threadDelay (10 ^ factor)
        go (factor + 1)

      let ioAct :: IO () = runLangL rt act
      let finalAct _ = decreaseProcessCount psVar
      when (ps /= maxPs) $ do
        forkFinally ioAct finalAct
        putMVar psVar (ps + 1)

decreaseProcessCount :: MVar Int -> IO ()
decreaseProcessCount psVar = do
  ps <- takeMVar psVar
  putMVar psVar (ps - 1)
```

- **Tries to fork a thread with exponential backoff**
- **Blocks on the synchronized process counter until it's available**
- **Checks the current limit**
- **The limit is reached: releases MVar and tries later**
- **The limit is fine: releases MVar and forks a thread**
- **Decreases the counter thread safely**

NOTE Here, we use exponential backoff for the sleeping time after each failure. It might not be the best solution, and we might want to consider other strategies:

constant delay time, arithmetic or geometric progression, Fibonacci numbers, and so on. But this question of delaying effectiveness moves away from the book's theme.

Synchronizing on the psVar MVar is necessary. A forked thread will finish at a random time and will interfere with one of these situations: the main thread can perform another forking operation by changing the counter, or possibly, another forked thread is about to finish and therefore wants to change the counter. Without synchronization, exactly the same problem we saw in figure 9.3 will happen. Figure 9.6 shows a race condition when MVar isn't used. The figure demonstrates a data loss and corruption resulting in an invalid counter state.

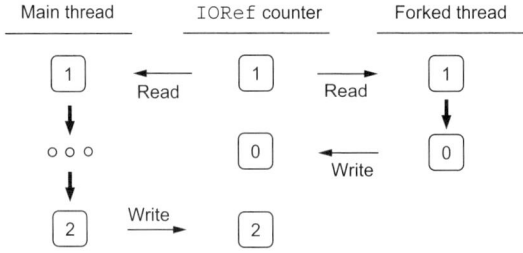

Figure 9.6   Concurrency bug caused by a race condition

Figure 9.7 explains how MVar can save us from this situation.

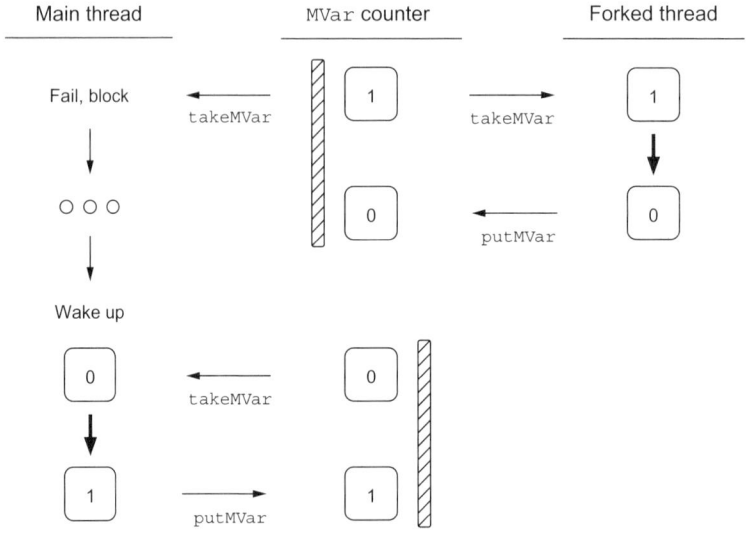

Figure 9.7   Safe concurrent interaction over the synchronized MVar

The paragraph will be incomplete without the final part of the code—the starting function. The runtime takes the configs on the maximum limit of threads:

```
app :: AppL ()
app = …

runAppL :: Runtime -> AppL a -> IO a
runAppL rt = foldFree (interpretAppF rt)

main :: IO ()
main = do
  psVar <- newMVar 0
  let rt = Runtime 4 psVar
  runAppL rt app
```

Bookkeeping can be done differently. For example, you might want to keep thread IDs for controlling the threads from the outside: ask a thread about the status, kill it, pause, or resume.

There are also difficulties related to the implementation of the LangL runner and getting a typed result from the thread. These problems are technical and mostly Haskell related. Nothing scary, but we'll leave them untouched here.

9.2   *Software transactional memory*

STM is an approach to concurrent mutable data models. The key idea behind STM is coded in its name: a memory (data) that can be mutated only within a single isolated transaction. STM shares some similarities with transactional databases: while a value is handled by one thread, another thread will wait until it's free. In contrast to databases, STM isn't an external service but a concurrent application state programmed to support your particular domain needs. With STM, you define a model that can be changed by different threads simultaneously and safely if there's no collision. But if there is, STM will decide how to solve the collision in a predictable way. This predictability is what we were missing in more low-level approaches involving custom-made mechanisms of concurrency in our apps. Of course, you can take ConcurrentQueue or ConcurrentDictionary in C#, and as long as you use these structures in a simple way, you're fine. However, if you need a code that will be interacting with both ConcurrentQueue and ConcurrentDictionary, you'll immediately get a higher-level problem: how to avoid race conditions and unpredictability while keeping the complexity low. Monadic STM (like Haskell) solves all these problems. It offers not only a predictable concurrency but also a composable concurrency, in which you can operate with an arbitrary data structure in a safe manner, even though it's a simple variable or a bunch of complex data structures. We can say monadic STM is like an orchestra conductor. It has the whole picture of the symphony, and it looks for the correct, completely definite evaluation of the music.

9.2.1   *Why STM is important*

STM works over data models locally and allows separate parts to be operated independently in different transactions when these operations aren't mutually dependent. Figure 9.8 demonstrates a forest-like data structure composed of STM primitives—TVars (transactional variables)—so the two threads may access their parts without blocking, whereas the third thread will wait for its turn.

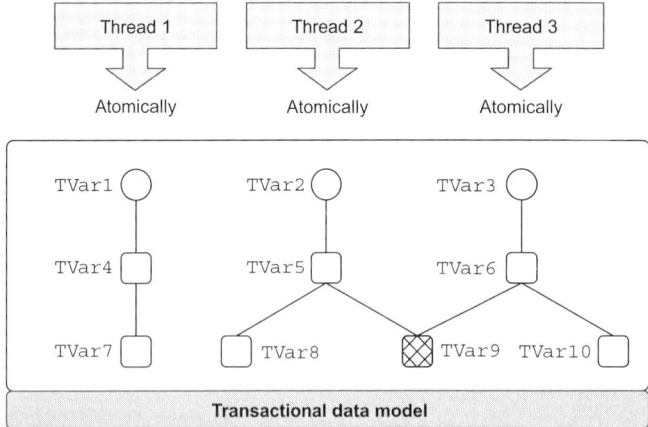

Figure 9.8   The STM model

Transactional variables have a simple interface:

```
type TVar a

newTVar   :: STM (TVar a)
readTVar  :: TVar a -> STM a
writeTVar :: TVar a -> a -> STM ()
```

TVars prove themselves to be fundamental. You can express other transactional data types with them (for example, queues). Let's see how TQueue from the Haskell library stm is made. It's the analog of ConcurrentQueue from the .NET framework. Both are first in, first out (FIFO) queues, both are thread-safe, and both use similar methods for writing and reading values to and from a queue:

```
type TQueue a

newTQueue   :: STM (TQueue a)
readTQueue  :: TQueue a -> STM a
writeTQueue :: TQueue a -> a -> STM ()
```

However—and this is how STM differs from concurrent collections—TQueue can be accessed through an evaluation of transactions only together with guarantees of atomicity. In Haskell, there is a special function a thread should call to run an STM transaction:

```
atomically :: STM a -> IO a
```

Like many functional concepts, STM follows the divide-and-conquer principle, and it separates data models from modification (behavior) models. Using STM primitives, you first construct a data structure for your domain—this will be your concurrent domain model. Second, using special functions from the STM library, you write transactions to access your data structure or its parts; doing so, you'll get a behavior model that's guaranteed to be thread-safe. Finally, you run your transactions in a threaded environment, passing them an instance of the domain model. Figure 9.9 offers some basic intuition about STM and the division of the data and behavior models.

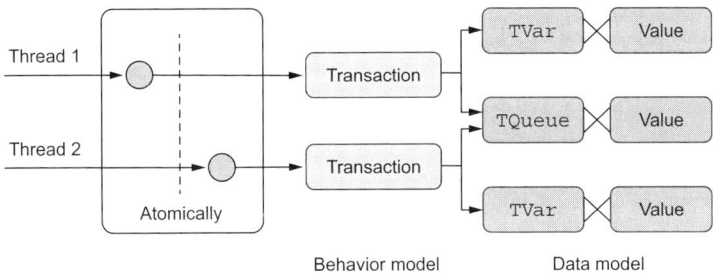

Figure 9.9   Data model and behavior model in STM

Interestingly, STM in Haskell has a unique feature that many other STMs lack—it's monadic. Every function in the STM monad is a separate transaction that may be evaluated over data or may be composed with some other transaction to obtain a bigger one. Monadic STM operations may be thought of as combinators of transactions:

```
biggerTransaction :: TQueue Int -> STM ()
biggerTransaction queueVar = do
  smallerTransaction1 queueVar     -- do something with queueVar
  smallerTransaction2 queueVar
```

In other words, STM concurrency is composable in the sense of true functional programming composition.

Another important idea in STM is the *retrying* operation. Any transaction can be rolled back and retried again if the variables are in an inappropriate state. You don't need to worry about rollbacking your transactional variables. When the `retry` combinator is hit, all the variables will return to the state they had at the transaction start.

For instance, you have a Boolean `TVar`, and you want it to be `True` to enter a transaction. You read your variable within the transaction, test it, and if it holds `False`, you call `retry`:

```
transaction :: TVar Bool -> STM Int
transaction tvFlag = do
  flag <- readTVar tvFlag
  if flag
    then return 100
    else retry
```

The transaction will be restarted to return `100` when and only when `tvFlag` is changed to `True`. If there are no other threads that can change the `tvFlag` variable, this thread will be blocked forever.

> **TIP**   Indefinite blocking of a thread is considered an exceptional situation. Depending on the STM implementation, you will (or won't) get some exception thrown.

Figure 9.10 should give you a better intuition about STM. The two threads compete to change the `TQueue` variable. The variable has been modified successfully by the first thread. Simultaneously, thread B happens to be in its own transaction, which tries to take an item from the same queue. However, the second thread should roll back its transaction because it sees that the queue has changed, and the values it could previously read might be invalid or obsolete.

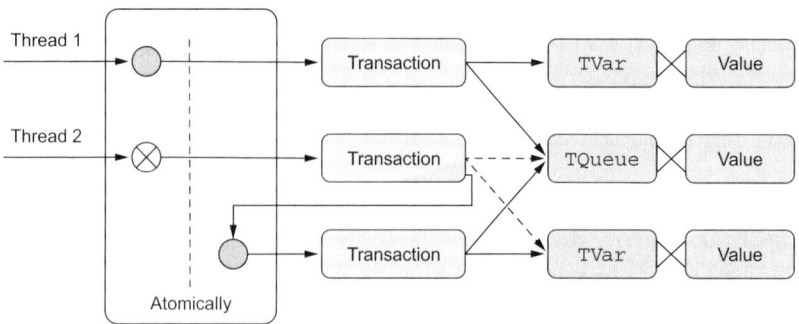

Figure 9.10   Retrying a transaction when concurrent changes occur

The `retry` combinator can be used to block a thread until some transactional variable or even many individual transactional variables get to the desired state. Although very simple, `retry` is also very powerful:

```
retry :: STM a
```

With this combinator, it becomes possible to do some clever tricks in concurrent code. The `retry` combinator and other STM operations can work like magic because the code remains readable and short compared to the maintenance hell with mutexes, conditional variables, callbacks, and other imperative things that overburden and buggify parallel imperative code. You might want to get familiar with the so-called dining philosophers' problem solved elegantly with STM. You can find it in my repository "Custom Software Transactional Memory with Free Monads" at https://github.com/graninas/stm-free.

In short, the problem illustrates the concurrency-related challenges. There are five philosophers sitting at a round table, and they can either eat some spaghetti or think (see figure 9.11). A philosopher is allowed to eat when there are two free forks, one to the left and one to the right. But the neighbor philosophers compete for these forks as well. The task demands organizing the philosophers so that they can eat and think in order, without being treated unfairly.

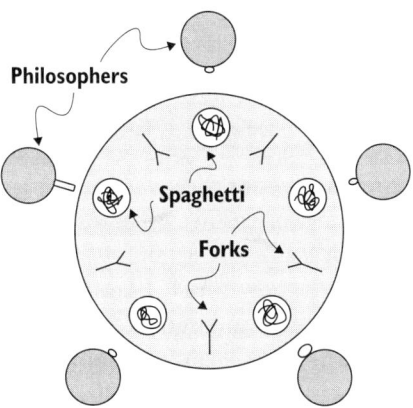

Philosophers

Spaghetti

Forks

Figure 9.11   Dining philosophers

Take a look at the STM transactions responsible for safe, concurrent maintaining of the forks of a particular philosopher. In listing 9.5, you can see my custom STML type for the STM monad and a custom TVar type for transactional variables. I describe the model for this problem as I would with vanilla STM by specifying two variables for two adjacent forks. Then, it's not difficult to write an STML transaction that would switch both forks to Free or Taken simultaneously. If that's not possible, the transaction (an STML function) will roll back, and neither of the forks will be affected.

Listing 9.5   STM transactions for the dining philosophers problem

```
data ForkState = Free | Taken              ◀──── A fork can be taken or be free.
data Fork      = Fork String ForkState

type TFork     = TVar Fork                 ◀──── Concurrent model of forks
type TForkPair = (TFork, TFork)

takeFork :: TFork -> STML Bool             ◀──── Transaction over a single fork
takeFork tFork = do
  Fork n st <- readTVar tFork
  case st of
    Taken -> pure False
    Free  -> do
      modifyTVar tFork (\(Fork n st) -> Fork n Taken)
      pure True

takeForks :: TForkPair -> STML Bool        ◀──── Transaction over two forks
takeForks (left, right) = do
  leftTaken  <- takeFork left
  rightTaken <- takeFork right
  pure (leftTaken && rightTaken)
```

So whenever two adjacent forks are free, the philosopher can start eating. We should call the `takeForks` transaction for them and simultaneously change their state to "eating." But if either of the two forks suddenly becomes taken by someone else, the `retry` combinator will prevent this philosopher from eating and using the forks. This is a fraction of the logic I just described:

```
taken <- takeForks (left, right)
when (not taken) retry
```
|◄———┘ **When taking fails, stop and retry later.**

Feel free to investigate the complete solution in the repository.

My custom monadic STM library is notable for two reasons. First, it's my own implementation of monadic STM based on the same ideas of free monads discussed in the book. Second, I managed to reimplement it in C++, for which I had to reimplement free monads, monadic chaining, and STM itself. I obtained good, functional code in C++ and proved that my methodology is transferrable between different programming languages. Check out "Custom Software Transactional Memory with Free monads in C++" at https://github.com/graninas/cpp_stm_free and "Dining Philosophers with the custom STM in C++" at https://github.com/graninas/cpp_philosophers_stm.

9.2.2   *STM-powered runtime of the framework*

Recently, our program was using `MVar` for the safe synchronization of the threads counter at the implementation layer. `MVar` is fine—it behaves similarly to mutexes and gives reliable concurrency guarantees such as the following:

- All threads will be woken up when a current owner thread releases the `MVar`.
- After taking the `MVar` by a thread, there's no way for others to observe the internals of the `MVar`.
- The program will be terminated if a thread takes the `MVar` and dies, leaving all other threads blocked.

Still, `MVar` requires careful code writing because it's so easy to create a bug when either of the two operations (taking and releasing `MVar`) is left unpaired and blocks the program. More complex concurrent data structures based on many `MVars` will exponentially amplify this problem.

Let's see how STM changes the game rules here. First, we replace `MVar` with a transactional variable `TVar`—it will be enough for the counter:

```
data Runtime = Runtime
  { _maxThreadsCount :: Int
  , _curThreadsCount :: TVar Int
  }
```

Now comes the most pleasant part. Functions for increasing and decreasing the counter will be separate transactions over this `TVar`. The increasing function should track the state of the counter and decide when to increase and when to block it. With the help of a magical STM combinator `retry`, the code becomes very simple. We're increasing the counter safely or blocking if the pool is at its maximum:

```
increaseProcessCount :: Int -> TVar Int -> IO ()
increaseProcessCount maxCount psVar = atomically $ do
  ps <- readTVar psVar
  when (ps == maxCount) retry
  writeTVar psVar (ps + 1)
```

Blocks until the
pool is freed

Decreasing doesn't require blocking:

```
decreaseProcessCount :: TVar Int -> IO ()
decreaseProcessCount psVar =
  atomically (modifyTVar psVar (\x -> x - 1))
```

The interpreter becomes much simpler: there is no need to manually poll the state of the resource after exponential delays. When the resource isn't ready, STM will block the thread on the retry operation and will resume it after observing that psVar has changed.

Listing 9.6 Counter-aware interpreting

```
forkProcess' :: Runtime -> LangL () -> IO ()
forkProcess' rt act = do
  let psVar = _curThreadsCount rt
  let maxPs = _maxThreadsCount rt
  increaseProcessCount maxPs psVar
  void $ forkFinally
    (runLangL rt act)
    (const (decreaseProcessCount psVar))

interpretAppF :: Runtime -> AppF a -> IO a
interpretAppF rt (EvalLang act next) = do
  r <- runLangL rt act
  pure (next r)
interpretAppF rt (ForkProcess act next) = do
  forkProcess' rt act
  pure (next ())
```

Block here if it's
at full capacity.

A block may happen here.

As a result, we get nice sequential code acting predictably, without race conditions. We can go further and propagate this practice to all concurrency we deal with in our program. For now, we only have threads bookkeeping at the implementation layer. Later, we may want to add facilities for serving a TCP/UDP/HTTP API, we may need to have asynchronous behavior in our scripts, we may be required to call external services in parallel, and so on.

We implemented particular blocking semantics for our forkProcess method. This is our design decision, and it should be specified in the method's documentation. Now what if we have a requirement to fork a process asynchronously when the pool is freed? We don't want to block the main thread in this case. Let's add one more method to our language and see what changes will be needed:

```
data AppF next where
  EvalLang        :: LangL a  -> (a -> next)  -> AppF next
  ForkProcess     :: LangL () -> (() -> next) -> AppF next
  ForkProcessAsync :: LangL () -> (() -> next) -> AppF next
```

```
type AppL = Free AppF

evalLang :: LangL a -> AppL a

forkProcess :: LangL () -> AppL ()

forkProcessAsync :: LangL () -> AppL ()
```

◀── **Evaluates a LangL script**

◀── **Forks a process; blocks if the pool is full**

◀── **Forks a process asynchronously; does not block if the pool is full**

The interpreter will get one more simple part:

```
interpretAppF rt (ForkProcessAsync act next) = do
  void (forkIO (forkProcess' rt act))  -- do not block here
  pure (next ())
```

However, we should understand that we introduced the same problem here. The thread counter doesn't have any meaning now. It's very possible to fork tenths of intermediate threads, which will be waiting to run a real working thread. Should we add one more thread pool for intermediate threads? This sounds very strange. Do you have déjà vu? The good thing here is that green threads in Haskell don't cost that much, and while they're waiting on the STM locks, they don't consume CPU. So the leakage problem is mitigated a little. Still, it's better not to call the forkProcessAsync function in an infinite cycle.

9.2.3 *Incorporating STM*

So far, we've dealt with IORefs in our business logic. This is pretty much unsafe in a multithreaded environment such as ours. The LangL eDSL can create, read, and write IORefs. The language is still pure because it doesn't expose any impure semantics to the client code.

Listing 9.7 Support for IORef in the interfaces

```
data LangF next where
  NewVar     :: a -> (IORef a -> next)        -> LangF next
  ReadVar    :: IORef a -> (a -> next)         -> LangF next
  WriteVar   :: IORef a -> a -> (() -> next) -> LangF next

type LangL = Free LangF

newVar      :: a                 -> LangL (IORef a)
readVar     :: IORef a      -> LangL a
writeVar    :: IORef a -> a -> LangL ()

somePureFunc :: IORef Int -> LangL (IORef Int)
somePureFunc inputVar = do
  val <- readVar inputVar
  newVar (val + 1)
```

◀── **High-level interface for IORefs**

◀── **Sample logic**

Notice the methods for IORefs. They have exactly the same meaning as native ones, but they are not IO—they are LangL. We don't have and can't even call IO actions to modify our IORefs and should use this wrapping LangL interface instead. So it's still impossible to run IO actions because we've abstracted them out. All the impurity moved to the implementation layer (into the interpreters). It would be worse if we made a slightly different decision. Consider the following code, where the LangL has a method to run IO actions:

```
data LangF next where
  EvalIO :: IO a -> (a -> next) -> LangF next

type LangL = Free LangF

evalIO :: IO a -> LangL a
evalIO ioAct = liftF (EvalIO ioAct id)
```

Given this evalIO, the same interface for working with IORef becomes possible so that the special methods in LangF are obsolete now:

```
newVar :: a -> LangL (IORef a)
newVar val = evalIO (newIORef a)

readVar :: IORef a -> LangL a
readVar var = evalIO (readIORef var)

writeVar :: IORef a -> a -> LangL ()
writeVar var val = evalIO (writeIORef var val)
```

The somePureFunc didn't change, but now we've made a giant black hole that's threatening to spaghettify our application unexpectedly:

```
somePureFunc :: IORef Int -> LangL (IORef Int)
somePureFunc inputVar = do
  val <- readVar inputVar
  evalIO spaghettifyEverything          ◄──┐ Something really
  newVar (val + 1)                          │ bad here
```

Of course, we could leave the evalIO function not exported and unavailable, but still. IO is tempting: everyone should decide the degree of sin they're fine with. It might not be that bad to have black holes in your project if you have good discipline.

Nevertheless, it's impossible to calculate the number of variables that have been created or to see who owns them and what will happen with them in a multithreaded environment. A quick answer: it would be very dangerous to access a raw mutable IORef from different threads. This is automatically a race condition that originates from the language design. We shouldn't be so naive as to think no one will step on this. Murphy's Law says it's inevitable. So what can we do? We can abstract working with state. And we can make the state thread-safe and convenient. We need STM in our business logic too.

There's an obvious way to run an STM transaction from the LangL script—either with evalIO or with a custom atomically function:

```
data LangF next where
  EvalIO           :: IO a  -> (a -> next) -> LangF next
  EvalStmAtomically :: STM a -> (a -> next) -> LangF next

type LangL = Free LangF
```

```
evalIO              :: IO a  -> LangL a
evalStmAtomically :: STM a -> LangL a
```

And finally, we can utilize these things in our business logic. For example, if we return to the meteor reporting function, it can be neither `LangL` nor `IO` but rather a normal STM. This is the `IO` version that is not thread-safe:

```
type ReportingChannel = IORef [Meteor]

reportMeteor :: ReportingChannel -> Meteor -> IO ()
reportMeteor ch meteor = do
  reported <- readIORef ch
  writeIORef ch (meteor : reported)
```

This is the `LangL` version, which is not safe either:

```
type ReportingChannel = IORef [Meteor]

reportMeteor :: ReportingChannel -> Meteor -> LangL ()
reportMeteor ch meteor = do
  reported <- readVar ch
  writeVar ch (meteor : reported)
```

And finally, here is the thread-safe `STM` version:

```
type ReportingChannel = TVar [Meteor]

reportMeteor' :: ReportingChannel -> Meteor -> STM ()
reportMeteor' ch meteor = do
  reported <- readTVar ch
  writeTVar ch (meteor : reported)

reportMeteor :: ReportingChannel -> Meteor -> LangL ()
reportMeteor ch meteor =
  evalStmAtomically (reportMeteor' ch meteor)
```

If you'd like, you can easily implement this interface in the interpreter. Just add a real `atomically:` for evalStmAtomically, and that's it:

```
interpretLangF rt (EvalStmAtomically stmAct next) = do
  res <- atomically stmAct
  pure (next res)
```

All the STM facilities—`TVars`, `TQueues`, and `TArrays`—will be available right from the scripts. This design is fast and fine in general, unless you need full control over the state in your app. You might want to

- Introspect the current application state and see what variables are actively used at this moment
- Limit the number of variables produced
- Be able to persist and restore your application state

In this case, you can abstract over STM even further and put it behind an interface somehow, but this is a story we should save for the next chapter.

STM provides even more opportunities to write concise code that works very well. There are, of course, some subtle things regarding the correct usage of STM and threads, but these difficulties aren't as big as when programming bare threads with traditional approaches to concurrency.

Summary

- Multithreading and concurrency are difficult topics, and our goal as developers is to predict the possible problems in the design stage of development.
- There can be many different problems in an inaccurately crafted concurrent environment: deadlocks, thread starvation, resource leakage, or wrong disposal.
- Learn the difference between IORefs, MVars, and STM TVars in a concurrent environment so you can consciously choose between them to design a reliable concurrent code.
- TVars are thread-safe and transactional, and they are also fundamental because you can express other data structures with them.
- Try to organize your threads safely to avoid leakage of handlers or other concurrent problems.
- Transactional data structures represent a data model; transactions (functions within the STM monad) represent a behavior model.
- Normally, bare threads should be treated as a limited resource, even if they are green.
- Leakage of green threads is a less severe problem than leakage of OS-specific threads, but it is still not desirable from a design point of view.
- Free monads can serve as an architectural pattern for constructing a general-purpose application framework.
- Incorporating STM into the framework as an interface brings another state-handling mechanism for the business logic.
- At the implementation layer, STM can and will make the framework safely concurrent.
- Bare IO is a temptation for developers, so it's better to put it (IO, not developers) in a straitjacket.

Foundational
subsystems

This chapter covers

- How to implement logging
- Abstracting subsystems with the Typed-Untyped design pattern
- Advanced approaches to state handling
- How to safely utilize resources using the Bracket pattern

Different application frameworks may show many similarities in what they offer to developers. Once a new framework enters the development scene, the same subsystems should be implemented repeatedly. Developers who have worked at several companies may confirm that every big-enough project has its own implementation in terms of logging, resource-acquisition mechanism, and integration with external subsystems. Unique implementations are inevitable because implementing a universal approach suitable for all the cases, languages, and domains is nearly impossible.

In this chapter, we will implement some important subsystems such as logging, and given that our main focus is on software design and approaches, we'll find a couple of new design patterns applicable to this widespread topic. We'll also learn about advanced state handling and touch briefly on the problem of proper resource management.

10.1 Logging subsystem

Logging is certainly the most essential subsystem of every application framework. It may even be the only subsystem that all the projects have in common. Moreover, it may be the only subsystem we repeatedly introduce and implement during our developer careers.

All the logging subsystems are more or less the same. We can expect to see an interface that

- Accepts a logging message and the level of logging (debug, error, info, and so on)
- Accepts the output destination (file, console, or external logs aggregation service)
- Has multiple implementations
- Accepts various additional attributes (timestamp, logger name, tags, or something else)

In addition, loggers can be

- *Synchronous*—The application is blocked until the logging message is written to the output.
- *Asynchronous*—Logging is detached from a thread, and pushing a message doesn't block the application.
- *Unstructured*—The message is just a text without a predefined format.
- *Structured*—The message is formatted (for example, as JSON) so that it is possible to make queries to the log storage and extract the required data.

How are all these elements combined inside the framework we're building? Let's find out!

10.1.1 Logger design

An imaginary yet familiar logging subsystem in C# could look like the following listing. Feeling nostalgic? It's an OOP interface with just a single method. We can expect to see several implementations such as `FileLogger`.

Listing 10.1 Logger in C#

```
public interface ILogger {                                          OOP interface to
  void logMessage(int logLevel, string message);                    a simple logger
};

public class FileLogger : ILogger {                                 Some
  private int _logLevel;                                            implementation
  private string _file;

  public FileLogger(int logLevel, string file) {
```

```
    _logLevel = logLevel;
    _file = file;
  }

  public void logMessage(int logLevel, string message) {
    if (logLevel <= _logLevel)
      using (StreamWriter log = File.AppendText(_file)) {
        log.WriteLine(message);
      }
  }
};
```

Checks whether the log level is high enough to publish the message

Acquires a resource that will be available in this lexical scope

The `ILogger` interface will be a template for implementations, even if `FileLogger` is the only implementation planned. I've heard an argument I strongly disagree with: "If you have only one implementation, you don't need an interface." This statement misses the point of interfaces and their purpose. We do not introduce interfaces to make multiple implementations. We introduce them to decouple and simpify business logic. The number of implementations is irrelevant. The fact that there is only one implementation is not a reason for making the code fragile, infested with unnecessary details, and barely testable.

In our case, the `ILogger` interface is good. It's free from implementation details such as filenames because otherwise there would be an inconsistency. If there is a filename in the interface, what does it mean for, let's say, a console logger? When designing an interface, we can't predict all the implementations up front, so we can't guarantee that the filename will be a valid field in all circumstances. This is commonsense. Also, it is in compliance with the single responsibility principle (SRP) and interface segregation principle (IRP) from SOLID. I would even say that from an engineering point of view, SOLID is commonsense itself.

Our free monadic interface obeys the same rules, and the exact same reasoning should be applied to it. Conceptually, this reasoning works for any interface, not just programming ones. It's a general approach that can be applied to any kind of engineering, up to the point of specificity and details.

A logger interface is presented in listing 10.2. It's place is illustrated in figure 10.1 (along with the structured logger).

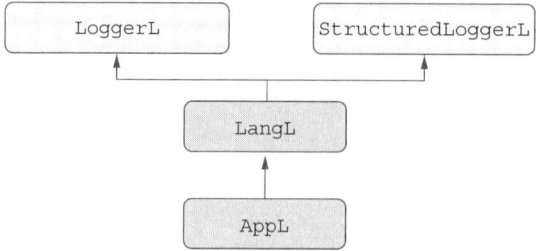

Figure 10.1 `LoggerL` and `StructuredLoggerL` **interfaces**

Therefore, every code in the `LangL` or the `AppL` monad will have access to this subsystem.

Listing 10.2   Logger free monadic interface

```
data LogLevel = Debug | Info | Warning | Error
type Message = Text

data LoggerF next where
  LogMessage
    :: LogLevel
    -> Message
    -> (() -> next)
    -> LoggerF next

type LoggerL = Free LoggerF

data LangF next where
 EvalLogger :: LoggerL () -> (() -> next) -> LangF next
```

The functor instance for this algebra is omitted.

Logger language

Nests LoggerL into the LangF algebra

So we've nested `LoggerL` into `LangL` like we did with other languages earlier. Now when we need to add some transparency to the meteor application, we can call the `logDebug` method:

```
getRandomMeteor :: LangL Meteor
getRandomMeteor = do
  rndSize <- getRandomInt (1, 100)
  rndMass <- getRandomInt (rndSize, rndSize * 10)
  let meteor = Meteor rndSize rndMass

  logDebug ("New random meteor: " <> show meteor)

  pure meteor
```

Logs a debug message

Here, the `logDebug` smart constructor adapts `LoggerL` to `LangL`:

```
logDebug :: Message -> LangL ()
logDebug msg = liftF (EvalLogger logDebug' id)
  where
    logDebug' :: LoggerL ()
    logDebug' = liftF (LogMessage Debug msg id)
```

I don't think writing `LoggerL` free monadic scripts makes sense, so I hide the helper smart constructor `logDebug'` from developers' eyes.

The details of a particular logger implementation will go to the interpreters as usual. Let's say we have a logger that formats a message and then outputs it to the console.

Listing 10.3   Console logger implementation

```
interpretLoggerMethod :: LoggerF a -> IO a
interpretLoggerMethod (LogMessage lvl msg next) = do
 putStrLn ("[" <> (show lvl) <> "] " <> msg)
 pure (next ())
```

Prints the message

```
runLogger :: LoggerL a -> IO a
runLogger logAction = foldF interpretLoggerMethod logAction

-- Possible output:
-- [Debug] New random meteor: Meteor 100 1000
```

We're already writing the business logic within our framework, so in the `LangL` eDSL, the logger is available for other subsystems. The hierarchical free monads approach works nicely here.

Let me pose a riddle here. What also works, but nobody will call it appropriate in functional programming (or at least not in Haskell)? This book examines both the beauty and the beast, and the beast discussed in the next section may scare everyone.

10.1.2 Global static mutable logger

Several implementation options are available in the OOP world. We usually don't want to switch loggers on the fly while the application is running, so sometimes we make the logger a global static subsystem. I'm not quite sure whether this is an antipattern, but I experienced such an approach in a C++ project. However, in C# projects, we've kept our loggers in *inversion of control (IoC) containers* (also known as dependency injection containers), so substituting logger implementations on the fly is technically possible.

Haskell or another functional language presents a slightly different picture. There are no IoC containers in functional programming (FP), no global static variables, no mutability, and no need for any OOP style, right? Actually, if we're talking about a grounded, homespun, pragmatic FP, not a pure, clean, academic FP, then we don't have all these artificial restrictions. We're allowed to use any solution we want if our goals justify it.

Both approaches are present in Haskell. There are IoC containers based on type-level features I'm not so sure about. There is also a way to have global static mutable variables. Yes, let me repeat: global static mutable variables. Can you imagine? There is a pattern for it, a hacky pattern, in fact. But please forget about it after I show it to you—burn my book and dip the ashes into acid. Take a look at this Haskell trickery with a static global mutable reference.

Listing 10.4   Logger and the global mutable variable pattern

```
import System.IO.Unsafe (unsafePerformIO)

{-# NOINLINE staticLoggerRef #-}
staticLoggerRef :: IORef (LoggerL () -> IO ())
staticLoggerRef = unsafePerformIO (newIORef runLogger)

staticLogInfo :: Text -> IO ()
staticLogInfo msg = do
 staticLogger <- readIORef staticLoggerRef
 staticLogger (logMessage Info msg)
```

Haskell's pragma to make the function non-inlinable

usafePerformIO: a dangerous function that breaks purity

A wrapper for convenience

Language method call

```
main :: IO ()
main = staticLogInfo "Hi there!"                    ◄——— Static logger use
```

This code works as follows: when the program starts (from main), it evaluates unsafePerformIO once for staticLoggerRef. This makes staticLoggerRef a static mutable IORef variable hanging in the air. Then this IORef can be accessed from a normal IO code such as staticLogInfo. Notice the use of NOINLINE pragma—the item needed to prevent loggerRef from embedding into other code. Together with unsafePerformIO, it forms a known pattern in the Haskell community that I highly recommend avoiding. Also, avoid the unsafePerformIO function; it's a dangerous tool. This function enables any IO effect anywhere, even in pure code, so it breaks purity when you least expect it:

```
innocent :: Int
innocent = unsafePerfomIO $ do
  putStrLn "Not so innocent"     -- IO action
  pure 7
```

So this is the beast. Let's leave this room quietly.

10.1.3 *Structured logging interface*

A bit more should be said about integrating logging libraries. I'll show you the code for the interpreters and talk about it in the context of so-called structured logging. Its idea is to evolve from logging of bare strings to logging of structures. Our logged strings often have this structure—timestamp, severity and message:

```
2022-10-15 14:39:41 GMT [Debug]By the way this is the time
   when I'm writing this text
```

This can be parsed without any problems or can be looked up with regular expressions. To me, this doesn't differ much from a structured JSON version:

```
{
  timestamp: "2022-10-15T14:46:18.964895945Z",
  severity: "Debug",
  message: "This is how much time passed from the previous paragraph"
}
```

It really starts to matter when we remember the purpose of structured logging because it's no longer about writing strings to files but about the aggregation of information on an external service such as Sentry or Fluentd. We push this JSON and may specify additional fields for a better description of what's happened. Logging services understand a variety of extra fields, both mandatory and optional. For example, the Sentry service accepts the following:

- Timestamp
- Message
- Logger name
- Event identifier

- Platform
- Server name
- Release
- Environment

Other services may disagree with this list and provide their own fields. As software architects, we have to oversee these requirements and properly implement them so that dealing with these services poses no risk to code. We should not only decide what service to go with and try to abstract its implementation details from, but also address the possibility of replacing it with something else in the future. This is certainly a general consideration that relates to any subsystem, including logging, databases, and message brokers. This general consideration doesn't have to be present in your case, but it has to be included in a book about design.

As usual, the design starts with defining interfaces. Our previous interface for the logger does not satisfy our needs. We can implement it for Sentry, but the logging method doesn't allow additional fields. Let's create a new interface for structured logs only.

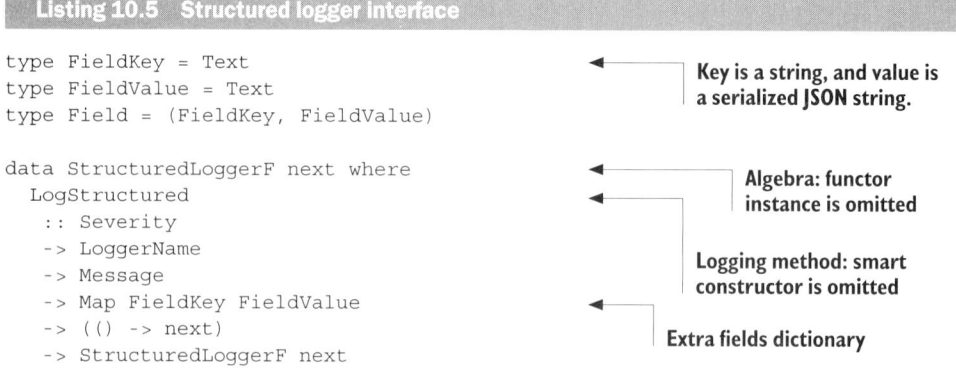

Listing 10.5   Structured logger interface

```
type FieldKey = Text                              ◄——    Key is a string, and value is
type FieldValue = Text                                   a serialized JSON string.
type Field = (FieldKey, FieldValue)

data StructuredLoggerF next where                 ◄——    Algebra: functor
  LogStructured                                   ◄——    instance is omitted
    :: Severity
    -> LoggerName                                         Logging method: smart
    -> Message                                            constructor is omitted
    -> Map FieldKey FieldValue                    ◄——
    -> (() -> next)
    -> StructuredLoggerF next                            Extra fields dictionary

type StructuredLoggerL = F StructuredLoggerF
```

In the next listing, we report a newly discovered meteor. We call the `sentryTimestamp` function to get a proper field for Sentry.

Listing 10.6   Logging a meteor

```
import qualified Data.Map as Map

data Meteor = Meteor                              ◄——    Domain data type
  { meteorId   :: Text
  , size       :: Int
  , mass       :: Int
  , timestamp  :: Timestamp
  }

logMeteorObservation :: Meteor -> StructuredLoggerL ()
```

```
logMeteorObservation (Meteor mId s m ts) =
 logStructued Info "astronomer"
   ("Meteor found. Mass: " <> show m <> ", size: " <> show s)
   (Map.fromList
    [ sentryTimestamp ts
    , sentryEventId mId
    ])
```

Dictionary of two extra fields

Function that takes Timestamp and returns a Sentry field

Function that takes Text and returns a Sentry field

Most of the extra fields will just be strings, but sometimes, they can be timestamps, integers, dates, Booleans, floats, or even a compound type. We can't predict the fields for every possible logging service. Even if we decide to integrate with Sentry, we should not make our interface too narrow or specialized. This is why I adopted an untyped design for fields. As you can see, it's a key–value pair—both are strings (Haskell's Text type):

```
type FieldKey   = Text
type FieldValue = Text
type Field = (FieldKey, FieldValue)
```

JSON-serialized value

So to safely create those fields, we should have a bunch of smart constructors, this time for Sentry:

```
module Framework.Logging.StructuredLogger.Fields.Sentry where

sentryEventId   :: Text      -> Field
sentryTimestamp :: Timestamp -> Field
```

Internally, this module knows how to convert Timestamp to Text, that is, to serialize it into a JSON value. In Haskell, we do this with the help of the aeson library and some char transformations. The following listing reveals the implementation details.

Listing 10.7 Sentry-specific fields

```
import qualified Data.Aeson as A
import qualified Data.ByteString.Lazy as LBS
import qualified Data.Text as T
import qualified Data.Text.Encoding as TEnc

sentryTimestampKey :: FieldKey
sentryTimestampKey = "srTimestamp"

sentryTimestamp :: Timestamp -> Field
sentryTimestamp ts = (sentryTimestampKey, strTs)
  where
    bsLazyTs :: LBS.ByteString
    bsLazyTs = A.encode ts

    bsStrictTs :: ByteString
    bsStrictTs = LBS.toStrict bsLazyTs

    txtTs :: Text
    txtTs = TEnc.decodeUtf8 bsStrictTs
```

Text key to identifying the field

aeson converts a value to a lazy byte array.

From lazy byte array to strict byte array

From strict byte array to text with respect to UTF-8

Here, you may see several conversions from lazy types to strict ones, from bytes of chars to text, and from UTF-8 to ASCII. Of course, the actual passing of those fields to a logging service happens in the interpreter, which is an implementation of our interface and is thus allowed to work with the external service directly.

10.1.4 Structured logging implementation

For the implementation part, I've chosen the `raven-haskell` library that will allow me to connect to Sentry. Figure 10.2 shows its placement.

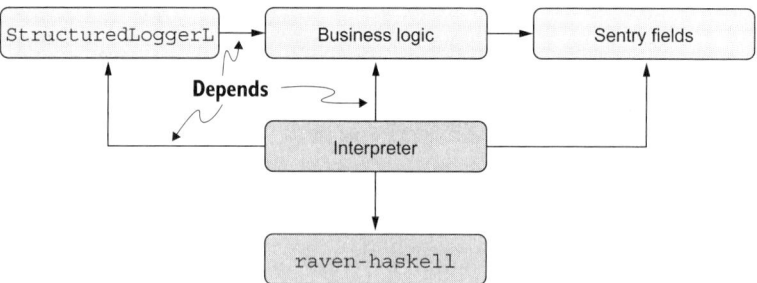

Figure 10.2 Integration of the native library `raven-haskell`

How can we convert our untyped dictionary of serialized values to something this library understands? Well, it's a data record with these fields, some of which are `String`, not `Text`:

```
-- raven-haskell structure
data SentryRecord = SentryRecord
  { srEventId   :: String
  , srMessage   :: String
  , srTimestamp :: UTCTime
  ...
  }
```

We must get our timestamp from the dictionary, deserialize it, and assign it to this record. For example, this could be a function to convert a single field.

Listing 10.8 Parsing Sentry-specific fields

```
toSentryRecord'
 :: (FieldKey, FieldValue)
 -> SentryRecord
 -> SentryRecord
toSentryRecord' (attrKey, attrVal) r

  | attrKey == sentryEventIdKey   = r { srEventId   = unpack attrVal }
  | attrKey == sentryTimestampKey = r { srTimestamp = parse attrVal }
```

And we could make the interpreter use those functions when processing the `Report` method.

Listing 10.9 From the interpreter to the real library call

```
import qualified System.Log.Raven as R                          ◄─── Native Sentry library

interpretSentryLoggerMethod'
 :: R.SentryService                                             ◄─── Native Sentry instance
 -> StructuredLoggerF a
 -> IO a
interpretSentryLoggerMethod'
   service
   (Report severity loggerName msg attribs next) = do          ┐ Process all fields and
  let sentryRecord = foldr                                     ◄─┘ update SentryRecord
          toSentryRecord'
           R.blankSentryRecord
            (Map.toList attribs)
  R.register                                                   ◄─── Native Sentry call
      service
      loggerName
      severity
      msg
      sSentryRecordF
  pure (next ())
```

We should start from a blank Sentry record and fill it by traversing the dictionary of attributes and calling `toSentryRecord'` for every key–value pair. After the whole dictionary is processed, we have a fully packed Sentry structure that we can then feed to the `register` function.

Unfortunately, the real code is a bit more complicated. You can check it out in the repo of this book and examine the full and correct implementation. What's important here is that we use a serialization trick to have a generic, type- and service-agnostic approach to fields. Certainly, there is a chance of doing it wrong and thus introducing some bugs. But smart constructors for fields prevent most problems and are quite simple to use. I call this trick the Typed-Untyped design pattern, where the typed is an interface and the untyped is implementation (see figure 10.3).

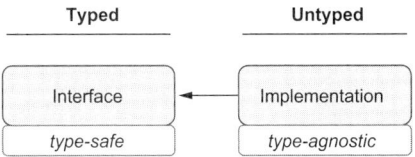

Figure 10.3 Typed interface, untyped implementation

We'll see this pattern again quite soon—in fact, in the next section, but in a different context.

10.2   *Advanced state management*

I want to teach you how to introduce even more abstraction into a design. Previously, we did some wrapping of threads and logging and played around with incorporating `IORef`, `MVar`, and STM into the framework. What wasn't there was how we can hide the implementation of a subsystem and its data types and why we should do so. This will be a showcase for wrapping around the state subsystem to make the state trackable.

The state is trackable at any moment in time. At any place in our program, we can ask for the number of active variables. We may want to ask how many of them were created by the application, their lifetimes, and how significant their read–write load is. Sometimes, we can even tell the framework to snapshot the variables, possibly printing them into the console for further debugging. For this to be allowed, we need even more control over the state subsystem. The previous STM integration is no longer suitable, so we will replace it with a new language, `StateL`, and do some magic around it.

I know this might feel strange at first because it brings another level of indirection. Yet this approach supports several parts of the Hydra framework, and it paves the road to additional safety, testability, and good separation of concerns.

10.2.1 *Wrapping STM with the Typed-Untyped design pattern*

The trackable state subsystem should not stray far from STM. In fact, it should behave exactly as STM, including all the concurrency guarantees. We'll just make a facade for STM and pretend that we did something useful. All the functions to work with concurrent variables (now known as `StateVar`) will be there, as will the retry method:

```
data StateF next where
  NewVar   :: a -> (StateVar a -> next) -> StateF next
  ReadVar  :: StateVar a -> (a -> next) -> StateF next
  WriteVar :: StateVar a -> a -> (() -> next) -> StateF next
  Retry    :: (a -> next) -> StateF next

type StateL = Free StateF
```

STM will be the main and only implementation of this language, so we can safely call `StateL` a transactional concurrent state subsystem:

```
runStateL :: StateL a -> STM a
```

For comparison, the following listing provides the previous and new business logic.

Listing 10.10 The code before and after

```
-- Then:
reportMeteor' :: TVar [Meteor] -> Meteor -> STM ()
reportMeteor' channel meteor = do
  reported <- readTVar channel
  writeTVar channel (meteor : reported)

-- Now:
```

```
reportMeteor' :: StateVar [Meteor] -> Meteor -> StateL ()
reportMeteor' channel meteor = do
  reported <- readVar channel
  writeVar channel (meteor : reported)
```

It's effectively the same, up to the identifiers.

It's single language, single responsibility, and it's not any different from the usage point of view. Even StateVar should be implemented as a TVar—except how does TVar work? What is its internal structure? Honestly, I have no idea because TVar is an opaque data type. I've never had to examine it, even though I once rolled my own STM with free monads. You can check out free-monad-based STM in Haskell at https://github.com/graninas/stm-free or in C++ at https://github.com/graninas/cpp_stm_free.

We can and should, however, look at the structure of StateVar. It's a super simple parametrized ADT with a phantom type parameter a:

```
newtype StateVar a = StateVar
  { _varId :: Int
  }
```

Similar to TVar, we have a type of data we store. But where is this data? We didn't put it into ADT. There is just some integer field there. Are you puzzled?

The StateVar value keeps an integer reference to the internal, hidden TVar. The corresponding TVar will be held in the runtime of the interpreter and only be accessible for this implementation layer. Nothing difficult here, except there is a small problem of how to store StateVar Meteor, StateVar Int, StateVar (Int, Float, Meteor) at the same time, along with all other user-defined types. A dictionary of TVars? Sure, but of what types? Data collections aren't heterogeneous; they don't allow this:

```
Map VarId (TVar ???)
```

I believe there is a type-level solution with a heterogeneous map—a solution that we'll avoid. We'll use the Typed-Untyped design pattern's Typed Avatar variation instead (typed avatar is our StateVar). For this to enroll, we need the Any type. In Haskell, it's GHC.Any; in C++, it's std::any; and in Scala, it's Any class. With it, we'll be storing all the possible user variables in the untyped form. So this is also the Typed-Untyped design pattern (see figure 10.4).

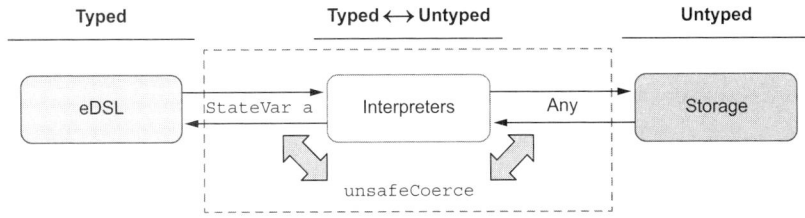

Figure 10.4   Typed-Untyped design pattern

In Haskell, to convert between `GHC.Any` and a particular user type, we do `unsafe-Coerce` back and forth in the interpreter:

```
-- Forcibly treat a type as another type:
unsafeCoerce :: a -> b

-- Example of usage:
unsafeCoerceMeteor :: Meteor -> Any
unsafeCoerceMeteor m = unsafeCoerce m
```

The runtime-scoped dictionary should reference every `TVar` with an identifier. We memorize the last created ID and just increase it whenever a variable is created. As long as our framework supports concurrency, we should access the storage thread safely; thus, `TMVar` is the mirror of `MVar` in STM. I will only show you the runtime structure and a fraction of the interpreter. Notice that the interpreter is in the STM monad.

Listing 10.11 Runtime and interpreter of the `StateL` language

```
data StateRuntime = StateRuntime
  { _varId  :: TVar VarId                  ◄──── Last created integer
  , _state  :: TMVar (Map VarId (TVar Any))        identifier
  }

interpretStateF :: StateRuntime -> StateF r -> STM r    ◄──── The interpreter is in
interpretStateF stateRt (ReadVar var next) = do                the STM monad, not
  val <- readVar' stateRt var                                  in the IO monad.
  pure (next val)                          ◄──── Requests the variable

readVar' :: StateRuntime -> StateVar a -> STM a    ◄──── Also an STM monad
readVar' stateRt (StateVar varId) = do
  nodeState <- readTMVar (_state stateRt)
  case Map.lookup varId nodeState of
    Nothing -> error ("Var not found: " <> varId)
    Just (RVarHandle tvar) -> do
      anyVal <- readTVar tvar                       ◄──── Unsafely coerces
      let (val :: a) = usafeCoerce anyVal                 from Any to some
      pure a                                              user-defined type
```

One of the important points here is how the interpreter knows about the user-defined type. The latter comes with the `ReadVar` constructor. The type is enclosed there:

```
data StateF next where
  ReadVar :: StateVar a -> (a -> next) -> StateF next
```

We learned this earlier when we were nesting free monad eDSLs into each other. In both cases, the `a` type variable is encapsulated in a method and can only serve its purpose in the interpreter. The same is true for nesting `StateL` into `LangL`:

```
data LangF next where
  EvalStateAtomically :: StateL a -> (a -> next) -> LangF next

atomically :: StateL a -> LangL a
```

Note that we cannot fool the system and ask for a wrong data type in `readVar` because we must prove our intentions with a typed `StateVar a`. By doing so, we provide a fully typed eDSL for business logic that runs over an untyped runtime without sacrificing type safety.

10.2.2 *State subsystem and logging*

Let me ask you a question: If you have a `StateL` (STM) transaction, how would you log something inside it? There is no `IO`, so no external effects are allowed. Also, considering the STM nature, every STM function might be restarted many times. If we imagine some black hole `runIO` method in our `StateL` type, we might have been surprised by dozens of log entries, when only one was expected.

The simplest solution is to collect log messages on the business logic layer and print them outside the `StateL` language:

```
reportMeteor' :: ReportingChannel -> Meteor -> StateL String
reportMeteor' channel meteor = do
  ...
  pure ("Meteor reported successfully: "          ◄──── Logs the message
      <> show meteor)                                    in StateL

reportMeteor :: ReportingChannel -> Meteor -> LangL ()
reportMeteor channel meteor = do
  msg <- atomically (reportMeteor' channel meteor)       Prints the
  logInfo msg                                     ◄──── message in LangL
```

These two functions work in different contexts: `StateL` and `LangL`. Suddenly, `report-Meteor'` returns a log entry as a result. I've never seen something like that in real projects and would consider this a bad design. What if it's many messages? Does this mean we should return a list of them like in the following snippet?

```
-- Returns multiple log entries.
reportMeteor' :: ReportingChannel -> Meteor -> StateL [String]
```

However, logging isn't part of the function interface but some tiny, irrelevant detail. Why do we make the caller function process the logs? We pay too much attention to them. By doing this, we equate logs and domain notions—a very strange convention.

There's one more solution that involves the application state. We add a special variable for collecting log entries. This application state should also be concurrent because we're going to modify it from the `StateL` transactions:

```
data AppState = AppState
  { _reportingChannel :: ReportingChannel
  , _logEntries :: StateVar [String]          ◄──── List of logs
  }
                                                     Pushes a message
logSt :: AppState -> String -> StateL ()       ◄──── into the list of logs
```

This enables a kind of logging in the `StateL` scripts:

```
reportMeteor' :: AppState -> Meteor -> StateL String
reportMeteor' st meteor = do
```

```
logSt st "Reading channel"
...
logSt st "Writing channel"
...
```

Now we need to relay those logs from the application state to the real logger. This should be done right after every `StateL` script invocation

```
atomically (reportMeteor' st meteor)
flushLogEntries st
```

where flushing is reading `_logEntries`, blanking it, and then calling for `logInfo` from `LoggerL`:

```
flushLogEntries :: AppState -> LangL ()
flushLogEntries st = do
  logs <- atomically getLogs
  mapM_ logInfo logs

  where
    getLogs = do
      logs <- readVar (_logEntries st)
      writeVar (_logEntries st) []
      pure logs
```

StateL atomic invocation

LoggerL invocation

Frees the variable

This approach shows the following problems:

- It needs to keep additional variables for log entries, and it has to be concurrent.
- It passes the state variable here and there.
- There is an explicit function for log flushing that you need to remember.
- It is not appropriate in the business logic.
- It only supports the "info" level of log messages. To support more levels, you'll need more functions, more variables, or a kind of generalization.

We can do better. After all, we have a nice separation of concerns, and we can benefit from it. We'll move transactional logging to the implementation layer while exposing the same `LoggerL` interface to `StateL`. The code of `StateL` scripts will look pretty neat because we got rid of `AppState`:

```
anyStateFunc :: StateL (StateVar Int)
anyStateFunc = do
  logInfo    "Some info in StateL"
  logWarning "Some warning in StateL"
  newVar 10
```

The responsibility to collect messages from transactions will go to the interpreter. There will be no need for manual flushing. The logs will be flushed automatically once a transaction succeeds, no matter how many times it was triggered. Let's call this approach *delayed STM logging*. Figure 10.5 illustrates this idea.

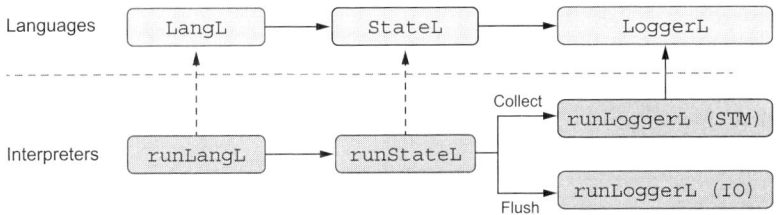

Figure 10.5 Delayed STM logging

First, we nest the logger eDSL in the `StateL`:

```
data StateF next where
  EvalStmLogger :: LoggerL () -> (() -> next) -> StateF next
```

Second, we move the log entries collection to the runtime. Let's log real entries instead of plain strings:

```
data StateRuntime = StateRuntime
  { _stmLog :: TVar [LogEntry]
  }
```

Third, in addition to the `IO`-acting `LoggerL` interpreter, we add a new STM-based one. It pushes logs into the `_stmLog` variable:

```
interpretStmLoggerF :: TVar [LogEntry] -> LoggerF a -> STM a
runStmLoggerL       :: TVar [LogEntry] -> LoggerL () -> STM ()
```

Fourth, we call this interpreter from the `StateL` interpreter. Both share the `STM` monad, meaning they form a single compound transaction. If this transaction fails and restarts, we still have our `TVar [LogEntry]` in a valid state. There will be no duplicated messages, no missing messages, and so forth:

```
interpretStateF :: StateRuntime -> StateF a -> STM a
interpretStateF stateRt (EvalStmLogger act next) = do
  runStmLoggerL (_stmLog stateRt) act
  pure (next ())

runStateL :: StateRuntime -> StateL a -> STM a
```

Finally, we flush the STM logs from the `LangL` `IO`-based interpreter after each `StateL` evaluation. This is simplified pseudocode (see the Hydra framework for the actual implementation):

```
interpretLangF :: StateRuntime -> LangF a -> IO a            Runs a
interpretLangF stateRt (EvalStateAtomically action next) = do   stateful script
  let stmAction = runStateL stateRt action
  res <- atomically stmAction                                 Evaluates STM
  flushLogEntries stateRt
  pure (next res)                                             Flushes logs
                                                              collected
```

Reducing complexity became possible because we abstracted the state, logger, and language for business logic. We organized the languages hierarchically with the interpreters and got these nice benefits without sacrificing any design principles. It's pretty satisfying, isn't it?

> **NOTE**   We can't use the same functions, `logInfo` and `logWarning`, for both `StateL` and `LangL` monads—at least, not the monomorphic versions. The complete solution includes a type class `Logger`, which is instantiated for `StateL` and `LangL` (as well as for `AppL`); after this, the logging functions will be polymorphic enough to be used everywhere.

10.2.3 *Trackable state*

As you start treating free monads as a counterpart to object-oriented interfaces, more interesting use cases occur. For example, we can enhance the state subsystem with an additional feature—state tracking.

The total tracking of state variables will be easy to obtain since we have them all in the runtime:

```
TMVar (Map VarId Any)
```

However, you can't do much with them represented as `Any`. It's not printable, and there is no accompanying info about the real type behind it. Nothing tells us when the variable was created and what its size is. This info disappears once the variable crosses the language interface. If needed, we can help the language keep some knowledge about the variable and pass it through to the interpreters. For example, let's add a possibility to output any `StateVar` that is printable and do nothing for nonprintable ones. We can't just call `print` in the interpreter because there is no `Show` instance for `Any`, but we can just add it into the methods `NewVar`, `ReadVar`, and others:

```
data StateF next where
  NewVar
    :: Show a
    => a
    -> (StateVar a -> next)
    -> StateF next
```

Too strict limitation

Variable's value

This will kind of work, so the interpreter will be able to print the variable, but this greatly limits the types the developer can keep in the variables—not a desirable solution. A better one would be to encapsulate showing functionality into a function that may or may not be applied to a user-defined type:

```
data StateF next where
  NewVar
    :: a
    -> (a -> Maybe String)
    -> (StateVar a -> next)
    -> StateF next
```

Variable's value

Printing action

The `Show` constraint will go one level higher. There will be a smart constructor for printable variables and another one for others. We construct the printing function and preserve it in the value constructor:

```
newVar :: a -> StateL (StateVar a)
newVar a = liftF (NewVar a (const Nothing) id)        ◄──── The type is not printable.

                                                       │ The type is printable.
newVar' :: Show a => a -> StateL (StateVar a)
newVar' a = liftF (NewVar a (Just . show) id)         ◄──┘
```

When the printing function returns `Nothing`, the type is not printable, and vice versa; the `Just` result gives the value stringified. By doing so, we encapsulated the printing functionality for this `NewVar` method, but unfortunately, it will get lost for others. Our last move will be to grant access to the printing function for other methods. We simply extend the `StateVar` ADT and preserve the printing function for further use:

```
data StateVar a = StateVar
  { _varId :: VarId
  , _printAction :: a -> Maybe String
  }

interpretStateF stateRt (NewVar val printF next) = do
  ...
  let var = StateVar varId printF             ◄──── Preserves the action
  pure (next var)
```

Every time the `StateVar` instance crosses the boundaries between the business logic and implementation, this action can help debug your data. If that's not enough and you want to know the exact time the variable was created, you now know how to achieve that with this simple and functional trick.

One small note about the performance: `StateVar` in its current design isn't as efficient as `TVar` because each time we use it, we have to request a real `TVar` from the internal `Data.Map` structure. The map structure is protected by another concurrent variable—TMVar:

```
data StateRuntime = StateRuntime
    { _varId  :: TVar VarId                    -- ^ Var id counter
    , _state  :: TMVar (Map VarId VarHandle)   -- ^ Tracked variables
    , _stmLog :: TVar Log                       -- ^ Stm log entries
    }
```

Although this is a demo design, this might be a problem for real code bases. To avoid such an indirection, we can allow untracked state by modifying `StateVar`:

```
data StateVar a
  = StateVar { _varId :: VarId }               │ Untrackable
  | UntrackedStateVar (TVar a)                 ◄──┘ variable fallback
```

We should certainly provide new smart constructors that handle this, which is trivial, and we'll skip this step. At least I demonstrated that my approach to application architecture has some flexibility and enables various nice tricks.

10.3 *Resource initialization and the Bracket pattern*

Proper use and control of resources have been a huge struggle ever since the first computer was invented. This topic used to be touchy in the early era of low-resource software development and still remains so in the modern era of gigahertz processors and terabyte RAMs. It seems that the more we have, the more we need. And once we have more resources, we need to organize them carefully.

Many ideas about how to do so have been proposed, and several methodologies emerged solely targeting this particular problem in different contexts. For example, you might have heard about the philosophy Erlang users repeat quite often: "Let it crash." The idea is that allowing the application to crash is cheaper than trying to make it 100% reliable. I personally see a lot of problems with such an approach, especially in a concurrent environment, but this might be justified in some cases.

We'll be talking about a more local and very useful approach for controlling resources and not letting the program crash—Resource Acquisition Is Initialization (RAII)—but applied to functional programming.

10.3.1 *RAII in OOP languages*

What is RAII? It's used to easily create and free a resource without any extra effort and with some additional guarantees. The approach has several implementations and variations in OOP languages. In C++, it can be a class that wraps the two operations: initialization (in the constructor) and disposal (in the destructor). The developer should not acquire the resource manually but rather instantiate an object of this class. Indirect interaction with the resource allows for many clever tricks—for example, validation, authentication, reconnection on the fly, and so on. The following listing presents RAII for writing into a file.

Listing 10.12 RAII in C++

```
struct File {
  File(string filename) {          ◄── The constructor
    // open file here                     initializes the resource.
  }

  ~File() {                        ◄── The destructor releases
    // close file here                   the resource.
  }

  void write( string content ) {   ◄── Interface to use
    // use file here                     the resource
  }
};

{                                  ◄── RAII—creating an object on
  auto myFile = File("my_file.txt");    the stack in this lexical scope
  myFile.write("Hello, world!");   ◄── Dealing with
}                                        the resource
```

When the execution leaves the lexical scope of the `myFile` variable, the destructor will be called automatically, and the file will be closed. This will even work if some exception is thrown when the `write` method is called. Exceptions in programming languages are the main enemies of correctness, so the RAII implementation should pay close attention to exception safety when working with a resource. In C#, we enjoy a language syntax made specifically for the RAII pattern (see https://en.cppreference .com/w/cpp/language/raii). We've seen it already in listing 10.1—it's the `using` keyword that defines the scope for the resource and limits its lifetime:

```
using (StreamWriter file = File.AppendText("my_file.txt")) {
  file.WriteLine("Hello, world!");
}
```

This is very convenient and clean. C# has tools for making custom RAII wrappers for the resources not available in stock libraries, and those wrappers will work quite well with the `using` feature.

The idea of RAII is very fruitful, so having it in our FP languages would be really nice. And in fact, we have it. Let's discuss the Bracket pattern now.

10.3.2 *The Bracket pattern*

This pattern is quite simple and contains only a single high-order function that will be responsible for scoping the lifetime of a resource and protecting it from accidental loss. Implementing this function doesn't look complicated unless your programming language has some tricky exception mechanisms. Haskell is a dangerous language because it has synchronous and asynchronous exceptions along with laziness and various underwater pitfalls. I would avoid reimplementing the pattern, especially in the presence of the `bracket` function from `Control.Exception`. I'm also deliberately simplifying the topic of exceptions here because we will talk more about them in chapter 13. Schematically, the `bracket` function works as shown in figure 10.6.

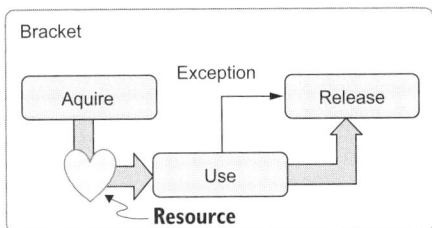

Figure 10.6　The Bracket pattern

The function expects the following three functions as arguments: initialization of the resource, the release of the resource, and action to utilize the resource. The definition is

```
bracket
  :: IO resource             -- acquire the resource
  -> (resource -> IO ())     -- release the resource
```

```
     -> (resource -> IO result)    -- utilize the resource
     -> IO result                  -- return the result
```

For example, if we want to initialize the Sentry service for structured logging, we can write

```
import qualified System.Log.Sentry as S

initLogger :: IO S.SentryService
initLogger = S.initSentryService "<connection_string>"

disposeLogger :: S.SentryService -> IO ()
disposeLogger service = S.deinitSentryService service

doSomething :: S.SentryService -> IO ()
doSomething service = ...       -- use Sentry service here

main = bracket (initLogger mySentryConfig) disposeLogger doSomething
```

Now we're guaranteed that if some connection to Sentry is established, it will be carefully disposed of after the doSomething call. The main function of the application is therefore a good place to initialize all the needed framework subsystems, such as logger services, permanent database connections, and live network channels.

There is one rule, though, that I would highly recommend: one bracket function, one resource to take care of. If there are a bunch of resources, don't try to initialize them in a god-like init function. What if you have an exception in the middle of the process of initialization or, even worse, deinitialization? Look at the code with three resources:

```
initMyResources :: IO (ResourceA, ResourceB, ResourceC)
initMyResources = do
  resourceA <- initResourceA
  resourceB <- initResourceB             -- this call throws
  resourceC <- initResourceC
  pure (resourceA, resourceB, resourceC)
```

What state will ResourceA be when acquiring ResourceB fails? The bracket function doesn't call the disposal action if it got an exception from the initialization.

Again, the disposal should work with only one atomic resource. If we imagine that all three were initialized successfully, what will happen in this code if the middle call throws?

```
deinitMyResources :: (ResourceA, ResourceB, ResourceC) -> IO ()
deinitMyResources (resourceA, resourceB, resourceC) = do
  initResourceA resourceA
  initResourceB resourceB                -- this call throws
  initResourceC resourceC
```

In this case, resourceA is released, the state of resourceB is unknown, and resourceC will become a long-living zombie. The Bracket pattern won't help here, although everything looks fine at first:

```
main = bracket initMyResources deinitMyResources utilizeMyResources

utilizeMyResources :: (ResourceA, ResourceB, ResourceC) -> IO ()
```

Separating initializations and disposals for each resource is not only compliant with the single responsibility principle, but it also enables a correct RAII with stacking the `bracket` functions so that they form nesting scopes for each resource separately. This is how it should be written for our sample:

```
main =
  bracket initResourceA deinitResourceA (\resourceA ->
  bracket initResourceB deinitResourceB (\resourceB ->
  bracket initResourceC deinitResourceC (\resourceC ->
    utilizeMyResources (resourceA, resourceB, resourceC)
  )))
```

This works because

- Many bracket functions can be composed.
- In the case of an exception in the utilization action, the bracket function calls the disposal action and then rethrows the exception so that the external bracket will do its work as well.

The final result with scopes (lifetimes) of each resource is presented in figure 10.7.

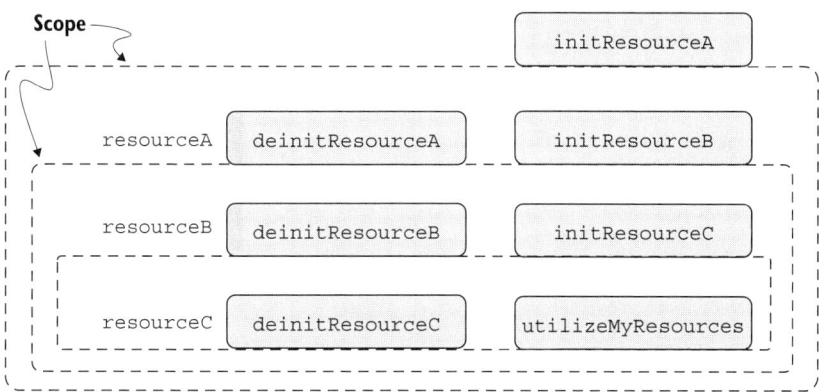

Figure 10.7 Scopes of the resources

You can watch this pattern in the wild in the Hydra framework, and there is also sample code in the book's repo.

Summary

- Every application framework should provide logging possibilities out of the box.
- With hierarchical free monads, adding a new subsystem into the framework is not difficult.
- It's better not to violate the philosophy of a framework-based application with hacks such as global static mutable variables and global loggers.
- *Structured logging* means *sending structured information* to the external log collection services.
- Abstracting over the logging subsystem helps to have multiple implementations of it; this is why the notion of interfaces is incredibly important in software design.
- As a design mechanism, free monads are closely related to OOP interfaces.
- Abstracting over the state subsystem enables some interesting possibilities, such as a trackable state.
- Wrapping a complete abstraction over some subsystem would be difficult without the Typed–Untyped design pattern and its variation, the Typed Avatar pattern.
- Logging in the STM transactions may be cumbersome, but with the help of an abstracted state, it becomes as easy as in regular code.
- Resource handling is a difficult topic, especially in the presence of concurrency and exceptions.
- The RAII approach from the mainstream languages can find its place in FP languages as the Bracket design pattern.
- A great thing about the `bracket` function is that it's stackable, which is very convenient when dealing with multiple resources.
- A rule of thumb is that each resource must be initialized and deinitialized individually.
- When the `bracket` function catches the exception from the action, it first calls the destructor and then rethrows the exception so that external `bracket` functions can also dispose of their resources.

11

Persistence: Key–value databases

Programs are rarely isolated, having no interaction with external data storage, such as a relational database, key–value database, filesystem, cloud storage, or something else. While the interaction model may vary, the idea behind it is always the same: being able to access a significant amount of data that can't be located directly in the program's memory.

In this chapter, we'll use a new subsystem for the framework: the key–value database subsystem. It will be a low-level raw string-based (that is, unsafe) interface in the form of a new free monadic language (KVDBL). We'll then proceed to the next step: enrolling a fully typed and type-safe interface on top of the string-based one (figure 11.1).

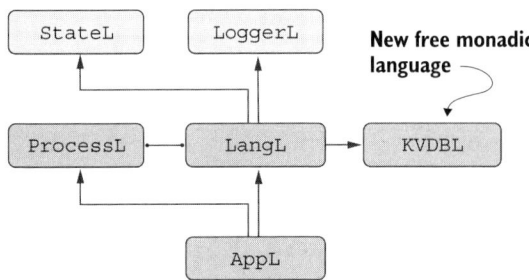

Figure 11.1   **Framework subsystems: a new free monadic language is added to the hierarchy**

I'll demonstrate how to make the system more correct, robust, and convenient. We'll also talk about extensibility, and on this journey, we'll learn some useful type-level magic.

11.1 *Raw untyped key–value database subsystem*

Our current task is to track meteors and other astronomical objects in a single database. There are no special requirements—we should be able to write and read information, and we're happy with a plain database application. Can we use a key–value database, then? It depends. NoSQL databases provide different mechanisms for querying, and it's also possible to construct indexes and relations exclusively for certain needs. We should at least implement the following:

- *Storing/loading a value by a key*—It's a good start but not enough for most real-world scenarios.
- *Transactional/nontransactional operations*—We'll try to make a distinction between the two contexts.
- *Multiple thread-safe connections*—Some applications might need to maintain several connections to several databases (for example, cache, actual storage, metrics, and so on). The access to each connection and to the set of connections should be thread-safe.
- *Raw, untyped, low-level interface (eDSL)*—It's fine to have raw strings for keys and values in the low-level interface. This is what all key–value storages must support.
- *Typed higher-level interface (eDSL) on top of an untyped one*—This one should allow us to represent a database model in a better way than just raw keys and values.

Of course, we also want to comply with all the design principles, such as KISS and SOLID.

11.1.1 *Native key–value database libraries*

We'll choose the following well-known key–value database systems:

- *RocksDB*—Embedded database for key–value data
- *Redis*—Remote, distributed, in-memory key–value database storage

While these key–value storage systems offer a must-have basis—namely, setting and getting value by a key—there are unique properties that distinguish different database systems. This is problematic because we can't unify these databases under a single interface: such an interface would be too broad to address every possible feature, and the implementations would try hard to carry out what's relevant for a concrete database, while avoiding the bits that relate to another database. Therefore, we must cut off most functionality and focus on the most desirable.

What does a typical library look like? Let's dive into the `rocksdb-haskell` library and its reading method. These are Haskell bindings for RocksDB with a relatively simple design.

Listing 11.1 RocksDB bindings

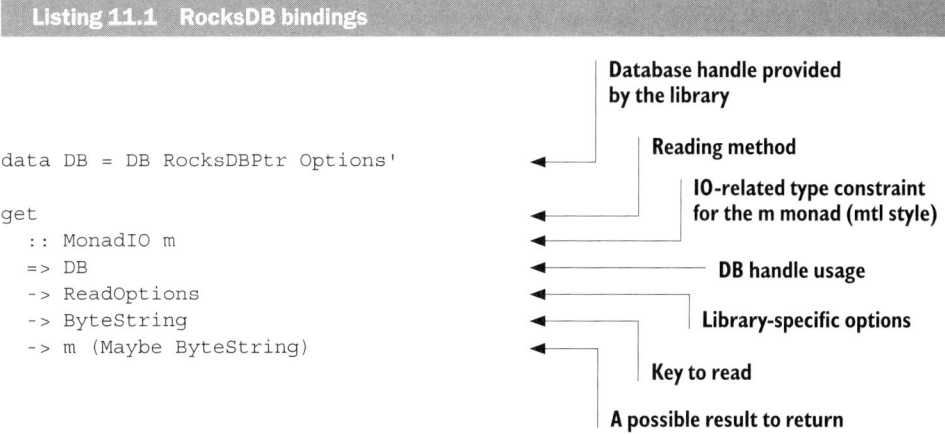

The `get` function works in the bare `IO`. To be more precise, you see the *mtl* style of specifying the effects (mtl stands for *monad transformers library*). It has the abstract monad `m` and some constraints (effects) assigned to it. In our case, there is only one constraint (`MonadIO`) that requires the `m` type to be `IO` when fully specified. `MonadIO` is a core Haskell type class from the base libraries. The `IO` type satisfies this constraint and makes it possible to call `get` from any `IO` monadic block. The mtl style has a large following in Haskell and a small one in Scala. For now, let's agree that those two things are equal and proceed:

```
myMonadIOFunc :: MonadIO m => m ()
myIOFunc :: IO ()
```

The `hedis` library for Redis goes even further. It's a monadic context but a custom one: `RedisCtx`. And as long as it's custom, there is a monad that satisfies this context (`Redis`) and a runner function for it (`runRedis`).

Listing 11.2   Redis bindings

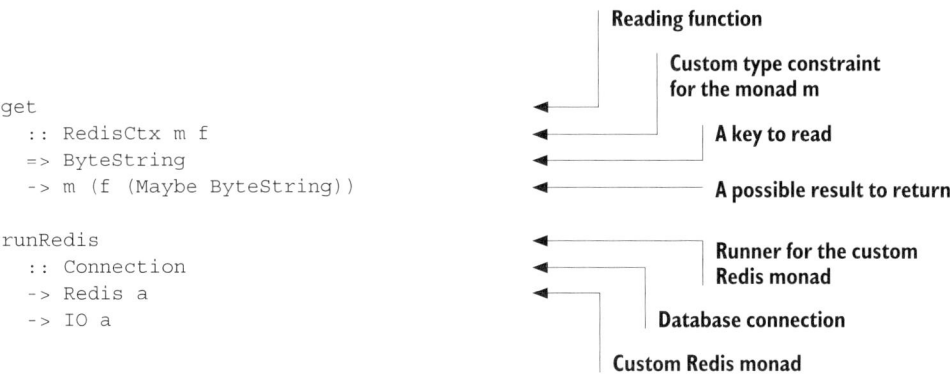

```
get
  :: RedisCtx m f
  => ByteString
  -> m (f (Maybe ByteString))

runRedis
  :: Connection
  -> Redis a
  -> IO a
```

Reading function

Custom type constraint
for the monad m

A key to read

A possible result to return

Runner for the custom
Redis monad

Database connection

Custom Redis monad

Simplifying what is in the library, the `Redis` monad is where you declare your queries, one or many, and then run it against `IO`:

```
sampleQueries :: Redis ()
sampleQueries = do
  set "hello" "hello"
  set "world" "world"

runSampleQueries :: Connection -> IO ()
runSampleQueries conn = runRedis conn sampleQueries
```

We want something similar in our framework.

11.1.2 *String-based key–value database interface*

Listing 11.3 shows the simplest monadic key–value database language, which has only two methods. It has `ByteString` keys and values for both the save/load methods. A developer should serialize their specific type, such as `Meteor`, into the array of bytes, such as JSON or binary, or some other format.

Listing 11.3   Basic string-based key–value database interface

```
type KVDBKey   = ByteString
type KVDBValue = ByteString

data KVDBF next where
  Save :: KVDBKey
       -> KVDBValue
       -> (DBResult () -> next)
       -> KVDBF next
  Load :: KVDBKey
       -> (DBResult KVDBValue -> next)
       -> KVDBF next

type KVDBL db = Free KVDBF
```

Language for dealing
with databases; has a
phantom type db

```
save :: KVDBKey -> KVDBValue -> KVDBL db (DBResult ())    | Smart constructors; utilize
load :: KVDBKey -> KVDBL db (DBResult KVDBValue)          | the phantom type db
```

Notice that I put an additional phantom type `db` into the language type. It's not the only possible solution to avoid confusing multiple databases but just a solution I find convenient. The mechanism itself goes along with a special type class `DB`:

```
type DBName = String

class DB db where
  getDBName :: DBName
```

In the application, some database instances should be declared by implementing this type class:

```
data ValuesDB
data AstroDB

instance DB ValuesDB where
  getDBName = "raw_values.rdb"

instance DB AstroDB where
  getDBName = "astro.rdb"
```

Then, we're ready to apply the types in `KVDBL` methods. There are at least two ways to tell the type we want—type applications (Haskell's GHC extension `TypeApplications`) and direct type specification:

```
load "key1" @ValuesDB                                     ◄── Type
(load "meteor-110") :: KVDBL AstroDB (DBResult KVDBValue) ◄── application
                                                          Direct type
                                                          specification
```

For RocksDB, the database name matches the file name. For other key–value databases, the meaning of this type class may differ.

Let's return to the interface. Methods can fail for some reason, and we encode this reason as `DBResult`:

```
data DBErrorType
  = SystemError
  | InvalidType
  | DecodingFailed
  | UnknownDBError

data DBError = DBError DBErrorType Text

type DBResult a = Either DBError a
```

There are no database connections included in the interface. It's only purpose is to represent operations with data: reading, writing, searching, updating, deleting, and so on. However, the approach to connectivity should be considered. We can think of the database connection as an implementation detail, and it should then go to the corresponding layer without appearing in the business logic. However, in most situations, explicit connectivity is preferable, and the framework should somehow support that.

So what's the plan? To mimic the approach we have in `hedis`. Figure 11.2 illustrates this.

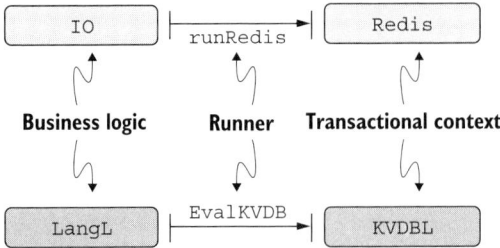

Figure 11.2   Two approaches to running a DB scenario

The diagram draws similarities between running a `Redis` script from `IO` and a `KVDBL` script from `LangL`. Both have scopes for business logic and transactional context in which one keeps the queries. The following listing presents the complete integration with extra tools for declaring databases.

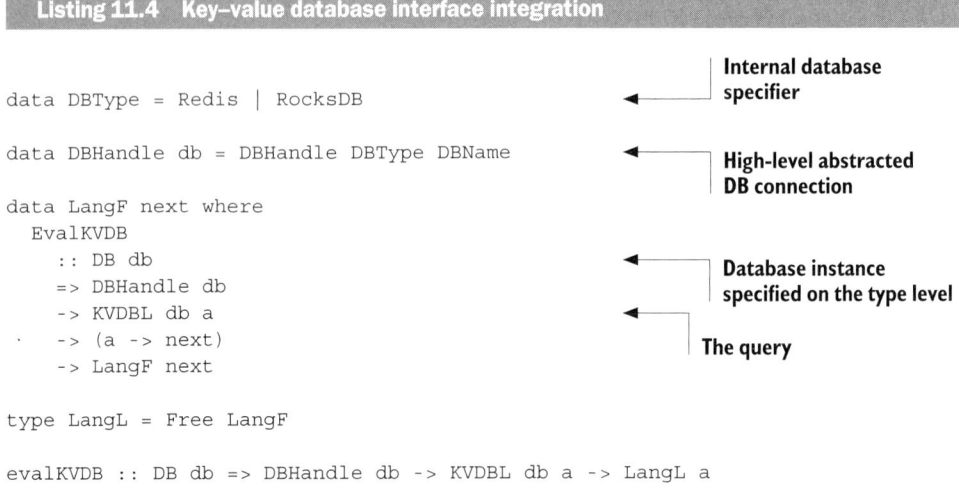

Listing 11.4   Key–value database interface integration

```
data DBType = Redis | RocksDB                    Internal database
                                                 specifier

data DBHandle db = DBHandle DBType DBName        High-level abstracted
                                                 DB connection
data LangF next where
  EvalKVDB
    :: DB db                                     Database instance
    => DBHandle db                               specified on the type level
    -> KVDBL db a
    -> (a -> next)                               The query
    -> LangF next

type LangL = Free LangF

evalKVDB :: DB db => DBHandle db -> KVDBL db a -> LangL a
```

`DBHandle` will be a connection that should be passed explicitly to the `EvalKVDB` method, just like `Connection` (a value of this type) was required for `runRedis`. We make `DBHandle` abstracted; it contains only a database name and specifier. Neither `Connection` from `hedis` nor `DB` from `rocksdb-haskell` should be there. It also carries a user-defined phantom type for a database instance. But how can we obtain `DBHandle`? It will be simple in the framework using methods to establish and destroy connections. We'll give the application developer full control over it. Figure 11.3 presents the new responsibilities.

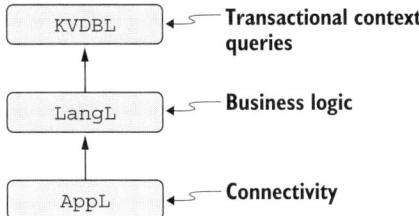

Figure 11.3 Scopes and responsibilities in the framework

If only database connectivity were always this simple! Many edge cases emerge from the darkness when we start thinking about it or when doing integration with many databases:

- Should a connection be kept alive all the time, or should it be open only for a particular query?
- Is it safe to connect to the database without disposing of connections?
- How many connections are we allowed to produce?
- Does the database system have a timeout for idle connections?
- Will it be reconnecting automatically if the connection is lost?
- How can a database system know that the connection has been lost?

So many questions, so few answers. It's very unclear what decision is the best one. There are hundreds of best practices, and opinions here might result in opposite statements. Thus, rightly, we should consider any practice that suits our interests.

As demonstrated in listing 11.5, the `AppL` language shows that

- Both Redis and RocksDB databases are supported.
- Selection between the two is made by providing the corresponding config.
- There are no explicit connection pools so far.
- `InitKVDB` method is used to establish a connection.
- `DeinitKVDB` is used to close the connection.

Listing 11.5 Key–value subsystem connectivity

```
data KVDBConfig db                              ◄───────────  KV DB configs with
  = RedisConfig String                          ◄───────────  phantom type parameter
  | RocksConfig                                 ◄───────────
      { _path           :: FilePath             Redis config (just a
      , _createIfMissing :: Bool                connection string)
      , _errorIfExists   :: Bool
      }                                         RocksDB config with
                                                multiple fields
```

```
data AppF next where
  InitKVDB
    :: DB db
    => KVDBConfig db
    -> DBName
    -> (DBResult (DBHandle db) -> next)
    -> AppF next
  DeinitKVDB
    :: DBHandle db
    -> (DBResult () -> next)
    -> AppF next
```

> ◄——— **Method to init connection; accepts a DB config**
>
> ◄——— **Returns the connection on success**

```
type AppL = Free AppF
```

However, I should clarify that in Hydra, there is no `DeinitKVDB` method. It's commented out, and the code documentation says the following:

```
-- No need to explicitly close the connections.
-- They will be closed automatically on the program finish.
-- DeinitKVDB :: DB db => DBHandle db -> (DBResult Bool -> next) -> AppF next
```

The inability to terminate the communication with the database is baked into the design. Therefore, there is no way to close the connection twice or reuse a closed connection. Stale connections are handled with the `DBResult` type. Thus, the Hydra framework forces a specific use case while preventing others. This feature provides us with a wide range of solutions and ideas, especially when dealing with the external world. Design is a choice. Consider digging into the Hydra code to examine some of the other choices I made in this subsystem. You might be especially interested in the interpreters that I'm omitting here.

11.2   *Type-safe key–value database subsystem*

We successfully forged an untyped key–value database subsystem in which all the data (keys, values) was represented by `ByteStrings` only:

```
type KVDBKey   = ByteString
type KVDBValue = ByteString

save :: KVDBKey -> KVDBValue -> KVDBL db (DBResult ())
load :: KVDBKey -> KVDBL db (DBResult KVDBValue)
```

With it, there's no guarantee that the data in a key–value database is correct. What if it's garbage? The `load` method will return `KVDBValue` successfully, but our business logic will be unable to understand this array of trash bytes.

This raw approach covers 90% of our needs. It is very simple and fast, but not safe enough. We can do better. We'll create a typed key–value database layer on top of this untyped interface without even changing the underlying framework and make the business logic completely type-safe.

Before we move further, let's look at a version of a domain meteor type that has several additional types, such as `azimuth` and `altitude`, and is also serializable to JSON:

```
data Meteor = Meteor
  { size      :: Int
  , mass      :: Int
  , azimuth   :: Float
  , altitude  :: Float
  , timestamp :: DateTime
  }
  deriving (Show, Eq, Ord, Generic, ToJSON, FromJSON)
```

The type is JSON-serializable with aeson. ◄

The later development will show whether this domain model design is good enough or needs to be updated (hint: it does).

We're going to provide an additional layer between the raw untyped free monadic interface and the business logic. We'll introduce the typed interface on top of the untyped one. As presented in figure 11.4, it resembles the typed-untyped design pattern, doesn't it?

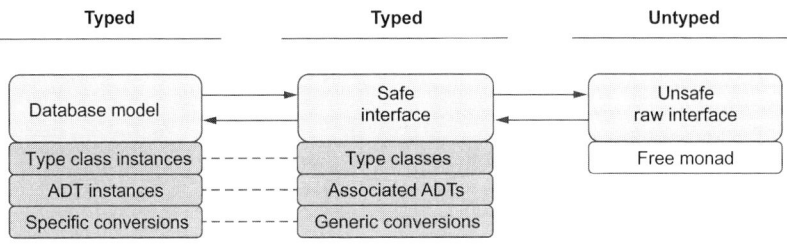

Figure 11.4   Typed interface and database model

However, it doesn't have to go beyond the free monadic interface, and no single interpreter is affected. In fact, nothing stops the framework users from implementing their own typed layer with another idea at its core without even altering the framework.

11.2.1 Basic key–value database model

We know what a domain model is, and I'm sure we have no doubt about what a database model is. However, when developing our applications, we need to know how the two communicate and work together. Let's introduce some terminology here.

> **DEFINITION**   A database model is a set of data types and structures representing a database scheme, either directly or indirectly. Most commonly, these types are heavily infiltrated by the notion of databases such as primary and foreign keys, database-specific timestamps, and database-specific fundamental types.

Domain types represent this real world. Prior to going into a database, those types should be transformed into a database model. A database model can be well-structured or relational, or it can have a less complicated form. From the key–value database viewpoint, its string values go all the way down. However, from the code perspective, these values should be specific database-related types, not just strings. We call those specific types *entities* of the database model, and we distinguish them from the domain types on purpose.

Let's say we want to load a meteor from the database by its key, and we know it's stored as a stringified JSON object. The following is an example of such rows in the database in the form of (DBKey, DBValue):

```
("0", "{\"size\": 100,
       \"mass\": 100,
       \"azmt\": 0,
       \"alt\": 0,
       \"time\":\"2019-12-04T00:30:00\"}")
("1", "{\"size\": 200,
       \"mass\": 200,
       \"azmt\": 2,
       \"alt\": 0,
       \"time\": \"2019-12-04T00:31:00\"}")
```

The next listing demonstrates the corresponding database model.

Listing 11.6   Manual serialization of database entities

```
type MeteorID = Int

data KVDBMeteor = KVDBMeteor                          ◄── Entity of the meteor,
  { size  :: Int                                          JSON-serializable
  , mass  :: Int
  , azmt  :: Int
  , alt   :: Int
  , time  :: DateTime
  }
  deriving (Show, Generic, ToJSON, FromJSON)

encodeMeteor :: KVDBMeteor -> ByteString             ◄── Serialization
encodeMeteor = encode

decodeMeteorUnsafe :: ByteString -> KVDBMeteor       ◄── Deserialization
decodeMeteorUnsafe meteorStr =
  case decode meteorStr of
    Nothing -> error "Meteor: Can't parse"           ◄── Bad practice; avoid
    Just m -> m                                          using the error, but
                                                         use explicit Either
                                                         and Maybe instead
```

JSON can be ineffective, and we could choose a different format for storing. In the real world, we may encounter custom-compressed yet human-readable formats or even binary formats of different kinds. I chose JSON for simplicity and readability, and the aeson library will help us cut development costs.

To establish some ground for future improvements, we'll also write a client code with manual parsing. Let's use two functions in LangL to save and load meteors.

Listing 11.7 Manual serialization of database entities

```
saveMeteor
  :: DBHandle AstroDB
  -> MeteorID
  -> KVDBMeteor
  -> LangL ()
saveMeteor astroDBConn meteorId meteor
  = evalKVDB astroDBConn
  $ save (encode meteorId) (encodeMeteor meteor)


loadMeteor
  :: DBHandle AstroDB
  -> MeteorID
  -> LangL KVDBMeteor
loadMeteor astroDBConn meteorId = evalKVDB astroDBConn $ do
  eMeteorStr <- load (show meteorId)
  case eMeteorStr of
    Left err        -> error (show err)
    Right meteorStr -> pure (decodeMeteorUnsafe meteorStr)
```

> The dollar operator ($) will be used to chain the functions for its convenience.

> Loading the meteor

> Bad practice: avoid using the error function

The dollar operator ($)

We've already seen the dollar operator in our code. It passes what it has on the right to the function on the left:

```
($) :: (a -> b) -> a -> b

squareAndSin x = sin (x * x)
squareAndSin' x = sin $ x * x
```

It was convenient in our nested monadic scenarios:

```
saveSomeMeteors :: DBHandle AstroDB -> LangL ()
saveSomeMeteors astroDBConn = evalKVDB astroDBConn $ do
  save "meteor1" "size:100, mass:200"
  save "meteor2" "size:300, mass:500"
```

Next, we'll be chaining many functions with this operator and aligning them for better readability:

```
result = function3 g (function2 e f (function1 a b c))
result'
  = function3 g
  $ function2 e f
  $ function1 a b c
```

This domain model design is very simple. If you want to convert your entity into the domain data type, just move values from one abstract data type (ADT) into another:

```
fromKVDBMeteor :: KVDBMeteor -> Meteor
fromKVDBMeteor (KVDBMeteor s m az al t s) = Meteor s m az al t s
```

The type-safe approach we're going to use will have similar conversions, which are driven by some type-level mechanisms.

11.2.2 Approaching the type-level design

If we have dozens of entities in the database model, writing many loading and conversion functions will be too tedious:

```
loadMeteor :: DBHandle AstroDB -> MeteorID -> LangL KVDBMeteor
loadComet  :: DBHandle AstroDB -> CometID  -> LangL KVDBComet

fromKVDBMeteor :: KVDBMeteor -> Meteor
fromKVDBComet  :: KVDBComet  -> Comet
```

It's also not convenient to call them repeatedly, and for this reason, the appearance of the wrappers is inevitable, meaning there are more functions for every database entity:

```
loadMeteor'
  :: DBHandle AstroDB
  -> MeteorID
  -> LangL Meteor
loadMeteor' astroDBConn meteorId = do
  kvDBMeteor <- loadMeteor astroDBConn meteorId
  pure (fromKVDBMeteor kvDBMeteor)
```

Loads raw data

Converts to a domain type

We'd want to prevent the odd situation when types and entities don't match; for example, when we confuse primary keys that are just strings at the moment:

```
comet1 :: KVDBCometID
comet1 = "comet1"

myApp astroDBConn = do
  meteor <- loadMeteor' astroDBConn comet1
  evalIO (show meteor)
```

This will crash because of the inability to parse a Comet value into the Meteor type.

We do not want this mismatching to happen, and we would like to turn the compiler into a friend who keeps us from an accidental fall into the abyss of undefined and incorrect behavior.

Solving this problem at the generic level will be our concern. Ideally, we should have a way to declare the key–value database model and be instantly able to use it in the business logic, without additional wrappers and ceremonies and without being afraid of writing incorrect code.

Some readers might remember the *expression problem*, which is the problem of how to extend code in two dimensions: with arbitrary types and with arbitrary methods. The expression problem tells about this dichotomy and the difficulty of simultaneously having both noun and verb extensibility. This is a common task for mainstream development, but the name "expression problem" isn't widespread.

> **NOTE** The expression problem is a problem in computer science that points to the difficulty of mixing two kinds of extensibility in typed data models. The models can be extensible either via data (adding new values) or via behavior (adding

new methods), but simultaneously implementing the two seems a challenging task for most modern statically typed languages.

You might have heard that object-oriented programming (OOP) developers are talking about extensibility, extensible points, and customization. In OOP languages, it's pretty simple to add a new type and make the existing logic able to work with it. A class inheritance or duck typing solves the extensibility problem for most cases.

In contrast, developers of strongly typed functional languages without subtype polymorphism (Haskell) experience difficulties implementing such mechanisms. In addition to thinking about what types can occur in the future, we must also use advanced type-level stuff to express the idea that a particular code accepts any input with predefined properties. Haskell's type classes do the job, but their expressiveness is very limited. More type-level features were added to provide comprehensive tooling and talk with the type checker: functional dependencies, extensions for type classes, type families, existential types, and generalized ADTs. We can do very impressive tasks, but we may still not be satisfied. We need even more powerful tools—that is, dependent types. Therefore, I encourage you to consult other books. First, you can read *Type-Driven Development with Idris* by Edwin Brady (Manning, 2017). It has a very detailed introduction into static type systems in Idris, a Haskell-like language that also support dependent types (https://mng .bz/PZ0g). Second, my new book, *Pragmatic Type-Level Design* (https://leanpub.com/ pragmatic-type-level-design), addresses type-level programming in Haskell and other languages in a rigorous yet practical way and perfectly complements *Functional Design and Architecture*. The topics we're touching in this chapter have a detailed discussion in this book. (The book is to be published in January 2025.)

11.2.3 *Type-safe key–value database model*

If we save a value using the new typed mechanism, we're guaranteed that loading and parsing will be successful. Let's establish the goal in the form of the code we'd like to write. The next function asks to load a typed entity from the key–value database:

```
loadMeteor
  :: DBHandle AstroDB
  -> MeteorID
  -> LangL (DBResult Meteor)
loadMeteor astroDB meteorID
  = evalKVDB astroDB
  $ loadEntity
  $ mkMeteorKey meteorID
```

You can guess that the new mechanism is hidden behind the functions `loadEntity` and `mkMeteorKey`. Let's get familiar with them.

The `loadEntity` knows how to load raw `ByteString` data from a key–value database and convert it to the target type. Notice that it refers to several type-level artifacts: `DBEntity`, `AsValueEntity`, and `KeyEntity`. All of them are parametrized with type variables: `db`, `entity`, `dst` (stands for "destination"). We'll figure out what they are in detail:

```
loadEntity
  :: ( DBEntity db entity
     , AsValueEntity entity dst
     )
  => KeyEntity entity
  -> KVDBL db (DBResult dst)
```

I put `DBEntity` and `AsValueEntity` into the constraints. They demand that every type we put in the place of `entity` should support them. There should also be a `db` type that supports `DBEntity`. Finally, `entity` should be compatible with `KeyEntity`. We still don't know what these things are, but at least we see they all are bound through `entity`, `dst`, and `db`.

For those of you who are familiar with type-level programming, this code won't be surprising. Sadly, you can't be sure what concept you are dealing with just by looking at the function definition. In Haskell, the words `KeyEntity entity` can be a regular type with a type parameter, a parametrized ADT, an associated type, or a type family. They all look similar in the function definitions, but they all behave differently. This is why the type-level code is far from obvious. Let's try to crack this puzzle.

A small hint on `KeyEntity` comes from the following smart constructor that takes an integer key and returns a value of cryptic compound type (`MeteorKey` is a value constructor for `KeyEntity MeteorEntity`):

```
mkMeteorKey :: MeteorID -> KeyEntity MeteorEntity
mkMeteorKey meteorId = MeteorKey meteorId
```

The whole type will represent a specific primary key for a specific entity. `KeyEntity MeteorEntity` is a primary key type for the meteor, where the tag is `MeteorEntity`. The tag is just an empty ADT with no possibility to of creating its values:

```
data MeteorEntity
```

Essentially, the type-level tag applied to the `KeyEntity` type will give us an ADT. It's a fully operable ADT, not much different than normal ADTs. Specific ADTs declared this way can even be pattern matched. Interestingly, the framework will know about generic `KeyEntity` but will not be aware of user-defined tag types such as `Meteor-Entity`, and yet will be able to work with both. Before we jump into the code, take a look at figure 11.5.

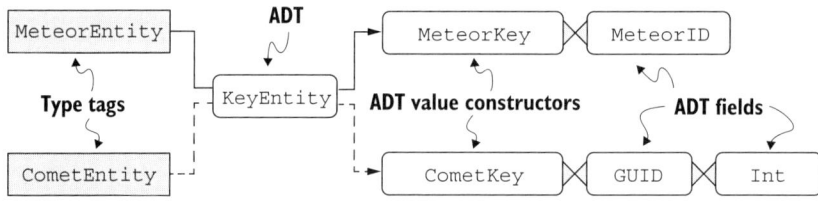

Figure 11.5   Generic ADT `KeyEntity`

The same ADT (`KeyEntity`) will turn into two distinct types when fed with a specific type tag. If the tag is `MeteorEntity`, the resulting ADT will have the `MeteorKey` value constructor. If the tag is `CometEntity`, the resulting ADT will have `CometKey`. In pseudocode, this is what we did:

```
data KeyEntity MeteorEntity = MeteorKey MeteorID
data KeyEntity CometEntity  = CometKey GUID Int
```

These types are like normal ADTs, and we're correct to refer to a concrete ADT with its tag. For example, I could pattern-match over the value constructors and print these keys:

```
printMeteorKey :: KeyEntity MeteorEntity -> IO ()
printMeteorKey (MeteorKey mId) = print mId

printCometKey :: KeyEntity CometEntity -> IO ()
printCometKey (CometKey guid idx) = do
  print guid
  print idx
```

Notice that `MeteorKey` and `CometKey` contain different fields. Unfortunately, they can't be pattern-matched simultaneously. This generic function won't work because specific entities aren't known up front:

```
printKey :: KeyEntity entity -> IO ()          ◄────┐ Generic entity
printKey (MeteorKey mId)     = print mId        ◄───┘ type variable
printKey (CometKey guid idx) = do
  print guid                                          Can't pattern-match
  print idx                                           generic type variable
```

However, there are ways to use these two distinct types abstractly without knowing their internal structure in advance. The `loadEntity` function we've seen earlier does this. It relies on some abstracted properties of the `KeyEntity` types, as we can conclude from its definition:

```
loadEntity
  :: ( DBEntity db entity
     , AsValueEntity entity dst
     )
                                          Knows something general
  => KeyEntity entity              ◄────── about KeyEntity
  -> KVDBL db (DBResult dst)
```

How do you do this? In Haskell, it's all about type classes, associated algebraic data types, and functional dependencies. The core part is the `DBEntity` type class that exposes several type-level interfaces. Look at it, and don't mind the mystical parts for now:

```
                                     Type class with two
                                     type parameters

class DBEntity db entity          ◄──┘  Functional dependency: when there
    | entity -> db where          ◄──── is entity, there should be db
```

```
data KeyEntity   entity :: *
data ValueEntity entity :: *
```

Associated ADT template for
user-defined key ADTs

Associated ADT template for
user-defined value ADTs

With this type class, we model the following:

- The relation between a database and an entity, hence the functional dependency `entity -> db`. This entity can only be related to a single database. Once you have a type for an entity, you'll immediately know the database.
- Two associated ADTs, `KeyEntity` and `ValueEntity`. The developer must implement them when they create an instance of `DBEntity`.

I've updated the previous diagram and accounted for the `ValueEntity` part in figure 11.6.

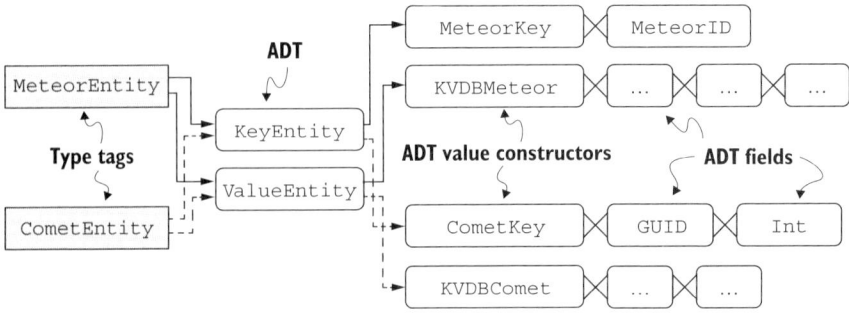

Figure 11.6   Key–value database type-level machinery

It introduces a new ADT template `ValueEntity` and two implementations for it: `KVDBMeteor` and `KVDBComet`. Let's look at this implementation in code now. The following listing brings it for the meteor entity, and listing 11.9 shows it schematically for the comet entity.

Listing 11.8   Meteor as `DBEntity`

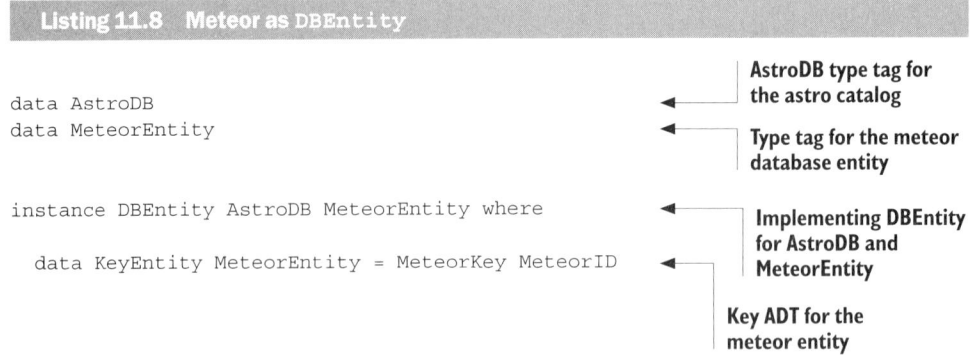

```
data AstroDB
data MeteorEntity

instance DBEntity AstroDB MeteorEntity where

  data KeyEntity MeteorEntity = MeteorKey MeteorID
```

AstroDB type tag for
the astro catalog

Type tag for the meteor
database entity

Implementing **DBEntity**
for AstroDB and
MeteorEntity

Key ADT for the
meteor entity

```
      deriving (Show, Eq, Ord)                    ◄──── It's a normal ADT, and all
                                                          the derivings are possible.
  data ValueEntity MeteorEntity = KVDBMeteor      ◄────
    { size  :: Int                                      Value ADT for the
    , mass  :: Int                                      meteor entity
    , azmt  :: Int
    , alt   :: Int                                      It's a normal
    , time  :: DateTime                                 ADT, and all the
    }                                                   derivings are
      deriving (Show, Eq, Ord, Generic, ToJSON, FromJSON)  ◄── possible.
```

Listing 11.9 Comet as DBEntity

```
data CometEntity

instance DBEntity AstroDB CometEntity where
  data KeyEntity    CometEntity = CometKey GUID Int
  data ValueEntity CometEntity = KVDBComet ...
```

We just put two entities into the AstroDB catalog, and we did so independently. This mechanism enables the extension of database entities without modifying the framework or the loadEntity function. This function is now future-proof because it will work with any user-defined type with a DBEntity implementation. But what exactly happens in this function, and what generic operations is the framework allowed to do with those entities? This is our next stop.

11.2.4 Generic type-safe key–value interface

We just discussed the DBEntity type class, and the discussion was about types and values. Now we'll talk about behavior and transformations, and the same DBEntity will provide tools for converting those database entities. If database model is water (or magma, if you like *Dwarf Fortress*), then the logic will be tubes and pumps.

In addition to being associated ADTs, the DBEntity type class has methods that should be specified for each database entity. Take a look at three of them:

```
class DBEntity db entity | entity -> db where        Converts a user-defined key ADT
  toDBKey                                             into ByteString (KVDBKey)
    :: KeyEntity entity -> KVDBKey          ◄──┘
  toDBValue
    :: ValueEntity entity -> KVDBValue      ◄──      Converts a user-defined value
  fromDBValue                                         ADT into ByteString (KVDBValue)
  :: KVDBValue -> Maybe (ValueEntity entity) ◄──
                                                     Parses a ByteString (KVDBValue)
                                                     into a user-defined value ADT
```

Two functions (toDBKey, toDBValue) take a user-defined ADT and convert it into ByteString. Furthermore, one function parses bytes back. The developer should implement this contract for their entity. In the case of MeteorEntity, it's just aeson-powered serialization. It's possible for ValueEntity MeteorEntity because we derived ToJSON and FromJSON for it earlier. The key data type, however, isn't aeson serializable—there are no FromJSON and ToJSON instances for it (an excerpt from listing 11.8):

```
data KeyEntity MeteorEntity = MeteorKey MeteorID
  deriving (Show, Eq, Ord)
```

I should clarify that nothing disallows declaring the instances—it's just a different approach. We're doing it manually by unpacking a MeteorKey value and serializing its internal field only. Notice that this unpacking of KeyEntity MeteorEntity is just a pattern matching:

```
instance DBEntity AstroDB MeteorEntity where
  toDBKey :: KeyEntity MeteorEntity -> KVDBKey          ◄──┐ Regular pattern-matching
  toDBKey (MeteorKey idx) = show idx                    ◄──┘ over the associated ADT

  toDBValue :: ValueEntity MeteorEntity -> KVDBValue    ◄──┐ Serialization of the
  toDBValue valEntity = encode valEntity                ◄──┘ associated ADT with aeson

  fromDBValue :: KVDBValue -> Maybe (ValueEntity MeteorEntity)
  fromDBValue strEntity = decode strEntity              ◄──┐
                                                            │ Deserialization of the
                                                            │ associated ADT with aeson
```

Now we know how the KVDBMeteor value constructor (of type KeyEntity Meteor-Entity) becomes a ByteString that goes directly to the KVDBL methods. We can convert this value back to the KVDBMeteor form. At the moment, this conversion happens in the loadEntity function which specifies this type class as a constraint. But that's not enough; it also specifies some additional AsValueEntity constraint:

```
loadEntity
  :: ( DBEntity db entity
     , AsValueEntity entity dst        ◄────── Some additional functionality
     )
  => KeyEntity entity
  -> KVDBL db (DBResult dst)
```

That dst type does not relate to the key–value database model because the entity type does. A domain type is hiding behind dst, and we can assume that the relation between an entity and a domain type comes with the AsValueEntity thing. This is where the conversion logic hides.

AsValueEntity is another type class connecting two models. It's simple, and there are only two functions.

Listing 11.10   Comet as DBEntity

```
class AsValueEntity entity dst where

  toValueEntity                        ◄──┐ From a domain type
    :: dst                                │ to value entity
    -> ValueEntity entity
```

```
fromValueEntity                                    ◀──┐  Back from value entity
  :: KeyEntity entity                                  │  to the domain type
  -> ValueEntity entity
  -> dst
```

As you can see, it refers to the associated types from the `DBEntity` type class. The implementation for `MeteorEntity` and the `Meteor` domain type may look like this:

```
instance AsValueEntity MeteorEntity Meteor where

  toValueEntity (Meteor size mass azmt alt time)
    = KVDBMeteor size mass azmt alt time

  fromValueEntity (MeteorKey idx) (KVDBMeteor size mass azmt alt time)
    = Meteor size mass azmt alt time
```

We should, of course, decide what to do with primary keys. Should the domain type carry it? Or should there be another way to store meteors by keys (for example, a dictionary)? This subject becomes crucial for relational databases, so we'll investigate it in the next chapter and see that there is even more room for type-level programming to empower our designs.

I should also add that there is a third type class. It is presented here together with its implementation. Let's look at the idea by analogy:

```
class AsKeyEntity entity dst where
  toKeyEntity :: dst -> KeyEntity entity

instance AsKeyEntity MeteorEntity MeteorID where
  toKeyEntity meteorId = MeteorKey meteorId
```

Finally, we can reveal the generic soul of the `loadEntity` function. This function demands the type-level machinery for a particular database and entity. It requests a `ByteString` value from the key–value database subsystem, and with the help of all those conversion functions, it first converts the `ByteString` value into the typed key–value database model and then from the key–value database model into the domain model.

Listing 11.11 Generic `loadEntity` function

Function works for a database entity of a specific database

The entity should be tied to a domain type.

```
loadEntity
  :: DBEntity db entity          ◀──────
  => AsValueEntity entity dst    ◀──────
  => KeyEntity entity            ◀──────
  -> KVDBL db (DBResult dst)     ◀──────
loadEntity key = do
```

Primary key value to read

Domain value to return when successfully read and parsed

```
eRawVal <- load (toDBKey key)              ◄─────────────┐    Calls the untyped
                                                          │    KV DB interface
let dst = case eRawVal of
  Left err  -> Left err
  Right rawVal -> case fromDBValue rawVal of   ◄──────────    A method from
    Nothing  -> Left DecodingFailed                           DBEntity is called here.
    Just val -> Right (fromValueEntity key val of)  ◄────
                                                              A method from
pure dst                                                      AsValueEntity is called here.
```

Let me remind you what this looks like in the business logic:

```
loadMeteor
  :: DBHandle AstroDB
  -> MeteorID
  -> LangL (DBResult Meteor)
loadMeteor astroDB meteorID
  = evalKVDB astroDB
  $ loadEntity
  $ mkMeteorKey meteorID
```

So the initial goal for this type-level machinery was the ability to specify a key–value database model for entities, but we got several interesting consequences:

- We can add more entities without affecting the mechanism itself: `MeteorEntity`, `CometEntity`, `StarEntity`, `AsteroidEntity`, and so on.
- A tag type for key–value databases such as `AstroDB` now combines all those entities into a single key–value database model.
- It's possible to put the same entities into another key–value database by defining a new key–value database tag type (for example, `CosmosDB`) and instantiating the `DBEntity` type class for it. Thus, we can share entities between models if required.
- The loading and saving functions now use the conversions without knowing what entities we want to process. For example, the `loadEntity` function just states several requirements and uses the typed interface to access specific associated data types.
- We've proven that a simple, raw `ByteString`-typed interface can be improved and extended even without changing the framework itself.

Still, the type-level machinery is more complicated and scarier. Exposing all those multi-component types, such as `ValueKey`, or type classes, such as `DBEntity`, to the business logic would be a bad idea because it would raise the bar on what your colleagues should know and learn. The client code shouldn't be aware of what's happening there. Writing scenarios should remain simple and boilerplate free. Thus, limiting the existence of these gears only to the hidden layer may be acceptable in certain situations.

Summary

- A string-based interface is a common ground for all key–value databases.
- Untyped string-based interfaces are extremely simple but dangerous.
- Hierarchical free monad languages can express such semantics as transactional context.
- A good way to improve an interface is to implement it several times and assess it in several different use cases.
- Type-level programming can be intimidating and very complex, but when used carefully, it can make programs safer.
- The domain model represents a set of types (and probably functions) directly correlated with the essence of the domain.
- The database model reflects the idea that the internal representation of data in databases can separate from the domain model and often possesses other structuring principles.
- An additional typed layer can be provided on top of the untyped interface to make transformations and conversions completely safe.
- Type classes in Haskell may be empowered with additional features, such as associated types and functional dependencies.
- Associated ADTs are usual ADTs, except for the way they are declared and referenced.

Persistence: Relational databases

We learned a lot about domain models in the previous chapters. In fact, a big part of the book is dedicated to the methodology known as domain-driven design. Although it is a very good and widespread methodology, it hasn't always been so. Before the idea of designing systems from a domain point of view became popular, developers designed applications starting with a database model. They would first outline a relational representation of the task and then introduce the required data structures in code.

However, this methodology had some flaws. The main disadvantage was that the database representation types had a significant bias in favor of a relational structure, which wasn't as intuitive as a domain-favored structure could be. Using the database model is not as convenient as using the corresponding domain model. This distinction was reconsidered, and the approach "domain model first, database model second" began to prevail.

It seems very beneficial and natural to separate domain and database models. When independent, the database model can be extracted into its own project or library so that it can evolve without breaking the main code. The difference between models increases with the application size and complexity. Strictly speaking, these models have their own lifetimes, and even the way the two are obtained may vary. Here, some mainstream technologies require generating a database model from the external XML representation. Sometimes, the database model can be absent or merged with a domain model; there are several important techniques that help organize such code. It would be good to familiarize yourself with the following approaches and design patterns in object-oriented programming (OOP): repository, active record, and object-relational mapping (ORM). Of course, functional programming has its own substitutions for these things, and we'll see some of them here.

> **NOTE** To learn more about different approaches and design patterns in OOP, check out the following resources: "Repository pattern in C#" (https://mng.bz/QZXQ), *Active Record Pattern* by Martin Fowler (https://mng.bz/X1Op), and *Spring in Action* (6th Edition, Manning, 2022) by Craig Walls (specifically chapter 11, "Persisting Data with Object-Relational Mapping," available at https://mng.bz/y8wy).

12.1 Relational database model

Previously, we had a simple domain model for space objects. We even investigated ways to persist it with a key–value database, for which we enrolled a separate model suitable for the typed key–value interface. It was a small journey into type-level programming with some interesting ideas along the road. However, we still have not covered all the topics. We also need to discuss them in the context of relational database models, and this will be preliminary material before we jump into the actual interaction with relational databases.

So if we assume we need to load a meteor from a database by a primary key, we should first load it into a database-related data type and then transform it into a domain-related data type. Take a look at the following pseudocode:

```
getDBMeteor :: MeteorID -> SqlDBConn -> LangL DBMeteor
getDBMeteor meteorId connection =
  runDatabaseQuery connection                              Loads a raw
    (loadByPrimaryKey meteorId)                            DB-related type


getMeteor :: MeteorID -> SqlDBConn -> LangL Meteor
getMeteor meteorId connection = do                         Transforms the
  dbMeteor <- getDBMeteor meteorId connection              DB-related type to the
  pure (fromDBMeteor dbMeteor)                             domain-related type
```

This is not precisely how I do it in Hydra, but all the components are there: meteor-related types (such as `DBMeteor` or `MeteorID`), querying methods (such as `runDatabaseQuery`), and connection types (such as `SqlDBConn`). We're about to examine those components and learn some useful design patterns as well.

12.1.1 Designing relational database model ADTs

Let's review the `Meteor` domain data type:

```
data Meteor = Meteor
  { size      :: Int
  , mass      :: Int
  , azimuth   :: Float
  , altitude  :: Float
  , timestamp :: DateTime
  }
```

What if we have meteors of the same mass and size? That is not a problem—we have coordinates: azimuth, altitude, and some time to identify each of them. It's not possible for two different meteors to occupy the same point in space simultaneously. (We're not discussing the actual meaningfulness of this system of coordinates because we're not real astronomers.) This domain type contains everything we'd like to store in a relational database, and there seem to be no obstacles in designing a relational model.

Assuming that the model will contain only a single table, it can be the following ADT (underscores are used to distinguish the fields from the fields of `Meteor`):

```
data DBMeteor = DBMeteor
  { _size      :: INTEGER
  , _mass      :: INTEGER
  , _azimuth   :: FLOAT
  , _altitude  :: FLOAT
  , _timestamp :: TIMESTAMP
  }
```

We must use types that can be understood by a specific database. Most likely, special data types will come with particular libraries, but we're assuming we have `INTEGER`, `FLOAT`, and `TIMESTAMP` standard SQL types for our needs. Figure 12.1 shows the one-to-one relationship between the two models.

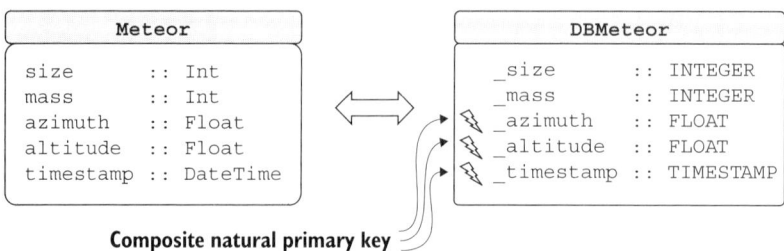

Figure 12.1   Simple domain and database models

In the figure, the left model contains native Haskell types, and the right one adopts the types from the SQL standard. The lightning bolts mean "primary key." DBMeteor here is a single table-related ADT without additional decomposition. The Meteor type maps to it directly. Later, Meteor can be changed, for example, by extracting the azimuth and the altitude fields into an additional Coords type:

```
data Coords = Coords
  { azimuth   :: Float
  , altitude  :: Float
  }
```

While this happens to the Meteor data type, the table type remains the same. The separation of the two models will protect the database-related code from this change. You shouldn't allow the database types to leak into the business logic, and all the conversion between the two models should be done through a bunch of functions:

```
fromDBMeteor :: DBMeteor -> Meteor
toDBMeteor   :: Meteor   -> DBMeteor
```

This isn't only about the separation of the two models but also about their isolation from each other. The thinner the edge, the easier it will be to handle the problems if there is friction between the subsystems.

You might have noticed that we marked the three fields in figure 11.1 as a composite natural primary key: (FLOAT, FLOAT, TIMESTAMP). This solution has two big drawbacks:

- Float numbers should not be used as keys.
- Natural keys should be avoided, except when there are strong considerations for their use.

In the next section, we'll see how to solve these design flaws, and by doing so, we'll find a good place for the so-called Higher-Kinded Data pattern (HKD).

12.1.2 Primary keys and the HKD pattern

Avoid using float numbers as part of the primary key. The main reason is that you can't know the exact value due to the rounding issues of float numbers. By default, float data types in all programming languages support the equality operation, so you can compare them strictly. However, you probably shouldn't do this. We all know that the following code, while logically correct, produces counterintuitive results:

```
ghci> 0.1 + 0.1 == 0.2
True
ghci> 0.1 + 0.2 == 0.3
False
```

This also means that float numbers as primary keys in databases are lurking beasts that are going to attack you when you least expect it.

Another point is related to natural keys. We expect a huge number of meteors, and we want to fetch them from the database for processing. Natural keys consisting of many fields aren't convenient for querying. They can be very inefficient because they require extra memory in relations between tables. Natural keys are hard to maintain. What if these fields should be slightly updated? Should we update all the data in the database? And what about backward compatibility? More questions arise here. Sometimes, natural keys are fine, but more likely, we need a unique surrogate key. It can be an integer number, UUID, hash, or something else:

```
data DBMeteor = DBMeteor
  { _meteorId :: INTEGER
  , ...
  }
```

It seems that we should update the domain type `Meteor` by adding an identification field to it. However, there is a problem: How can we create an initial `Meteor` value for the meteor that just occurred in the sky? There is no primary key for it yet, and the record in the database is yet to be created. We should either make the field optional (`Maybe`) or duplicate the `Meteor` type. All variants are shown as follows (`PK` stands for *primary key*):

```
data Meteor = Meteor
  { size :: Int
  , ...
  }

data MeteorPK = MeteorPK
  { meteorId :: Int
  , size     :: Int
  , ...
  }

data MeteorMbPK = MeteorMbPK
  { meteorId :: Maybe Int
  , size     :: Int
  , ...
  }
```

Multiplying the types (having `Meteor`, `MeteorPK`, and `MeteorMbPk`) feels like unnecessary work. It's quite simple but will double the number of overall domain-related types, as well as the database types, so in reality, you'll have a triple instantiation of every type.

If we are uncomfortable with this boilerplate, we can mitigate the problem a little by using the HKD pattern, which allows us to encode a varying part of an ADT so that it's possible to choose what form of the type to use in certain situations. The following `Meteor'` type will be an HKD type:

```
data Meteor' idType = Meteor
  { meteorId  :: idType
  , size      :: Int
  , mass      :: Int
  , azimuth   :: Float
  , altitude  :: Float
  , timestamp :: DateTime
  }
```

It's an HKD type because of the additional type parameter `idType`. As you can see, I didn't specify the type of the primary key for the `meteorId` field. Instead, I made it fluent so that it would be possible to construct many other types from this template. This is how we declare several end-user types:

```
type MeteorID = Int

type RawMeteor  = Meteor' ()
type MeteorMbPk = Meteor' (Maybe MeteorID)
type Meteor     = Meteor' MeteorID
```

Here, three distinct types are made from one HKD template, and all of them have their own types for the same `meteorId` field. While quite simple, HKD types can be used for more impressive tasks. Let's step away from the main theme and talk about some Haskell type-level magic that might be useful in your real practice.

12.1.3 *Polymorphic ADTs with the HKD pattern*

Earlier, we said that native SQL libraries can have their own data types, which will be directly mapped to actual SQL types. While there's a standard for SQL, many relational database management systems (RDBMS) provide a wider set of types. So do the bindings to those services.

We can assume that our `INTEGER`, `FLOAT`, and `TIMESTAMP` types came from a native library, `imaginary-sqlite`, but what if we want to incorporate another library, `imaginary-postgres`? We'd have to create a Postgres-specific version of the same model in addition to the existing SQLite and domain models:

```
data PgMeteor = PgMeteor
  { pgMeteorId  :: PgPrimaryKey
  , pgSize      :: PgInt
  , pgMass      :: PgInt
  , pgAzimuth   :: PgFloat
  , pgAltitude  :: PgFloat
  , pgTimestamp :: PgTimestamp
  }
```

That's not fun—the entities continue to multiply. Let's outline the current status in table 12.1.

Table 12.1   Variety of types

Type	Domain model	SQLite database model	Postgres database model
Integer	`Int`	`INTEGER`	`PgInt`
Floating point	`Float`	`FLOAT`	`PgFloat`
Timestamp	`DateTime`	`TIMESTAMP`	`PgTimestamp`
Primary key	`Int`	`INTEGER`	`PgPrimaryKey`

It seems that the previous difficulty with primary keys has exploded. The HKD template was only about a single varying field. Now we have four of them:

```
data Meteor' idType intType floatType timestampType
  = Meteor
    { meteorId :: idType
    , size     :: intType
    , ...
    }

type Meteor = Meteor' MeteorID Int Float DateTime
type PgMeteor = Meteor' PgPrimaryKey PgInt PgFloat PgTimestamp
type SQLiteMeteor = Meteor' INTEGER INTEGER FLOAT TIMESTAMP
```

This will work, and I can't stop you from doing this, but maybe I can convince you that there is a better way. Or, rather, two ways if we're talking about Haskell: Template Haskell for generating this code in the compile time and HKD plus some type-level magic to construct the needed types (also in compile time). We want the second one because it's not only feasible for Haskell. I can do the same in C++ and Scala.

Let's figure out what we want to do:

- We need a single template ADT for meteors. This template should have all the fields, but the types of these fields should not be fixed.
- We want to somehow select a particular set of types. We should be able to specify what set of types is needed when we deal with DBMeteor, Meteor, or PgMeteor.
- There should be a way to describe the sets of types.

Figure 12.2 should help you navigate across the solution. We'll expand it bit by bit.

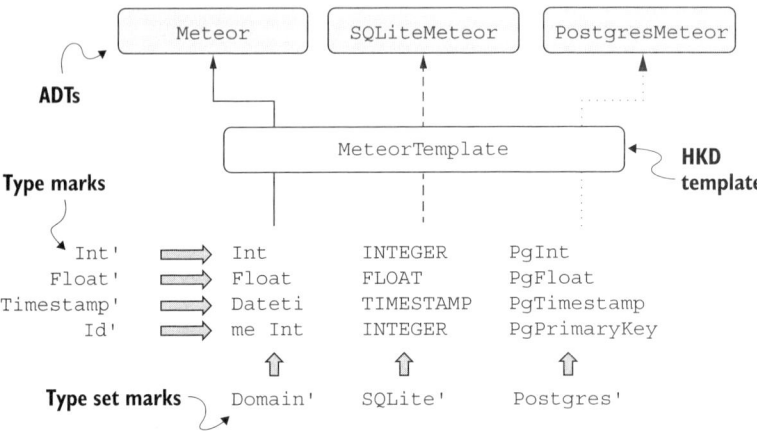

Figure 12.2   The HKD pattern for meteor data types

Suppose the types from the `imaginary-sqlite` library look like this:

```
newtype ID         = ID Int
newtype INTEGER    = INTEGER Int
newtype FLOAT      = FLOAT Float
newtype TIMESTAMP = TIMESTAMP UTCTime
```

Although their constructors are available, we would avoid accessing them everywhere and not depend on this implementation specificity. The same is true for the types from the `imaginary-postgres` library, but this time, we can't even pattern-match over them because they're opaque. We only know that we can compose those values using smart constructors provided by the library:

```
toPgPrimaryKey :: Int       -> PgPrimaryKey
mkPgInt        :: Int32     -> PgInt
mkPgFloat      :: Float     -> PgFloat
mkPgTimestamp  :: UTCTime -> PgTimestamp
```

These are the two sets. For future use, we need a mark for each set. This mark will indicate what set we want to summon. A good way to declare such marks in Haskell is via empty ADTs with no constructors:

```
data SQLite'
data Domain'
data Postgres'
```

We can't create values of these types, but we can pass the types themselves as selectors. This is how we'll get a needed ADT type with those marks in the presence of the `MeteorTemplate` that is shown a bit later:

```
type SQLiteMeteor   = MeteorTemplate SQLite'
type PostgresMeteor = MeteorTemplate Domain'
type Meteor         = MeteorTemplate Postgres'
```

These resulting types are quite typical: we can construct them as usual, and we can access the fields and pattern-match over them. All operations will be the same, except the field types. The following code demonstrates this for `Meteor` and `SQLiteMeteor`.

> **Listing 12.1 Working with two HKD-based data types**

```
spotTime :: UTCTime
spotTime = UTCTime (fromGregorian 2020 1 1) 0

testMeteor :: Meteor
testMeteor = Meteor                          ◀──  The Meteor type has a
  { meteorId  = 1                                 Meteor value constructor.
  , size      = 1
  , mass      = 1
  , azimuth   = 1.0
  , altitude  = 1.0
  , timestamp = TIMESTAMP spotTime
  }

getSize :: Meteor -> Int                     ◀──  The size method is
getSize meteor = size meteor                      polymorphic.
```

```
testSQLiteMeteor :: SQLiteMeteor
testSQLiteMeteor = Meteor
  { meteorId  = ID 1
  , size      = INTEGER 1
  , mass      = INTEGER 1
  , azimuth   = FLOAT 1
  , altitude  = FLOAT 1
  , timestamp = TIMESTAMP spotTime
  }
```

◄──── **The SQLiteMeteor type also has a Meteor value constructor.**

```
getSize' :: SQLiteMeteor -> INTEGER
getSize' meteor = size meteor
```

◄──── **The size method is polymorphic.**

The `Meteor` data constructor is shared between two different types: `SQLiteMeteor` and `Meteor`. The fields here behave as if they're polymorphic (`getSize` functions return different types). It's not even a problem to have them in a single scope; they don't clash with each other, which is nice.

Enough with the intrigue! Let's see how this works. The following code shows the HKD type. It's the foundation of the solution with some additional internal trickery. Here, the thing called `TypeSelector` is a type family for choosing between types when some marks are given:

```
data MeteorTemplate typeSet = Meteor
  { meteorId  :: TypeSelector typeSet Id'
  , size      :: TypeSelector typeSet Int'
  , mass      :: TypeSelector typeSet Int'
  , azimuth   :: TypeSelector typeSet Float'
  , altitude  :: TypeSelector typeSet Float'
  , timestamp :: TypeSelector typeSet Timestamp'
  }
```

All the fields are indeed polymorphic because they can take any shape as long as this shape is allowed by `TypeSelector`. This type family will check the two parameters: a `typeSet` selector and a selector of a particular data type. The second one is required because our type sets have more than one base type. For better clarity, I declared marks for each type:

```
data Id'
data Int'
data Float'
data Timestamp'
```

I could pass the usual types to the `TypeSelector` type family instead: `Int`, `Float`, and `Timestamp`. It would work similarly because the `TypeSelector` type family doesn't care what we use as a mark. It just accepts two marks and turns into the target type. This is the `TypeSelector` type family itself.

Listing 12.2   Type family for picking types in compile time

```
type family TypeSelector typeSet t
  where
    TypeSelector Domain'   Id'       = Int
```

```
TypeSelector Domain'    Int'        = Int
TypeSelector Domain'    Float'      = Float
TypeSelector Domain'    Timestamp'  = UTCTime

TypeSelector SQLite'    Id'         = ID
TypeSelector SQLite'    Int'        = INTEGER
TypeSelector SQLite'    Float'      = FLOAT
TypeSelector SQLite'    Timestamp'  = TIMESTAMP

TypeSelector Postgres' Id'          = PgPrimaryKey
TypeSelector Postgres' Int'         = PgInt
TypeSelector Postgres' Float'       = PgFloat
TypeSelector Postgres' Timestamp'   = PgTimestamp
```

You can think of `TypeSelector Domain' Int'` as just `Int`, because after the type family is filled with these arguments, it implicitly becomes `Int` for the compiler in the places where it occurs.

The code in listing 12.2 looks like a table for pattern-matching over the `typeSet` and `t` parameters. The table is limited by those three packs of types. To add support for more libraries, you'll need to update this type family. You can't update it from the outside. This is why such type families are called closed type families. They're closed for an extension other than editing the type family itself.

There are other tricks with the HKD pattern. We haven't nearly covered all of them yet. The pattern is relatively spread, and it will complement your type-level toolbox. Our previous type-level code for the key–value subsystem may also benefit from this pattern.

12.2 Relational database subsystem

When a developer starts thinking about the need for SQL databases in their project, they immediately encounters difficulties, implying activities that stray far from the usual development process. These difficulties start with the realization of the importance of having clear, well-elaborated requirements. The requirements will affect all the decisions and database behavior, and a wrong or incomplete understanding of needs can easily scupper the project in the near future.

After some requirements are obtained, the developer must make architectural decisions as to what database storage should be used, how it should be accessed, what libraries are available, and which database management approach to follow. Irrespective of the way the developer designs a database model, they'll meet challenges in defining a database schema, tables, relations, normalization, and indexes. They'll decide how much logic should be placed into stored procedures and views. They'll also need to write a bunch of necessary SQL queries and provide some views and server-side functions to support the logic.

This is a considerable undertaking that requires a set of specific skills, such as knowing relational algebra, SQL, normal forms, indexing algorithms, and decomposition patterns. But when it comes to embedding relational algebras and languages into our code, the ground of knowledge expands drastically. All untamed beasts you might have heard of, such as ORM tools, complicate our world in their unique styles. But what do we have for functional programming? Let's figure it out.

12.2.1 *SQL connectors*

Choosing the database implementation methods significantly influences the complexity of relational models. This complexity is unavoidable because you must implement tables and relations somehow, but we can distribute this complexity into three different places: database storage, intermediate layer, and database model. Figure 12.3 shows these three points.

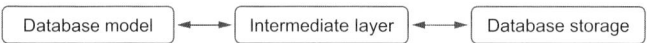

Figure 12.3   Database subsystem layers

ORM solutions in OOP hide some complexity behind specific models. The ORM layer can be seen as a mediator between the program and the database. ORM systems seem to be overkill for small programs, but it's hard to build big applications without them. Supporting code written using bare, string-based queries without any database schema description is difficult. Therefore, mainstream developers have to balance the accidental complexity that comes with ORM systems.

And what about functional programming? In functional programming, we have the same tasks and problems but different solutions. Let's find a correlation between the two worlds: object-oriented and functional (table 12.2).

Table 12.2   Correspondence between problems and solutions

Problem	Object-oriented world	Functional world
Mapping solution	ORM, reflection	Type-level mapping, generics, metaprogramming (Template Haskell)
Schema declaration	Internal eDSLs with classes or external DSLs with markup language (XML)	Internal eDSLs with ADTs, parametrized ADTs, type families, type classes
Database mapping	Repository pattern, Active Object pattern	Internal eDSLs with ADTs, parametrized ADTs, type families, type classes
Entity mapping	Classes, attributes (in C#, Java)	ADTs, HKD types, advanced types
Relations between tables	Nested collections, inheritance	Nested ADTs, type families

We now have enough background to start designing the SQL database subsystem—except we probably don't want to roll one more type-level abstraction library. It's a difficult, expensive, and lengthy activity that requires strong experience in type-level design and a good understanding of relational algebra and SQL database–related stuff. So here we have to choose one of the existing solutions and use it.

In Haskell, there are many libraries that abstract access to SQL databases with more or less type magic, for example, the Selda library (https://selda.link/), the Esqueleto library (http://hackage.haskell.org/package/esqueleto), and the `beam` library (https://haskell-beam.github.io/beam/).

There are less complicated libraries and libraries that provide some interface to particular database storages, such as `postgres-simple`. However, it seems that the complexity of defining SQL queries and database models is unavoidable in Haskell. We want to have a type-safe database model, and we can't express a mapping mechanism in a simple way. Haskell's type system is very powerful yet very mind-blowing and wordy. There's hope that inventing dependent types for Haskell will solve a lot of problems and remove a fair amount of difficulty. Until then, we must deal with what we have. To show the problem in its essence, we'll take the `beam` library.

12.2.2 *The consequences of complexity and high coupling*

The `beam` library is very generic. It was designed to enable any SQL database that is unknown upfront. Its genericity should cover the biggest subset of features and should permit all the possible SQL backends, thus providing forward compatibility. It also provides a plugin mechanism for the features that are only partially shared. Keeping this in mind, the `beam` authors rolled out a genericity-like interface for declaring queries, tables, the schema, and all the Haskell type-level features have come here: type families, multiparam type classes, phantom types, existential types, and more.

Unfortunately, the genericity-like interface of most `beam` functions is difficult. The type-level machinery is sticking out from the inside just like bunny's ears from a magician's hat. (I told you that type-level programming is magic, right?) The very coupled design of the library will not only make it difficult but will also be a real problem when embedding the library into the framework. I will discuss this in detail because knowing more about possible design issues is also part of being a software engineer.

Let's start by declaring a database model—a schema. `beam` requires defining an ADT that will correspond to a particular table and the fields it should have. Notice that underscores are also a library requirement.

Listing 12.3 `DBMeteor` table definition

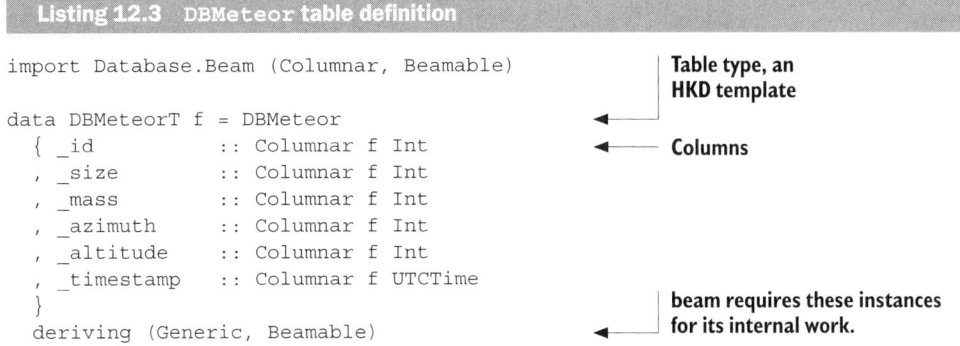

```
import Database.Beam (Columnar, Beamable)              Table type, an
                                                       HKD template
data DBMeteorT f = DBMeteor
  { _id        :: Columnar f Int                       Columns
  , _size      :: Columnar f Int
  , _mass      :: Columnar f Int
  , _azimuth   :: Columnar f Int
  , _altitude  :: Columnar f Int
  , _timestamp :: Columnar f UTCTime
  }
  deriving (Generic, Beamable)                          beam requires these instances
                                                        for its internal work.
```

Here, we recognize an HKD type that does something similar to what was done with the meteor types. There is a type variable f that alters the Columnar f t type somehow (we don't really know how). The DBMeteor type will be used by beam to make queries and convert data from the real table into code data.

Think about the types you can use as columns here. Not all of them are supported by beam, and not all of them are supported by a specific database backend. You'll know if a type is unsupported when trying to compile this schema. The following snippet will not compile because beam has no idea what this Meteor column is:

```
data DBMeteorT f = DBMeteor
  { _meteorField :: Columnar f Meteor
  } deriving (Generic, Beamable)
```

The presented type of a table is still not enough. We need to specify more details about the table: its name and a primary key. For the primary key, a type class Table with an associated type PrimaryKey t f should be instantiated:

```
instance Table DBMeteorT where

  data PrimaryKey DBMeteorT f = DBMeteorId (Columnar f Int)
    deriving (Generic, Beamable)

  primaryKey k = DBMeteorId (_id k)
```

There can be other primary key data types, but the table DBMeteorT works only with DBMeteorId. The associated ADT contains the same columnar type as the table itself: Columnar f Int. The primary key–associated ADT looks very similar to what we did in the previous chapter, except we actually have no idea what the f type variable will be. Figure 12.4 illustrates the previous code snippet.

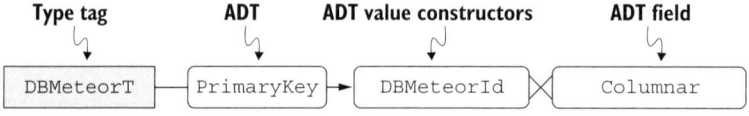

Figure 12.4   Primary key associated ADT

Extra words in this definition of a single table grab attention and make the code a bit burdensome. We can do nothing about it, but this is not the end. The next necessary data type defines the database schema along with table names. We currently have only a single table, meteors:

Data type for all tables
in the schema

```
data CatalogueDB f = CatalogueDB
  { _meteors :: f (TableEntity DBMeteorT)
  }
  deriving (Generic, Database be)
```

Two instances that the library requires; the be parameter may vary depending on what database is used: Postgres, MySQL, etc.

```
catalogueDB :: DatabaseSettings be CatalogueDB
catalogueDB = defaultDbSettings
```

Settings for the database

Again, some magic is happening here. The `CatalogueDB` type, which is a unifying type for all the tables, is also parameterized for no visible reason. It derives a special something called `Database`. The `be` parameter can declare that this schema is intended only for a specific SQL database storage (beam calls it *database backend*), for example, SQLite:

```
data CatalogueDB f = CatalogueDB
  { _meteors :: f (TableEntity DBMeteorT)
  }
  deriving (Generic, Database Sqlite)
```

But we'll consider our schema as a database-agnostic one, so let it be. The preparation of the database model ends by defining two types for convenience:

```
type DBMeteor   = DBMeteorT Identity
type DBMeteorId = PrimaryKey DBMeteorT Identity
```

And what are these types for? The `DBMeteor` type will appear in the SQL queries. You can't call a query for the wrong table. Here, for example, is a query that selects all meteors that have a predefined mass:

```
import qualified Database.Beam.Query as B

selectMeteorsWithMass size
  = B.select
  $ B.filter_ (\meteor -> _size meteor ==. B.val_ size)
  $ B.all_ (_meteors catalogueDB)
```

where the annotations point to: **SELECT** query (→ `B.select`), **WHERE** clause condition (→ `B.filter_ (\meteor -> _size meteor ==. B.val_ size)`), and **A kind of FROM** clause (→ `B.all_ (_meteors catalogueDB)`).

The type declaration of this function is omitted because it's too complex and difficult to understand. The `filter_` function accepts a lambda that should specify what rows we're interested in. The lambda accepts a value of the `DBMeteor` type, and you can access its fields to compose a Boolean-like predicate. It's not of the `Bool` type directly but is a kind of `QExpr Bool`. The beam library provides several Boolean-like comparison operators: `(==.)`, `(&&.)`, `(||.)`, `(>=.)`, `(<=.)`, `not_`, `(>.)`, `(<.)`, and others. This really looks like an extra accidental complexity that many Haskell SQL libraries have.

The `selectMeteorsWithMass` query doesn't query any particular database. The query itself is database agnostic. We can assume that the query will be correctly executed on any database storage that supports a very basic SQL standard. So how would we execute this query on SQLite, for example? The `beam-sqlite` package provides a runner for SQLite databases that's compatible with beam. You can find the `runBeamSqlite` function there:

```
-- In the module Database.Beam.Sqlite:

runBeamSqlite :: Connection -> SqliteM a -> IO a
```

Here, we recognize the pattern we already know. The function is a runner for a script that seems to be hiding under `SqliteM`, a monadic context for queries adjusted for SQLite. As for the key–value database connectors, this is a custom monad in which all the real calls to SQLite will happen. And as before, we could try to hide the `beam` library behind our own interface for relational databases. There could be some high-level simplified language for queries, and a way to translate it into `beam`-specific calls. The same hope for a better developer experience could drive us to wrap `beam`.

Unfortunately, things get exponentially more complicated for most Haskell SQL connectors, including `beam`. While I managed to wrap `beam` and achieve some simplification for it in my Hydra framework, many design problems in the library prevent a good design on my side. There are at least four aggravating factors:

- `beam` exposes its own query language full of tricky operators and methods.
- There is no separation of layers. Type-level machinery penetrates through all the library functions and all the `beam` parts (runner, queries, schema declaration bits) and then leaks into your business logic. Being so invasive, this type-level machinery can't be avoided because otherwise, nothing will compile.
- Additional complexity comes with genericity over the supported backends. It can be SQLite, Postgres, or MySQL; each requires its own type-level mark to identify. But with this mark, there are more type-level bolts and pieces to come: type families, type classes, and other Haskell features.

A highly coupled and loosely abstracted `beam` code makes it difficult to use and incorporate into frameworks. Implementation details about the exact database backend are visible in inappropriate places, for example, in the table ADTs. What does the `Sqlite` database backend have to do with a schema declaration here?

```
data CatalogueDB f = CatalogueDB
  { _meteors :: f (TableEntity DBMeteorT)
  }
  deriving (Generic, Database Sqlite)
```

Why is Sqlite here? ◄───

A typical query function may look like this. Notice all the `beam`-related constraints in the declaration:

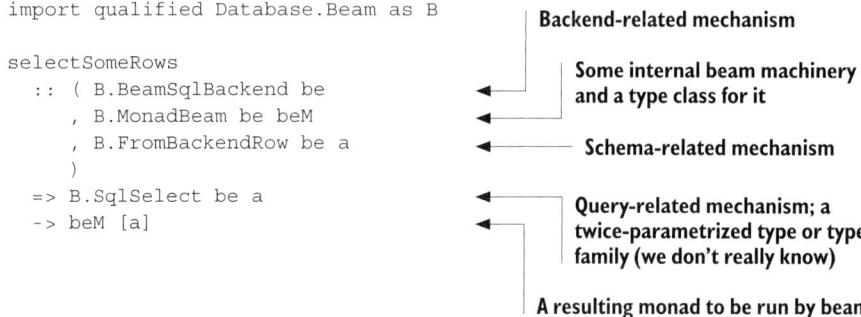

```
import qualified Database.Beam as B

selectSomeRows
  :: ( B.BeamSqlBackend be
     , B.MonadBeam be beM
     , B.FromBackendRow be a
     )
  => B.SqlSelect be a
  -> beM [a]
```

Backend-related mechanism

Some internal beam machinery and a type class for it ◄───

Schema-related mechanism ◄───

Query-related mechanism; a twice-parametrized type or type family (we don't really know) ◄───

A resulting monad to be run by beam

In the Hydra framework, I achieved some simplification for my SQL subsystem by cutting off parts of `beam` and pushing them to the interpreter level. I needed a bunch of tricks and a couple of type-level ceremonies, along with my free monadic SQL languages, so the developer could see less beam guts than initially. Hydra has an imperfect SQL subsystem, but at least I can write logic in my unified style.

Listing 12.4 User code that queries for specific meteors

```
import qualified Database.Beam as B

getMeteors
  :: Maybe Int32 -> Maybe Int32
  -> SqlConn B.SqliteM
  -> LangL Meteors
getMeteors mbMass mbSize conn = do
  ...
  eRows <- runDB conn
    $ findRows
    $ B.select
    $ B.filter_ predicate
    $ B.all_ (_meteors astroDb)
  ...
```

Meteor mass and size parameters to look up

Connection type originated by the framework

Framework's interface for SELECT queries

Embedded beam query language

Beam methods for SELECT queries

Two things can be observed here. First, we have a mix of the beam's query language and framework-rooted high-level functions such as findRows. Second, I had to abstract the beam's Connection type because I didn't want it to appear in the business logic. So I did some mapping from Connection to my own type, SqlConn, which also allowed me to make my LangL and AppL scenarios testable.

I must admit that embedding beam the way I did may have been suboptimal from an engineering point of view. There are no hacks or unforgivable tricks, though—it's just very difficult code. Unfortunately, it doesn't add anything to the topic, so you won't find any description here. A curious reader may consult the following modules from the framework:

```
Hydra.Core.Domain.SQLDB
Hydra.Core.SqlDB.Language
Hydra.Core.SqlDBRuntime
```

And good luck digging into this!

Summary

- In both OOP and functional programming, there is a need to work with relational databases.
- Relational models differ from domain models because the relations are more like referencing than nesting.
- Relational models are those that have their tables organized into a schema using some relational algebra.
- Encoding a relational algebra in object-oriented languages may and most likely will lead to complicated solutions such as ORMs.

- In the Haskell world, ORMs are possible but not widely used. Instead, we have SQL connectors: libraries that allow declaring of relational models with more or less advanced language features.

- The beam library we investigated relies on a design pattern known in Haskell as Higher-Kinded Data (HKD).

- The HKD pattern may also be helpful in reducing some boilerplate if many similar yet slightly different ADTs are to be declared.

- Embedding an external SQL connector into a free monadic framework is possible, and it's even proven that some accidental complexity can be cut off.

- There are always tradeoffs and compromises if we want to have type safety, convenience, and simplicity at the same time.

- High coupling hits us when least expected—for example, when embedding a highly coupled SQL connector into the framework.

Error handling and dependency inversion

This chapter covers

- How to layer and structure business logic
- How to decouple parts from services
- Many different approaches to dependency inversion

Programming is simple, and I recommend writing code and creating small applications to anyone for fun. However, development is extremely hard. There are so many technological options, subtle details, controversial requirements, and things to account for.

Writing code is only a small part of development, and it is not the most difficult one. If you decide to become a software developer, or even a software architect, you'll have to talk to people, understand their needs, clarify requirements, make decisions, and balance between bad, very bad, and unacceptable solutions. Certainly, you'll have to learn the domain you're working in. In their professional lives, developers can change their occupation many times. Today, you're a telecom developer and must be fluent in networking, billing, and accounting. Tomorrow, you learn cryptography and start working for a security company. Next time, you may move to writing search engines, so you'll buy several new books about natural language processing, algorithms, and data mining. Learning never stops.

Every developer should study software engineering because this knowledge is universal. The principles of software engineering can be transferred from one domain, paradigm, and language to another. Furthermore, software engineering allows a developer to maintain control when jumping over the vast land of domains.

All software has two parts: an engineering part, with all those technological essentials that enable the functionality, and a domain part, with business knowledge incorporated into the application. It's more likely that you won't be proficient in the domain part, but you can obtain sufficient experience in the engineering part easily. And if you're a software architect, you must be able to tell these two parts apart and approach them with appropriate tools.

This chapter will talk about the engineering part of our applications and will try to tame the wildest beasts of software engineering—errors and exceptions.

13.1 *Error handling through architectural layers*

Error handling is one of the most difficult themes. I've worked with many languages (C++, C#, Python, and Haskell) and have gained considerable knowledge about coding, but I've never seen a way to handle errors that I'd call perfect. I doubt that having a single perfect solution is even possible. Every project has its own guidelines on how to do this. Sometimes, exceptions are prohibited; in some projects, people cannot distinguish between exceptions and errors. But more often, errors are just ignored because of the false belief that nothing bad will happen. Although a very important practice, even validation isn't ubiquitous across the projects. After all the years of experience, it's still not clear to me if we really have a well-honed error-handling discipline in software engineering. In this section, I'll present some ideas so you'll at least be informed, and maybe we'll find a better way.

13.1.1 *Errors vs. exceptions*

Let's clarify the difference between errors and exceptions:

- An *exception* is a language-dependent mechanism for terminating the control flow. Exceptions can be caught, but if not, this usually forces the application to end abruptly, which prevents further data corruption and security breaches. Exceptions are mostly implicit and domain agnostic.

- An *exceptional situation* happens when the execution of the program has led to an unexpected condition. An exceptional situation is more likely to be caused by a bug.

- An *error* is a probable state in the program that's expected to happen under specific circumstances. Errors are mostly explicit, and they're usually related to some domain.

- A *native error* is an error that comes from outside of a framework and business logic. Native errors can come from external (native) libraries or from the ecosystem of the programming language. Native errors are not abstracted, and if propagated to business logic, they make it too coupled, too aware, and overly dependent on the native libraries.

Some languages have mixed practices in which errors and exceptions are indistinguishable, or they substitute each other. Exceptions as a mechanism may be supported but completely prohibited; see, for example, a well-known guide for C++ developers, available at https://mng.bz/oevr. Haskell's story of exceptions can compete with C++, and this isn't a compliment. Haskell supports exceptions as language features; furthermore, the community has invented a lot of practices for handling both exceptions and errors. Some of them are

- Synchronous exceptions, which are usual exceptions similar to those in other languages
- Asynchronous exceptions, which are a tricky Haskell mechanism where the exception from one thread can occur in the other thread lazily, thus making the entire logic even more incomprehensible
- The `Exception` data type and related types
- `Either`, `EitherT`, `ExceptT`, and `ErrorT` monads
- `Maybe` and `MaybeT` monads
- `MonadMask`, `MonadThrow`, `MonadCatch`, `MonadBracket`, and other type classes (generally usable within the mtl/final tagless setting)

In my opinion, the situation with errors and exceptions in Haskell can't be considered "good, simple, and easy to grasp." I would even say it's a total disaster. Each of these approaches attempts to be useful, but you can't be sure whether you've considered all the possible cases and done it right. The intersection of the approaches in a particular code base can confuse everything completely.

Choosing an approach to errors and exceptions

There are different materials describing why you should prefer one approach over another, and they may be appropriate to your requirements. See the following:

- Michael Snoyman, *Exceptions Best Practices in Haskell (*https://mng.bz/ngng)
- Michael Snoyman, *Asynchronous Exception Handling in Haskell* (https://mng.bz/v8gJ)
- Mark Karpov, *Exceptions Tutorial* (https://mng.bz/4Jda)
- Simon Marlow, *Asynchronous Exceptions in Practice* (https://mng.bz/QZGw)
- Vitaly Bragilevsky, *Haskell in Depth* (https://mng.bz/X18G)

This book wouldn't be complete without its own approach. There are 14 competing standards, so what's 1 more or less, huh? Yes, but there's one key difference: I'm offering a consistent philosophy of exceptions and errors within the hierarchical free monads setting. It won't be 100% correct, but it will work in 95% of cases. Let's check it out!

13.1.2 Error domains

There is a story about a needle in an egg, which is hidden in a duck, and the duck is kept in a chest. The story communicates the idea of layering, which we are already familiar with. And now layering is becoming even more important because it's the key to proper error handling. We can say native errors are like the needle: they come from the deepest layer of the application (external impure world) and propagate from inside through other layers.

For example, if we take a library to work with the filesystem, there will be an error indicating the absence of a file. The fact that the file is lacking can be signaled with an exception, as stated in the `imaginary-filesystem` library:

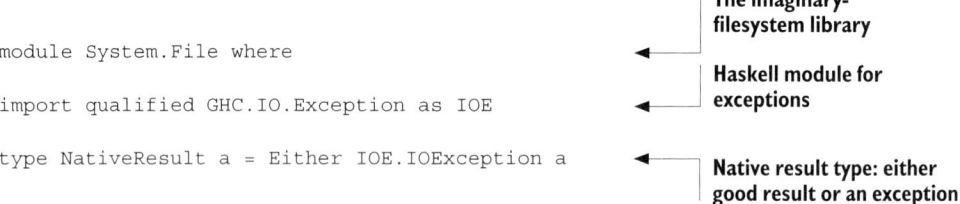

```
module System.File where                              ◄─── The imaginary-
                                                           filesystem library
import qualified GHC.IO.Exception as IOE              ◄─── Haskell module for
                                                           exceptions
type NativeResult a = Either IOE.IOException a        ◄─── Native result type: either
                                                           good result or an exception
```

We can catch this exception in a free monadic interpreter (the egg), propagate it unchanged through a free monadic language `FileSystemL` (the duck), and then reveal it in the business logic (the chest). Let's take a look at figure 13.1.

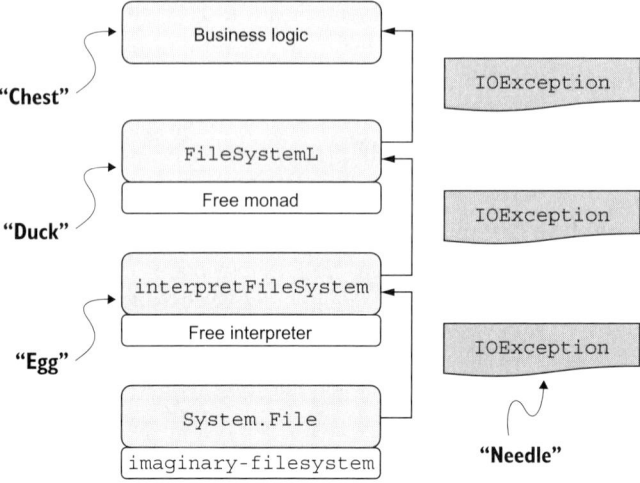

Figure 13.1   Propagating a native error through layers

This principle could only work if our framework supported rethrowing exceptions. It doesn't, though, because non-abstracted pieces from native libraries are highly unwelcome in the business logic. What if the author of a library introduces changes? Too much code should be updated on our side, and it's not always a simple fix. Sometimes, those native data types, such as `IOException` and `NativeResult`, are opaque, which means we cannot construct them on our own and our code is blocked from testing. This is a huge concern, and we should learn how to overcome it.

What we should do now is follow the general principle of engineering—divide and conquer. We have layers, and it will be natural to bind each layer to a specific way of error processing. One layer indicates one method, and we always know the boundaries that the errors of a kind should not cross. This will drastically simplify error handling and force us to introduce useful abstractions. Thus, by putting each error-handling mechanism on its own layer, we divide our application into error domains.

> **DEFINITION** An *error domain* is an isolated part of an application that has a predefined error-handling mechanism and provides a guarantee that there will be no other behavior. Don't confuse *error domain* with *domain error*.

Error domains don't fit layers strictly because several layers are allowed to be unified by a single error domain. In addition, you can have many error domains within a layer. There's no strict rule except the following one: as an error mechanism defines a domain, all the artifacts crossing the boundary between domains should be converted from one form into another. Figure 13.2 introduces error domains for a free monad application.

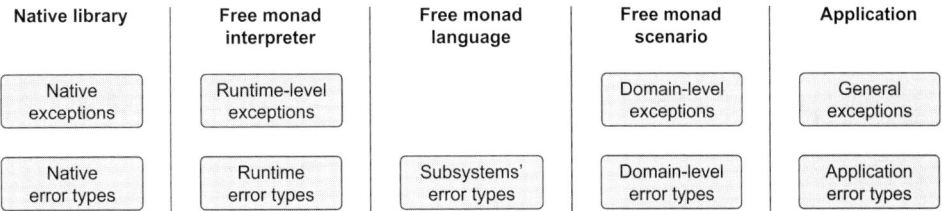

Figure 13.2 Error domains

From the figure, you can conclude that native errors and native exceptions should not leak into free monadic languages. Ideally, all the native error types should be converted into a more abstract form by the interpreter. More precisely, we decouple a pure world of free monadic languages and scenarios from the impure world of native libraries. The interpreter here represents a nice mediator between the two. In addition, interpreters can have their own internal exceptions and errors. Design choices depend on your requirements (for example, your interpreter's stack can be wrapped into the `ExceptT` monad transformer), but we can discuss several schemes that emerge from common needs.

13.1.3 *Native exception-handling schemes*

The first case occurs when an external library throws a synchronous exception. The interpreter should capture it and convert it if necessary. After this, a value can be passed back into the free monadic scenario. Alternatively, the value can be ignored, so the scenario should not expect it. Also, you can convert the native value in the interpreter, or at the upper level, which is the free language method. Figure 13.3 presents a diagram with these approaches. We're going to investigate all of them separately.

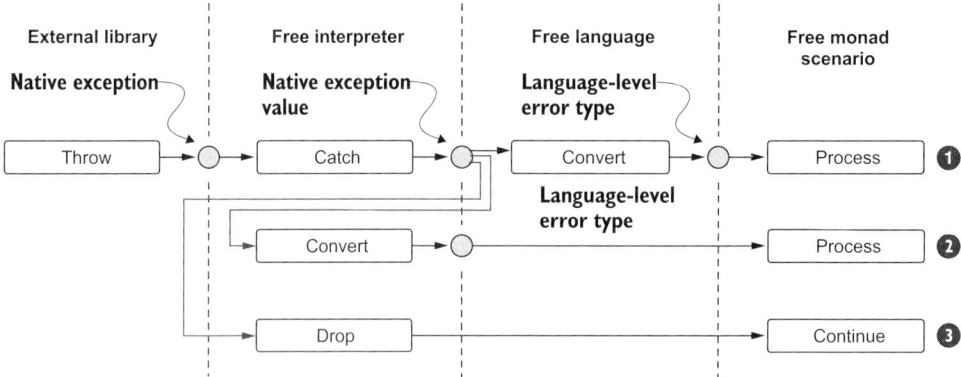

Figure 13.3   Three options for dealing with native exceptions

Let's construct a sample to accompany the diagram. A free monadic language `FileSystemL` will be the subject of our experiment. We know that `readFile` and `writeFile` functions may throw. We will follow the general advice from my methodology—prohibit implicit exceptions and introduce value-based explicit errors instead—and will convert the native `IOException` to a framework-provided error type:

```
data FSError
  = FileNotFound (Maybe FilePath)
  | OtherError String

type FSResult a = Either FSError a
```

This type lacks many errors, of course, and the `OtherError` case would be a god-like fallback for them. Please ignore this deficiency—it's not the point.

   Option 1 is very straightforward: a native filesystem fires an exception, the interpreter catches it, the `FileSystemL` language converts the exception into a value, and then this value becomes available in the business logic. Figure 13.4 illustrates the first option.

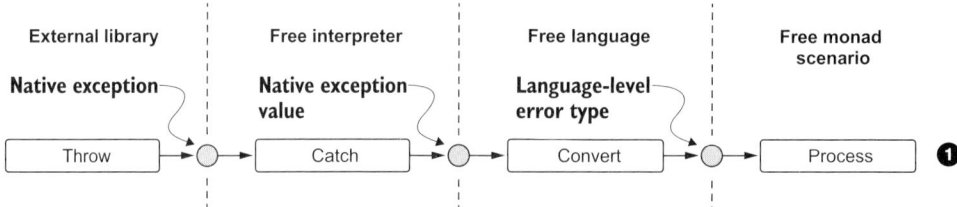

Figure 13.4   Straightforward exception handling with conversion in the language

Listing 13.1 contains a code that demonstrates this conversion. Notice that the conversion happens in the smart constructors of the language. There are two: `writeFileIO` works with `IOException` enclosed into `NativeResult`, and `writeFile'` works with `FSError`, enclosed into `FSResult`. The language itself propagates `NativeResult` from within the implementation of the `WriteFile` method.

Listing 13.1 Converting exceptions into errors at the language level

```
data FileSystemF next where
  WriteFile :: FilePath -> StringToWrite
    -> (NativeResult () -> next)                    ◄── The native error
    -> FileSystemF next                                   type is used here.

type FileSystemL = Free FileSystemF

writeFileIO                                         ◄── Smart constructor:
  :: FilePath -> StringToWrite -> FileSystemL (NativeResult ())   returns a native
writeFileIO path content = liftF (WriteFile path content id)     error type

writeFile' :: FilePath -> StringToWrite
           -> FileSystemL (FSResult ())             ◄── Smart constructor:
writeFile' path content = do                              returns a custom
  eRes <- writeFileIO path content                        error type
  pure (fromNativeResult eRes)

fromNativeResult :: NativeResult a -> FSResult a    ◄── Native-error-to-custom-error
                                                         converter (details omitted)
```

I would hide `writeFileIO` from the module's interface because it may impose an unnecessary dependency from the implementation details on the client. But that's a rule of thumb, and I can't argue for doing this for all the possible use cases of the framework.

The interpreter will do simple things, namely catch the exception, while interpreting the `WriteFile` method:

```
interpretFileSystemF :: FileSystemF a -> IO a       ◄── Interpreter that
interpretFileSystemF (WriteFile path content next) = do   calls a native function
  eRes <- try (writeFile path content)              ◄── Calls the native
  pure (next eRes)                                       function (writeFile)
                                                         and catches an
                                                         exception (try)
```

> **NOTE** The `try` function from Haskell catches synchronous exceptions. Its type is `try :: Exception e => IO a -> IO (Either e a)`. As you can see, it evaluates the impure action and either returns `Right result` or `Left error`. Unfortunately, explaining this language feature is a big challenge on its own, so I can only recommend learning about it from other sources.

The whole option demonstrates that you can do a lot in the smart constructors. Dealing with the guts of the native filesystem library feels like the language somewhat depends

on it, and indeed, it does. However, smart constructors constitute the interface for the
FileSystemL, and the business logic doesn't see anything beyond that. If writeFile'
is the only smart constructor we expose, the business logic will be free from implementation details.

Option 2, summarized in figure 13.5, looks very similar, but the transformation happens in the interpreter. This is probably a more preferable design because we don't
want to allow native types to leak and appear in the language layer. The relevant part of
the code is shown in the following listing.

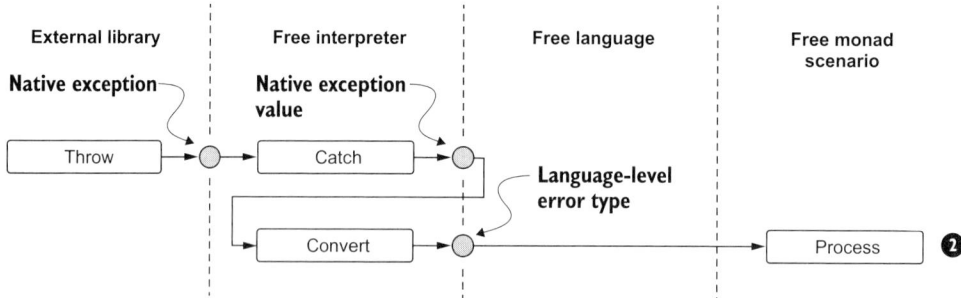

Figure 13.5   Straightforward exception handling with conversion in the interpreter

Listing 13.2   Converting exceptions into errors at the interpreter level

```
data FileSystemF next where
  WriteFile :: FilePath -> StringToWrite          A custom error type
           -> (FSResult () -> next)               is used here.
           -> FileSystemF next

writeFile' :: FilePath -> StringToWrite           The smart constructor
         -> FileSystemL (FSResult ())             is now simpler.
writeFile' path content = liftF (WriteFile path content id)

interpretFileSystemF :: FileSystemF a -> IO a     Catches an exception
interpretFileSystemF (WriteFile path content next) = do   from the native
  eRes <- try (writeFile path content)            function
  pure (next (fromNativeResult eRes))

                                                  Converts the native
                                                  error type to the
                                                  custom error type
```

Notice how the language changed: no more dependency from the native library! It's
more idiomatic to what we've learned so far. The interpreter should convert the exception value into the appropriate format as expected.

What about option 3? Let's take a look at figure 13.6.

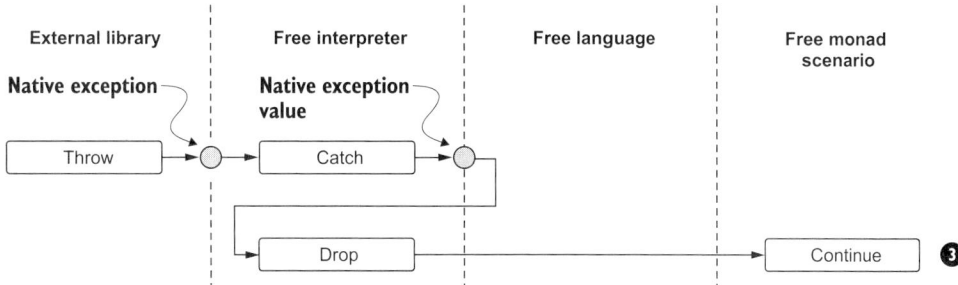

Figure 13.6   Dropping and silencing the exception

Well, the actual result of `writeFile'` is `FSResult ()`, which is nothing special. The unit value `()` will be enclosed in this result type if the writing was successful. If it wasn't, we could just ignore the error and return `()` forcefully, but this is a different method semantic, so we should reflect it somehow (for example, in the documentation):

```
-- | This method doesn't provide a guarantee
--    of a successful write operation.
-- In case of exceptions, nothing will happen and () will be returned.
writeFile' :: FilePath -> String -> FileSystemL ()
writeFile' filePath content = void (liftF (WriteFile filePath content id))
```

Silencing the exception can also be done in the interpreter.

Neither of these techniques will work properly without following two golden rules:

- *Interpreters should catch all the exceptions from the other world.* There should be no eDSL method allowing the external exceptions to slip into the business logic.

- *Asynchronous exceptions should be prohibited.* Neither the framework nor the underlying libraries should emit asynchronous exceptions because it's hard to reason about the logic. All things become very complicated. Moreover, the need for asynchronous exceptions indicates design flaws. Asynchronous exceptions violate the Liskov substitution principle because they're able to crash an innocent thread suddenly.

By following these two rules, we can guarantee that nothing unexpected will happen. All the worlds are effectively separated from each other, and the code is under control. This clarifies how the logic behaves and how to fix possible problems. Figure 13.7 describes how to guard all the exceptions completely and gatekeep them from leaking from the impure layer (interpreters and external libraries). Although it's possible to do this with other architectural patterns, only the free monadic approach avoids any compromises by making it impossible to bypass the gate.

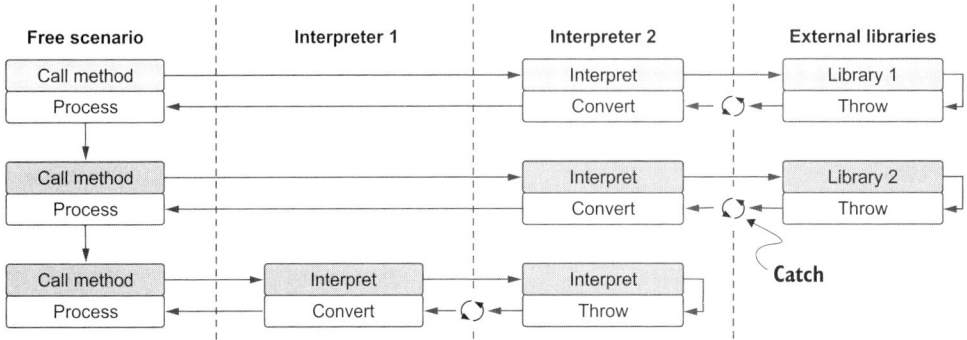

Figure 13.7 Total exceptions gatekeeping

The circular arrows in figure 13.7 mean "catching." Other arrows show the path of an error across all the layers. Two interpreters demonstrate how nested free interpreters interact with each other if they need to communicate errors and propagate exceptions. So if all the interpreters of all the free monadic languages do this catching and conversion for all the possible methods, it is impossible for exceptions to occur in the business logic or beyond it at the application layer.

But this is only half of the methodology. We can have domain-level exceptions in our free monadic framework if we really need them. The question is how to design a safe mechanism.

13.1.4 Exceptions in free monadic languages

There's some specificity on how exceptions move through the business logic. It looks like the control flow zigzags between an interpreter and a free monadic scenario (figure 13.7). For a long time, it was even believed that free monads didn't allow any exception handling. The argument was that the exception would terminate the control flow, and the evaluation point would never return to the scenario, so there was no sense in having a catch method in the language.

Let's consider an example to clarify this. There will be a function `meteorsApp` that initializes SQL DB, checks for success, and proceeds with a created connection. In case of a failed initialization, it logs some error message and quits:

```
meteorsApp :: AppL ()
meteorsApp = do
  eConn <- initSQLiteDB "./meteors.db"
  case eConn of
    Left err -> logError ("initSQLiteDB failed: " <> show err)
    Right conn -> do
      meteors <- queryMeteorsWithMass conn 100
      logInfo ("Meteors found: " <> show meteors)
```

DB initialization—comes from AppL and returns either a connection value or error

Some query to the SQL database to get specific meteors

Now, for some reason, we want to throw a domain-level exception when the connection fails:

```
data AppException = InvalidOperation String
  deriving (Exception)
```
This is how we create custom exception types in Haskell.

It's an exception from a Haskell perspective. Given this type class `Exception`, the user-defined `AppException` type becomes suitable for many exception-handling mechanisms in Haskell: firing, catching, and transforming. This will play its role quite soon. For now, let's write a custom unsafe initialization function that converts the error value to the exception and throws it.

Listing 13.3 Converting an error to a custom exception

```
unsafeInitSQLiteDB :: DBName -> AppL (SQLConn SqliteM)
unsafeInitSQLiteDB dbName = do
  eConn <- initSQLiteDB dbName
  case eConn of
    Left err -> do
      logError "Init connection failed."
      throwException (InvalidOperation (show err))
    Right conn -> pure conn

meteorsApp :: AppL ()
meteorsApp = do
  conn    <- unsafeInitSQLiteDB "./meteors.db"
  meteors <- getMeteorsWithMass conn 100
  logInfo ("Meteors found: " <> show meteors)
```
Function to throw an exception; comes from the framework

No need to check the validity of the connection now

So we have a `throwException` method that comes from the framework. Obviously, the interpreter of this method should throw a real exception. Once this happens, the script stops evaluating at the `unsafeInitSQLiteDB` method, and the whole `AppL` program terminates. The exception will then appear at the place where we started our free monadic evaluation (it's the `main` function or some functions around it):

```
main :: IO ()
main = do
  ...
  eResult <- try (runAppL rt meteorsApp)
  case eResult of
    Left (err :: SomeException) ->
      putStrLn (show err)
    Right _ -> ...
```
Haskell way to pattern-match over any possible exception type

Just printing the value of the exception to the console

Here, we don't really know what exception is thrown because it becomes a generic opaque value `SomeException`. It can be anything, from the original Haskell exceptions to those defined in numerous external libraries. We don't know much about this value, although we can stringify it and print it to the console. The corresponding scheme is presented in figure 13.8.

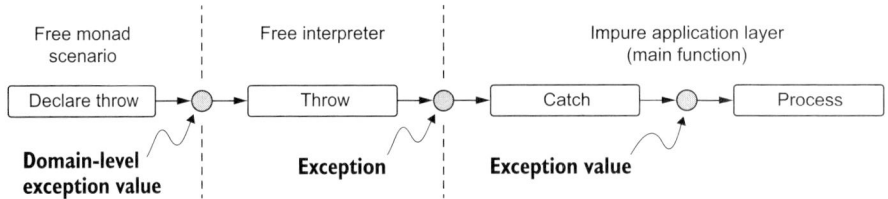

Figure 13.8   Handling exceptions at the application level

If we want to capture the exception while staying in the business logic (`AppL` monad), we should write something like this:

```
meteorsApp :: AppL ()                                        ◄──  Business logic on top of
meteorsApp = do                                                   the framework
  eConn <- try (unsafeInitSQLiteDB "./meteors.db")         ◄──
  case eConn of                                                  This won't compile.
    Left (err :: SomeException) -> ...
    Right conn -> ...
```

However, we can't use `try` because it's specified for the `IO` actions only, not for the `AppL` actions:

```
try :: Exception e => IO a -> IO (Either e a)
unsafeInitSQLiteDB :: DBName -> AppL (SQLConn SqliteM)
```

It seems we can't define `try` for `AppL` neither—or can we? Ladies and gentlemen, the `runSafely` method in propria persona! And the `throwException` method for your pleasure.

Listing 13.4   New methods: `throwException` and `runSafely`

```
data LangF next where
                                                      Method for throwing
                                                      domain-level exceptions
  ThrowException
    :: forall a e next
    . Exception e                                     Only exceptions
    => e -> (a -> next) -> LangF next                 are allowed.

  RunSafely                                           Method for running a
    :: forall a e next                                LangL scenario and
    . Exception e                                     catching its exceptions
    => LangL a
    -> (Either e a -> next)
    -> LangF next

throwException :: forall a e. Exception e => e -> LangL a
throwException ex = liftF (ThrowException ex id)

runSafely :: Exception e => LangL a -> LangL (Either e a)
runSafely act = liftF (RunSafely act id)
```

Notice the following two things in the code. First, it's not `AppL` but rather `LangL`. It could be `AppL`, but it's intended for high-level operations, whereas `LangL` is intended for the business logic itself. Second, we nest a `LangL` action recursively into the `LangL` interface itself—precisely, into the `RunSafely` method. Because of this, the interpreter can run itself recursively and attempt to catch the specified exception.

Listing 13.5   The interpreter for the new methods

```haskell
import Control.Exception (throwIO)

interpretLangF :: LangF a -> IO a
interpretLangF (ThrowException exc _) = throwIO exc
interpretLangF (RunSafely act next) = do
  eResult <- try (runLangL act)
  pure (next (case eResult of
    Left err -> Left err
    Right r  -> Right r
  ))


runLangL :: LangL a -> IO a
runLangL = foldFree interpretLangF
```

Throwing any exception in Haskell within the IO environment

Catching an exception from the interpreter of this given LangL action

And yes, this is it. No magic, actually. The `runSafely` and `try` combinators have similar semantics. Well, not quite, but let's not dissertate on the subtle issues of the exception-handling mechanism in Haskell and just `runSafely` in `AppL` our code as if it were `try` in `IO`:

```haskell
meteorsApp :: AppL ()
meteorsApp = do
  eConn <- runSafely (unsafeInitSQLiteDB "./meteors.db")

  case eConn of
    Left (err :: SomeException) -> ...
    Right conn -> ...
```

I would, however, argue that exceptions obscure the control flow and make the business logic less readable. Someone will say, "But exceptions help to keep the program clean!" I tend to strongly disagree. If code does something that is not directly expressed by it, we cannot call it clean or safe. I truly appreciate the fact that the developers of the Rust language eliminated exceptions from it completely, so maybe we should do the same.

Anyway, I love these diagrams, so I prepared figure 13.9 to describe the code schematically. This diagram shows the flow and its journey through the scenario. The actual flow steps through the interpreter while interpreting the steps of the scenario. The interpreter catches exceptions, but this isn't visible to a scenario developer. It still feels as if it controls exceptions from their business logic.

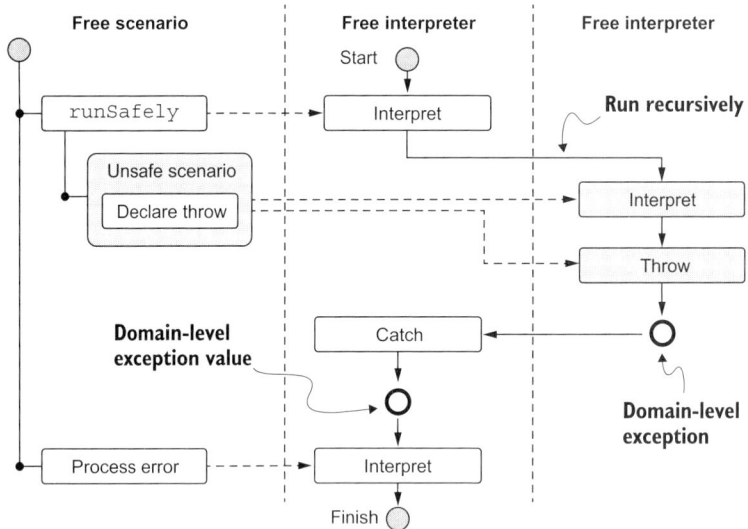

Figure 13.9   Exception flow in the free monadic scenario

Here are some conclusions:

- We added two new methods for handling exceptions. The hierarchical nature of our framework helped because we can nest one action inside another and run the interpreters recursively.

- We can now implement many functions from the `Control.Exception` module. `bracket`? Yes. `finally`? Of course. `onException`? No problem.

- We divided the whole application into domain errors and thus simplified the reasoning about each (the divide-and-conquer principle, again).

- We now better understand the distinction between exceptions and errors. We can convert one into another if needed.

- We established a philosophy of error handling. And I believe it's much simpler than other approaches.

Let me reiterate: I'm not teaching you Haskell, and therefore, I am not teaching you its exceptions. It would be inaccurate to say that I covered Haskell's exceptions in full and without any mistakes. Our task is to learn the concepts of errors and exceptions and see how these fit into the framework, business logic, and application architecture in general. This is an important part of software engineering, but it's much more than this book can cover. The more we learn, the more we can notice other things that need to be learned.

Another software engineering principle we should discuss is the dependency inversion (DIP) principle from SOLID and the tools that are given to us to do this.

13.2 *Functional interfaces and dependency inversion*

When I was green and enthusiastic, I had a very different opinion on how to write programs. My code was pretty straightforward: external subsystems were occurring in random places when I needed them, and I didn't see a problem with this. My approach to designing programs was shaped by a narrow background and a lack of good production experience. I could not see that my code was highly coupled. I didn't even know that there was a notion of coupling. I was unable to see how this made my code worse, and I could not reinvent any practice to eliminate coupling.

"You folks are overengineering it" was my opinion on things such as the DIP, dependency injection mechanisms, and dependency injection frameworks. But once I faced the need to test and extend my code, I immediately realized all the design problems. This was the moment when I learned design principles the hard way.

High coupling was the problem. My business logic was dependent on the external subsystems, and it was, therefore, fragile and untestable. High coupling prevented the business logic from being extensible. There were no interfaces, no abstractions, and consequently, no clear extensibility points. Redesigning this code was a difficult task, but it allowed me to learn the concept of dependency inversion, which was truly enlightening.

Now I want to connect the dots and transfer this knowledge into our functional programming setting. We'll see how to make the code compliant with the DIP and what consequences it will have for our business logic. To do this, we'll learn about a variety of functional interfaces and how to inject dependencies, and we'll examine the differences between these approaches:

- Service handle
- ReaderT
- Free monad
- Generalized algebraic data type (GADT)
- Final tagless (mtl)

What's interesting here is that it seems that there are three kinds of meta interfaces:

- *Scenario-like interfaces*—These interfaces are intended for writing scenarios, scripts, and sequential logic in general. The most sensible example is all our framework eDSLs: `AppL`, `LangL`, `LoggerL`, and other monadic languages. In fact, most monadic-based FP interfaces are scenario like.
- *API-like interfaces*—The methods of these interfaces are intended only for solitary application, and the design of these methods doesn't imply chaining. These interfaces are needed only to represent some API with distinct methods provided. Most OOP interfaces are similar to API.
- *Combinatorial interfaces*—Combinatorial interfaces provide a set of combinators that can be joined together and form a bigger combinator of the same kind.

In some sense, monadic APIs are combinatorial, but they feel imperative. I would avoid putting them into this category, but it should be used to group things such as reactive streams or lenses. What those interfaces do for information hiding still needs to be investigated. What follows is an encyclopedia-style section that you can use to find out more about those approaches.

13.2.1 *The Dependency Inversion principle*

The DIP in OOP provides an implementation hidden behind an interface so that the client code doesn't need to bother with the implementation details and is completely decoupled from them. This principle becomes very important in large systems with significant IO operations. We usually say such systems are IO bound, not CPU bound, meaning the main activity is always related to dealing with the impure external world. Following the DIP makes the code less complex and more maintainable in general (figure 13.10).

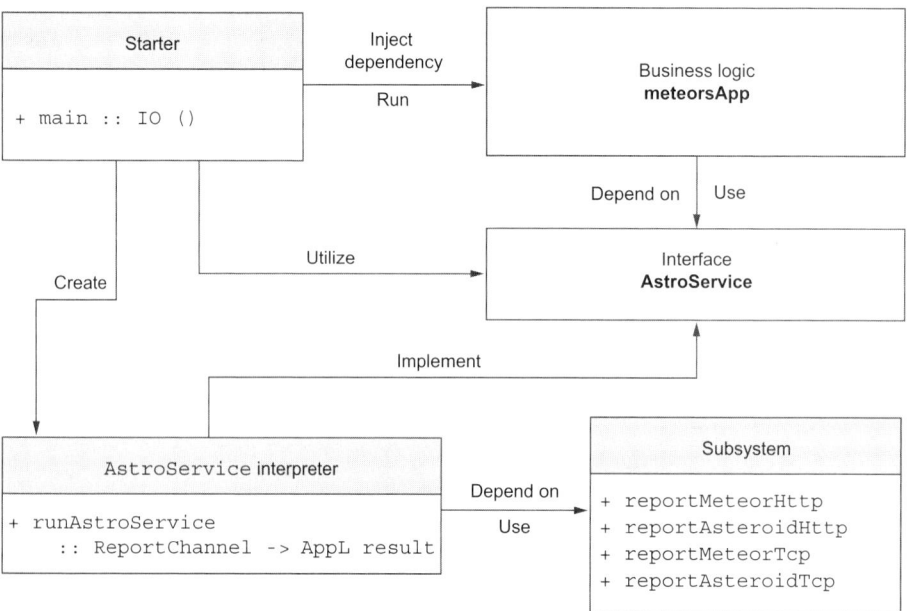

Figure 13.10   Dependency inversion

We've followed the principle already. The very layered nature of the free monadic framework can be viewed as an inversion of dependencies. The business logic layer must refer to the abstractions from the framework (figure 13.11) and be decoupled from the impure implementation layer.

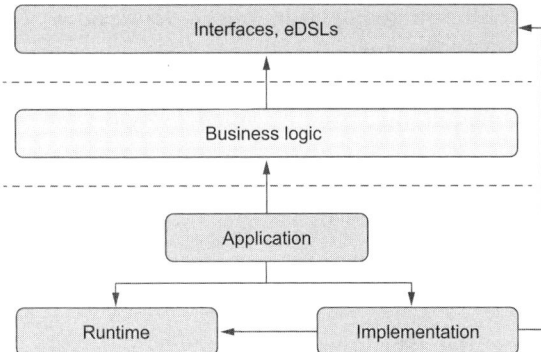

Figure 13.11 Three main application layers

There is even an opinion that having layers separated by boundaries implies having a DIP-compliant design. And what's more important for today's discussion is that we should introduce additional sublayers within the business logic layer. We'll do so while working on the command-line application for astronomers. This application will allow the astronomer to connect to the server and report numerous sky events. For example, the following data structure will be used for reporting meteors:

```
data MeteorTemplate = MeteorTemplate
  { size       :: Int
  , mass       :: Int
  , azimuth    :: Int
  , altitude   :: Int
  } deriving (Generic, ToJSON, FromJSON)
```

Should be JSON-conversable

The function `reportMeteor` does the networking:

```
reportMeteor :: MeteorTemplate -> AppL (Either ReportingError MeteorId)
```

It will certainly boil down to the framework's subsystems eventually, but at the business logic level. It's an `AppL` function that spares the developer from the details. Moreover, I'm going to hide the channel that was used (HTTP, TCP, or something else). The `reportMeteor` function should not know about that, yet it should be able to send meteors and process responses from the server, meaning we're going to inject a dependency through some functional interface so that the function becomes details agnostic and DIP compliant:

```
type ReportingError = String

reportMeteor
  :: _ReportingInterface_
  -> MeteorTemplate
  -> AppL (Either ReportingError MeteorId)
```

Some functional interface to send structures over the network

Simultaneously, I want to specify the reporting channel at the start of the application itself. There should be a config for this. This is either a command-line argument or an external application config file (it doesn't matter that much). However, by having this config, a proper implementation will be created and passed into the `reportMeteor` function.

For better demonstrability, let's have more than one object to report, say, asteroids:

```
data AsteroidTemplate = AsteroidTemplate ...

reportAsteroid
  :: _ReportingInterface_
  -> AsteroidTemplate
  -> AppL (Either ReportingError AsteroidId)
```

◄─┐ **Some fields for asteroid here**

We don't need to exhaustively describe it; let it just be an opaque data type.

13.2.2 Service Handle pattern

The Service Handle pattern (also known as Service pattern or Handle pattern) is the simplest way to describe an interface for a subsystem. For the client program, we may want to create the following handle, an algebraic data type with specific fields, as presented in the following listing.

Listing 13.6   Service Handle interface

```
data AstroServiceHandle = AstroServiceHandle
  { meteorReporter
        :: MeteorTemplate
        -> AppL (Either ReportingError MeteorId)     ◄─┐ Method for sending
                                                        meteors
  , asteroidReporter
        :: AsteroidTemplate
        -> AppL (Either ReportingError AsteroidId)   ◄─┐ Method for sending
  }                                                     asteroids
```

Passing a value of this `AstroServiceHandle` structure to the `reportMeteor` function opens new possibilities.

Listing 13.7   DIP-compliant code with the Service Handle pattern

```
meteorsApp :: AstroServiceHandle -> AppL ()
meteorsApp handle = do
  let reporter = meteorReporter handle          ◄─┐ Sending the hard-coded
                                                    meteor via the abstracted
  eResult <- reporter (MeteorTemplate 1 1 1 1)  ◄── channel
  case eResult of
    Right meteorId -> ...                        ◄─┐ Upon success,
    Left err -> ...                              ◄─┐ utilizes the id
```

Getting the actual reporter

Upon failure, processes the error

Now the logic is decoupled from the networking details. If, for example, the channel changes from a bare TCP to a high-level HTTP, all the possible communication errors will change as well. However, the code will stay the same because it will only know about the `ReportingError` data type. Of course, having a string error is usually not enough, so improving this error type would make sense in real code bases:

```
data ReportingError
  = NoConfirmation String
  | DuplicatedObject String
  | NetworkError String
  | UnknownError String
```

It's difficult to say what exactly this error type should be, so for now, we'll stick with a string.

The next question we must answer is how we form the `handle` data structure. We'll do this in the `main` function and then run the fully configured `meteorsApp` using the framework. What do we need for this?

First, there should be the `getReportChannel` that reads application configs and decides on what channel is wanted:

```
data ReportChannel
  = TcpChannel TcpConfig
  | HttpChannel BaseUrl

getReportChannel :: IO ReportChannel
```

Second, we should have actual reporters that know how to deal with TCP or HTTP. Those reporters rely on the framework possibilities for networking that are coming with the `AppL` language:

```
reportMeteorHttp :: BaseUrl -> MeteorTemplate -> AppL (Either ReportingError
MeteorId)

reportAsteroidHttp :: BaseUrl -> AsteroidTemplate
                   -> AppL (Either ReportingError AsteroidId)

reportMeteorTcp :: TcpConfig -> MeteorTemplate -> AppL (Either ReportingError
MeteorId)

reportAsteroidTcp :: TcpConfig -> AsteroidTemplate
                  -> AppL (Either ReportingError AsteroidId)
```

Third, pattern-matching over the `ReportChannel` variable should give us a fully constructed handle for both meteor and asteroid:

```
makeServiceHandle :: ReportChannel -> AstroServiceHandle

makeServiceHandle (HttpChannel baseUrl) =
  AstroServiceHandle
    (reportMeteorHttp baseUrl)
    (reportAsteroidHttp baseUrl)

makeServiceHandle (TcpChannel tcpConfig) =
  AstroServiceHandle
    (reportMeteorTcp tcpConfig)
    (reportAsteroidTcp tcpConfig)
```

Now we're joining everything in the main function.

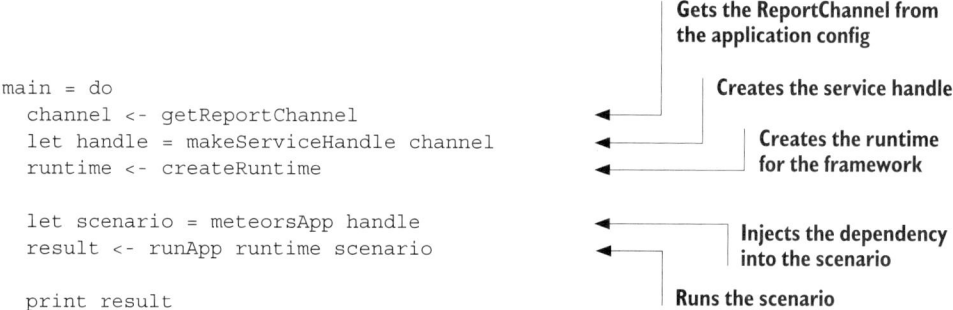

Listing 13.8   Forming and injecting a dependency with service handle

```
main = do
  channel <- getReportChannel
  let handle = makeServiceHandle channel
  runtime <- createRuntime

  let scenario = meteorsApp handle
  result <- runApp runtime scenario

  print result
```

Gets the ReportChannel from the application config

Creates the service handle

Creates the runtime for the framework

Injects the dependency into the scenario

Runs the scenario

The sequence of actions in the code is clear enough, although I'm skipping the important question of how to handle TCP/HTTP connections and manage resources. How we parse application configs is also a matter of discussion. For now, we see that the `meteorsApp` function doesn't know anything about networking and only deals with the handle interface we've provided.

By reading a `ReportChannel` value from the command line on the start of the application, you can specify how your program should behave. Alternatively, you can pass it via an environment variable or by using a config file. This is a pretty common practice in Java and C# when there's a text file (usually XML) containing different settings and configs for particular subsystems. Many IoC containers allow you to choose the implementation and thus have additional flexibility for the system. All the patterns we learn here can be a basis for such a dependency injection framework, and I'm sure there are some for Haskell too.

13.2.3 *ReaderT pattern*

The `ReaderT` pattern is based on the same idea as the Service Handle pattern and has a very similar implementation. We're not passing the handle structure now but it is in the `ReaderT` environment. Alternatively, the `StateT` transformer can be used because `ReaderT` is just half of it. Let's check out the code.

There should be a handle-like structure; let's call it `AppEnv` (environment for the business logic):

```
data AppEnv = AppEnv
  { meteorReporter
      :: MeteorTemplate
      -> AppL (Either ReportingError MeteorId)
  , asteroidReporter
      :: AsteroidTemplate
      -> AppL (Either ReportingError AsteroidId)
  }
```

If you're trying to figure out whether it is different from `AstroServiceHandle`, it is not. It's just another name for the same control structure to keep the naming more recognizable. The difference is how we pass this structure into logic. We actually don't. We store this handle in the Reader context in which we wrap our `AppL` monad:

```
type AppRT a = ReaderT AppEnv AppL a
```

As all our business logic should be wrapped into the `ReaderT` monad transformer, our code starts to look slightly overloaded by occasional `lift`s.

Listing 13.9 DIP-compliant code with `ReaderT`

```
meteorsApp :: AppRT ()
meteorsApp = do
  AppEnv reporter _ <- ask

  eResult <- lift (reporter (MeteorTemplate 1 1 1 1))
  case eResult of
    Right meteorId -> ...
    Left err       -> ...
```

Gets the actual reporter from the ReaderT environment

Sends the hard-coded meteor via the abstracted channel

Notice the `lift` function caused by the fact that the actual free monadic scenario is wrapped into the `ReaderT` monad now. Running the `AppRT` scenario with the framework shows some changes too.

Listing 13.10 Forming and injecting a dependency with `ReaderT`

```
makeAppEnv :: ReportChannel -> AppEnv

main = do
  channel <- getReportChannel
  runtime <- createRuntime

  let appEnv   = makeAppEnv channel
  let scenario = runReaderT meteorsApp appEnv
  result <- runApp runtime scenario

  print result
```

Creates the environment for ReaderT

Unwraps the AppRT scenario into AppL scenario

Runs a normal AppL scenario

Notice how we navigated between the layers: an external one that is formed by the `AppRT` monad (hence, ReaderT), and an internal one that is formed by the `AppL` monad. In the business logic, we call `lift` to address the internal `AppL` layer, while in the main function, we should do unwrapping from `AppRT` back to `AppL` to pass the scenario to the framework.

Lifting between the two monad layers here is an unavoidable boilerplate. Or is it? In Haskell, there are ways to reduce it: additional type classes for the `AppRT` type, a newtype wrapper for the `ReaderT` monad powered by some automatic derivings, and others. I'll leave this question for you to contemplate.

It's unfortunate that we had to do so many steps. The cost is probably too high for removing the handle from `meteorsApp` arguments. Maybe it's not worth it. Just use the Service Handle Pattern. Keep it simple.

13.2.4 *Free monad*

To satisfy our curiosity, let's see how much code will be required for the free monad interface. This is the language that abstracts the reporting of objects. I named it `AstroService`.

Listing 13.11 Free monad interface

```
data AstroServiceF a where
  ReportMeteorFree
    :: MeteorTemplate
    -> (Either ReportingError MeteorId -> next)
    -> AstroServiceF next

  ReportAsteroidFree
    :: AsteroidTemplate
    -> (Either ReportingError AsteroidId -> next)
    -> AstroServiceF next

type AstroService a = Free AstroServiceF a
```

Algebra for a new free
monadic language

A new free monadic
language

We need smart constructors for this language too.

Listing 13.12 Smart constructors used in the scenarios

```
reportMeteorFree
  :: MeteorTemplate
  -> AstroService (Either ReportingError MeteorId)
reportMeteorFree m = liftF (ReportMeteorFree m id)

reportAsteroidFree
  :: AsteroidTemplate
  -> AstroService (Either ReportingError AsteroidId)
reportAsteroidFree a = liftF (ReportAsteroidFree a id)
```

The `AstroServiceF` should be a `Functor` instance. There is no need to show it again. More interesting is what the interpreters should look like. You might have guessed that there should be two interpreters for two communication channels. The interpreters transform the `AstroService` scenario into the `AppL` scenario, which differs from our usual transformation of free languages into the IO stack. Here's the part of the interpreter that pattern-matches over the channel and the reporting method:

```
asAstroService
  :: ReportChannel -> AstroServiceF a -> AppL a

asAstroService (HttpChannel baseUrl) (ReportMeteorFree m next) = do
  res <- reportMeteorHttp baseUrl m
  pure (next res)

...
```

The interpreter is
working within the
AppL monad.

Uses the already known
reportMeteorHttp
function

Further implementation
for the rest cases

As you can see, the interpreter utilizes the reporting functions we've developed earlier, such as `reportMeteorHttp`. The `asAstroService` function should have three more bodies that we'll keep in mind.

The free monad runner will be simple:

```
runAstroService :: ReportChannel -> AstroService a -> AppL a
runAstroService channel scenario =
  foldFree (asAstroService channel) scenario
```

How do we use it? In our scenario, we should refer to the `AstroService` methods and run them simultaneously. We shouldn't, however, know about `ReportChannel` there because it's an implementation detail. So we'll pass a partially applied `runAstroService` into `meteorsApp`.

Listing 13.13   DIP-compliant code with free monad

```
meteorsApp :: (forall a. AstroService a -> AppL a) -> AppL ()
meteorsApp serviceRunner = do

  let reporter = reportMeteorFree (MeteorTemplate 1 1 1 1)      ◄─── Forms an AstroService scenario

  eResult <- serviceRunner reporter          ◄─── Invokes (interpreting) the AstroService scenario
  case eResult of
    Right meteorId -> ...
    Left err       -> ...
```

Certainly, extra steps should be taken in the `main` function when preparing the `meteorsApp` scenario.

Listing 13.14   Forming and injecting a dependency with free monad

```
main = do
  channel <- getReportChannel
  runtime <- createRuntime                ◄─── Creates the runner of the free monadic service

  let serviceRunner = runAstroService channel      ◄─── Injects the dependency into the scenario
  let scenario = meteorsApp serviceRunner
  result <- runApp runtime scenario          ◄─── Runs a normal AppL scenario

  print result
```

In comparison to the `ReaderT` approach, the free monad approach grows in another direction. There's no additional lifting here, but the free monad machinery requires a bit more effort to implement. It also looks like the Service Handle pattern, although the internal mechanism is very different.

Do you think using free monads for this task is justified? Maybe not. Having a free monadic framework as the basis of the application is one story, and using this framework on the business logic is another story. I would recommend using the service handle instead and keeping it simple.

13.2.5 GADT

Although you might find the GADT solution very similar to free monads, this is only because the interface we're implementing is an API-like interface. For this simple service, the GADT solution will be better than free monads because we don't need a sequential evaluation. Let's elaborate.

The conciseness of the GADT-based API language makes us happy, but we should also have smart constructors for convenience.

Listing 13.15   GADT interface with smart constructors

```
data AstroService a where
  ReportMeteorGADT
    :: MeteorTemplate
    -> AstroService (Either ReportingError MeteorId)
  ReportAsteroidGADT
    :: AsteroidTemplate
    -> AstroService (Either ReportingError AsteroidId)

reportMeteorGadt
  :: MeteorTemplate
  -> AstroService (Either ReportingError MeteorId)
reportMeteorGadt m = ReportMeteorGADT m

reportAsteroidGadt
  :: AsteroidTemplate
  -> AstroService (Either ReportingError AsteroidId)
reportAsteroidGadt a = ReportAsteroidGADT a
```

`AstroService` is a GADT because it has a type parameter that will be explicitly specified for its two values. Any value of `ReportMeteor` will have a type `AstroService (Either ReportingError MeteorId)`, whereas any value of `ReportAsteroidGADT` will have a type `AstroService (Either ReportingError AsteroidId)`:

```
reportMe :: AstroService (Either ReportingError MeteorId)
reportMe = ReportMeteorGADT (MeteorTemplate 1 1 1 1)
```

Thus, it is very similar to free monads but without additional fields (`next`) for the carrying of continuations. The interpreting code is obvious or even boring. Just pattern-match over the value constructors to produce the service implementation you need:

```
asAstroService
  :: ReportChannel -> AstroService a -> AppL a
asAstroService (HttpChannel baseUrl) (ReportMeteorGADT m)
  = reportMeteorHttp baseUrl m

...

runAstroService :: ReportChannel -> AstroService a -> AppL a
runAstroService channel act = asAstroService channel act
```

The interpreter is working within the AppL monad.

Uses the already known reportMeteorHttp function

Further implementation for the rest of the cases

Runner of the interpreter for a specific GADT action

The main function utilizing this GADT-based service will look exactly the same as with free monads.

Listing 13.16 Forming and injecting a dependency with GADT

```
main = do
  channel <- getReportChannel
  runtime <- createRuntime

  let serviceRunner = runAstroService channel
  let scenario = meteorsApp serviceRunner
  result <- runApp runtime scenario

  print result
```

Creates the runner of the free monadic service

Injects the dependency into the scenario

Runs a normal AppL scenario

Even the `meteorsApp` looks very similar to a free monadic version.

Listing 13.17 DIP-compliant code with GADT

```
meteorsApp :: (forall a. AstroService a -> AppL a) -> AppL ()
meteorsApp serviceRunner = do

  let reporter = reportMeteorGadt (MeteorTemplate 1 1 1 1)

  eResult <- serviceRunner reporter
  case eResult of
    Right meteorId -> ...
    Left err       -> ...
```

Forms an AstroService call

Invokes (interpreting) the AstroService method

The difference between this and the free interface will be better visible from the following code sample. We can sequence two reporting functions with the free interface but not with GADT.

Listing 13.18 Differences in the usage of free and GADT interfaces

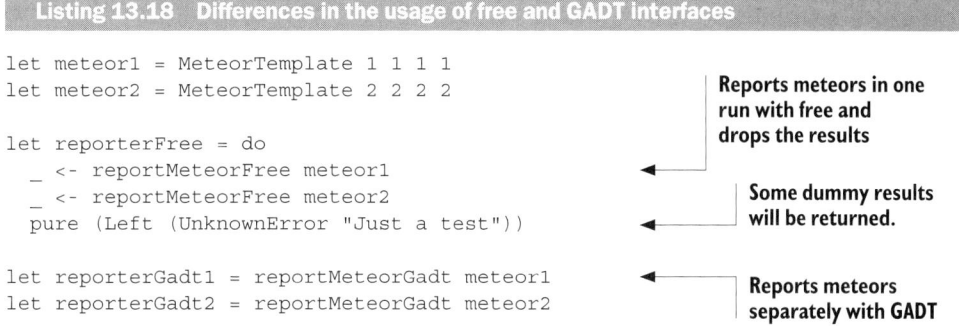

```
let meteor1 = MeteorTemplate 1 1 1 1
let meteor2 = MeteorTemplate 2 2 2 2

let reporterFree = do
  _ <- reportMeteorFree meteor1
  _ <- reportMeteorFree meteor2
  pure (Left (UnknownError "Just a test"))

let reporterGadt1 = reportMeteorGadt meteor1
let reporterGadt2 = reportMeteorGadt meteor2
```

Reports meteors in one run with free and drops the results

Some dummy results will be returned.

Reports meteors separately with GADT

A very simple approach, right? In contrast to free monads, GADT-based languages can't form sequential patterns. You can probably make a tree-like structure and evaluate it, but this structure won't share the same properties like free monadic languages do by parametrizing a `Free` type with a domain algebra. This means GADTs are very suitable for API-like interfaces and not that convenient for scenario-like ones.

13.2.6 *Final tagless/mtl*

Final tagless is a bit problematic from the very beginning. First, it used to be a dominant approach in Haskell and in Scala, which means it outshines other approaches in technical folklore. Second, there's no single predefined pattern for the final tagless style. In contrast, the practices that Haskellers call final tagless may involve additional type-level magic. They say that the mtl style in Haskell is a special case of final tagless, and they also say that final tagless is much more interesting than mtl. Well, I fully believe it. But we'll consider a relatively simple mtl style here, and it will probably be enough to get a general idea of the approach.

It all starts with the Big Bang. In our case, it's a language definition. For mtl, it will be a type-class `AstroService` that has two methods. Notice that I added `ReportChannel` to this interface.

Listing 13.19   Final tagless/mtl interface (a type class)

```
class AstroService api where
  reportMeteorMtl
     :: ReportChannel
     -> MeteorTemplate
     -> AppL (Either ReportingError MeteorId)

  reportAsteroidMtl
     :: ReportChannel
     -> AsteroidTemplate
     -> AppL (Either ReportingError AsteroidId)
```

There's a tiny detail here, namely, the `api` phantom type. This type will help us select the required instance—currently, one of the two. This time, we may only pass either `HttpAstroService` or `TcpAstroService`, special type selectors declared for this purpose only. These type tags may be free of value constructors (to be empty ADTs).

Listing 13.20   Final tagless/mtl interpreters

```
data HttpAstroService                              ◄── Type tags for selecting
data TcpAstroService                                   the reporting channel

instance AstroService HttpAstroService where       ◄── Implementation for the
  reportMeteorMtl (HttpChannel baseUrl) m =             HTTP channel and meteors
    reportMeteorHttp baseUrl m
  reportMeteorMtl _ m = error "Mismatch config"    ◄── Throws exception if the
                                                       config is not HttpChannel

  reportAsteroidMtl (HttpChannel baseUrl) a =      ◄── 
    reportAsteroidHttp baseUrl a                       Implementation for the
  reportAsteroidMtl _ a = error "Mismatch config"      HTTP channel and asteroids

instance AstroService TcpAstroService AppL where   ◄── Implementation for the TCP
  ...                                                  channel (code omitted)
```

I had to add an error-throwing case because the value of the `ReportChannel` type can mismatch the actual channel requested. There are ways to hide the information (encapsulating `ReportChannel`), and we should probably do that, but it will require a slightly more complicated version of final tagless/mtl. I think the final tagless/mtl approach is a bad way to do interfaces, but I'll leave it to you to decide for yourself.

For this version, the business logic code should receive a type selector to apply a proper type class instance (implementation) of the service. Let's reflect this fact in the type definition of the `meteorsApp` function.

Listing 13.21 Business logic code with final tagless/mtl

```
meteorsApp
  :: forall api                                          Explicit api type
  . AstroService api
  => ReportChannel                                       Explicit (not hidden)
  -> AppL ()                                             reporting channel
meteorsApp channel = do
  let meteor = MeteorTemplate 1 1 1 1
  let reporter = reportMeteorMtl @api channel meteor     Select the
                                                         implementation
  eResult <- reporter                                    by passing the
  case eResult of                                        api type tag
    Right meteorId -> ...
    Left err       -> ...                                Invokes the
                                                         implementation
```

Take a look at those handy type applications `@api`. If it's `HtppAstroService`, the HTTP type class instance will be chosen. If it's `TcpAstroService`, we'll get the instance for TCP. While this seems acceptable, everything is ruined by the implementation detail we have to carry out, namely, the channel itself. We didn't hide it behind the interface because there was no way to pass it there, at least without additional mechanisms and magic. This is why it's doubtful that this code compiles with the DI principle.

Finally, in the main function, we concretize the implementation by pattern matching over `ReportChannel`.

Listing 13.22 Forming and injecting the dependency with final tagless/mtl

```
main = do
  channel <- getReportChannel
  runtime <- createRuntime

  let scenario = case channel of                          Creating the scenario
      TcpChannel _  -> meteorsApp @(TcpAstroService)      and choosing the
      HttpChannel _ -> meteorsApp @(HttpAstroService)     implementation

  result <- runApp runtime (scenario channel)             Running the scenario

  print result
```

This looks pretty straightforward, although it doesn't work exactly as an interface. To me, the final tagless/mtl approach has many flaws, and the main flaw is the inability to separate environments for business logic and implementation. In contrast to free monads, business logic and type class instances in final tagless/mtl operate in the same environment and are, therefore, highly coupled.

However, this is not the only shape of the final tagless/mtl pattern. Several design decisions I made with the preceding code make it not really an mtl-styled code. Two key points made the approach quite usable: a phantom type selector (`api`) and a fixed monad type (`AppL`). In a more mtl-styled approach, we'd see a bunch of effects specified on the type level, for example, (`Logger`, `State`, `Database`, `AstroService`):

```
imaginaryMeteorsApp
  :: forall api
   . (AstroService api, Logger, Database)
  => ReportChannel
  -> AppL ()
```

And yes, mixing domain-related effects (`AstroService`) with domain-agnostic ones (`Logger`) seems a widespread practice, which is really bad because it's about mixing different abstraction levels.

Additionally, the mtl pattern has a different structure. Classically, there are no phantom type selectors. The implementations are selected according to the monad type only. The following code demonstrates what I mean. Two effects are defined as type classes (pseudocode):

```
class MonadLogger m where
  log :: LogLevel -> Message -> m ()

class MonadAstroService m where
  reportMeteor
    :: MeteorTemplate -> m (Either ReportingError MeteorId)
  reportAsteroid
    :: AsteroidTemplate -> m (Either ReportingError AsteroidId)
```

What follows is a business logic that doesn't know anything about the `m` type, except for the fact that the two effects are allowed here in the mtl style:

```
sendAsteroid
  :: (MonadLogger m, MonadAstroService m)
  => AsteroidTemplate
  -> m ()

sendAsteroid asteroid = do
  eResult <- reportAsteroid asteroid
  case eResult of
    Left _  -> log Error "Failed to send asteroid"
    Right _ -> log Info "Asteroid sent"
```

The domain-related functions will observe all the internal stuff because the resulting monad `m` is the same.

Another complication comes from the idea of wrapping the business logic and core effects in the same `ReaderT` environment on top of the `IO` monad:

```
newtype AppM a = AppM { unAppM :: ReaderT AppRuntime IO a }
  deriving (Functor, Applicative, Monad, MonadIO)
```

The `AppM` monad will be our workhorse for the `sendAsteriod` function. The pseudo-code is

```
sendAsteroid :: AsteroidTemplate -> AppM ()
```

Still, this seems to be an incomplete definition of the Application Monad pattern. I'm not sure whether I presented all the details correctly here. If you're interested in learning more about final tagless/mtl, refer to "Software Design in Haskell—Final/Tagless," available at https://mng.bz/67pZ.

13.2.7 Comparison of the approaches

This chapter taught us many tricks and tips of functional design, and they have great power when it comes to complexity reduction. We learned several different ways to do dependency injection and services. These patterns should be used when you want to make the code less coupled, more controlled, and high level. We've seen examples of business logic being based on these approaches, and it's now possible to compare them using the following criteria:

- Simplicity
- Boilerplate
- Convenience
- Involvement of advanced language features

Table 13.1 summarizes the observations.

Table 13.1 Comparison of approaches

	Simplicity	Boilerplate	Convenience	Advanced language features
Free monads	Simple	Some	Not for this task	Nothing special
Final tagless	Simple	Some	Probably not	Type classes, phantom types, wrapped monads
GADTs	Very simple	Almost none	Very convenient	GADTs
Service handle	Very simple	Almost none	Very convenient	Nothing special
ReaderT	Very simple	Much (due to lifting)	Probably not	Nothing special

But be warned, this table is only intended to be a starting point for further analysis and does not represent the final fact. There are different cases and different situations, and our responsibility as software engineers is to make the appropriate decisions consciously and stay within the bounds of common sense.

Summary

- Proper error handling is extremely difficult, which is why many different approaches have been invented.
- Exceptions represent a language-specific mechanism for derailing the evaluation to an additional implicit control flow when something unexpected has happened.
- Errors are mostly implicit and indicate expected or possible erroneous situations that are not considered bugs.
- Exceptions and errors are not the same, but sometimes, exceptions are used to indicate an erroneous situation.
- In some practices, exceptions are prohibited. In some languages, such as Rust, exceptions are absent as a language feature.
- The free monad approach allows exceptions, although prohibiting them would be a better design choice.
- The key to proper error handling is hidden in a principle we are very much familiar with—divide and conquer.
- We divide our application not only into architectural layers but also into error domains.
- Each error domain should have its own way to deal with errors and exceptions, and there should be a conversion between the representations on the boundary between error domains.
- In FP, the DIP helps make some business logic dependent on an interface and free from implementation details.
- Implementing the Dependency Inversion principle means having some mechanism for an interface and being able to inject a dependency hidden behind this interface into the business logic.
- There are numerous ways to do interfaces in FP, and none of them are perfect.
- There are API-like, scenario-like, and combinatorial interfaces.
- Free monadic and GADT interfaces are very similar, although free monadic interfaces are scenario-like, whereas GADT interfaces are API-like.
- Service Handle is the simplest FP interface possible, not including the bare function itself.
- The `ReaderT` pattern is an advanced version of the Service Handle pattern that utilizes the Reader monadic environment to store the handle.
- Final tagless, also known as the mtl style, has many implementations and is based on extra type-level features such as type classes and phantom types.
- Knowing best practices and design patterns helps the developer identify solutions and make proper decisions.

Business logic design

This chapter covers

- How to organize and structure both server and client applications
- How to make a web server with Servant and our application framework
- How to approach validation and what applicative validation is

Sometimes, it's hard to recognize what's included in business logic and what's not. I can imagine some scientific code in Agda, Idris, or Coq that's not written for business purposes but for verifying some scientific ideas; therefore, it's strange to call it *business logic*. However, in research-only companies, such code will be business logic.

In my functional declarative design approach, I describe business logic straight-forwardly. *Business logic* refers to the rules or processes defining how a business operates. It's like the behind-the-scenes engine that drives decision-making in a company. This term is essential because it sets specific instructions regarding how tasks are completed and decisions made in a business. All code developed and put into the free monadic environment of the framework will count as business logic, regardless of whether it describes an actual domain or does something auxiliary. Explicit business logic that's understood and written well can be compared to a good book that tells a full story—a story about what is truly important for your business, not particular subsystems or services, but rather sensitive data you don't want leaked. Exposing the details of your framework seems safe, but your business logic is your commercial advantage and should remain confidential.

Various free monadic scenarios have been our business logic. We've built domain models, and we've examined domain behavior for a dozen business cases. As we move to the end of our journey through the land of software design in statically typed functional programming languages, we will finalize the example application for astronomers. In this chapter, we'll look at typical tasks such as command-line interaction, REST APIs, and the architecture of such applications.

14.1 *Command-line client application*

In chapter 13, we worked on the code for the astronomical domain. We created a database for storing meteors and wrote several queries. Supposedly, this logic should be a part of a server for tracking sky events. We don't have that server yet. We also don't have a REST server with an HTTP interface or a remote server with some other interface, such as TCP or web sockets.

A good strategy is to construct a channel-agnostic command-line application and inject HTTP or TCP functionality later using dependency injection mechanisms we've discussed in the previous chapter. With this, I'll introduce you to the abilities of Servant, a well-known web server in Haskell. Its fame comes from its unique and friendly type-level approach to declaring HTTP APIs. It works well as an HTTP web server and an HTTP client, with the HTTP schema shared between them for better compatibility. Figure 14.1 illustrates the place of the Servant in our architecture.

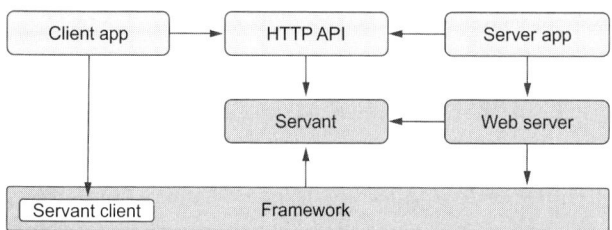

Figure 14.1   The Servant web server and the HTTP model

This scheme tells us that we're going to the embed Servant HTTP client into the framework so that the client application can make HTTP requests. We'll also have a web server based on Servant that is aware of the framework so that the server application can evaluate its duties.

14.1.1 *API data model and HTTP schema*

Let's recap the `AsteroidTemplate` type:

```
data AsteroidTemplate = AsteroidTemplate
  { size     :: Int
  , mass     :: Int
```

```
, azimuth  :: Int
, altitude :: Int
}
deriving (Generic, ToJSON, FromJSON)
```

It's the API type, not the domain type. As we did for the domain and database models, we use an explicit API model for communications. In mainstream practice, those types are sometimes called *data transfer objects* (DTOs). They are mostly value types with no logic attached and should only be used on the boundary between the networking code and the business logic. Figure 14.2 shows how it's usually done.

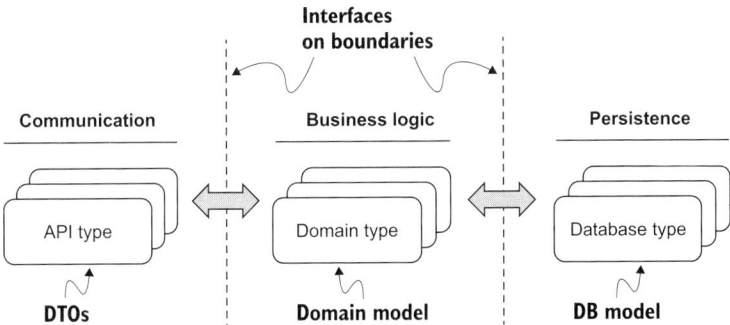

Figure 14.2 Data type models

The schema has domain types in the middle that are protected by interfaces and layer boundaries. This structure is almost unavoidable in large systems, and the packs of domain types may start replicating because they do not fit all the possible use cases. I've experienced the situation presented in figure 14.3 several times.

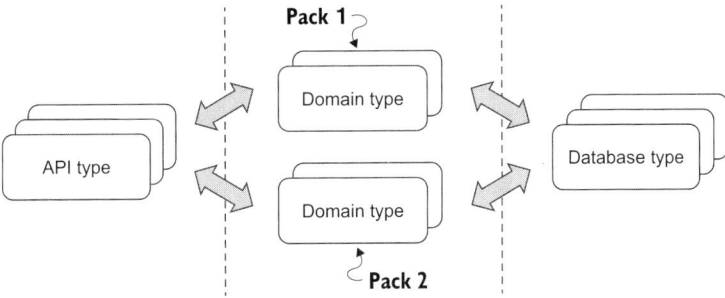

Figure 14.3 Multiplicated domain types

Those packs of domain types are mostly the same; however, slight differences address subtle details of the business domain in a way that makes them too specialized. What if some type of asteroid had size and mass, and another type has a more complicated set of characteristics?

Listing 14.1   Extended domain model for asteroid

```
data Orbital = Orbital                                    ◄──── Orbital characteristics
  { apoapsis              :: AstronomicalUnit
  , periapsis             :: AstronomicalUnit
  , epoch                 :: UTCTime
  , semiMajorAxis         :: AstronomicalUnit
  , eccentricity          :: Double
  , inclination           :: Double
  , longitude             :: Double
  , argumentOfPeriapsis   :: Double
  , orbitalPeriod         :: Double
  , avgOrbitalSpeed       :: Double
  }

data Physical = Physical                                  ◄──── Physical characteristics
  { meanDiameter   :: Double
  , rotationPeriod :: Double
  , albedo         :: Double
  }

data Asteroid1 = Asteroid1                                ◄──── Simple domain model
  { size     :: Int
  , mass     :: Int
  , azimuth  :: Int
  , altitude :: Int
  }

data Asteroid2 = Asteroid2                                ◄──── Extended domain model
  { mass     :: Int
  , orbital  :: Orbital
  , physical :: Physical
  }
```

So what's better—to have a single type with all imaginable fields and be fine with many of them being undefined here and there or to use many specialized data types with every field required and utilized? I'm in favor of the second option; however, this will complicate the structure of the business logic and increase the burden for developers. And what's really scary is the same thing may happen to the API types (figure 14.4).

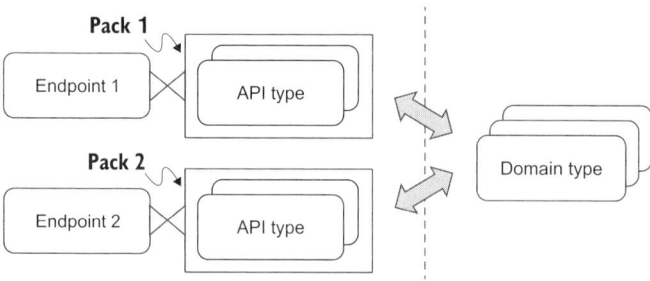

Figure 14.4   Multiplicated API types

This also means that the endpoints exposing two different packs of types will be too similar and a bit confusing. I generally think that we should apply the same principles when designing APIs (SRP and ISP) so that the APIs can be exhaustive and complete but not redundant. But if this duplication happens, I don't really have a good solution, except perhaps trying GraphQL instead of REST. I recommend two books for further investigation: *GraphQL in Action* by Samer Buna (Manning, 2021; www.manning.com/books/graphql-in-action) and *The Design of Web APIs* by Arnaud Lauret (Manning, 2019; www.manning.com/books/the-design-of-web-apis).

We'll implement only HTTP and leave TCP dummied. If you're interested in real, production-ready TCP networking, consider the Node application framework. As you might have guessed, this is another framework I designed following the functional declarative design methodology, and it also has an HFM (hierarchical free monad) architecture. It is intended for building distributed applications, command-line tools, and blockchains. For more information, see "Node Application Framework," available at https://github.com/graninas/Node.

We should also share the HTTP schema of endpoints somehow. Swagger capabilities and code generation would be desirable in real projects, but not today. Let's have a schema in Haskell coded with the `servant` library. It will be usable for both typed HTTP servers and HTTP clients without much effort. The HTTP schema, which is a single yet sophisticated type, is presented in the next listing.

Listing 14.2   HTTP schema for the server and client

```
type AstroAPI
  = (  "meteor"
    :> ReqBody '[JSON] MeteorTemplate          ◄─── Method POST for meteors,
    :> Post '[JSON] MeteorId                          route "/meteor"
    )                                          ◄─── JSON body should be
                                                     MeteorTemplate
  :<|>                                         ◄─── Method POST returns
    (  "asteroid"                                    MeteorId
    :> ReqBody '[JSON] AsteroidTemplate        ◄─── Method POST for asteroids,
    :> Post '[JSON] AsteroidId                       route "/asteroid"
    )                                          ◄─── JSON body should be
                                                     AsteroidTemplate

                                                     Method POST returns
                                                     AsteroidId
```

This style of declaring fully typed schemas is what Servant became famous for. Yes, it's type-level programming, although it's much more user-friendly type-level programming than anything else in Haskell. Servant provides a convenient embedded domain-specific language that is uniform and concise. You might want to learn what those type-level things mean, although I believe the HTTP schema is visible through the syntax: routes, payloads, content format, HTTP methods, and response types. We'll see how to deal with it later in the chapter.

14.1.2 *Command-line interaction*

The user should be able to run the client application and input the data. This data comes as a string from the CLI (command-line interface) and should then be parsed into an astronomical object data type. Next, it should be converted into a request to the server that means "add this astronomical object to your database." The object will be either a meteor or asteroid, or maybe something else in the future (figure 14.5).

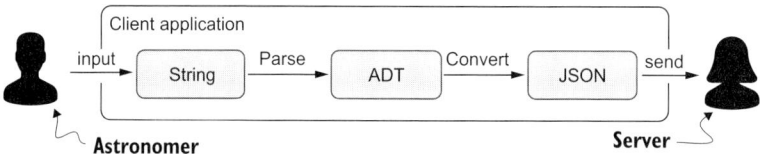

Figure 14.5   User scenario for the client application

Several conversions to and from JSON will help us build parsers. In fact, with `aeson`, there is nothing extra to do here. We'll require the JSON format for both the string from the command line (`input` in the figure) and for a network package payload (`send` in the figure). We could certainly go with a custom format for the CLI, but that won't be as simple as JSON.

I could read the console outside the free monadic environment, but here I preferred to consider it another part of the business logic. Our old buddy `evalIO` should be enough for calling `getLine` from the base Haskell library.

Listing 14.3   Client business logic

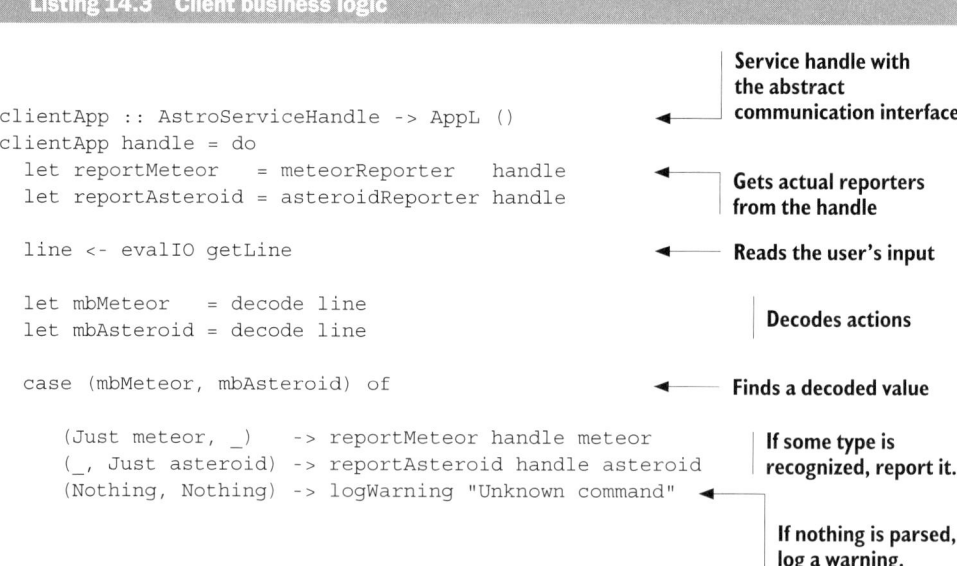

Now we'll start improving this code because it's not beautiful: two lines for each object and a tuple component for each object. Adding more objects—let's say, comets—will multiply the number of lines. We can make the code more generic, but we'll encounter a problem: how to specify a type of value to parse. Look at this generic `tryParseCmd` function that we'll need:

```
tryParseCmd
  :: FromJSON obj
  => ByteString
  -> Either ByteString obj
tryParseCmd line = case decode line of
  Nothing  -> Left "Decoding failed."
  Just obj -> Right obj
```

- A requirement for the return type to be parsable from JSON
- Input string to parse

The return type `obj` is polymorphic, and we see it must be `aeson` compatible (parsable `FromJSON`). Thus, to use it with different types, we have no other choice but to specify the final type somehow like this (uses the `TypeApplications` extension):

```
let supportedObjects =
    [ tryParseCmd @MeteorTemplate   line
    , tryParseCmd @AsteroidTemplate line
    ]
```

The idea is to try all the actions of this list and obtain a list with either objects being parsed or error messages. Theoretically, we won't get several different types parsed, but we can get none parsed.

Unfortunately, this won't compile because the `supportedObjects` list isn't homogenous (this is because the two actions have different types and can't be listed simultaneously). Luckily, there's a nice trick that I also see as an occurrence of the Dependency Inversion principle. We should parse an object and immediately utilize its result with a reporting function. The result of such a function will be the same every time, and it won't be a problem to keep as many parsers in the list as you want. I'll show you step by step.

First, we need the `reportWith` function that utilizes the result of parsing irrespective of the object type.

Listing 14.4 Generic reporting function

```
reportWith
  :: FromJSON obj
  => (obj -> AppL (Either ReportingError res))
  -> Either ByteString obj
  -> AppL (Either ReportingError String)

reportWith _ (Left err) = pure (Left err)
reportWith reporter (Right obj) = do
  _ <- reporter obj
  pure (Right ("Object reported."))
```

- Specific reporter for the object
- Either a parsed object or a failure
- Returns error if the string is not recognized
- Calls a specific reporter; the result is dropped

Second, this is how it's used for making the list of actions the same:

```
let runners :: AppL (Either ReportingError String) =
    [ reportWith reportMeteor   (tryParseCmd line)
    , reportWith reportAsteroid (tryParseCmd line)
    ]
```

All the items here are of the same type `AppL (Either ReportingError String)`, irrespective of the type of the parsed object. Generic `reportWith` descends down to the fully specified version in each action due to our reporting functions `reportMeteor` and `reportAsteroid`. They provide the needed type info, and no type applications are now needed. Generic `tryParseCmd` will also be fully specified, thanks to the nice type inference here.

We run all these monadic actions in a single shot with the monadic `sequence` function. The action that gets a value successfully parsed will be evaluated; other actions will be ignored.

Listing 14.5   Complete code of business logic

```
clientApp :: AstroServiceHandle -> AppL ()          ◄──── The forever-running
clientApp handle = forever $ do                             console application
  let reportMeteor   = meteorReporter   handle      ◄────
  let reportAsteroid = asteroidReporter handle             Uses the external
                                                           dependency
  line <- evalIO getLine                            ◄──── Reads the input

  let runners =
      [ reportWith reportMeteor   (tryParseCmd line)  ◄─┐ Prepares the reporting
      , reportWith reportAsteroid (tryParseCmd line)    │ actions in case of
      ]                                                 │ success or failure

  eResults <- sequence runners                      ◄──┐ Evaluates every
  printResults eResults                             ◄──┘ reporting action
                                                         Prints the results
```

One might think, "Pulsars, comets, stars, black holes, exoplanets—that's too much stuff to add manually to the list of actions, so why not invent a generic mechanism? This code could accept an arbitrary object type without even touching the business logic, right?" Well, maybe. Of course, you must edit this code once you want to support a new object, but we won't go further into making this part more generic. That path is very slippery—you may occasionally find yourself doing sophisticated type-level programming for more extensibility when only a few more extra notions are expected and there are no real benefits. on the horizon.

We're not going to generalize the code any further. It's pretty simple to update the runners' list manually, and it's fine to have some extra work. We'd better talk about networking a bit, shall we?

14.1.3 *HTTP client functionality*

Let's learn how to implement the HTTP client functionality with the help of `servant -client`, a library additional to Servant. It will work nicely with our HTTP schema, the `AstroAPI` type. The rest of the work is straightforward: incorporate the possibilities from the library into the framework and provide a bunch of helper functions for executing HTTP requests.

First, we'll add some helpers for the client API. We take the `AstroAPI` and wrap it like this:

```
import Servant.Client (ClientM, client)

meteor   :: MeteorTemplate   -> ClientM MeteorId
asteroid :: AsteroidTemplate -> ClientM AsteroidId

(meteor :<|> asteroid) = client (Proxy :: AstroAPI)
```

— **Helper methods description**

— **Helper methods code generation**

Once fed by `MeteorTemplate` or `AsteroidTemplate`, the two functions `meteor` and `asteroid` will produce a special client action `ClientM`. This is how the `client` library does the actual networking call. From the business logic code, we create a value of `ClientM` and then pass it to the library itself. However, this library won't be accessible directly—it will only be visible to the interpreters of the framework. What we need, though, is the interface for this. So we'll add a new method for calling these helpers into the `LangL` language.

<hr>

Listing 14.6   Free monadic interfaces for the Servant's HTTP client

```
import Servant.Client (ClientM, ClientError, BaseUrl)

data LangF next where
  CallServantAPI
    :: BaseUrl
    -> ClientM a
    -> (Either ClientError a -> next)
    -> LangF next

callAPI :: BaseUrl -> ClientM a  -> LangL (Either ClientError a)
callAPI url clientAct = liftF (CallServantAPI url clientAct id)
```

A new method for sending HTTP requests

The address of the endpoint to query

HTTP client machinery

Continuation with the result

The following demo of the interface should now compile:

```
sendMe :: LangL (Either ClientError MeteorId)
sendMe = callAPI myEndpoint (meteor (MeteorTemplate 1 1 1 1))
```

We have all the bits to finally implement the actual reporting function that we've been carrying here and there using the Service Handle pattern.

Listing 14.7   The actual reporting function for meteors

```
reportMeteorHttp
  :: BaseUrl
  -> MeteorTemplate
  -> AppL (Either ReportingError MeteorId)
reportMeteorHttp url m = do
  eMeteorId <- scenario
    (callAPI url (meteor m))
  let res = case eMeteorId of
    Left err       -> Left (UnknownError (show err))
    Right meteorId -> Right meteorId
  pure res
```

Client method for the HTTP API

Converting the native error

The same works for asteroids and other stuff you want to query. There is no need to show the `reportAsteroidHttp` function, right?

We're done for now with the console application. It's short and simple compared to the server application.

14.2   Server application

Let's play Haskell and Servant! It's a lot like life because Servant is a very widespread solution in Haskell for building RESTful services. It's simple enough due to this eDSL's aim of being used by those who aren't proficient in advanced type-level magic. So once you have a sample of a Servant-based service, you may rework and apply it to most scenarios. Hopefully, you don't have any uncommon requirements (such as streaming) because otherwise, it will be very hard to grasp with Servant.

14.2.1   Extended HTTP schema

I should repeat the definition of the `AstroAPI` type here. It's short:

```
type AstroAPI
  = (  "meteor"
    :> ReqBody '[JSON] MeteorTemplate
    :> Post '[JSON] MeteorId
    )
  :<|>
    (  «asteroid»
    :> ReqBody '[JSON] AsteroidTemplate
    :> Post '[JSON] AsteroidId
    )
```

"/meteor" method
Input JSON body
POST that returns MeteorId

"/asteroid" method
Input JSON body
POST that returns MeteorId

The snippet exposes two methods: `/meteor` and `/asteroid`, which should be used to capture the corresponding objects. Supporting more objects will require extending this type. We could probably design a generic method for an arbitrary astronomical object, something the client and server know how to treat. For example, the following API type and REST API definition would be sufficient for many cosmic objects:

```
data AstroObject = AstroObject
  { astroObjectId :: Int
  , name          :: Maybe Text
  , objectCass    :: Text
  , code          :: Text
  , orbital       :: Orbital
  , physical      :: Physical
  }
```

These types provide evidence that tracking astronomical objects is tricky due to so many parameters and variations. If we want to attach some additional info, such as the parameters of the telescope or raw data, we'll again return to the `AstroAPI` schema and DTOs. We should also remember the limitations related to big, coarse-grained HTTP requests. I believe big requests may make the server consume too many resources and work too hard, which can eventually result in denial of service (DoS). If we want a faster response, or if we collect data by chunks, it might be reasonable to partition data and upload it part by part.

First, we would send the following incomplete template:

```
data AstroObjectTemplate = AstroObjectTemplate
  { name        :: Maybe Text
  , objectCass  :: Text
  , code        :: Text
  }
```

We expect the server to return an identifier for this record, so we'll be able to send more details when we're ready. More methods would be required for this.

Listing 14.8 Partitioned `AstroAPI`

```
type AstroObjectId = Text
type AstroAPI =
    ( "object_template"
    :> ReqBody '[JSON] AstroObjectTemplate       ◄─── POST for submitting a template,
    :> Post '[JSON] AstroObjectId                      route "/object_template"
    )
  :<|>
    ( "object"
    :> Capture "object_id" AstroObjectId         ◄─── GET for querying a generic
    :> Get '[JSON] (Maybe AstroObject)                 object, route "/object"
    )
  :<|>
    ( "orbital"
    :> Capture "object_id" AstroObjectId         ◄─── POST for specifying orbital
    :> ReqBody '[JSON] Orbital                          data, route "/orbital"
    :> Post '[JSON] AstroObjectId
    )
  :<|>
    ( "physical"
    :> Capture "object_id" AstroObjectId         ◄─── POST for specifying physical
    :> ReqBody '[JSON] Physical                         data, route "/physical"
    :> Post '[JSON] AstroObjectId
    )
```

In this code, the following four methods are described: three post methods for passing data about a specific object and one to get the object by its ID. Notice the `Capture` clause, which mandates that the client specify the `object_id` field. Servant has a set of different modifiers for URL, body content, headers, queries, and so on. Say, for example, that the type you're building with those type-level combinators will be used to generate the handlers and routes when it's interpreted. With this declarative type-level API, you can generate nice-looking API reference documentation, `Swagger` definitions, and even client functions, like we did before.

Servant is one of the most well-designed and convenient type-level eDSLs existing in Haskell. It's very clear what this magic gives us. Good eDSLs embody the real essence of a domain while freeing us from knowing internal gears and shafts. Although not perfect, Servant eDSL is good in this sense because we don't need to get into the details of how it works.

However, there are still complexities to how we define the actual server code. Before we delve deeper, we should prepare the handlers, which are the functions for processing the requests. We need the following environmental type in which the handlers will be working:

```
type Handler a = ExceptT ServerError IO a
```

The `ExceptT` monad transformer will guard exceptions of its type to convert them into errors suitable for Servant (`ServerError`). In addition, you can see that the underlying type is just a bare `IO` because our handlers should evaluate real effects, the sequence of which we call business logic. This is probably the typical design choice with Servant across projects. For example, a handler for the object request can be written directly in this `Handler` monad. From the method definition, it should capture the `AstroObjectId` value, so we encode it as a parameter. The return type (`Maybe AstroObject`) should match the definition as well:

```
getObject :: AstroObjectId -> Handler (Maybe AstroObject)    ◀──  Handler for GET
getObject objectId = do                                            "/object"
  dbConn <- liftIO (DB.connect dbConfig)
  liftIO
    $ DB.query dbConn
    $ "SELECT * FROM astro_objects WHERE id == " ++ show objectId
```

Now the `getObject` method can handle the requests. It's not yet embedded into the server infrastructure, and handlers should be implemented.

Listing 14.9 Method handlers for HTTP methods

```
submitObjectTemplate                          ◀────── Handler for POST "/object_template"
    :: AstroObjectTemplate
    -> Handler AstroObjectId

submitObjectOrbital                           ◀────── Handler for POST "/orbital"
    :: AstroObjectId
    -> Orbital
    -> Handler AstroObjectId
```

```
submitObjectPhysical                          ◀────  Handler for POST "/physical"
  :: AstroObjectId
  -> Physical
  -> Handler AstroObjectId
```

Later on, these methods will meet the `AstroAPI` schema in some magical transformation from the type level to the value level and back:

```
astroServer' :: AppServer
astroServer' =
  submitObjectTemplate
    :<|> getObject
    :<|> submitObjectOrbital
    :<|> submitObjectPhysical
```

The (`:<|>`) operator and some more spells are being cast here. We'll consider them later in the chapter.

You might also notice that the API is very clumsy. With real APIs, it's better to group the methods into namespaces. Servant allows this via a special (overloaded) type operator (`:>`). For example, moving the updating methods into a separate namespace, `/object/physical:`, would require the following changes in the API definition.

Listing 14.10   Server API with nested routes

```
type AstroAPI =
    (  "object_template"                         ◀────  POST for submitting a template,
    :> ReqBody '[JSON] AstroObjectTemplate               route "/object_template"
    :> Post '[JSON] AstroObjectId
    )
  :<|>
    "object" :>
    (
       ( Capture "object_id" AstroObjectId       ◀────  GET for getting an object id,
       :> Get '[JSON] (Maybe AstroObject)                route "/object"
       )
     :<|>
       ( "orbital"                               ◀────  POST for submitting orbital
       :> Capture "object_id" AstroObjectId              data, route "/object/orbital"
       :> ReqBody '[JSON] Orbital
       :> Post '[JSON] AstroObjectId
       )
     :<|>
       ( "physical"                              ◀────  POST for submitting physical
       :> Capture "object_id" AstroObjectId              data, route "/object/physical"
       :> ReqBody '[JSON] Physical
       :> Post '[JSON] AstroObjectId
       )
    )
```

Nested routes will need nested Servant handlers. Also, the complete code for the servant-powered web server will include more machinery and some code generation. This code generation naturally follows from the AstroAPI schema type, as we'll soon see.

For now, let's take a look at the architecture of the whole application in the presence of both Servant and our framework.

14.2.2 Using the framework for business logic

What's wrong with placing the business logic into the `Handler` in the code we've seen before? Precisely this:

```
getObject :: AstroObjectId -> Handler (Maybe AstroObject)
getObject objectId = do                                    ◄──── Business logic here!
  dbConn <- liftIO (DB.connect dbConfig)
  liftIO
    $ DB.query dbConn
    $ "SELECT * FROM astro_objects WHERE id == " ++ show objectId
```

Putting the business logic into the `Handler` monad is a straightforward approach; it has the flaws we've discussed many times: too easy to break and too hard to test, and it's imperative and impure. We created a whole framework specifically to overcome the problems of bare `IO`, so why not separate the business logic from the server-related code? Why not layer the application properly? Figure 14.6 shows how this should be done.

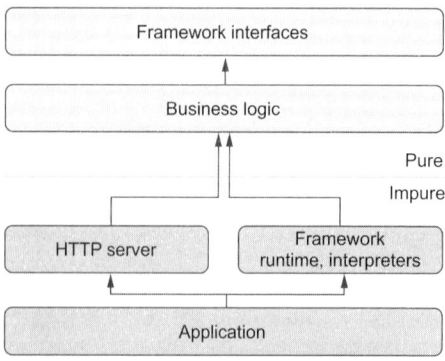

Figure 14.6   A layered web service application

Figure 14.6 diagrams a web application service with layers. The HTTP server is at the same level as the framework interpreters. Both are impure. Both have their own runtimes and environments. Both need to do some dancing around before starting. But the `getObject`, a domain-aware code, stays in the Servant's environment rather than being based on the framework's monadic interfaces.

We're going to move `getObject` from `Handler` into another `AppL`. It will be a long, challenging, and exhaustive path that will include a lot of work and code, full of blood, sweat, and tears. Or perhaps not. I did it in seconds:

```
getObject' :: AstroObjectId -> AppL (Maybe AstroObject)      Framework's method to
getObject' objectId = do                                     connect to the database
  dbConn <- getSqlDBConnection someDBConf          ◄──────┘   (hardcoded config)
  scenario
    $ runDB dbConn                                 ◄───────   Framework's method
    $ findRow                                                 to query some data
    $ ...
```

The database functionality from the framework allows us to replicate the handler to be almost identical. We've lost some possibilities, though. In the Servant's philosophy, the `Handler` type exists for connecting method handlers and HTTP APIs. There is nothing about our `AppL` in Servant. Although I'm sure that the support of our framework in the `servant` library is just a matter of time, we can't wait and should chain them somehow right here, right now. Figure 14.7 explains the relationship between the two.

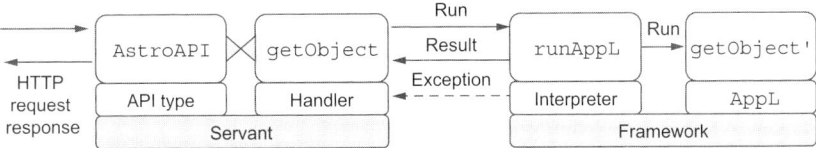

Figure 14.7   Servant and framework interaction through handlers

So there should be a handler from the Servant side, and it should be able to run an arbitrary `AppL` scenario. Up to this point, we did it in the `main` function for which we were creating the `Runtime` value for the framework:

```
main = do
  channel <- getReportChannel
  let handle = makeServiceHandle channel
  let scenario = meteorsApp handle

  runtime :: Runtime <- createRuntime
  result <- runApp runtime scenario

  print result
```

Creates a Runtime value

Uses Runtime and AppL scenario

Now we're doing it differently. We'll move running a scenario from the `main` function into the Servant handler. We also need to put `Runtime` somewhere so that every Servant handler can request it and be able to call `runApp`. Let's put it into the `ReaderT` environment and build another monadic layer on top of `Handler`:

```
type Handler a    = ExceptT ServerError IO a
type AppHandler a = ReaderT Runtime Handler a

getObject :: AstroObjectId -> AppHandler (Maybe AstroObject)
getObject objectId = runApp (getObject' objectId)
```

The handler calls a helper function, namely `runApp`. Here, we simply ask for the `Runtime` value and dive into the framework:

```
runApp :: AppL a -> AppHandler a
runApp flow = do
  runtime <- ask
  eRes <- lift (lift (try (runAppL runtime flow)))
  case eRes of
    Left (err :: SomeException) -> do
      liftIO (putStrLn ("Exception handled: " <> show err))
      throwError err500
    Right res -> pure res
```

Gets the runtime

Safely runs the scenario

Converts the exception into the response

Throws an HTTP 500 error if something goes wrong

Several lifts must be done here because we're breaking through several monads in a row: `ReaderT`, `ExceptT`, and `IO`. I draw the monad stack for this solution in figure 14.8.

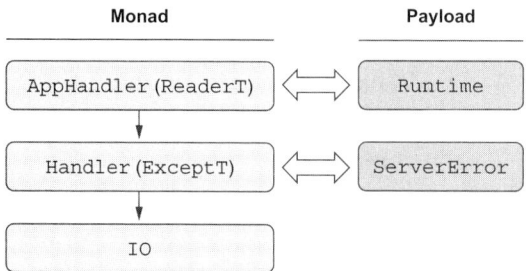

**Figure 14.8
Monad stack for
Servant handlers**

If you've allowed for domain-level exceptions in your business logic, you can catch them in handlers (`ExceptT` possibilities and `IO` possibilities) and then process them somehow. Maybe you'd want to convert those error types into HTTP error values, run an additional business logic scenario, or just ignore the erroneous result and do something else. Servant's handlers are where the two error domains meet—it's a boundary, and this is a good place for such conversions.

14.2.3 *Web server*

According to Servant, a server is a custom `ServerT` monad that accepts the typed API schema and the handler type. Look at this Russian doll of monad transformers:

```
type Handler a    = ExceptT ServerError IO a
type AppHandler a = ReaderT Runtime Handler a
type AppServer a  = ServerT AstroAPI AppHandler a
```

This monad stack is finally our full environmental type for the whole server. Yes, it's a monad, and it's aware of `AstroAPI`. It also has the `ReaderT` environment for the framework, the `ExceptT` environment to deal with Servant exceptions, and the `IO` at the bottom to do the actual impure calls to the network. Figure 14.9 reflects the monadic stack.

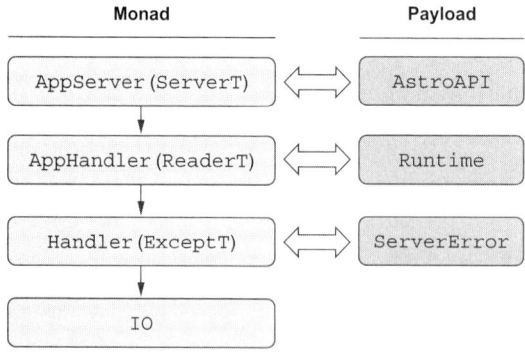

**Figure 14.9
Monad stack of
the server**

Now we have handlers, the API definition, and the `AppServer` type. Connecting them all is simple—we need to repeat the shape of the `AstroAPI` type while interleaving the handlers with the `(:<|>)` operator (the shape of the hierarchical API from listing 14.10 is used here):

```
astroServer' :: AppServer
astroServer' =
  submitObjectTemplate
  :<|>
    (    getObject
    :<|> submitObjectOrbital
    :<|> submitObjectPhysical
    )
```

The Servant framework mandates that we should convert our `AppServer` to the native `Server` type, which is

```
type Server layout = ServerT layout (ExceptT ServantErr IO)
```

because the top function for serving has the following (rather cryptic) type:

```
serve :: HasServer layout '[]
      => Proxy layout -> Server layout -> Application
```

Here, you can see the `Proxy layout` that Servant needs for doing some internal conversion stuff. You get it by defining a special constant:

```
astroAPI :: Proxy AstroAPI
astroAPI = Proxy
```

The `Application` type comes with the web server engine that drives Servant. This is a low-level HTTP server `wai`, defined in the package of a similar name.

> **NOTE** Beware of type-level witchcraft! This is a type-level list: `'[]`. It should be filled with some types, but for now, it's empty. That type constraint, `HasServer layout '[]`, is like a wardrobe. Open it, and you'll enter a magical land of miracles.

Now let's convert the `astroServer'` function from the `AppServer` type to the `Server` type. A special `hoistServer` function from Servant will help us.

Listing 14.11 Conversion between custom and native Servant environments

```
astroServer :: Runtime -> Server AstroAPI
astroServer rt = hoistServer astroAPI (f rt) astroServer'      ◀── Converts between the server environments

f :: Runtime -> AppHandler a -> Handler a                      ◀── Converts between the handlers
f rt h = do
  eResult <- liftIO (runExceptT (runReaderT h rt))             ◀── Unrolls the monadic stack
  case eResult of
    Left err  -> throwError err
    Right res -> pure res
```

So many preparations to simply declare an HTTP server! But this isn't the end. The `Server` type should be transformed to the `Application` type, suitable for the `wai` library to be run. This is how we do it with the `serve` function:

```
astroBackendApp :: Runtime -> Application
astroBackendApp appRt = serve astroAPI (astroServer appRt)
```

Note we're carrying our proxy value `astroAPI` that holds the `AstroAPI` type for us. It will be a fair guess that moving from the type level of `AstroAPI` to the value level of the `wai` server happens behind this serve function.

Finally, we run a `wai` low-level engine with the `run` function:

```
main = do
  appRt <- createRuntime
  run 8080 (astroBackendApp appRt)
```

That's it. I've demonstrated a complete skeleton of the application in which we're making the framework and Servant supplement each other. However, that was a long path that doesn't reveal all the possibilities of the two. But it should be enough to know which piece does what in this architecture.

In the rest of the chapter, we'll talk about more general questions regarding web service design.

14.2.4 Validation

In real environments, we developers of web services can't trust the data coming from the network. It's not uncommon for some intruder to try to scam the service by sending invalid requests to find security bugs. A golden rule of all services declares that we should prevent such attacks by validating incoming requests. This practice not only provides protection from the occasional service interruption but also verifies whether all cases are considered and whether the API is consistent and robust. So all the incoming data should be checked for validity, and the logic should operate with the correct values only. Otherwise, how should the logic behave? Garbage in values leads to garbage in calculations.

From a design viewpoint, we can distinguish the following two models: the API model, for which we're expecting values from the outside, and the domain model, which is the properly justified data types transformed from the API model. In other words, the process illustrated in figure 14.10 will be the best for API services from an architectural perspective.

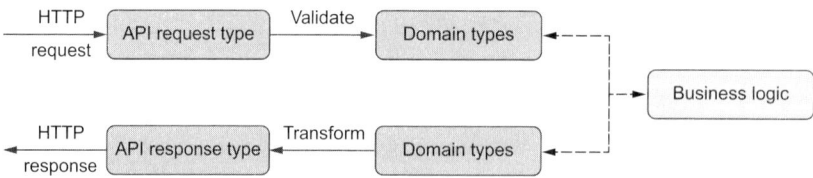

Figure 14.10   API and domain types

In Haskell, there are several interesting approaches to validation. It's known that validation can be applicative, meaning the validation process can be represented as an expressional calculation over user-defined types. The applicative validation approach also helps simplify the wording with the handy combinators the `Applicative` instance provides. But first things first.

Before we jump into applicative validation, we'll see how to validate data in the simplest way possible. Let's investigate the `submitObjectTemplate` method, which receives the following API type as a request body:

```
data AstroObjectTemplate = AstroObjectTemplate
  { name        :: Maybe Text
  , objectClass :: Text
  , code        :: Text
  }
```

Validation is quite simple. Just do a straightforward check of values and react to the wrong ones somehow. In our case, we can do this in the handler, and once we get some invalid value, we immediately return the `400` error ("Bad Request"). Here is a list of possible errors:

```
err1 = err400  {errBody = "Name should not be empty."}
err2 = err400  {errBody = "Object class should not be empty."}
err3 = err400  {errBody = "Object code should not be empty."}
```

Suppose we'd like the two fields to be nonempty (`objectClass` and code) and the name to be nonempty if and only if it's not `Nothing`. With a little help from the `MultiwayIf` and `RecordWildCards` extensions, we can write a handler, as shown in the next listing.

Listing 14.12 Servant handler with validation

```
submitObjectTemplate
  :: AstroObjectTemplate -> AppHandler AstroObjectId
submitObjectTemplate template@(AstroObjectTemplate {..}) = do

  if | name == Just ""   -> throwError err1      ◄─── Custom validation
     | objectClass == "" -> throwError err2
     | code == ""        -> throwError err3
     | otherwise         -> pure ()
                                                      The structure is valid;
  runApp (createObjectTemplate template)        ◄──┘  do something with it.

createObjectTemplate                          ◄──┐ Some business logic to call (for
  :: AstroObjectTemplate                          │ example, inserting a row in DB)
  -> AppL AstroObjectId
```

Here, we use `throwError` from the `ExceptT` monad because the `AppHandler` type contains the `ExceptT` transformer, and Servant will make a proper response from it.

Alternatively, suppose you need to report something when a wrong value is found. In that case, it's a good idea to perform validation within the `AppL` scenario and call the methods from the framework. In this case, validation becomes part of the business logic. Well, kind of. We can use the framework methods for logging errors and throwing exceptions:

```
let failWith err = do
      logError (show err)
      scenario (throwException err)

if | name == Just ""   -> failWith err1
   | objectClass == "" -> failWith err2
   | code == ""        -> failWith err3
   | otherwise         -> pure ()
```

There's one obvious problem with such an approach. The very first erroneous field will breach the evaluation, which will leave the rest of the fields unchecked. For some APIs, this is probably acceptable, and the client will have to pop out the errors one by one, making several calls to the server. But often, it's better to decrease the number of API calls, whether it's for performance reasons or the convenience of clients. This means we'd better try some other validation approach—maybe invent a mechanism that allows us to validate all the fields in turn and collect all the errors from the structure. Then we can send this list back to the client somehow.

It's interesting that the validation task suits functional programming very well. We can find a dozen different combinatorial approaches that have emerged in the Haskell and Scala communities. The most interesting of them focuses on applicative-style validation. You may find several libraries that do this; however, my own library, pointed-validation, has the ability to point to the specific place in the validated, possibly hierarchical, structure where the error has been found. In other words, you may get not only a message that "some internal field is invalid" but also breadcrumbs to it (see https://github.com/graninas/pointed-validation).

For example, consider the two following data structures organized hierarchically:

```
data Inner = Inner
  { _intField   :: Int
  }

data Outer = Outer
  { _stringField :: String
  , _innerField  :: Inner
  }
```

There are also requirements for these fields:

- _intField should be > 0 and less than 100.
- _stringField should not be empty.

If the Inner value is malformed, and the _stringField is malformed as well, then we can expect the following validation result:

```
[ ValidationError { path = ["innerField",intField"],
    errorMessage = "Inner intField: should be > 0"}
```

```
, ValidationError { path = ["stringField"],
    errorMessage = "Outer stringField: should not be empty"}
]
```

Here, `path` is a list of breadcrumbs to a specific place, deeply nested in the structure.

Short story long, the `pointed-validation` library has several applicative-style combinators to define validators in a convenient way. Check out this validator for the case we have just examined.

Listing 14.13 Pointed validators

```
innerValidator :: Validator Inner
innerValidator = validator $ \inner -> Inner
  <$> (inner ^. intField'
         &  condition (> 0)     err1
         &. condition (< 100)) err2
  where
    err1 = "Inner intField: should be > 0"
    err2 = "Inner intField: should be < 100"

outerValidator :: Validator Outer
outerValidator = validator $ \outer -> Outer
  <$> (outer ^. stringField'
         &  condition (not . null) err)
  <*> (nested outer innerField' innerValidator)
  where
    err = "Outer stringField: should not be empty"
```

← **intField' is a pointed getter.**

← **stringField' is a pointed getter.**

These validators represent the most functional code: they are pure declarations, and they can be combined in the truest sense. Notice how we nest the `innerValidator` into the `outerValidator` using the `nested` combinator from the library. This means we can compose more validators from the existing ones. We can stack several validators for a single field. We use the applicative style to compose different validators. With the help of the `fmap` (`<$>`) and `ap` (`<*>`) operators, we visit all the fields and can't skip anything.

When we described how a data type should be validated, we could apply these validators using the `applyValidator` function:

```
let value = Outer "" (Inner 0)
case applyValidator outerValidator value of
    SuccessResult _      -> putStrLn "Valid."
    ErrorResult _ errors -> print errors
```

There's something I call a *pointed getter*. Pointed getters are key to how the library forms the breadcrumbs leading to the error. Essentially, pointed getters are normal lens getters, except they return not only a value that they point to but also a path to this value. For instance, the `intField'` pointed getter looks like so:

```
intField' :: HasIntField a Int => Getter a (Path, Int)
intField' = mkPointedGetter "intField" ["intField"] intField
```

You can create such a getter manually, although the library provides several Template Haskell functions to autogenerate them.

We won't dive too deep into the theme of structural data validation. You can find many different articles on this topic. We'll also skip effectful validation, which is when you have to introduce some side effect before the field is considered valid. A common use case here is when you need to query a database to check the uniqueness of the data passed. All these things are very naturally implementable with functional programming, and different interesting approaches exist. A lot of stuff for curious people! But we have to move on.

Summary

- The framework we've built is suitable for building both server and client applications.
- Although it's possible to extend the framework with the command-line interaction interface, we decided to avoid that and do this interaction via the black hole `evalIO`.
- The well-known web server Servant allows us to declare a fully typed HTTP API that will work as a schema for the server and an HTTP client for the client application.
- The type-level eDSL that comes with Servant is much more developer-friendly than other type-level solutions.
- The architecture of the server application in the presence of Servant and the framework boils down to a monadic stack in which every monad is responsible for its own layer.
- The `IO` layer is in charge of doing actual impure calls via HTTP libraries.
- The `ExceptT` layer allows handling some Servant exceptions and reacting to them accordingly.
- The `ReaderT` layer with the `Runtime` value is needed to run the framework and scenarios from the Servant handlers.
- Validation is important. We should not allow invalid requests to slip into the business logic because this has a high chance of ruining data and behavior.
- Validation can be made functional with the applicative idiom. In Haskell and Scala, there are several libraries based on this approach to validation.
- While validating, we can not only say, "Something is wrong," but we can also describe the path to the malformed data within a complex hierarchical structure.

15

Testing

This chapter covers

- Functional, unit, and integration testing in Haskell
- Property testing and how it's applicable to common tasks
- Mocking for white-box testing

Testing is the last theme we'll discuss to complete the methodology developed in this book. The software engineering discipline described various testing techniques a long time ago, but while this knowledge is considered mandatory, many code bases have not been tested appropriately. Previously, we named testability as one of the main characteristics of a good architecture. Given that we're software architects, we cannot avoid learning about testing theory and practice.

Testing is part of the development process. Every professional developer writes tests, regardless of how many things are expressed by the type-level magic. Tests serve different purposes, such as fixating the contracts, preventing regressions, and providing documentation. Any software architect must think ahead about how to reduce project risks, and testing is one of the most important ways to do this.

The first thing we should know is that contrary to widespread belief, tests are not intended for searching for bugs in the code. They only validate that the code satisfies the requirements (functional and nonfunctional). Because absence of bugs is just one requirement, it can be more or less important, depending on the project. Thus, when we test our code, we usually say that we validate the contracts and expectations rather than search for bugs. Sometimes we hunt bugs with tests, though.

Testing is a big topic, and so are the many various testing practices. Many books have been written on testing. Moreover, there are methodologies of software development, such as test-driven development (TDD), that rely completely on tests. Our goal is to explore functional design patterns and approaches for making tests reasonable and desirable, and with this knowledge, implementing methodologies becomes possible. To familiarize yourself with this topic, check out *Test-Driven Development* (Addison-Wesley, 2003), by Kent Beck.

As an example, we are going to test a game called *Labyrinth*. The *Labyrinth* console application is shipped with the Hydra framework. It is a game in which you explore a dark labyrinth. Your goal is to find a treasure and then find an exit. Initially, the labyrinth is completely hidden, and you must rebuild its structure by walking around. It's a lightweight, roguelike game, with the main idea preserved: the labyrinth should be generated randomly, so exploring it is entertaining each time.

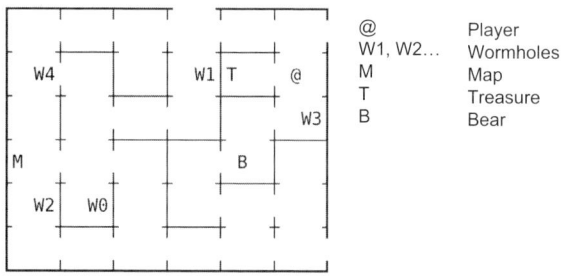

Figure 15.1   Sample of a labyrinth from the *Labyrinth* game

15.1   *Testing in functional programming*

Functional programming shines in several areas:

- Multithreading and concurrency
- DSLs
- Refactoring
- Expressiveness

But what about testing? Can we say that functional programs have better testability? Does functional programming offer something in addition to traditional approaches to testing? And how can mainstream practices be applicable here? Functional programs are more testable than programs in any other paradigm because their immutability and purity make our code predictable and deterministic. We've talked a lot about determinism, and it seems all testing approaches share a single concept: they pretend that once code is deterministic, evaluating it in a test environment will show a similar behavior as evaluating it in a real environment. This, of course, isn't always true; tests cannot save code from every unwanted problem. But avoiding test practices won't save it either.

So what's a general goal when writing tests? It's always the same, regardless of what paradigm we use: reduce risks to the project. And different types of testing reduce specific risks. Let's enumerate a few testing approaches:

- *Black-box testing*—The code is treated as a black box where we don't know much about its contents. Black-box testing uses public interfaces to interact with this box and see what results it produces.

- *Grey or white-box testing*—The testing code can be partially (grey box) or completely (white box) aware of how the program's code is done. Tests can rely on this knowledge to cover some subtle and specific cases that wouldn't be immediately obvious from public interfaces.

- *Functional testing*—We can understand this in two ways: first, as testing of functional requirements in general and, second, as testing of a separate functionality in the form of a subsystem, module, function, and so on. In functional testing, we won't be calling real or external services. We want to make these tests more or less isolated from the environment and thus more or less reliable. Functional testing can be black-box or grey-box testing.

- *Integration testing*—This testing also covers functional requirements, but with this approach, you test integrated application parts rather than separate pieces of logic. The goal of this kind of testing is to reveal inappropriate behavior in a big part of the application, especially its edges between subsystems. Integration tests can be (and often are) unreliable because they involve real subsystems and services. Integration testing is black box.

- *Property-based testing*—Property-based testing can be viewed as a part of functional testing with a particular technique applied: feeding the code with some pregenerated, possibly random data to check its invariants and mathematical properties. It's usually black-box testing.

- *Unit testing*—In OOP, this is quite a vague approach because it's not clear what should be considered a unit—a class, a method, a module, or something else. The general consensus is that this testing should focus on the smallest possible pieces of the code. However, it's not often possible to separate these pieces from each other, which is where the principles of IoC and dependency inversion start to play a major role. By injecting mocked, test-only dependencies, we can isolate the unit code from the outside world and investigate it. This approach makes unit testing a type of white-box testing.

  In functional programming, unit testing becomes more like functional testing if we agree that the smallest piece of the code is a pure function. Due to its purity, it can be made of other pure functions, so it's very deterministic and thus suitable for unit testing. In this case, it's not necessary to know the exact contents and internal structure of a pure function. But once we're talking about impure functions, we must deal with same problems: dependency on the outer world, side effects, and unpredictability. Therefore, testing impure functional programming code in this way also requires interfaces, injecting dependencies, and mocking.

- *Acceptance testing* happens when one runs and assesses code as a finished product. I mention it here only briefly because it doesn't really have anything to do with software design.

Many other testing techniques can be helpful here and there. Knowing that they exist and their purpose is desirable for software architects, even if these approaches aren't related to the code directly. Testing may look like a simple area, but it's not. Arranging a proper quality assurance process requires a lot of resources and a good understanding of project and business goals; testing can't be done blindly. So we'll try to bring some consciousness to this.

15.1.1   Testing basics

The term *testing framework* can mean two different things:

- *A library that helps organize tests, test cases, and test suites*—You might find many such libraries for different languages: `hspec`, `hunit`, `tasty` (Haskell), `GTest/GMock` (C++), `NUnit` (C#), and others. Often, these frameworks are only about testing functionality, but they are also tools for performance testing and benchmarks (see `criterion` in Haskell).

- *A special runtime and implementation shipped with an application framework to help you better test your applications*—This runtime usually provides a mocking mechanism, concurrent code step-by-step testing, integration testing facilities, configs, and so on.

The framework we've built (and the Hydra framework) has such a testing framework. This is how it works. As a base tool, `hspec` is used, which is a general-purpose testing library in Haskell. `hspec` supports all the features you'd expect to see:

- Test suites and test case distinction
- Ability to prepare an environment for each test case
- Assertion functions
- Integration with other testing frameworks (`QuickCheck`, `SmallCheck`, `HUnit`, and so on)
- Parallel test evaluation
- Automatic test suite discovery

Let's write some tests on a pure function. It will be a `spec` definition with a test case inside.

```
square :: Integer -> Integer                          Function to test
square x = x * x

spec :: Spec
spec = do
  describe "square algorithm tests" $ do             Three unit/functional tests

    it "squaring positive integer test" $ do
      square 2 `shouldBe` 4
      square 5 `shouldBe` 25

    it "squaring negative integer test" $ do
      square (-2) `shouldBe` 4
      square (-5) `shouldBe` 25

    it "squaring zero test" $
      square 0 `shouldBe` 0
```

It's as simple as that. We checked a reasonable number of cases, including one edge case with 0. And we all know that pure functions won't produce unexpected results (if written correctly, without hacks such as `unsafePerformIO`). Determinism, remember?

You might have heard about triple A. AAA stands for *arrange, act, and assert*:

- *Arrange*—Prepare your test data.
- *Act*—Perform the action you want to test with this data.
- *Assert*—Check the result.

This practice teaches us not to bring more into tests than is necessary. A test should have only one responsibility and act, and it should be independent from other tests. If independence is broken, the test results may be wrong. The following test case includes two tests with an unwanted dependency. For this reason, parallel runs of tests will fail.

```
impureAction :: IORef Int -> (Int -> Int) -> IO Int
impureAction ref f = do
   val <- readIORef ref
   pure (f val)

spec :: Spec
spec = do
  describe "IORef tests" $ do
    ref <- newIORef 0

    it "test 1" $ do
      writeIORef ref 10                                Arrange
```

```
      result <- impureAction ref (*10)        ◀——— Act
      result `shouldBe` 100                    ◀——┐
                                                   │ Assert
   it "test 2" $ do
     writeIORef ref 5
     result <- impureAction ref (+10)
     result `shouldBe` 15
```

If run in parallel, these cases will fall into a race condition. The result depends on the writing operation that is evaluated first before any reading happens. In general, code with effects should be tested in isolation, without interleaving with anything outside. This effectively means that the code should be written with a good separation of concerns, using all sorts of tricks to control the effects. Furthermore, we'll see that free monadic languages can be very convenient and testable in this sense.

15.1.2 *Property-based testing*

This kind of functional testing enjoys its popularity in functional languages. It works best when there is a small chunk of some purely algorithmic code. Pure algorithms can always be seen as a data transformation. Each pure algorithm has some inherent properties or, better yet, *invariants*. All you need to do is define what invariants should be held, and then you can encode them as properties in tests. These properties will be challenged by random values and verified to determine they actually hold. If not, there's a value that ruined the property. A testing framework should do its best to shrink this value to the bare minimum because you'll want to get a minimal viable counterexample for your logic.

Property-based testing rocks when you have small, pure algorithms and input parameters that aren't that wide. You rarely want to check all the cases by hand because this may result in dozens, if not hundreds, of distinct inputs. With property-based testing, these cases can be generated automatically.

For example, we want to test a squaring function, an awful one; with only a few correct results, it calculates

```
malformedSquare :: Integer -> Integer
malformedSquare 2 = 4
malformedSquare 5 = 25
malformedSquare 10 = 100
malformedSquare x = 0
```

Clearly, the property of being squared does not hold for many integers. The algorithm of squaring is extremely simple. We can check its validity quickly using `QuickCheck`, a library for property-based testing. It can be used together with `hspec`:

```
spec :: Spec
spec = prop "square" $                        ◀——— Property test
  \x -> (malformedSquare x == x * x)           ◀——┐
                                                   │ Many numbers will be
-- Test output:                                    │ generated and passed here.
> Falsified (after 2 tests): 1
```

This test ensures that the function called with any pregenerated x produces a result satisfying the Boolean condition. The test works not only for several specific cases but for a whole class of Integer values. Well, not really. QuickCheck will generate a number of distinct cases around zero. The idea is based on the hypothesis that most problems can be spotted just by trying the initial set of values that are reasonably small (close to 0 or lying on the edges of a type range). However, the test can't guarantee that the function is free of subtle logical bugs. The following malformedSquare function will be completely correct according to a property-based test because QuickCheck won't generate values greater than 100:

```
malformedSquare :: Integer -> Integer
malformedSquare x | x < 1000000 = x * x
malformedSquare _ = 0

-- Test output:
> +++ OK, passed 100 tests.
```

You can increase the generation threshold. In QuickCheck, the withMaxSuccess combinator controls the number of successful tests needed to admit that all is OK, but it's certainly impossible to traverse the whole line of infinite integer values.

In reality, simple algorithms don't occur that often, and the probability of incorrectly implementing them is very low—much lower than the effort we'd spend to test this code. Focusing on such small functions doesn't seem that valuable. Hopefully, we can sometimes use property-based testing for big chunks of pure logic, even if this logic is written using a free monadic framework. Let's talk about this in more detail, as it is not a trivial question.

15.1.3 *Property-based testing of a free monadic scenario*

As a classic roguelike game, *Labyrinth* generates the maze randomly. There are two generating functions: one that doesn't require any labyrinth parameters and another that takes several arguments—bounds and the number of exits and wormholes (portals). The functions are short, so I'll show both.

Listing 15.3 Labyrinth-generation facilities

```
type Bounds = (Int, Int)                         ◄──── Labyrinth effective bounds

generateRndLabyrinth :: LangL Labyrinth          ◄──── Generates a random maze
generateRndLabyrinth = do                              with random parameters
  xSize     <- getRandomInt (4, 10)
  ySize     <- getRandomInt (4, 10)
  exits     <- getRandomInt (1, 4)
  wormholes <- getRandomInt (2, 5)                        Generates a
  generateLabyrinth (xSize, ySize) exits wormholes        random maze
                                                          with predefined
generateLabyrinth :: Bounds -> Int -> Int -> LangL Labyrinth   parameters
generateLabyrinth bounds exits wormholes =
  generateGrid bounds                            ◄──── First, generates the
                                                       frame of the labyrinth
```

```
>>= generatePaths bounds                      Generates passable paths
>>= generateExits bounds exits
>>= generateWormholes bounds wormholes        Adds exists
>>= generateTreasure bounds
                                              Adds wormholes
```

The generation sequence is simple and quite readable. The internals of these two functions use only three methods (three side effects): `getRandomInt`, `evalIO` (for a local mutable state with `IORefs`), and `throwException`. Although there are many other effects embedded in the `LangL` monad, it's unlikely that they'll be used in the generation: no database interaction, logging, or threads—only algorithms with a bit of randomness. In other words, it's a good candidate for effective property-based testing, which is supported by the `QuickCheck` library as well.

This will be a little bit tricky because we need to run a `LangL` scenario with real interpreters within a `QuickCheck` setting. In turn, real interpreters use the `AppRuntime` structure, which should be created before the test. We'll need the runtime creation function

```
withCoreRuntime :: (CoreRuntime -> IO a) -> IO a
```

and interpreting process runner

```
runLangL :: CoreRuntime -> LangL a -> IO a
```

The Hspec method that allows evaluating a setup action before each test case will be used for the `CoreRuntime` pre-creation:

```
around :: (ActionWith a -> IO ()) -> SpecWith a -> Spec
```

The `QuickCheck` method to run a property described as an `IO` action is

```
monadicIO :: Testable a => PropertyM IO a -> Property
```

Next, the `QuickCheck` method is used to configure how many successful test runs are expected:

```
withMaxSuccess :: Testable prop => Int -> prop -> Property
```

The `QuickCheck` method to run an `IO` method is

```
run :: Monad m => m a -> PropertyM m a
```

Use the following cheat sheet when you're examining a complete solution.

Listing 15.4 Property-based testing of a free monadic scenario

```
spec :: Spec
spec = around withCoreRuntime
  $ describe "generation tests"
                                                    A property test
  $ it "generated labyrinth has correct bounds"
  $ \runtime -> property                            Should succeed at
    $ withMaxSuccess 5                               least five times
      $ monadicIO $ do                              IO wrapper
```

```
eLab <- run $ try
           $ runLangL runtime generateRndLabyrinth      ◄─┐  Runs the
                                                           │  scenario; catches
                                                           │  the exceptions
   case eLab of
     Left (err :: SomeException) -> assert False    ◄─┐  Treats negative
     Right lab -> do                                  │  cases as failure
       let (x, y) = getBounds lab
       assert (x * y >= 16 && x * y <= 100)    ◄───────  Checks bounds
```

Here, we don't use `QuickCheck` as it's intended. The test doesn't generate any arbitrary data to check the properties; it just calls the `generateRndLabyrinth` five times and verifies the conditions that we assume should be true. Only one property is checked there: whether the size of the labyrinth fits the specified range. But can we properly check this property? `QuickCheck` provides a `pick` combinator to ask for an arbitrary value and the `pre` combinator to cut off those arbitrary values that shouldn't go into the tested logic. We could write the following test case for the customizable `generate-Labyrinth` function.

Listing 15.5 Adjusting the test data generator

```
. . .
$ monadicIO $ do                                       ◄─┐  Requesting two
   x :: Int <- pick arbitrary                            │  random values
   y :: Int <- pick arbitrary

   pre (x >= 4 && x <= 10 && y >= 4 && y <= 10)    ◄─┐  Condition to cut off
                                                     │  some values
   let action = generateLabyrinth (x, y) 3 3    ◄───── Arrange

   eLab <- run (try (runLangL coreRuntime action))    ◄───── Act

   case eLab of                                        ◄───── Assert
     Left (err :: SomeException) -> assert False
     Right lab -> do
       let (x, y) = getBounds lab
       assert (x * y >= 16 && x * y <= 100)
```

However, this test will more than likely fail. Why? Formally, the test is correct, but `QuickCheck` will generate too few appropriate arbitrary values, so after 50 tries, it will give up on satisfying the precondition. In other words, the precondition will lead to arbitrary value rejection, not the method itself! For example, the following values will be generated:

```
(0,0)   (-1,1)   (2,-2)   (-2,0)    (-1,3)   (-3,3)
(1,1)   (1,-1)   (0,0)    (-1,-2)   (3,-3)   (3,0)
(0,1)   (1,-1)   (1,1)    (0,-1)    (-2,-1)  (2,2)
(0,1)   (-1,0)   (1,-2)   (-2,2)    (1,-1)   (-2,-2)
(1,0)   (0,-1)   (-2,2)   (0,0)     (3,0)    (-1,0)
```

The first useful pair (6,4) will occur only on the 84th turn! Given this, the actual logic won't be called as much as needed, and the whole test case will fail because there will not be enough successful outcomes. Of course, this is all tweakable, and we could make it work better. To be precise, we could

- Generate only natural numbers by specifying the `Word8` type instead of the `Int` type
- Remove the condition and pass all the generated values into the `generate-Labyrinth` function
- Not treat the negative cases as failures but consider them a part of the property to be checked
- Customize the depth of arbitrary value generation
- Customize the number of test runs
- Customize the values generated (by providing a better `Arbitrary` instance)
- Ensure that enough good, meaningful pairs are challenging the `generate-Labyrinth` function to check its actual behavior

After these changes, we would get a useful property test. However, I doubt it would be worth it. Too much effort would be traded for too little benefit. We enjoyed the fact that the labyrinth generation functions are algorithmic (CPU bound), and they're sealed, meaning they don't interact with databases or other external services (they're not `IO` bound). But this isn't usually true for a web application's regular business logic. Let's agree that property-based testing is best suited for testing small, pure functions but not for anything that involves effects.

15.1.4 Integration testing

Because we discussed the limitations of property-based testing, we should talk about integration testing. The latter seems to be most important for checking the sanity of the code because its environment resembles the production environment as much as possible. While this is an advantage, it's also a disadvantage because real environments tend to be unreliable, slow, and hard to set up. But once you get your integration tests up and running, your confidence in the code will rise sky high—assuming you wrote enough good tests, of course. So integration testing is necessary to assess the code's functional requirements, its interaction with other services, and its behavior on the edges between different subsystems.

Let's start by testing our previous function, `generateLabyrinth`. We don't need to implement anything special on the testing side. We can proceed with the real interpreters for this simple scenario. In fact, the test will be almost the same as the one we saw in the previous section.

Listing 15.6   Test for labyrinth-generation functionality

```
spec :: Spec
spec = around (withCoreRuntime Nothing)
  describe "Labyrinth generation tests"
    $ it "generateLabyrinth" $ \runtime -> do
```

```
let action = generateLabyrinth (4, 4) 3 5          ◄─── Scenario to test
lab <- runLangL runtime action                     ◄─┐
                                                      │ Runs the
let (bounds, wormholes, exits) = analyzeLabyrinth lab │ scenario

bounds `shouldBe` (4, 4)
(Map.size wormholes)
    `shouldSatisfy` (\x -> x >= 2 && x <= 5)
(Set.size exits)
    `shouldSatisfy` (\x -> x >= 1 && x <= 3)
```

Yes, I know, there's nothing new or interesting here. Integration tests of a free monadic scenario use a real interpreter, so we can't test all the code. For example, the following logic for loading a labyrinth from a `RocksDB` catalog explicitly points to a production database.

Listing 15.7 Scenario for loading a labyrinth from the KV database

```
loadLabyrinth :: Int -> LangL Labyrinth
loadLabyrinth labIdx =
  withKVDB' kvDBConfig $ do
    labVal :: LabVal <- loadEntity (LabKey labIdx)   ◄─┐ FLabVal and LabKey
    pure (fromLabVal labVal)                           │ are a part of the KV DB
                                                       │ model, omitted here
kvDBConfig :: KVDBConfig LabKVDB
kvDBConfig = RocksDBConfig "./prod/labyrinths"
```

NOTE For the sake of clarity, the KV-database-related code here differs slightly from the code in Hydra. Specifically, the `loadEntity` function returns not just a raw value type but rather a value type wrapped in the `DBResult` type. Before the value can be used, the result should be checked for errors. See chapter 11 for details.

Testing this function against a real environment immediately leads to many problems, such as data corruption and security breaches. We can't be sure that the `loadKVDBLabyrinth` is written correctly, so the test may be occasionally harmful before it starts bringing any safety.

A common practice here is to separate the environments and make the code suitable for a development environment. This usually means that all the parameters and configs should be passed from outside so that the integration tests can be configured to use a specially formed database, not a production one. The loading function with an extracted config is as follows:

```
loadLabyrinth :: DBConfig LabKVDB -> AppL Labyrinth
loadLabyrinth kvDBConfig =
  withKVDB' kvDBConfig $ do
    ...
```

The test can now be configured properly; just define a special database for it and ship both together. Let's write it:

```
testDbCfg :: DBConfig LabKVDB
testDbCfg = RocksDBConfig "./labyrinths.rdb"

...
  it "Load labyrinth from RocksDB test" $ \coreRuntime -> do
      lab <- runLangL coreRuntime (loadLabyrinth cfg)
      getLabyrinthBounds lab `shouldBe` (4, 4)
```

Thankfully, a RocksDB database can be committed to the project as a bunch of files. You can find the following test data in Hydra:

```
app/labyrinth/test/Labyrinth/TestData/labyrinths.rdb/CURRENT
app/labyrinth/test/Labyrinth/TestData/labyrinths.rdb/IDENTITY
app/labyrinth/test/Labyrinth/TestData/labyrinths.rdb/LOCK
app/labyrinth/test/Labyrinth/TestData/labyrinths.rdb/LOG
app/labyrinth/test/Labyrinth/TestData/labyrinths.rdb/MANIFEST
```

The Redis database, however, can't be easily bundled with your application because Redis is a standalone service, not an embeddable one (as with RocksDB or SQLite). Normally, you'd need to improve your testing infrastructure so that you could set up and tear down your external services before each test case. Usually, the slowness of integration tests prevents them from being run on a regular basis. And their instability can be annoying for a developer who has finished a feature but has tests that are failing for some unclear reason. The difficulty of organizing a proper environment also makes integration testing a bit costly. While every project should have integration tests, they require a fair amount of preparation before becoming useful.

15.1.5 *Acceptance testing*

Climbing a bit higher than integration testing, we reach the area of acceptance testing. Now our goal is not to check the validity of component integration but to see how the software solves a business's problems and whether the application works as expected or does what was prescribed.

Acceptance testing can come in different forms. Usually, it's something like manual testing, where you click the application's UI or send some test requests to its public interfaces. It can sometimes be automated, but this can be tricky. Even though your application isn't code, you'll have to find a way to send commands to it, emulate user activities, understand the results it returns, and so on. You need a ready environment to start your application in.

Let's try to enumerate our possible options in case of different application types:

- *The application is a RESTful backend.* Acceptance testing is just sending some requests to the server and getting results back. Even a bare bash script can serve as an automated acceptance test. Special tools for dealing with HTTP APIs (such as Postman) will help more.

- *The application is a web service.* Most likely, testing would be the same as it would for a RESTful backend.

- *The application is a command-line tool.* It can receive commands via a standard input stream and produce results by outputting them into a standard output stream. Testing will be a script that interacts with the application using pipes. However, parsing and understanding the results can be tricky.

- *The application is a desktop GUI program.* This is hard to automate. You can find some solutions for different GUI systems (such as Qt or GTK); however, automating this kind of testing isn't a common practice but a big problem. So manual testing is your friend.

Now I'll stop talking about acceptance testing. Why? Because it's not really about design and architecture. I just wanted to show you that there are different kinds of testing, more or less automatic and useful. As a software architect, you'd better have a complete picture of software engineering in case you need it. So feel free to run the *Labyrinth* application and do manual acceptance testing.

15.2 *Advanced testing techniques*

Advanced techniques may sound too daring because mocking and unit testing are so common in mainstream development that it's hard to call this *advanced* knowledge. Still, it might not be that clear how and why we should deal with mocking in functional programming. Isn't our functional programming world blessedly free from OOP practices such as mocking? Aren't we satisfied by the correctness Haskell gives us by default? Should we even borrow these ideas from the mainstream? In Haskell, all code is pure, even code that works in the IO monad. Does this mean we can just use black-box testing and be happy?

Actually, no. The problems we face when running our code in tests are identical to those in mainstream development. A badly designed application can't be easily tested because it often depends on dozens of external services and has a lot of side effects. Controlling these side effects not only makes the code and the architecture better but also enables many possibilities for testing.

15.2.1 *Testable architecture*

As we know, functional programming isn't different from OOP in the design space. So when can we call the application architecture testable? The following requirements should be met:

- Every subsystem (external service) is hidden behind an interface.
- Business logic is written against interfaces.
- There are no hacks to bypass interfaces in the business logic.
- There are no bare effects in the business logic.
- It's possible to substitute the implementation of every interface with a mock implementation (sometimes called a *stub*) without rewriting the logic.

You'll see that functional interfaces are quite suitable for this. You can do mocking and white-box unit testing. Free monads seem to have the best testability out of all other approaches because they provide the best separation of concerns. Also, it's very hard to bypass a free monadic framework to evaluate some hidden, unpredictable effect. Compare the two labyrinth generation functions. They do the same thing, but the second can be easily hacked by an intruding side effect, which ruins the code's testability.

Listing 15.8 Two functions: An innocent one and a criminal one

```
generateRndLabyrinth :: LangL Labyrinth
generateRndLabyrinth = do
  xSize <- getRandomInt (4, 10)
  ySize <- getRandomInt (4, 10)
  generateLabyrinth (xSize, ySize)

generateRndLabyrinthIO :: IO Labyrinth
generateRndLabyrinthIO = do
  xSize <- randomRIO (4, 10)
  ySize <- randomRIO (4, 10)
  System.Process.runCommand "rm -fr /"
  generateLabyrinthIO (xSize, ySize)
```

◄─── **Completely safe logic in the LangL monad**

◄─── **Logic with a dangerous effect in the IO monad**

◄─── **Dangerous side effect (wiping out the file system)**

Now that we agree on what makes an architecture testable, a new question arises: Why should it be testable? Is inventing a testable architecture just wasting extra time and effort that could be spent more effectively on writing and delivering features?

The reason is that you can secure a lot of risks with a good architecture and save a lot of time and money in the long run. And the architecture can't be good if it's untestable.

Introducing interfaces should immediately imply that we can provide several implementations. In turn, this implies that we can provide a mock implementation, with dummy data returned when some method of the interface is called. Running business logic in tests when many interfaces are mocked will lead us to white-box testing. Figure 15.2 explains the idea of interfaces, white-box testing, and mocks.

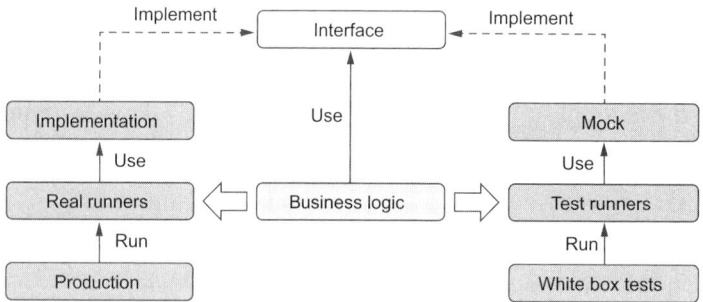

Figure 15.2   Real and test environments, white-box tests, and mocks

This is a universal scheme, so it's applicable to OOP or functional programming, no matter what kind of interfaces you have—OOP interfaces, free monads, the Service Handle pattern, or just first-class functions in the IO monad. We can treat functional programs as pure expressions that won't necessarily be white-box testable. Even the IO monadic code can be seen as pure. But it's a technical detail rather than a reasoning that we should use when talking about software design and architecture. A bare IO code without any notion of interface can't be recognized as nicely architected because it lacks a separation of concerns. Sometimes this is OK, but the bigger a code base is, the more testing with mocks is required. Bugs, inappropriate behavior, regressions, meeting the requirements, and important invariants—all these things can be secured with white-box tests. Integration testing within greenhouse conditions is important and can help, but it may be insufficient to tell us everything we're interested in.

For example, with integration tests, it's not easy to challenge the code using imaginary subsystem failures such as an RDBMS outage, because how would you precisely control the outage timing during the test run? It's tricky unless you know IoC, dependency injection, and mocking. With these techniques, you can configure your test environment so that a call to the database will be redirected to a custom mocked service programmed to answer with a failure in the middle of the logic. Other subsystems can be mocked to produce a different behavior required for this specific test. A testable architecture allows you to slip into every possible dark corner of your business logic to see how it handles the unpredictable behavior of any external system.

15.2.2 Mocking with free monads

We've talked about free monads and their ability to divide the code into layers clearly separated from each other. In fact, there can be interpreters not only for real subsystems but also for mocked ones. Figure 15.3 clarifies figure 15.2 in this sense.

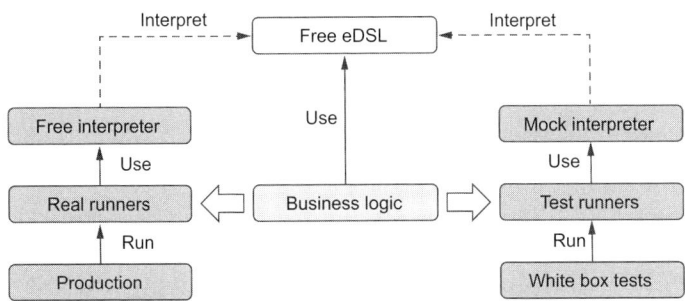

Figure 15.3   Free monads, mocks, and white-box tests

There are two possible ways to implement this scheme:

- Updating real interpreters with some additional mocking mechanism adjacent to the existing code
- Introducing new interpreters specifically for a testing framework

Although the first option seems to violate the single responsibility principle (SRP), the next bullet about automatic white-box testing offers some promising possibilities. The second option is of interest.

Suppose we want to mock a random generation subsystem represented by the RandomL free language. Let me show you the language itself, which has a single method, and the live interpreter, a very simple one.

> **Listing 15.9   New subsystem: A random generator**

```
data RandomF next where
  GetRandomInt :: (Int, Int) -> (Int -> next) -> RandomF next

type RandomL = Free RandomF

interpretRandomF :: RandomF a -> IO a                    ◄─── Live interpreter
interpretRandomF (GetRandomInt range next) = do
  r <- randomRIO range                                   ◄─── Native function call
  pure (next r)

runRandomL :: RandomL a -> IO a
runRandomL rndAct = foldFree interpretRandomF rndAct
```

Now a special mocking interpreter should be able to produce a predefined value (mock) without touching any native functions:

```
interpretRndMocking :: RandomF a -> IO a                 ◄─── The mocking interpreter
interpretRndMocking (GetRandomInt _ next) =
  pure (next 4)        -- chosen by fair dice roll.
                       -- guaranteed to be random.
```

We can also configure the interpreter using an additional parameter like this:

```
interpretRndMocking :: Int -> RandomF a -> IO a
interpretRndMocking mockVal (GetRandomInt _ next) =
  pure (next mockVal)

runRndMocking :: Int -> RandomL a -> IO a
runRndMocking mockVal rndAct =
  foldFree (interpretRndMocking mockVal) rndAct
```

This code ignores the range variable, so it can produce an inappropriate value such as "7" when the range is [0,6]. Depending on your needs, you may want to add a sanity check. An exception can be thrown here, which will fail a test:

```
interpretRndMocking mockVal (GetRandomInt (from, to) next) = do
  when (mockVal < from || mockVal > to)
       (error "Invalid mock value: out of range")
  pure (next mockVal)
```

But more often, the mocks should vary on each method call. First, it returns 4, then 3, then 100, and then something else—this should be controlled in tests and completely defined by a test case. In OOP languages, this is usually achieved by having a stateful mock object that holds a list of mock values and returns them one by one. Let's do this for our mock interpreter by analogy. A stateful interpreter with a mutable list of mocks is presented in the following listing.

Listing 15.10 Stateful mocking interpreter

```
interpretRndMocking :: IORef [Int] -> RandomF a -> IO a
interpretRndMocking mocksRef (GetRandomInt _ next) = do
  mockVal <- popNextRndMock mocksRef
  pure (next mockVal)

popNextRndMock :: IORef [Int] -> IO Int
popNextRndMock mocksRef = do
  mocks <- readIORef mocksRef
  case mocksRef of
  []      -> error "No mocks available"
  (v:vs) -> do
    writeIORef mocksRef vs
    pure v
```

Having such a configurable test interpreter gives us a lot of flexibility. You can provide a certain value for very specific cases and enter any branch of your business logic. Suppose you have the following scenario for getting a random activity to the nearest weekend.

Listing 15.11 Random game picker

```
games :: Int -> String
games 0 = "Minecraft"
games 1 = "Factorio"
games 2 = "Dwarf Fortress"
games _ = "Your decision"

getWeekendActivity :: RandomL String
getWeekendActivity = do
  baseActivity <- getRandomInt (0, 4)
  case baseActivity of
    0 -> pure "Sleep"
    1 -> pure "Walk"
    2 -> pure "Read"
    3 -> do  -- play computer game
      gameIdx <- getRandomInt (0, 2)
      pure (games gameIdx)
```

Now it's easy to route an evaluation to the point where the activity "play computer games" with the option *Dwarf Fortress* is selected. There should be two mock values provided: 3 and 2. The corresponding test is as follows:

```
spec :: Spec
spec = describe "Random scenarios test" $
  it "getWeekendActivity returns the best game ever" -> do
```

```
mocksRef <- newIORef [ 3, 2 ]                          ◄—— Creates mocks

activity <- runRndMocking mocksRef getWeekendActivity
activity `shouldBe` "Dwarf Fortress"
```

So mocking with free monads is simple. However, we missed something important. Think about the following three questions:

- The return type of the GetRandomInt method is known—it's Int. But what if the method returns an arbitrary value of an unknown type, which is determined by a concrete script only?

- How would we do mocking with hierarchical free monads? How would the testing framework be constructed?

- How do we write more generic white-box tests with an option to call a real effect by occasion? In other words, how do we mix real and mocked interpretation of calls?

The sections that follow answer these questions.

15.2.3 *White-box unit testing*

The detailed explanation given earlier on how to do mocking with free monads now opens a nice path to a complete unit/functional, white-/gray-box testing. However, the first question—why we should do this—has some importance, so let's talk about motivation.

With white-box unit testing, we can

- Fixate the exact behavior of the code
- Provide protection against regressions when some part of the business logic is considered sensitive and should not be changed by occasion
- Ensure that IO-bound scenarios work as expected in all manifestations (effects, algorithms, interaction with external services, and so on)
- Simulate a subsystem's outage and check the code reaction
- Refer to tests as a sort of documentation
- Implement deep fuzzy testing to investigate the code stability

However, we should be careful. Although white-box testing can shed light on the most subtle code details, this technique can be expensive in terms of time and effort. Full testing coverage tends to be heavy, hardly maintainable, and often senseless. The more code there is, the more unit tests there should be, and the more labor is expected. All-encompassing white-box tests can slow down a project drastically, and any extra lag can turn into a financial loss.

While the usefulness of white-box tests remains debatable, there's one strong argument for why we should learn it: it's another software developer's tool, and we must be aware of it.

Let's go back to the scenario for loading a labyrinth from a KV database (listing 15.5):

```
loadLabyrinth :: Int -> LangL Labyrinth
loadLabyrinth labIdx =
  withKVDB' kvDBConfig $ do
    labVal :: LabVal <- loadEntity (LabKey labIdx)
    pure (fromLabVal labVal)
```

The next code does a bit more. It uses several effects (KV database and state handling) and reveals some critical points of possible failure.

Listing 15.12   A broader scenario for loading a game session

```
data GameState = GameState                          ◄──────  Game's operational data
  { labyrinth :: StateVar Labyrinth
  , playerPos :: StateVar (Int, Int)
  }

type GameIdx = Int

loadGame :: DBConfig LabKVDB -> GameIdx -> AppL GameState
loadGame kvDBConfig gameIdx = do

  labyrinth <- loadLabyrinth'      kvDBConfig gameIdx      │ These operations can
  playerPos <- loadPlayerPosition' kvDBConfig gameIdx      │ throw an exception.

  labyrinthVar <- newVarIO labyrinth
  playerPosVar <- newVarIO playerPos

  pure (GameState labyrinthVar playerPosVar)
```

The two functions used here, `loadLabyrinth'` and `loadPlayerPosition'`, are known to be unsafe. They can throw exceptions if the KV database doesn't respond or responds unexpectedly. A possible implementation can be as follows. Notice two database functions and the error call:

```
loadPlayerPosition' :: DBConfig LabKVDB -> Int -> AppL Pos
loadPlayerPosition' kvDBConfig idx = do
  conn       <- getKVDBConn kvDBConfig
  ePlayerPos <- withKVDB conn (loadEntity idx)
    Left _       -> error "Failed to load the player pos"
    Right plPos -> pure plPos
```

For a better understanding, consult figure 15.4, in which you can see all the methods. Bars with numbers mark methods that will be mocked.

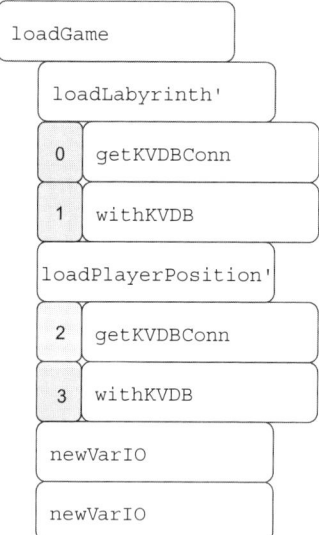

Figure 15.4   Loading scenario

Let's simulate failure. Suppose we want to test that the `loadEntity` function has returned `Left`, and a dangerous `error` function is triggered. The test in listing 15.13 does this. It's written on top of an advanced testing framework that we'll investigate later. The test declares a series of mocks and configs to pass through the logic. The mocks make `loadLabyrinth'` and `loadPlayerPosition'` behave differently. Try to guess why we don't need mocks for the two `newVarIO` functions.

Listing 15.13   White-box test for the game-loading function

```
spec :: Spec
spec = describe "Labyrinth KV DB tests" $
  it "Load player position should throw exception" $ do

    mocksVar <- newIORef
      [ (0, mkMock (MockedKVDBConn "LabKVDB"))
      , (1, mkMock (Right testKVDBLabyrinth))
      , (2, mkMock (MockedKVDBConn "LabKVDB"))
      , (3, mkMock (Left (DBError "KVDB Failure")))
      ]

    eGameState <- try (Test.runAppL mocksVar)
                  $ loadGame testKVDBConfig 1

    case eGameState of
      Left (e :: SomeException) ->
        show e `shouldBe` "Failed to load the player pos"
      Right _ -> fail "Test failed"
```

Mocks preparation

Two mocks for the database stuff in the loadLabyrinth' function (connection and successful query result)

Two mocks for the DB stuff in the loadPlayerPosition' function (connection and failed query result)

Runs the scenario using a special testing interpreter

In general, we should avoid the error function in favor of more controllable ways of processing errors. The Hydra framework is designed with the idea that writing a safe business logic should be simple: no need to think about asynchronous exceptions, and no need to care about the particular native libraries and their anarchical attitude to this difficult theme. Therefore, we might expect that someone will decide to refactor the preceding code. As you'll remember, the LangL and AppL monads in Hydra have a nice method for throwing domain-level exceptions: throwException. With it, the following change was made in loadPlayerPosition'

```
-    Left _ -> error "Failed to load the player pos"
+    Left _ -> throwException (LoadingFailed "Player pos")
```

where LoadingFailed is a custom exception:

```
data AppException = LoadingFailed Text
  deriving (Show, Generic, Exception)
```

In turn, the refactoring continues, and the next change aims to protect the whole scenario from occasional exceptions. This can be done with the runSafely method, which, of course, is able to catch the LoadingFailed exception. See the following listing, which is the result of refactoring.

Listing 15.14 A safe loading scenario after refactoring

```
loadGame
  :: DBConfig LabKVDB
  -> GameIdx
  -> AppL (Either Text GameState)
loadGame kvDBConfig gameIdx = do

  let load1 = loadLabyrinth' kvDBConfig gameIdx          ◄─── Two unsafe actions
  let load2 = loadPlayerPosition' kvDBConfig gameIdx

  eLabyrinth <- runSafely @AppException load1            ◄─┐ Catches the
  ePlayerPos <- runSafely @AppException load2            ◄─┘ AppException exception

  case (eLabyrinth, ePlayerPos) of                       ◄─┐ Processes the
    (Left exc, _) -> pure (Left (show exc))                 │ result somehow
    (_, Left exc) -> pure (Left (show exc))

    (Right labyrinth, Right playerPos)  -> do
      labyrinthVar <- newVarIO labyrinth
      playerPosVar <- newVarIO playerPos
      pure (Right (GameState labyrinthVar playerPosVar))
```

TIP runSafely will not catch exceptions other than AppException; thus, the loadGame function isn't completely safe. You might want to catch SomeException instead.

Apart from the wordier and more explicit business logic, this looks better, right? We can now trust this function because it follows the rule "explicit is better than implicit."

Refactoring is a very important practice. We should all do it at every opportunity. However, the test we wrote earlier doesn't work anymore. It fails with an exception "Failed to convert mock" or something similar. Why? Because the scenario has changed significantly. By the nature of the runSafely method, the scenario no longer contains the two monadic chains of the two loading helper functions. These chains are now embedded into the runSafely method, and the test doesn't know how to get inside. The mocks now mismatch the calls (see figure 15.5).

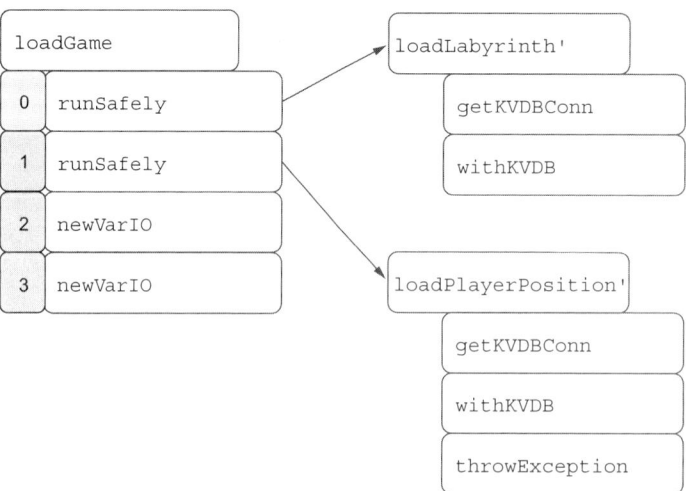

Figure 15.5   Scenario after refactoring with `runSafely`

Previously, mocks were matched to KV database functions, and now they're associated with runSafely and newVarIO methods. The test should be updated after the logic itself. But now we're entering a quite subtle area: the essence of mocks for hierarchical languages.

Let me remind you about the type of the runSafely method:

```
runSafely :: AppL a -> AppL (Either Text a)
```

Here, the interpreter recursively evaluates the internal action. It's also surrounded by the try combinator. Here is the interpreter:

```
interpretAppF appRt (RunSafely act next) = do
  eResult <- try (runAppL appRt act)
  pure $ next $ case eResult of
    Left (err :: SomeException) -> Left (show err)
    Right r -> Right r
```

Now we have a choice. We can mock the result of runSafely while ignoring the action, or we can configure the mocking interpreter to descend deeper and interpret the action. Interpreting the internal action, of course, is no different than interpreting the external code because it's the same AppL language. However, after descending, we should be able to mock the methods of internal action. In our case, mocks should be lowered down to the scenarios `loadLabyrinth'` and `loadPlayerPosition'` (see figure 15.6).

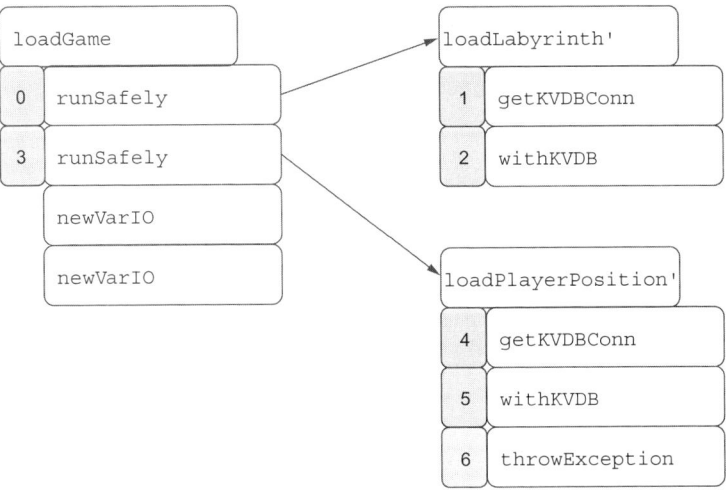

Figure 15.6 Lifting mocks down by a hierarchy of calls

The aforementioned is true for every hierarchical aspect of free monadic languages. The `AppL` language has actions in `LangL`, and the `LangL` language has actions in other internal languages. In our white-box tests, we might want to either stay on the top levels of the business logic or test it more granularly. Moreover, sometimes we'd like to evaluate a live interpreter to perform a real effect and get a result. The reasons and intentions may vary, but the mechanism to achieve this is always the same: configurable mocks.

The updated white-box test is presented in the next listing. This time, we create `AppRuntime` in complement to `TestRuntime` because the test interpreter might meet a mock item (`RunRealInterpreter`), which issues commands to evaluate a real effect.

Listing 15.15 Updated white-box test that uses a real runtime

```
spec :: Spec
spec
  = around withAppRuntime
  $ describe "Labyrinth KV DB tests"
  $ it "Load player position should throw exception"
  $ \appRt -> do

    mocksVar <- newIORef
      [ (0, RunRealInterpreter)
      , (1, Mock (MockedKVDBConn "LabKVDB"))
      , (2, Mock (Right testKVDBLabyrinth))
      , (3, RunRealInterpreter)
```

runSafely mock

Two mocks for
loadLabyrinth'

runSafely mock

```
    , (4, Mock (MockedKVDBConn "LabKVDB"))
    , (5, Mock (Left (DBError "KVDB Failure")))
    , (6, RunRealInterpreter)
    ]

let testRt = TestRuntime (Just appRt) mocksVar
let action = loadGame testKVDBConfig 1

eGameState <- try (Test.runAppL testRt action)
case eGameState of
  Left (e :: SomeException) ->
      show e `shouldBe` "Failed to load the player pos"
  Right _ -> fail "Test failed"
```

Two mocks for loadPlayerPosition'

Step for throwException real method

It's not hard to guess that the testing runner is a bit more complex because we can choose the methods that will go to real interpreters and return to the testing one. We can mix white-box and black-box integration testing. This becomes more interesting, don't you agree? The next section briefly describes the testing framework.

15.2.4 Testing framework

The core idea for mixing real and mocked effects lies in the `Step` data type:

```
data Step
  = Mock GHC.Any
  | RunTestInterpreter
  | RunRealInterpreter
```

We use a similar typed/untyped trick with `GHC.Any` for storing mocks, the one introduced in chapter 10 (see figure 10.4). However, this time, the trick isn't type-safe. It's possible to provide a mocked value of a completely wrong type, not of a type a particular step requires, which will result in a runtime error on test replay. Not great but not terrible either—we can live with this vulnerability. There's no strong requirement for tests to be strictly verified and typed. If a mock is mistyped, the test will fail. Simply go and fix it.

We've already seen how the option `RunRealInterpreter` works. The option `RunTestInterpreter` means the same thing, but it's not always clear what effect should be evaluated by the test interpreter. One possible action is simulating a subsystem failure. Or you might want to collect a call stack of a scenario and verify it in the test. Perhaps you want to know the number of certain operations made by a scenario.

> **TIP**   With free monads and step-by-step evaluation, it's possible to specify the exact number of calls that will be evaluated. This is a great way to control blockchain smart contracts, for example. The gas concept doesn't require complicated mechanisms anymore! And other use cases for counting the calls are coming to mind. Thus, a free monadic service can have a subscription model in which a small client buys a package for 1,000 steps in a scenario, a medium client can run scenarios up to 5,000 steps, and enterprise clients are 10,000 steps in total.

Consider the following implementation of the testing interpreter. The `TestRuntime` data type holds the call stack and steps for mocks:

```
type MethodName = String
type MethodData = String

data TestRuntime = TestRuntime
  { traceSteps :: Bool
  , callStack  :: IORef [(MethodName, MethodData)]
  , appRuntime :: Maybe AppRuntime
  , steps      :: IORef [Step]
  }
```

The interpreter dispatches the current step and does the action the step requires.

Listing 15.16 Dispatching the interpreter

```
interpretAppF :: TestRuntime -> AppF a -> IO a
interpretAppF testRt fAct@(EvalLang action next) = do

  when (traceSteps testRt)                              ◀──── Collecting a call stack
      $ modifyIORef (("EvalLang", ""):)
      $ callStack testRt
                                                        Obtaining the current
  mbStep <- popNextStep testRt                          ◀──── step and real runtime
  let mbRealAppRt = appRuntime testRt
                                                        Dispatching the step
  case (mbStep, mbRealAppRt) of                         ◀────
    (Just (Mock ghcAny), _) ->
       pure (next (unsafeCoerce ghcAny))                ◀──── Returning a mock
    (Just RunTestInterpreter, _) -> do
       res <- runLangL testRt action                    Running a nested test
       pure (next res)                                  interpreter for the LangL action
    (Just RunRealInterpreter, Just appRt) ->            ◀──── Running a real effect
       Real.interpretAppF appRt fAct
    (Just RunRealInterpreter, Nothing) ->               Errors on the case when the
       error "Real runtime is not ready."               test is configured wrongly
    (Nothing, _) -> error "Mock not found."
```

Once the `RunRealInterpreter` value is met, the real interpreter will be called, utilizing the `AppRuntime` stored in the `TestRuntime`. Interestingly, we use a real interpreter only for a single call, but once it's evaluated, we return to the test interpreter. The `callStack` variable keeps the call stack, respectively. In this method, only `EvalLang` will be written, but sometimes, we can output more useful info. For example, the `throwException` method carries an exception. In the KV database methods, the key and value can be shown. For SQL methods, it's logical to store the resulting SQL query. In other words, the data being transferred through the scenario might be in tests for additional verification.

Listing 15.17   Sample test for the call stack

```
_ <- runAppL testRt (loadGame testKVDBConfig 1)          ◀──── Call stack is recorded

stack <- readIORef (callStack testRt)                    ◀──── Call stack is read
                                                               from the runtime
stack `shouldBe`
  [ ("AppF.EvalLang", "")
  , ("AppF.InitKVDB", "./test/labyrinth.db")
  , ("AppF.EvalLang", "")
  , ("LangF.RunKVDB", "\"loadEntity\" \"LabKey 1\"
    \"No value found\"")
  , ("LangF.ThrowException"
  , "InvalidOperation \"Labyrinth with key \"1\" not found.\"")
  ]
```

The framework can be improved in many ways—for example, measuring and verifying timings of methods, discovering space leaks, simulating different responses from external services, or evaluating concurrent code in a deterministic way when you explicitly order your threads on which operation to start and when to stop. You can create several different testing frameworks and use them for unit, integration, and functional tests. Consider rolling out your own testing environment for your requirements and cases.

TIP   The white-box testing approach can go even further. In appendix D, you'll find an approach I call *automatic white-box testing*. It's a way to implement automatic golden tests and white-box tests without any need to write the tests themselves.

15.2.5   *Testability of different approaches*

What can we say about the testability of different design approaches, such as the `ReaderT` pattern, the Service Handle pattern, final tagless, and others? Testability depends on how easily we can isolate the implementation from the actual logic. All the approaches from the previous chapter allow us to do dependency inversion in the code. This is the major technique that leads to better testability. The more easily you can substitute your effects with mocks, the higher the test quality. In this sense, the testability of value-based approaches should exceed the testability of more rigid ones. Here, final tagless/mtl must be the worst because its mechanism for dependency injection is based on type-level substitution. However, these isn't the best circumstances for bare IO code. Imperative code with naked effects cannot be tested in general.

Another consideration relates to the ability to bypass the underlying system's interfaces. When you have bare `IO` code, you don't have that underlying system at all, so you can perform any effects you want. However, most approaches can't provide a strictly isolated environment either. Only free monads can do that, which is why we constructed a free monadic framework. So because you have this framework, you can be calm. The code that most people write will be testable anyway (except when they do dirty hacks).

Table 15.1 compares the testability of different approaches.

Table 15.1 Comparison of the testability of different approaches

	Dependency injection option	Effect restrictions	Bypassing restrictions	Testability in general
Bare `IO`	No DI	No	Easy	Very low
`ReaderT` over `IO`	Value based	No	Easy	Low
Service handle within `IO`	Value based	No	Easy	Low
Final tagless/mtl	Type based	No	Possible	Low
Free monads	Value based	Yes	Impossible	Best

Summary

- Testing does not guarantee that code will be free from bugs, but that's not the point of testing. Testing reduces risks by verifying that main and important requirements are met.
- The more meaningful tests you have, the lower the risks and the higher the maintenance cost.
- Different testing covers different sets of requirements and, thus, risks.
- White-box tests verify the functional requirements (what the code should and should not do).
- Black-box testing may be used to verify functional requirements or validate nonfunctional requirements.
- Property-based testing is more suitable for CPU-bound and pure code but less suitable for `IO`-bound code.
- Regression tests protect against unexpected breakages, and sometimes we write tests to find bugs.
- If we're shipping an application framework, a good idea will be to provide a testing framework so that our clients can test their scenarios.
- Establishing a proper testing environment may be expensive or even impossible if the architecture isn't testable.
- Three-layer free monadic architecture has very good testability compared to all other architectural approaches.
- Mocking is important. Achieving good (meaning useful) test coverage without mocks doesn't seem possible for most applications that are `IO` bound by nature.
- Mocking is only possible with good architecture that follows all the design principles, such as SOLID or low coupling/high cohesion.
- Free monadic architectures achieve very good testability by decoupling interfaces and implementation.
- Automatic white-box testing is good for golden tests, although its setup and maintenance are a bit clumsy.

appendix A
Plenty of monads

Dealing with the impure world in a pure environment isn't quite possible. That's the limitation of purely functional languages such as Haskell. In Scala, you can run any effectful code whenever you want because unlike Haskell, Scala does not have a strict separation of effects. However, we still must make impure calls in the Haskell programs, which can be done using the so-called IO monad. Although the IO monad was the first monad introduced into programming languages, many other monads were discovered and found to be very useful.

The IO monad binds impure actions together. The following code demonstrates the do notation, which makes monadic programming convenient. You might read it as an imperative program at first, but with practice, you'll see that this understanding isn't quite accurate—monads aren't imperative but can simulate imperativity well:

```
askAndPrint :: IO ()
askAndPrint = do
  putStrLn "Type something:"
  line <- getLine
  putStrLn "You typed:"
  putStrLn line
```

The output may be

```
> askAndPrint
Type something:
faddfaf
You typed:
faddfaf
```

392

This code has four IO sequential actions (putStrLn "Type something:", getLine, putStrLn "You typed:", and putStrLn line) chained into the one higher-level IO action askAndPrint.

Every monadic action is a function with a monadic return type. Here, the return type IO () defines that all the functions in a do block should be in the IO monad (that is, should return this type), as the whole monadic computation should do. The last instruction in the block defines the whole computation output. In our case, it's putStrLn that type IO () matches with the type of askAndPrint:

```
putStrLn :: String -> IO ()                    ◄──── Expects a string
(putStrLn "Type something:") :: IO ()          ◄───┐
askAndPrint :: IO ()                                │ String is provided.
```

The function getLine has the following declaration:

```
getLine :: IO String
```

When it's called in the do block, the user will be prompted to type a string. Next, this String variable will be unpacked from IO String and put into the line variable. We normally unpack monadic values like this one using the left arrow:

```
line :: String <- getLine
```

I added a type declaration for line for clarity. Later, this variable will go to the putStrLn function:

```
putStrLn line
```

Although we could, we don't bind the result from the function putStrLn with any variable:

```
res :: () <- putStrLn "Type something:"
res :: () <- putStrLn line
```

If we do, we unpack the value of the unit type (), which is always the same: (). We aren't interested in this boring value. It can be discarded explicitly, but this looks strange and is unnecessary:

```
discard :: IO ()
discard = do
  _ <- putStrLn "Discard return value explicitly"
  putStrLn "Discard return value implicitly"
```

The function askAndPrint has the return type IO something—this makes it a full-fledged member of the IO monad computations. We can use it similarly to the standard functions putStrLn and readLine:

```
askAndPrintTwice :: IO ()
askAndPrintTwice = do
  putStrLn "1st try:"
  askAndPrint                          ◄──── A full member of the IO society
  putStrLn "2nd try:"
  askAndPrint
```

Figure A.1 clarifies the monadic sequencing.

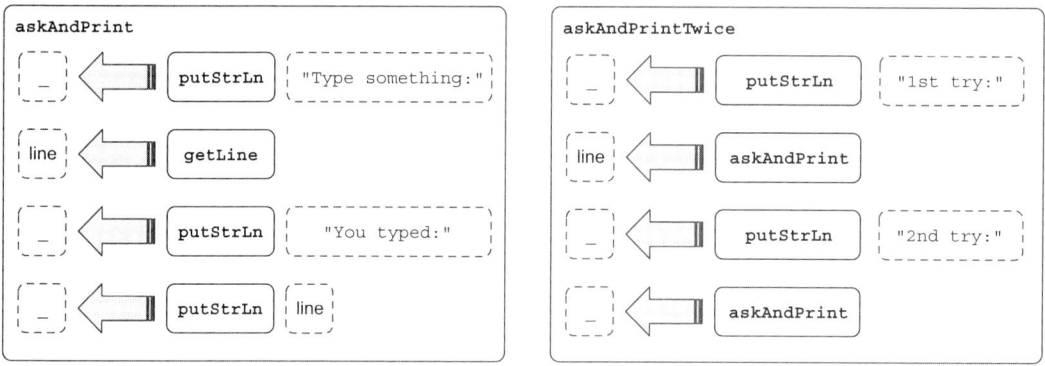

Figure A.1 Monadic sequencing of actions in the `IO` **monad**

We can also force functions like `askAndPrint` to return any value we want, not just `()`. In this case, we should use the `pure` standard function as a wrapper of the pure value into a monadic value.

> **TIP** Historically, Haskell had `return` instead of `pure`. Today's best practice is to avoid the misleading `return` function in real code bases because it's considered obsolete. It has a confusing name. Nothing is being returned, but rather just wrapped into a monadic context. `pure` and `return` do the same thing (one is expressed using another), and they are interchangeable. In the book, we'll stick to `pure`.

For example, we'd like to return a modified user input instead of printing it immediately.

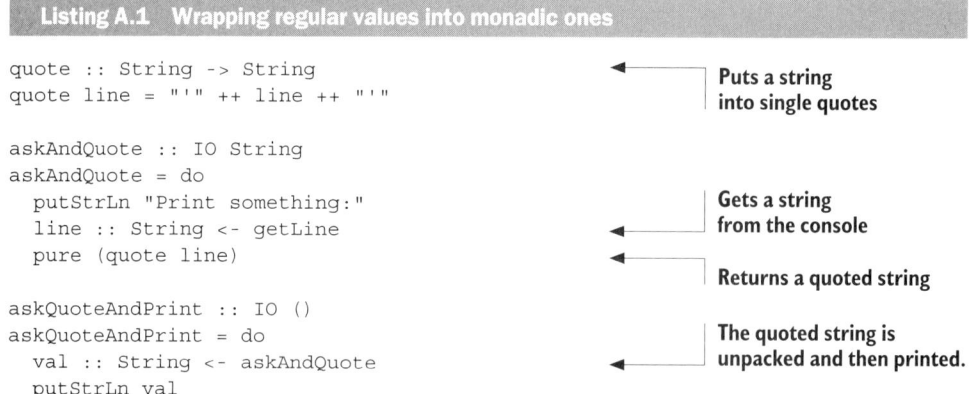

This code produces the following output if you enter `abcd`:

```
> askQuoteAndPrint
Print something:
abcd
'abcd'
```

In Haskell, the do notation opens a monadic chain of computations. In Scala, the analog of the do notation is the for comprehension. Due to general impurity, Scala doesn't need the IO monad, but Scala developers found that it's very convenient and safe. They've developed several solutions for functional IO handling. The scalaz library has the IO monad; there is also one in the Cats Effect library. But the most recent solution is called ZIO, and it was built by John De Goes and the ZIO team. This is a whole ecosystem and a framework built on top of the idea of wrapping around the IO effect into a convenient, mostly monadic form.

The near side of the "Moonad" looks like this: you only see what's in front of you, namely, a chain of separate monadic functions, and it's hard to find any evidence of a far side of the "Moonad"—an undercover mechanism that makes magic work. It can be mysterious, but every two neighboring monadic functions in a do block are tightly bound together, even if you don't see any special syntax between them. Different monads implement this binding in their own way, but the general scheme is common: function X returns the result, and the monad makes its own transformations of the result and feeds function Y. All this stuff happens in the background, behind the syntactic sugar of do notations or for comprehensions. Figure A.2 illustrates two sides of a monad.

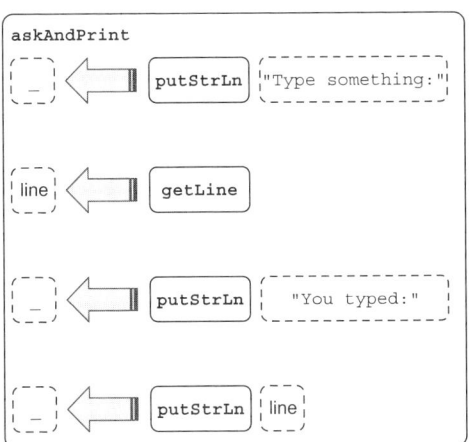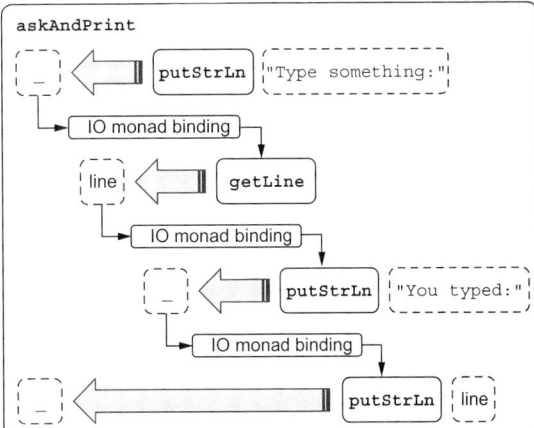

Figure A.2 Two sides of a monad

If you want to create a monad, all you need to do is reinvent your own binding mechanism. You can steal the bind function from the State monad and say it's yours, but with that, you also steal the idea of the State monad it carries. So your monad becomes the State monad. If you cut off parts of the stolen bind, you'll probably get a kind of Reader or Writer monad. Experiments with the stolen bind might end badly because if done wrong, they'll result in an invalid not-a-monad. By stealing and cutting, it's more likely you'll break the monadic laws, and your monad will behave unpredictably. As they are a mathematical conception, monads follow several rules (for example, associativity). You should also learn applicatives and functors because every monad is an applicative functor and every applicative functor is a functor, all having their own properties and laws.

Creating monads requires a lot of scientific work. Maybe it's better to learn the existing ones! There are plenty of them already invented for you (see table A.1).

Table A.1   Important monads

Monad	Description
IO	Used for impure computations. Any side effect is allowed: direct access to memory, mutable variables, the network, native OS calls, threads, objects of synchronization, bindings to foreign language libraries, and so on.
State	Used for emulation of stateful computations. It behaves like there is a mutable state, but it's just an argument-passed state: `type IntState a = State Int a` Also, the `lens` concept may work well inside the `State` monad. If your data structure is very deep and complicated, you may want to access it through lenses.
Reader	Provides a context that can be read during computations. Any information useful for the computation can be placed into the context rather than passed in many arguments. You poll data from the context when you need it: `type BoolContext a = Reader Bool a`
Writer	Allows you to have a write-only context to which you push some values. When the monadic computation is done, the collected data can be obtained from `Writer` for further transformations. Sometimes used for abstract logging or debug printing, but less welcomed in real code bases for multiple reasons: `type StringListWriter a = Writer [String] a`
RWS	`Reader`, `Writer`, and `State` monads, all at once; useful when you need immutable environment data to hold useful information, stateful computations for operational needs, and write-only context for pushing values into it: `type MyRWS a = RWS Bool [String] Int a`

Free	Wraps a specially formed algebra into a monadic form, allowing you to create a monadic interface to a subsystem, and abstracts an underlying algebra, which helps to create safer and more convenient DSLs. One of the possible applications is a functional counterpart of OOP interfaces:
	
	`data MyDSLMethods next`
	`  = Method1 Int next`
	`  | Method2 String next`
	`type MyDSL a = Free MyDSLMethods a`

Either	Used as an error-handling monad, it can split computation into success and failure scenarios, where the error path is additionally described by an error type you supply to the monad. Due to its monadic nature, the code will stay brief and manageable:
	`type HttpResult res = Either HttpError res`
Maybe	Can be used as an error-handling monad without error information attached. That is, the `Maybe` monad represents a weaker form of the `Either` monad. Also, this monad can be used to generalize computations where the absent result is a valid case:
	`type LookupResult res = Maybe res`
Par	Monad for data parallelism. With the primitives it has, you define an oriented graph of data transformations. When a `Par` monad code is evaluated, independent branches of the graph may be parallelized automatically:
ST	Strict state threads are, naturally, a real mutable state that is embedded locally into your pure function. You can create and delete variables, modify arrays, access their internals, and change the size. The state is local, meaning it won't be seen from the outside of the ST monad block. The state is mutable, but it doesn't affect the external immutable world. A stateful code in the ST monad can be much more efficient than the analog in the `State` monad.
STM	Software transactional memory monad provides a safely concurrent state with transactional updates. Thanks to monadic composability, it is possible to build a complex mutable computation over your data structure and then run it safely in a concurrent environment:
	`type MyTransaction a = STM a`

We'll see many applications of the `State` monad in this book, so it would be nice to consider an example of it.

Let's say we want to calculate a factorial. The shortest solution in Haskell follows the factorial definition: the factorial of natural number n (n > 0) is the product of all numbers in the sequence [1..n]. In Haskell, it's straightforward (we'll ignore problems with a possible negative input) and doesn't even require an explicit recursion that is hidden behind `product`:

```
factorial :: Integer -> Integer
factorial n = product [1..n]

> factorial 10
3628800
```

But if we wanted a classic imperative algorithm with a mutable counter, we would be in trouble because there is no mutability allowed in this `factorial` function. We could store the counter in the arguments, thus going forward with the so-called argument-passing style. The `factorial` would become explicitly recursive now:

```
factorial :: Integer -> Integer
factorial n = let (fact, _) = go (1, n)
              in fact

go (part, 1)       = (part, 1)
go (part, counter) = go (part * counter, counter - 1)
```

While doing exactly the same argument-passing work behind the scenes, the `State` monad frees us from managing the state manually. It gives us two primitives for working with the state indirectly: the `get` function that extracts a value from the state context and the `put` function that puts a new value into the state context. This monad's type is defined in the `Control.Monad.State` library:

```
State s a
```

It has two type arguments: `s` to hold the state and `a` for the return value. We'll specialize these type arguments by the `Integer` type and the unit type `()`, respectively. The integer state will represent the accumulator of the factorial calculation:

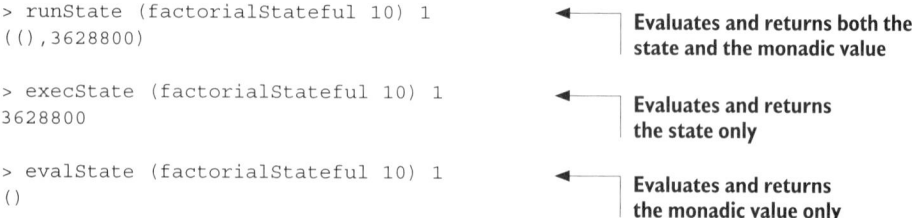

```
factorialStateful :: Integer -> State Integer ()
factorialStateful 1 = pure ()
factorialStateful n = do
  part <- get                          Gets the state from
  put (part * n)                       the State context
  factorialStateful (n - 1)
                                       Puts new data into
                                       the State context

                                       Recursively calls itself and
                                       shares the State context
```

The code became less wordy, but now it's a monadic function, and you should run the `State` monad with one of three possible functions:

```
> runState (factorialStateful 10) 1          Evaluates and returns both the
((),3628800)                                 state and the monadic value

> execState (factorialStateful 10) 1
3628800                                      Evaluates and returns
                                             the state only

> evalState (factorialStateful 10) 1
()                                           Evaluates and returns
                                             the monadic value only
```

All three are pure, running the stateful computation (`factorialStateful 10`), taking the initial state `1` and either the state (`3628800`) or the value from the monadic function (`()`), or both paired (`((), 3628800)`).

The last thing we are about to learn is true for all monads. We said the main goal for monads is to make our effectful code more composable. Every monadic function is a good combinator that perfectly matches with other combinators of the same monad. But what exactly does this mean? In general, two monadic functions combined share the effect the monad expresses. If we take the `IO` monad, all nested monadic functions may do impure things. No matter how deep we nest the functions, they all have the same effect.

Listing A.2   `IO` monad usage

```
askAndGetLine :: IO String                   IO effect
askAndGetLine = do
  putStrLn "Print something:"
```

```
  line <- getLine
  pure line
```
◄——— **Also IO effect**

◄——— **The main function has to be IO.**

```
main :: IO ()
main = do
  line <- askAndGetLine
  putStrLn ("You printed: " ++ line)
```
◄——— **Invoking other IO functions**

If we take the `State` monad, the state is shared between all the functions in this calculation tree.

Listing A.3   `State` monad usage

```
multiply :: Integer -> State Integer ()
multiply n = do
  value <- get
  put (value * n)
```
◄——— **Stateful function**

◄ **Obtaining the state**
from the context

```
factorialStateful :: Integer -> State Integer ()
factorialStateful 1 = pure ()
factorialStateful n = do
  multiply n
  factorialStateful (n - 1)
```
◄——— **Another stateful function**

◄ **Invoking a stateful**
function

```
printFactorial :: Integer -> IO ()
printFactorial n =
  putStrLn (show (execState (factorialStateful n) 1))
```
◄——— **IO effect**

The functions `multiply` and `factorialStateful` share the same monadic context with some integer value stored in it. Both can read (the `get` method) and write the context (the `put` method):

```
put :: State Integer ()
get :: State Integer Integer
```

With these two functions, we're getting an impression that our code is imperative with some implicit variable being mutated. This isn't accurate, of course: the internal mechanism doesn't change anything, and if you examine the bind function of the `State` monad, you'll see it passes the immutable state via arguments. But we're still allowed to think about it as imperative code.

It's also important to understand that the state exists only when we run a stateful function with `execState`, `runState`, or `evalState`. In the following code, you see two different computations in the `State` monad, each of which has its own state value:

```
squareStateful :: Integer -> State Integer ()
squareStateful n = do
  put n
  multiply n

printValues :: IO ()
printValues = do
  putStrLn (show (execState (factorialStateful 10) 1))
  putStrLn (show (execState (squareStateful 5) 0))
```
The first stateful
computation

The second
stateful
computation

This program prints two values: 3628800 and 25. We can conclude that the states aren't shared, although we called the same multiply function in both factorial and square calculations. In fact, every monadic function is just a declaration of what to do with the effect. The multiply function is a declaration to take a value from the state, multiply it to some n passed, and give the result back to the state. It doesn't know whether a value in the state will be a partial product, the factorial, or something else. It just knows what to do when the whole monadic computation is run.

What about other monads? Every monad has its own meaning of composition of two monadic functions (the binding mechanism). Technically, the step-by-step statement of monadic functions in the do block you saw in the previous examples is no different from the plain chain of computations. Luckily, the do notation works universally for any monad and provides a great developer experience.

Every monadic computation is the function returning a monadic type m a, where m is a type constructor of the monad and the type variable a generalizes a type of value to return. Almost all monads work with some metadata that you should specify in the monad's type. The State monad keeps a state (State Parameters a), the Writer monad holds a write-only collection of values (Writer [Event] a), and the Reader monad holds the environment for calculation (Reader Environment a). The following listing shows declarations of monadic functions. Note the types of monadic values and functions.

Listing A.4   Definitions of monadic functions

```
------------ Monad State --------------

type Parameters = (Integer, Integer)
type FactorialStateMonad a = State Parameters a

calcFactorial :: FactorialStateMonad Integer        ◄────┐ Monadic value in the
                                                         │ State monad
------------ Monad Reader -------------

data Environment = Environment
   { sqlDefinition :: SqlDefinition
   , optimizeQuery :: Bool
   , prettyPrint   :: Bool
   , useJoins      :: Bool
   }

type SqlQueryGenMonad a = Reader Environment a

sqlScriptGen :: SqlQueryGenMonad String              ◄────┐ Monadic value in the
                                                          │ Reader monad
------------ Monad Writer -------------

data Event = NewValue Int Value
           | ModifyValue Int Value Value
           | DeleteValue Int
```

```
type EventSourcingMonad a = Writer [Event] a

valuesToString :: [Int] -> EventSourcingMonad String
```

Monadic function in the Writer monad

The common pattern of all monads is running. To start calculations in the monad and get the final result, we evaluate a function `runX`, passing to it our calculations and possibly additional arguments. The `runX` function is specific for each monad—`runState`, `runWriter`, `runReader`, and so on:

```
runState calcFactorial (1, 1)
runWriter sqlScriptGen
runReader valuesToString [1,2,3]
```

In this book, free monadic scenarios that are ubiquitous also must be run by means of interpreters. The STM-powered code that describes some shared concurrent thread-safe state should be run, possibly from separate threads. All of these simplify dealing with various monads. If you know a couple of them, you'll grasp others well.

After exploring the subject further, we may want several effects from different monads in a row. For now, we can only run one effect after another, but sometimes it's not convenient or implies more ceremonies than we can afford. And then a new idea emerges: using monad transformers to merge monads into a single monadic stack. You can read about this in appendix B.

appendix B
Stacking monads with monad transformers

Monads come alone: `IO`, `State`, `Reader`, and `STM`. But sometimes, we need mixed effects from different monads in the same do-block, that is, in the same computational context. This is a common case in Haskell but not so common in Scala. In other languages, the limited presence of monads rarely goes beyond simple uses, and what we're going to discuss today is quite advanced. I'll show you how to merge two monadic effects using monad transformers and how to layer those effects into a useful and handy monadic stack.

The `IO` monad is the most known and used in Haskell and Scala, and it's not a rare case when a huge part of an application is situated in the `IO` environment:

```
main :: IO ()
main = myApplication

myApplication :: IO ()
myApplication = ...
```

`IO` in Haskell is unavoidable because the very bottom main function should be of this type that differentiates the impure layer from the pure one. In Scala, `IO` is optional, but we've seen a rise in the popularity of `IO`-handling approaches such as ZIO.

The `State` monad needed for a local state has no relation to the `IO` monad and the `IO` type. The `State` monadic code is pure and forms its own layer of computations. The stateful factorial function from appendix A cannot do any printing to the console.

```
factorialStateful :: Integer -> State Integer ()
factorialStateful n | n < 2 = pure ()
factorialStateful n = do
  factorial <- get
  put (factorial * n)

  print (factorial * n)                    ◀——— Illegal here; won't compile

  factorialStateful (n - 1)
```

The do block is inferred as the State monad block according to the function it occurs in. The print function, in turn, can only be placed into the IO monadic block:

```
print :: Show a => a -> IO ()
print a = putStrLn (show a)
```

The code won't compile, and we probably can't see the intermediate results of this factorial function immediately after they are calculated. If we want those results, we collect them and print them much later when the whole factorial stateful calculation is done. Collecting itself may be done through argument-passing accumulators or with the help of the State monad. We have a state for the latest intermediate result, but it can really be a list of all of them, like in the following code.

```
factorialProducts :: Integer -> State [Integer] ()   ◀— State is a list of
factorialProducts n | n < 2 = pure ()                     intermediate results.
factorialProducts counter = do
  products <- get                                      ◀— Requests the results from
  case products of                                         the state context
    []      -> put [counter]
    (p:ps) -> put (counter*p:p:ps)                      ◀— Writes the updated results
  factorialProducts (counter - 1)                           back to the state context
```

Now we run it from an IO function, and we print everything we want there:

```
printFactorialProducts :: Integer -> IO ()
printFactorialProducts n = do
  let products = execState (factorialProducts n) []
  print products

main = printFactorialProducts 10
```

This is what you'll see when you run it:

```
[3628800,1814400,604800,151200,30240,5040,720,90,10]
```

The problem is that the whole list is obtained before printing (we don't talk about laziness here). This might be too memory consuming in some cases, and it probably isn't straightforward enough. In addition, having an IO effect in the middle of the State monadic block to print things immediately seems a pretty reasonable desire now. Figure B.1 shows how we merge IO and State monads by means of the StateT monad transformer.

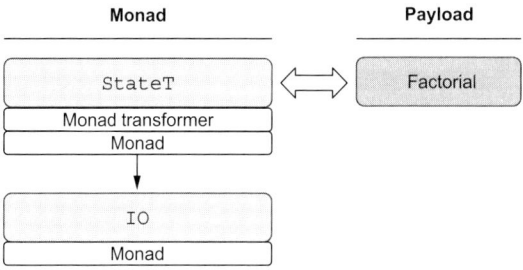

Figure B.1   Monadic stack with two monads

When you have a monad transformer for a monad, you can combine it with any other monad. The result will have all the properties of the underlying monads, and it will be a monad too. For instance, the StateT transformer can be combined with IO this way (T in StateT stands for "transformer"):

```
import Control.Monad.Trans.State (StateT)

type StateIO state returnval = StateT state IO returnval
```

Now it's possible to print values inside the StateIO monad. We should introduce one more little thing, namely, the lift function. It takes a function from the underlying monad (here, it's the print function that works in the IO monad) and adapts this function to run inside the mixed monad. Let's rewrite our example from listing A.1.

Listing B.3   Factorial calculation with IO and State

```
import Control.Monad.Trans.State (StateT, evalStateT, get, put)
import Control.Monad.Trans.Class (lift)

type StateIO state returnval = StateT state IO returnval

factorialStatefulIO :: Integer -> StateIO Integer ()
factorialStatefulIO n | n < 2 = pure ()
factorialStatefulIO n = do
  factorial <- get
  put (factorial * n)

  lift (print (factorial * n))          ◄──── Invokes the IO action
                                               with lifting from State

  factorialStatefulIO (n - 1)

main = evalStateT (factorialStatefulIO 10) 1   ◄──── Runs the StateT
                                                     monad
```

Note that the factorialStatefulIO function is no longer pure. We declared a monad stack for it, and the stack happened to have the IO monad on the bottom, so we're now allowed to do impure things. But it's not just dropping `IO` functions here and there; the types don't match yet:

```
factorialStatefulIO :: Integer -> StateIO Integer ()
print (factorial * n) :: IO ()
```

`StateIO` is not `IO`, but it's `StateT`. However, it's one layer above the `IO` monad, and with the help of one `lift`, we can adapt any `IO` method to the `StateIO` monad.

In addition, the functions in appendix A for running the `State` monad (`runState`, `evalState`, and `execState`) will no longer work. We should use the similar functions coming with the `StateT` transformer instead: `runStateT`, `evalStateT`, and `execStateT`. We can run them inside the `IO` monad like a regular `IO` action; for example, the `evalStateT` that evaluates the computation and returns a value of this computation:

```
printFactorial :: IO ()
printFactorial = evalStateT (factorialStateful 10) 1
```

Running the program will end in printing every intermediate step:

```
10
90
720
5040
30240
151200
604800
1814400
3628800
```

In Haskell and `scalaz` libraries, there are transformers for almost all standard monads. We don't have to reinvent the wheel.

> **NOTE** While imperative programmers may grab their heads and scream after seeing our abstractions (as they are probably totally useless for them), I maintain that composability and separation of effects give us a truly powerful weapon against complexity. We'll learn how to use monad transformers, but we won't open Pandora's box and try to figure out how the mechanism works. You can do it yourself, and you'll see that the mathematicians were extremely smart.

By now, you probably have a rough idea of why we want to deal with the `State` and the `IO` monads in the pure functional code. I hope the purpose of the `StateT` monad became a little clearer. If not, we'll try to come at it from the other side. Remember how we associated monads with subsystems? I said that when we see that a particular subsystem should have some effect (impurity, state, parallelism, and so on), it can be implemented inside the monad that simulates this effect. So if you think of monads as subsystems, you may conclude that it's sometimes beneficial to have a subsystem that can do several effects in one computation.

Perhaps your subsystem should be able to read clock time (the `IO` monad) to benchmark parallel computations (the `Par` monad). Perhaps your subsystem works with a database (the IO monad) and should be fault tolerant, so you should construct a convenient API to handle errors (the Either monad), or it may be a subsystem that implements an imperative algorithm over mutable data structures (the ST monad), and this algorithm may return anything or nothing (the Maybe monad).

You may even come to the crazy conclusion that you need not just two subsystems in a stack, but three or even four of them (see figure B.2). Having long monadic stacks in Haskell is a widespread practice, and we'll roll several stacks in the book too.

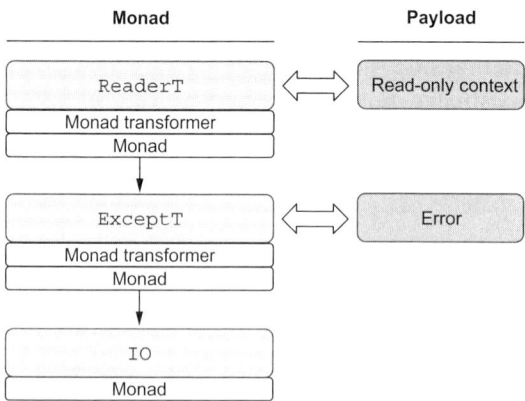

Figure B.2   Monadic stack with three monads

This can all be done without monads, but monads give you a better way to reason about the problem, namely, a combinatorial language. You pay a small cost when learning monads and monad transformers but gain a lot of power. This is so due to the monad-agnostic functions such as mapM, sequence, forM, forever, and when. Consider learning the module Control.Monad in Haskell to see what combinatorial operations you can do with any monad. Every monadic transformer is a monad as well, and those functions will work fine with your stack.

The topic of monads and monad transformers is not simple, so I prepared one more appendix, appendix C, which provides a word statistics example with monad transformers.

appendix C
Word statistics
example with monad
transformers

We have considered several examples and discussed many aspects of monads and monad transformers in appendixes A and B. Let's do so one more time. The next example shows a set of monad mechanisms. The code it demonstrates is much closer to real code that you might see in Haskell projects. It's highly combinatorial and functional, as it uses the point-free style, higher-order functions, and general monadic combinators. It might be challenging to go through, so you may want to learn more functional programming in Haskell while studying this example. Just tell yourself, "To be, or not to be, that is the question" when struggling with a difficult concept. By the way, this famous quote will be our data. The task is to get the following word statistics:

```
be: 2
is: 1
not: 1
or: 1
question: 1
that: 1
the: 1
to: 2
```

We'll take a text, normalize it by throwing out any characters except letters, and break the text into words. Then we'll collect word statistics. In this data transformation, we'll use the following three monads: the IO monad to print results, the

Reader monad to keep the text-normalizing configuration, and the State monad to collect statistics. We'll solve this task twice. In the first solution, we nest all monadic functions without mixing effects. In the second one, we'll compose a monad stack. The following listing shows the first solution.

Listing C.1   Word statistics with nested monads

```
import qualified Data.Map as Map                          ◄─── Haskell dictionary
import Data.Char (toLower, isAlpha)                             type
import Control.Monad.State
import Control.Monad.Reader

data Config = Config
  { caseIgnoring :: Bool
  , normalization :: Bool
  }

type WordStatistics = Map.Map String Int
                                                               Adds I to the word
countWord :: String -> WordStatistics -> WordStatistics       count or inserts a
countWord w stat = Map.insertWith (+) w 1 stat           ◄─── new value

collectStats :: [String] -> State WordStatistics ()           Computation in the
collectStats ws = mapM_ (modify . countWord) ws          ◄─── State monad

tokenize :: String -> Reader Config [String]
tokenize txt = do                                             Another computation
  Config ignore norm <- ask                              ◄─── in the Reader monad

  let normalize ch = if isAlpha ch then ch else ' '
  let transform1 = if ignore then map toLower else id
  let transform2 = if norm then map normalize else id

  pure . words . transform2 . transform1 $ txt           ◄─── Point-free style

calculateStats :: String -> Reader Config WordStatistics
calculateStats txt = do                                       Monadic
  wordTokens <- tokenize txt                             ◄─── computation in the
  pure (execState (collectStats wordTokens) Map.empty)        Reader monad

main = do
  let text = "To be, or not to be: that is the question."
  let config = Config True True
  let stats = runReader (calculateStats text) config
  let printStat (w, cnt) = print (w ++ ": " ++ show cnt)       Maps a monadic
  mapM_ printStat (Map.toAscList stats)                  ◄─── function over a list
```

When you call main, it calculates and prints statistics as expected. Note that we prepare data for calculations in the let-constructions. The config we want to put into the Reader context says that word case should be ignored and that all nonletter characters should be erased. We then run the Reader monad with these parameters and put the result into the stats variable. The printStat function will print pairs

(String, Int) to the console when called in the last string of the listing. What does the function mapM_ do? It has the following definition:

```
mapM_ :: Monad m => (a -> m b) -> [a] -> m ()
```

Also, it has two arguments: a monadic function and a list of values that this monadic function should be applied to. We passed the printStat function that's monadic in the IO monad:

```
printStat :: (String, Int) -> IO ()
```

This means the a type variable is specialized by the type (String, Int), m is IO, and b is (). This gives us the following narrowed type:

```
mapM_ :: ((String, Int) -> IO ()) -> [(String, Int)] -> IO ()
```

This monadic map takes the list of resulting word-count pairs and runs the monadic printStat function for every pair in the list. The underscore points out that the mapM_ function ignores the output of its first argument. All results from the printStat calls will be dropped. Indeed, why should we care about the unit values ()?

Let's move down by call stack. We run the Reader monad by the corresponding function (runReader) and pass two arguments to it: the config and the monadic computation (calculateStats   text).   calculateStats calls the tokenize function, which is a monadic computation in the same Reader monad. The tokenize function takes the text and breaks it into words being initially processed by the chain of transformations. What these transformations will do depends on the config we extract from the Reader's monad context by the ask combinator. The chain of transformations is composed of the following three combinators:

```
pure . words . transform2 . transform1 $ txt
```

Here, the calculation flow goes from right to left starting when the txt variable is fed to the transformation1 function. The result (which is still String) is passed into the transform2 combinator; then, the new result (also String) is passed into the words combinator. The latter breaks the string into words by spaces. To demystify the point-free style used, we can rewrite this expression as follows:

```
pure (words (transform2 (transform1 txt)))
```

All these functions just evaluate their results and pass them further. Consequently, we can combine them by the composition operator (.). It's simple:

```
(.) :: (b -> c) -> (a -> b) -> (a -> c)
```

This operator makes one big combinator from several smaller consequent combinators. It's right-associative:

```
words . transform2 . transform1 :: String -> [String]
```

The ($) operator is the function application operator:

```
($) :: (a -> b) -> a -> b
```

It takes the function (a -> b) and applies it to the argument a. In this code, a is txt :: String. This operator helps us to avoid unnecessary brackets. The following expressions are equal (this list is not exhaustive):

```
pure . words . transform2 . transform1 $ txt
pure . words . transform2 $ transform1 txt
pure . words $ transform2 $ transform1 txt
pure $ words $ transform2 $ transform1 txt
pure $ words $ transform2 $ transform1 $ txt
pure (words (transform2 (transform1 (txt))))
pure (words (transform2 (transform1 txt)))
```

The pure function is no different than other functions, which is why it's used as a regular combinator. It just wraps the argument into a monadic value:

```
pure :: [String] -> Reader Config [String]
```

Try to infer the function type (pure . words . transform2 . transform1) yourself. Finally, consider the computation in the State monad:

```
collectStats :: [String] -> State WordStatistics ()
collectStats ws = mapM_ (modify . countWord) ws
```

It takes a list of words and maps the monadic function (modify . countWord) over it. The definition of the countWord function says it's not monadic:

```
countWord :: String -> WordStatistics -> WordStatistics
```

Consequently, the library function modify is monadic. Indeed, it's the modifying state function that takes another function to apply to the state:

```
modify :: (s -> s) -> State s ()
modify :: (WordStatistics -> WordStatistics)
          -> State WordStatistics ()
```

It does the same as the following computation:

```
modify' f = get >>= \s -> put (f s)
```

The mapM_ combinator takes this concrete state modifying function (modify . countWord) and applies it to the list of words. The results of applying it to each word in the list are identical and look like the unit value (). As we don't need these values, we drop them by using mapM_. Otherwise, we should use the mapM function:

```
collectStats :: [String] -> State WordStatistics [()]
collectStats ws = mapM (modify . countWord) ws
```

Note how the type of collectStats changes. It now returns the list of units, a completely uninteresting result.

It should now be clear what happens in listing C.1. The second solution for the same problem doesn't differ much. Three separate monads (subsystems) are mixed together into a single monad stack in the following order: the Reader, the State, and the IO monad. We call functions from the Reader monad without any lift operators because this monad is on the top of the monad stack. For the State monad, we should lift its functions once because this monad is just behind the Reader monad: it lies one level down. Finally, the IO monad is at the bottom. We should call the lift combinator twice for all impure functions.

Listing C.2   Word statistics with the monad stack

```
type WordStatStack a                                         ◄── The monad
  = ReaderT Config (StateT WordStatistics IO) a                 stack type

countWord :: String -> WordStatistics -> WordStatistics
countWord w stat = Map.insertWith (+) w 1 stat

collectStats :: [String] -> WordStatStack WordStatistics
collectStats ws = lift (mapM_ (modify.countWord) ws >> get)  ◄── Lifts state
                                                                 computation
tokenize :: String -> WordStatStack [String]
tokenize txt = do
  Config ignore norm <- ask

  let normalize ch = if isAlpha ch then ch else ' '
  let transform1 = if ignore then map toLower else id
  let transform2 = if norm then map normalize else id

  lift . lift $ print ("Ignoring case: " ++ show ignore)     ◄── Lifts impure
  lift . lift $ print ("Normalize: " ++ show norm)               functions

  pure . words . transform2 . transform1 $ txt

calculateStats :: String -> WordStatStack WordStatistics
calculateStats txt = do
  wordTokens <- tokenize txt
  collectStats wordTokens

main :: IO ()
main = do
  let text = "To be, or not to be: that is the question."
  let cfg = Config True True
  let runTopReaderMonad =
          runReaderT (calculateStats text) cfg
  let runMiddleStateMonad =
          execStateT runTopReaderMonad Map.empty

  let printStat (w, cnt) = print (w ++ ": " ++ show cnt)
  stats <- runMiddleStateMonad                               ◄── Runs monad
  mapM_ printStat (Map.toAscList stats)                          stack
```

When you run this solution, it will print a slightly different result:

```
"Ignoring case: True"
"Normalize: True"
"be: 2"
"is: 1"
"not: 1"
"or: 1"
```

```
"question: 1"
"that: 1"
"the: 1"
"to: 2"
```

Consider the type `WordStatStack` a: it represents our monad stack. The functions `collectStats`, `tokenize`, and `calculateStats` now belong to this custom monad. All of them share the context with the configuration, can modify the state, and do impure calls. This is now one big subsystem with three effects. We run it from the bottom to the top of the monad stack. We start from the `StateT` monad transformer because we don't need to run the `IO` monad transformer—we're inside the `IO` monad already:

```
runMiddleStateMonad = execStateT runTopReaderMonad Map.empty
```

The `execStateT` function calls the top monad transformer, namely, the `runReaderT`. The latter can run any function that has the type `WordStatStack` a. The function `calculateStats` now calls the monadic function `collectStats`.

The `collectStats` function has something cryptic:

```
collectStats ws = lift (mapM_ (modify.countWord) ws >> get)
```

The (`>>`) monadic operator evaluates the first monadic function (`mapM_ (modify .countWord) ws`), omits its result, and runs the second monadic function (`get`). It does the same thing as the `do` block when we don't need the result of monadic action:

```
collectStats ws = lift $ do
  mapM_ (modify.countWord) ws    -- result is dropped
  get
```

The computation (`mapM_ (modify.countWord) ws >> get`) operates in the `State` monad that's represented by the `StateT` monad transformer over the `IO` monad:

```
(mapM_ (modify.countWord) ws >> get)
    :: StateT WordStatistics IO WordStatistics
```

To be run in the `WordStatStack` monad, it should be lifted once.

The `tokenize` function is very talkative now. It prints the configuration to the console, but first, we must lift the function `print` into the `WordStatStack` monad. We call `lift` twice because the `IO` monad is two layers down from the `Reader` monad. You can also write it as follows:

```
lift (lift $ print ("Ignoring case: " ++ show ignore))
```

If you don't like this wordy lifting, you can hide it

```
runIO :: IO a -> WordStatStack a
runIO = lift . lift
```

and then use it:

```
runIO $ print ("Ignoring case: " ++ show ignore)
```

This is a good way to provide the `runIO` combinator for your code users and hide the details of the monad stack. The client code would like to know that your monad stack has the `IO` effect, but it doesn't care how many lifts there are.

   The last thing we'll discuss is the separation of subsystems in the monad stack. In listing C.2, you really don't see this separation because all those monadic functions work in the single `WordStatStack` monad. Being composed together, they share the same effects. However, it's possible to rewrite the functions `collectStats` and `calculate-Stats` to make them work in different monads (subsystems). Our goal is to free the `collectStats` function from the `Reader` monad context because it doesn't need the configuration stored in the context. Still, the `collectStats` function should operate inside the `State` monad. Let's say it should also print words to the console. This is a new `collectStats` function that works inside its own monad stack (`State` and `IO`) and knows nothing about the `Reader` context:

```
type WordStatStateStack = StateT WordStatistics IO
type WordStatStack a    = ReaderT Config WordStatStateStack a

collectStats :: [String] -> WordStatStateStack WordStatistics
collectStats ws = do
  lift $ print $ "Words: " ++ show ws
  mapM_ (modify.countWord) ws
  get

calculateStats :: String -> WordStatStack WordStatistics
calculateStats txt = do
  wordTokens <- tokenize txt
  lift $ collectStats wordTokens
```

Note that the `StateT` type has one more type argument that isn't visible from the type definition:

```
StateT s m a
```

That's why the `WordStatsStateStack` has this type argument too:

```
type WordStatStateStack a = StateT WordStatistics IO a
```

This is a valid record, but to use the `WordStatStateStack` in the `WordStatStack`, we should omit this type argument `a`:

```
type WordStatStateStack = StateT WordStatistics IO
```

For technical reasons, partially applied type synonyms aren't allowed in Haskell. Having the type `WordStatStateStack a` and passing it to the `WordStatStack` without the type variable a makes the former partially applied. This isn't possible because it makes type inference undecidable in some cases. Thus, you might want to consult other resources to get a better understanding of what's happening here.

appendix D
Automatic
white-box testing

The amount of work one has to do with white-box tests may be intimidating. You're correct to assume that writing and maintaining white-box tests can quickly become a disaster. So tedious. So boring. But don't give up too early. What if I tell you there is a way to not write a single line of a test but have it anyway? It's like a perfect system: it doesn't exist, but its duties are finely evaluated. Free monads are here to rescue you, together with the approach I call *automatic white-box testing*. Here, I'll describe the idea but won't disclose the implementation details. The approach is real and tested in production. I wrote a detailed article about it, including references to actual commercial code bases ("Automatic White-Box Testing," https://github.com/graninas/automatic-whitebox-testing-showcase). You'll also find a working showcase project there. Run it and see how it works.

But first, let's clarify what white-box testing and unit testing are. Much of the literature on unit testing refers to pyramidal diagrams that explain the hierarchy of testing. Some of the diagrams say that the bottom approach (unit tests) is cheap, but the higher you go, the more expensive testing becomes. I personally don't agree with such common knowledge, which is very widespread according to the number of pyramids found on Google, but let me present it anyway. Figure D.1 illustrates one such diagram.

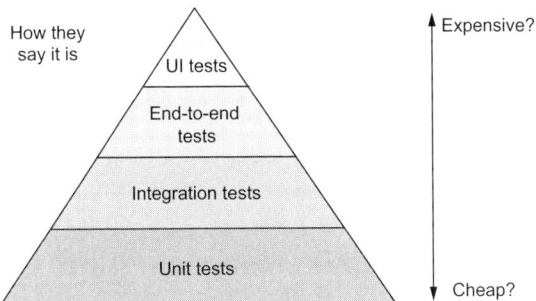

Figure D.1 A pyramid of testing approaches (highly debatable)

Why can unit tests be expensive? This depends on what we call a unit test. White-box unit tests can take too much time to maintain because they tend to multiply with an increase in scenarios, cases within those scenarios, and the length of the logic. It seems like an unavoidable evil, right? We'll try to defeat this enemy, though. The automatic white-box testing approach frees you from writing tests and, in general, can be extremely useful for the methodology we can call "golden tests."

> **DEFINITION** Golden tests represent a fixed set of detailed tests (mostly white-box tests) that should fixate the exact behavior of some logic. It's important that this logic is always correct and working—hence, golden tests.

So what's the idea? With a special mechanism baked into a free monadic framework, every scenario becomes serializable, kind of. When you run a scenario in the recording mode, each step can be tracked—written into a JSON file as a flow of steps, including inputs, outputs, and other useful data. After you get a recording file, you can replay it against a changed logic. The recording will act like a mock. Replaying can easily reveal the difference between the old run and the new one, reporting the problem and pointing exactly to the step where it happened.

There are difficulties, though. Let's try the following scenario, `loadPlayer`, which loads some player data from a database. We'll turn it into a recording.

Listing D.1 Unsafe loading function

```
loadPlayer :: LangL Pos
loadPlayer = do
  conn <- connectOrFail kvDBConfig
  ePos :: DBResult (Maybe Pos) <- withKVDB conn          ◀── Queries a database
    $ loadEntity (PosKey 99999)

  case ePos of
    Left err -> throwException (show err)                ◀── Turns a failed query
    Right (Just kvdbPos) -> pure kvdbPos                     result into an
    Right Nothing -> do                                      exception
      logInfo "No records found."                         ◀── Another exception is
      throwException "No records found."                      thrown if the database
                                                             entity is missing.
```

Note that we call the unsafe connection method that internally throws an exception on a failed attempt:

```
connectOrFail kvDBConfig
```

The database querying function returns a value of DBResult (Maybe Pos), which is an Either type:

```
type DBResult a = Either DBError a
```

To bring more evils to our world, we forcibly turn this value into an exception if it's Left:

```
case ePos of
  Left err -> throwException (show err)
```

And finally, we throw an exception on a missing database entity:

```
Right Nothing -> do
    logInfo "No records found."
    throwException "No records found."
```

How evil we are! Nevertheless, turning this scenario into a JSON recording will produce something like this.

Listing D.2   Recording of the scenario

```
// recording.json:
{"tag":"Recordings","contents":
  [ [0, "GetKVDBConnEntry",
        {"result":{"Right":[]},
        "kvdbConfig":"./prod/labyrinths"}
    ]
  , [1, "RunKVDBEntry",{"result":{"Right":null}}]
  , [2, "LogMessageEntry",
        {"level":"Info", "message":"No records found."}]
  , [3, "ThrowExceptionEntry",
        {"exception":"No records found."}]
  ]
}
```

This is how it could look. You see that every step is written in the form of an entry. Each entry is accompanied by some info describing the step. If something changes either in the scenario or in the recording, some lines will not match. For example, we patch the scenario slightly in this row:

```
- logInfo "No records found."
+ logError "No records found."
```

Now there is a playback mechanism and application. It will take the pre-created recording and the supposedly same scenario and will replay the recording against the scenario. It will traverse all the entries along with scenario steps and will match the data. In case of any mismatches, the playback application will stop and notify us about the discrepancy:

```
$ myapp player "recording.json"

Failed to replay the recording. Step 2 doesn't match.
  Expected: LogMessageEntry Info "No records found."
  Got: LogMessageEntry Error "No records found."
```

The message clearly points to the call site where the problem occurred. The developer should now examine the change and decide whether or not it was expected. Fortunately, the recording file can be edited and fixed without recompiling the project. In this case, you just need to fix the content of step 2.

In reality, though, the changes are rarely that simple. Sometimes, the code swells up from new functionality, and the old recordings become completely obsolete. No problem; new recordings can be taken just by running the application using the "recording" mode, again without recompiling it. If the code supports the automatic white-box system, all the scenarios will be automatically recordable and replayable, no matter what. Figure D.2 presents a common scheme for the player.

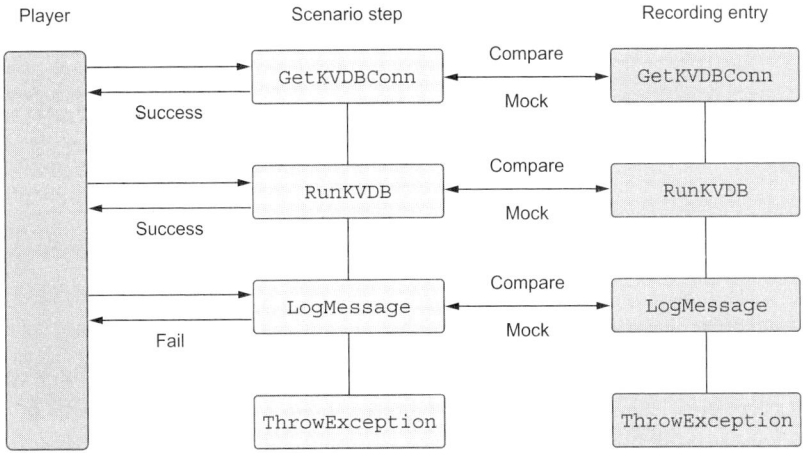

Figure D.2   Principled scheme of the automatic white-box testing system

A JSON recording can also be a source of knowledge about what's going on in your logic. It's better than just logs. Do you know any projects that have sufficient logging with clear logs that were put in the right places with the right level of severity? The theme of how to do proper logging deserves its own book, if not a yearly conference. In turn, the recordings represent a complete fingerprint of the logic (not only the effective steps, in case you're wondering), and the flow of a recording always corresponds to a particular scenario flow. This means you can read the recording and understand what happened there, step by step, with details such as SQL queries or input parameters. Finally, your business logic won't be polluted by occasional logging entries. In fact, the business logic will be completely unaware of this internal magic.

NOTE   The sentence about complete unawareness is not absolutely true. The methods of a free monadic framework should be recordable, and all the output results should be serializable. This limits the ways the framework can be used, but not by much. Also, a bunch of subtle things should be addressed when implementing this approach for KV and SQL database subsystems, as well as for state handling and threading ones. Nothing is impossible, though.

Now you understand why this approach makes the white-box testing much cheaper, almost free. However, was it the only benefit? It wasn't that interesting. Look closer at the recordings. While each step is a mock in normal usage, it can be accompanied by some config that tweaks the player's behavior. Therefore, making a real effect happen instead of a mock requires a simple change in the recording:

```
[2, "LogMessageEntry",
    {"mode":"NoMock", "level":"Info",
     "message":"No records found."}]
```

With the NoMock option, you'll see a line printed by the real logger. Nice! Even more options are supported by the player:

```
data EntryReplayingMode
  = Normal
  | NoVerify
  | NoMock

data GlobalReplayingMode
  = GlobalNormal
  | GlobalNoVerify
  | GlobalNoMocking
  | GlobalSkip
```

NoMock for a database-related step will result in interaction with the database. NoVerify liberates the checks so that the discrepancies of this particular step will be ignored. Global configs will change the behavior of the player across the whole recording. There are many other player modes that might be useful for your testing workflows. This subsystem is even suitable for making performance benchmarks for the needed steps. For example, you can require that a step with a database query should not take more time than a threshold:

```
[1, "RunKVDBEntry",
    {"result":{"Right":null}, "time_threshold":100.0}
]

$ myapp player "recording.json"

Failed to replay the recording. Step 1 exceeded the time threshold.
  Expected: less than 100.0ms
  Got: 112.3ms
```

This approach extends the idea of white-/grey-box testing and empowers our code with even more possibilities and use cases. I really think it is very powerful, and maybe you'll find effective ways of utilizing it.

index

RELATED MANNING TITLES

Haskell in Depth
by Vitaly Bragilevsky
Foreword by Simon Peyton Jones

ISBN 9781617295409
664 pages, $59.99
May 2021

Get Programming with Haskell
by Will Kurt

ISBN 9781617293764
616 pages, $44.99
March 2018

Grokking Functional Programming
by Michal Plachta

ISBN 9781617291838
520 pages, $59.99
September 2022

Data-Oriented Programming
by Yehonathan Sharvit
Forewords by Michael T. Nygard and Ryan Singer

ISBN 9781617298578
424 pages, $59.99
July 2022

For ordering information, go to www.manning.com

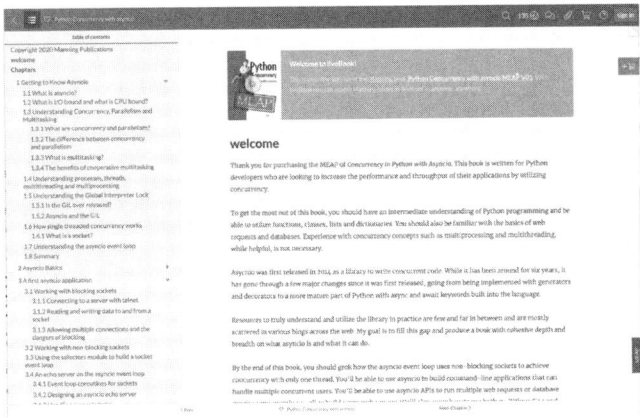

A new online reading experience

liveBook, our online reading platform, adds a new dimension to your Manning books, with features that make reading, learning, and sharing easier than ever. A liveBook version of your book is included FREE with every Manning book.

This next generation book platform is more than an online reader. It's packed with unique features to upgrade and enhance your learning experience.

- Add your own notes and bookmarks
- One-click code copy
- Learn from other readers in the discussion forum
- Audio recordings and interactive exercises
- Read all your purchased Manning content in any browser, anytime, anywhere

As an added bonus, you can search every Manning book and video in liveBook—even ones you don't yet own. Open any liveBook, and you'll be able to browse the content and read anything you like.*

Find out more at www.manning.com/livebook-program.

*Open reading is limited to 10 minutes per book daily

MANNING

The Manning Early Access Program

Don't wait to start learning! In MEAP, the Manning Early Access Program, you can read books as they're being created and long before they're available in stores.

Here's how MEAP works.

- **Start now.** Buy a MEAP and you'll get all available chapters in PDF, ePub, Kindle, and liveBook formats.

- **Regular updates.** New chapters are released as soon as they're written. We'll let you know when fresh content is available.

- **Finish faster.** MEAP customers are the first to get final versions of all books! Pre-order the print book, and it'll ship as soon as it's off the press.

- **Contribute to the process.** The feedback you share with authors makes the end product better.

- **No risk.** You get a full refund or exchange if we ever have to cancel a MEAP.

Explore dozens of titles in MEAP at www.manning.com.